WHERE TO RETIRE

America's Best and Most Affordable Places

WHERE TO RETIRE

John Howells

GATEWAY
BOOKS

Printed in the United States of America

Gateway Books
Oakland, CA

Distributed by Publishers Group West

Library of Congress Cataloging-in-Publication Data

Howells, John
    Where to retire : America's best and most affordable places / John Howells. -- 2nd ed.
      p.   cm.
    Includes bibliographical references (p.   ) and index.
    ISBN 0-933469-19-5 : $14.95
    1. Retirement, Places of--United States--Case studies. 2. Quality of life--United States--Case studies.   3. Social Indicators--United States--Case studies.   I. Title
HQ1063.2.U6H68   1995
646.7'9--dc20   94-34062
                                                  CIP

10 9 8 7 6 5 4 3 2 1

This book is dedicated to all those lively, enthusiastic retirees who unselfishly helped fill in the details of this endeavor. Seeing how these people create adventurous and interesting lifestyles somehow makes a person look forward to growing old and enjoying retirement to the fullest.

Other Gateway books by John Howells:

Choose Mexico, *by John Howells and Donald Merwin*
How to retire on $800 a month in comfortable, safe and picturesque surroundings.

Choose Costa Rica, *by John Howells*
How to enjoy the superb winter and summer climate as a part-year or year-round resident. It covers all aspects of legal requirements, costs, medical care, housing, recreation and investment opportunities.

Choose Spain, *by John Howells and Bettie Magee*
How to enjoy Spain and Portugal through leisurely travel or retirement. A complete guide to the Iberian Peninsula for those who want a different way of travel.

RV Travel in Mexico, *by John Howells*
A handbook for the RV traveler who is ready to enter the exciting adventures of mobile living in Mexico. A guide to smooth traveling, finding the safest places to stay, and how to truly enjoy the unique experiences that Mexico has to offer. Lists hundreds of RV parks throughout the country.

Retirement on a Shoestring, *by John Howells*
How to plan for the retirement years on a limited budget while enjoying a good quality of life. Howells offers detailed and easy-to-follow strategies to enable those with only Social Security income to make their dollars go much further.

Contents

Introduction

In 1991, the first edition of *Where to Retire* reviewed some 150 communities as desirable places to retire. In this latest edition, we've added a few communities and deleted some. This is not because certain places have suddenly become undesirable. We've simply found other communities that are more deserving of mention. In any case, the listed cities and towns in this book are not to be taken as recommendations, but rather as suggestions, a sort of "menu" of interesting places to visit, with an emphasis on how it might be to *live* there. You'll need to do much research on your own to decide which place, if any, will become your dream retirement home.

As the title suggests, this book focuses more on *where* to retire than *how* to retire. It's designed for those who are approaching retirement with a vague notion that they should move away from their home towns after they retire, but aren't sure *where*.

Further, we hope to help you decide what could be an equally important question: "*Why* should I move after retirement?" Maybe you shouldn't. Many people assume that relocating is an obligatory part of retirement. Actually, most *don't* move away when they retire. About 75 percent of all retirees stay put. For some, moving to a new town and starting over just doesn't make sense. But for others, finding a new home can be exciting and can contribute to a longer, happier life.

The *why* of moving to a new town or state when you retire requires a good deal of self-examination. You need to examine your goals, motives and present lifestyle to be sure you really need to relocate. People often think of retirement as being on a "permanent vacation." Nothing wrong with that. But before you pack up the proverbial lock, stock and barrel to move to that beach town or mountain village where you've enjoyed spending your regular two-week vacations, ask yourself the question: "Will I be happy living there year-round?" Will you become bored with trout fishing after a couple of months? Will you enjoy the beach during the winter, when your summer resident friends have left?

Another question is, "Will I easily make new friends there?" In popular vacation spots, year-round residents tend to adopt a "we-them" attitude toward seasonal visitors. If you aren't skilled at making new friends, you could be a permanent "outsider." Therefore, you really should spend some time in your new location before settling permanently—preferably in the off-season. You may discover drawbacks you'd never noticed before, items such as no intercity bus service, no air transportation, terrible restaurants or unfriendly natives. In the final analysis, the community you choose is more important than climate, recreational opportunities or any other attraction. My standard advice to those thinking about moving to another location upon retirement is to try it out for six months before deciding.

However, the truth is, most readers follow my recommendations about as faithfully as does my wife. Real estate folks tell me that couples often come to a place they've never seen before, and if they like it, they'll put down a deposit, then return home to sell their old homestead.

On the other hand, you may find the aforementioned drawbacks unimportant. Maybe you find your closest friends at work. And, when you retire, you'll be "dropping out" of the workplace and leaving your friends at the office behind. You'll have to make new friends anyway, so why not try it in a more agreeable environment?

In my younger days, my family and I moved around a lot—and we loved it. After working on 40 daily newspapers around the United States, we acquired an intimate knowledge of what it feels like to enter a new town, set up housekeeping and make friends. Later, while researching and writing this and other books on retirement, my wife and I traveled many thousands of miles, criss-crossing the nation several times by air, auto and motorhome. We evaluate each new city or town as if we were going to live there. Over and over we ask ourselves: "Could we be happy here? Can we recommend this place for retirement?"

One of the few things my wife and I completely agree on is: you can't find an ideal retirement place by studying statistics. A computer can't swallow a bunch of numbers and then spit out the "ideal" place for you to spend the rest of your lives! It isn't that simple. You must look beyond statistics. You must see your new home through your own eyes.

Even if statistics are interpreted rationally and accurately, there remains the common fallacy that there is a "best" place for retirement. What is ideal for you could be excruciatingly boring for me. What I might consider a wonderful climate could be far too warm for you. The choice of a retirement location is as personal as the choice of an automobile or a vacation resort. Just as there is no one best car or ideal vacation, there is no perfect retirement spot.

Statistics can be useful, of course, and we'll present a lot of them in this book. But we use them for making comparisons, not for drawing conclusions. How many people live in a town, the number of people per square mile, and the cost of houses are interesting facts. But, more importantly than how many people, what *kind* of people are they? Will you find something in common with them? Will you fit in and make friends readily? Will you be in a minority religiously or politically? Will your friends and family be eager to visit you in your new location, or will they be appalled because they can't find good restaurants and the most exciting thing to do in your town is visit the local dairy? Giving a locality a high rating because of good hunting and fishing means little to someone who thinks outdoor sport is sitting in a beer garden. Museums, operas and other cultural events would raise the ratings for some folks, but not for those who consider video cassette rentals their prime entertainment.

Housing statistics are particularly liable to be misleading. Low monthly rents or inexpensive real estate aren't nearly as important as the quality of life that goes with inexpensive property. Just because you can buy a three-bedroom house for $29,000 doesn't mean you'll be happy living there. Statistics show where the average selling price of homes is the lowest, but not *why* housing is so cheap. That's important.

Sometimes special circumstances make real estate a true bargain. For example: when a local industry closes its doors, when a major employer goes bankrupt or when an Air Force base closes, real estate prices may plummet. Displaced families try to bail out. Nobody is happy about tragedies like this, yet retirees can reap a benefit from disaster. High unemployment doesn't affect retired folks who don't need to work; the lower costs of labor, housing and services make life easier for them. A depressed community welcomes retirees as clear assets to bolster its economy. The money we spend helps local businesses and creates jobs.

On the other hand, a common reason property prices are depressed is that, given a choice, anyone with a brain larger than a ping-pong ball wouldn't want to live there! During our travels we've encountered some appallingly dull, boring towns where the most exciting thing to do is sit on the front porch, swat flies and wait for some fool to buy your house.

Research Methods

This book evaluates over 160 different communities, and by extension, hundreds more in surrounding localities. How are judgments made?

Understand, it would be impossible for one couple to visit all the potential retirement locations in the United States. What we've tried to do is select logical areas of the country where retirement is practical and illustrate a few cities, towns or villages that are typical of that region.

Our research has been ongoing for more than nine years, starting with our first retirement book. In each location, my wife and I try to envision ourselves living there. We visit senior citizen centers and chambers of commerce; we interview managers and residents of retirement complexes and we chat with retired couples. The last cross-country research trip ended in April, 1994.

In each location we visit at least one real estate office and interview salespeople. When staff members come from somewhere else, we ask why they chose this particular area to retire. It turns out that many people in real estate sales are retired. These retiree-salespeople enjoy the sociability of their jobs, the chance to meet new people and, of course, the chance to pick up a few commissions. They're especially helpful because they understand the problems involved in moving away for retirement.

We learn which neighborhoods retirees prefer, and we visit to see for ourselves. Sometimes we pose as buyers or renters looking for retirement property. This helps when looking at large retirement complexes, where potential customers tour in groups, since we find opportunities to talk with prospective buyers to find out what brings them to that particular place for retirement.

We scout neighborhoods for shopping, quality of supermarkets and access to freeways. We visit mobile home parks and talk to tenant organizations. We check classified advertisements in newspapers, comparing prices of houses, apartments, mobile homes and farms. We compare the number of help-wanted ads with that of work-wanted ads. This tells us something important about the economy.

We use U.S. government publications, drawing statistics from the Bureau of Census, Department of Labor and National Oceanographic Administration weather charts. The FBI's crime statistics are carefully tabulated, and consultations are made with noted sociologists and police officials. The government's price index and the American Chamber of Commerce Researchers Association supply us with trends. Computers are essential in our task, but not our primary tools.

Over the years, we've investigated hundreds of retirement areas and examined many different lifestyles before making the final selections for this book. However, because a town is *not* described here doesn't necessarily mean it wouldn't be a great place to retire.

In this ongoing process, we've discovered some of our preconceptions about retirement to be erroneous. It's been a great learning process, and we are happy to share this knowledge with you.

Chapter 1

Finding Your Shangri-La

I once interviewed a couple who, when they retired from their jobs in Hawaii, realized they couldn't afford to stay in Hawaii after retirement. They studied magazine articles and retirement guides, checked the recommendations and finally zeroed in on a small Ozark lake town. They called a real estate agent there who assured them he could find any number of homes selling in their desired $40,000 range. The couple asked him to start looking for a house and to arrange to store their furniture, which they sent ahead by ship.

When they arrived, they fell in love with a good-sized house, right on the lake, nestled among mature pine trees. They paid a fraction of what they received for their Oahu condominium and banked the rest. They looked forward to a change in seasons—something they truly missed in Hawaii—and learning how to fish in fresh water.

Before long, they discovered several conditions the guidebooks hadn't mentioned—subtle things statistics can't evaluate. First of all, they were used to entertaining friends, either exchanging home visits or going to exotic restaurants on Waikiki Beach. They enjoyed cocktails and conversation before dinner, wine during and a brandy after. To their dismay, they discovered that their new home was in a dry county. Forget the cocktails.* They really hadn't expected exotic restaurants; but this area was too small to support even a McDonald's, Wendy's or other fast-food mill. To make matters worse, most mom-and-pop restaurants closed in October, when the tourist trade fell away.

Much of this was irrelevant, since they had little in common with their immediate neighbors and had no success in making friends they would have enjoyed entertaining. They liked to play bridge, but they

---

* Many Southern states allow cities and counties to prohibit the sale of liquor. So, if you enjoy a martini before your steak is served, you might think twice about where you settle. Dry counties rarely have outstanding restaurants anyway. The profit margin is too small to hire a really good chef. Dry county establishments are usually formica lunch-counter type places, serving daily specials like meatloaf garnished with canned vegetables and mashed potatoes topped with imitation gravy.

found no partners. They were mildly Catholic, but their neighbors were aggressively Baptist. True, the husband did enjoy lake fishing, but his wife neared terminal boredom, sitting in a rowboat watching a bobber make circles in the water. She realized that she missed the ocean and wished they had chosen Florida or California instead of the Ozarks.

The next shocker came when they decided to list their property and try some other place for retirement. Houses just weren't selling. That's why they bought so cheaply in the first place; the usual reason for bargains: more sellers than buyers. The couple managed to get rid of the house, although at a substantial sacrifice. Eventually they moved to Florida, a state not highly rated by their retirement guidebook.

They would have saved themselves time, money and effort had they investigated on their own and not blindly accepted someone else's evaluation. A trip to their dream town and a few weeks in a rental unit could have told them everything they needed to know.

Doing Your Own Research

Magazine articles and guidebooks commonly grade retirement communities, ranking the top places from one to ten, as if they were rating major league baseball teams. With a baseball team, we can check the scores; can't argue with that. But cities and towns don't receive scores except in somebody's mind. The fact that a freelance writer likes a city and ranks it number one in his magazine article, doesn't prove a thing. For all we know, maybe the writer has never even *seen* the place!

Favorable ratings are too often awarded on the basis of conditions that don't affect retirees. For example: good schools, high employment and a booming business climate will boost a town's popularity rating, while horrible weather and high taxes are often ignored. Quality grammar schools and juvenile recreational programs matter less to retirees than quality senior citizen centers and safe neighborhoods. Full employment and thriving business conditions spell high prices and expensive housing. Also, cultural amenities, such as museums and operas, receive high marks in retirement analysis. Yet, how many times a month will you be going to the opera? The museum? Would you rather live in a town with two golf courses and no museums, or two museums and *no* golf courses? To find your ideal location, you're going to have to do your own ranking.

Ideally, you'll start your retirement analysis early. A great way to do this is by combining research with your vacations. Instead of visiting the same old place each year, try different parts of the country. Check out each location as a possible place to live. Look at real estate, apartments and house rentals. What about libraries? (An appalling number are closing because of lack of funds.) Does this town offer the types of cultural events you enjoy? A cultural event could be anything from concerts and stage plays, or square dance lessons and quilting bees, to bowling tournaments and beer drinking. The point is, will you be happy there?

Don't forget to drop in on the local senior citizens' center. Most folks are surprised to learn that these are often lively, stimulating places, not simply spots where old fogies gossip and play cards. Talk to the director and the members of the center to see what kinds of services are available should you move there. A dynamic and full-service senior center can smooth your transition into a new neighborhood. Here is where you get involved with community affairs, make acquaintances and learn something about the area from insiders.

Another important consideration is public transportation. A number of smaller towns in the United States were cut off from intercity bus service when Greyhound Corporation shut down its less-profitable runs. If you choose to live in a town without passenger train service or intercity buses, be sure you're comfortable with depending on your automobile for basic transportation. Some very small towns don't even have taxis.

The local chamber of commerce office can be an excellent source of information. Although some offices hire minimum-wage employees who couldn't possibly care less if you moved there, the better ones are staffed by volunteers—often retirees—who will help any way they can, short of paying your moving expenses.

What to Look For

Following is a list of requirements my wife and I personally consider essential for a successful retirement relocation. Your needs may be different; feel free to add or subtract from the list, and then use the list to measure communities against your standards.

1. Safety—Can you walk through your neighborhood without fearful glances over your shoulder? Can you leave your home for a few weeks without dreading a break-in?

2. Climate—Will temperatures and weather patterns match your lifestyle? Will you be tempted to go outdoors and exercise year-round, or will harsh winters and suffocating summers confine you to an easy chair in front of the television set?

3. Housing—Is quality housing available at prices you're willing and able to pay? Is the area visually pleasing, free of pollution and traffic snarls? Will you feel proud to live in the neighborhood?

4. Nourishment for Your Interests—Does your retirement choice offer facilities for your favorite pastimes, cultural events and hobbies, be it hunting, fishing, adult education, art centers, or whatever?

5. Social Compatibility—Will you find common interests with your neighbors? Will you fit in and make friends easily? Will there be folks from your own cultural, social and political dimension?

6. Affordability—Are goods and services reasonable? Can you afford to hire help from time to time when you need to? Will your income be high enough to be significantly affected by state income taxes? Will taxes on your pension make a big difference?

7. Medical Care—Are local physicians accepting new patients? Does the area have an adequate hospital? (You needn't live next door to the Mayo Clinic; you can always go there if your hospital can't handle your problem.) Do you have a medical problem that requires a specialist?

8. Distance from Family and Friends—Are you going to be too far away, or in a location where nobody wants to visit? Would you rather they *wouldn't* visit? (In that case, you'd do better even farther away.)

9. Transportation—Does your new location enjoy intercity bus transportation? Many small towns have none, which makes you totally dependent on an automobile or taxis. How far is the nearest airport with airline connections? Can friends and family visit without driving?

10. Senior Services—Senior centers should be more than merely places for free meals and gossip; there should be dynamic programs for travel, volunteer work and education. What about continuing education programs at the local college?

Newspaper Research

If you can't or don't care to travel, you can do research at the local library and by mail. Almost all libraries subscribe to a variety of out-of-town newspapers; these are extremely valuable research tools.

The most important part of an out-of-town paper is the classified section. Check real estate prices, rentals and mobile home parks; compare them with your hometown newspaper and you begin to get a picture of relative costs. Contrast help-wanted ads with work-wanted ads. This tells you wage rates, should you consider working part-time, and clues you in on what kind of competition you will have for jobs. A scarcity of help-wanted ads indicates unemployment. This won't matter if you don't plan on working, but it's important if you need to work part-time.

Mobile home parks advertise monthly park rentals, giving you an idea of what that style of living costs. Should there be an undersupply of vacancies, you can expect rentals to be expensive. Comparing prices of used items such as furniture, appliances and automobiles against your local paper's classifieds tells you a great deal about local living costs.

Display advertisements provide supermarket and department store specials to compare; particularly if national chains operate both there and in your home town. Sometimes identical specials will be priced differently from one locality to another, a further measure of costs. Ads will tell you whether large discount stores are available for shopping convenience and economy.

A newspaper's editorial page broadcasts the publisher's political stance. A paper that slants news stories to match its owner's opinions makes uncomfortable reading if you happen to be on the other side of the political fence. A publisher can profoundly influence the thinking of a community. When his newspaper is the only source of local news, the publisher's opinions are often accepted as clear truths by your neighbors. Being the only conservative in a neighborhood of liberals (or vice versa), can make you feel lonely. Particularly revealing are newspaper campaigns for or against services and spending for senior citizens.

You learn a lot about how safe a community is by the way crime is reported in the news columns. If a bicycle theft or a reckless-driving arrest makes front page headlines, rest assured, the crime situation isn't too serious—assuming, of course, you aren't a bicycle thief and don't occasionally drive your Buick on the sidewalk. But if chain-saw murders, car-jackings and drive-by shootings are buried on page 27, look out!

A good newspaper will list senior citizen activities, cultural events, community college classes and other undertakings that might interest you. A paper with a large section devoted to senior citizen news reflects a high level of interest in our well-being. Look for news about retiree political-action groups; when we band together to vote, the level of services and benefits rise in proportion to our voting strength.

If your local library doesn't carry a paper from the town you're interested in, you can usually get a copy by writing to the town's chamber of commerce. You can also write to the newspaper office (look in the phone directory section of your library for the name of the paper). Some real estate brokers will gladly mail you copies of the local newspaper, because they know you will probably use their services when and if you decide to buy.

Libraries have out-of-town telephone books, also full of valuable information. The "Yellow Pages" paint an unabridged picture of a town's business life: banks, supermarkets, shopping centers and other commercial enterprises. Check for local and intercity bus service and taxi companies. Look under the listing for "airlines" or "airports" to see if there is a local airport and which airlines service it. See how many hospitals there are. A telephone book also gives an up-to-date listing for the chamber of commerce office and the senior citizens' center.

Private Retirement Communities

Year by year, retirement becomes more of a big business, prompting impressive corporate investment. Planned retirement communities, often of astounding size, are popping up all over the country. Arkansas, Tennessee and North Carolina lead the trend, with other states following suit. Arizona's Sun City West, for example, has 7,100 acres, with more than 15,000 homes. Often these places are "hermetically sealed" developments; that is, to enter the property you must be a member of that development or have good reason to be there. Wanting to price property is usually a good enough reason to visit, although a few developments permit you to purchase only by invitation of other residents. Round-the-clock guards staff the gates, scrutinizing everyone who enters. Occasionally, after the project is sold out, the original developers are no longer interested in staffing the gates with expensive security guards. It then becomes the responsibility of the owners' associations.

Many complexes restrict buyers to 55 and older. Youngsters may visit, but not live there. This impacts the community in two ways. Obviously, your lives will be more tranquil, without gangs of kids riding bikes, playing boomboxes and knocking baseballs through your living room window. But more important than that, you'll enjoy a lower crime rate. Burglaries, vandalism and theft usually occur in direct proportion to the number of teenagers in the neighborhood. The other side of the coin is that many retirees prefer living in mixed-age neighborhoods; they find young children and teenagers fun to be with.

Developers look for inexpensive land for their new complexes. They buy square miles of desert or large tracts of forested land in places like the Ozarks and Appalachians. They can then afford to put in roads and utilities, dam up streams to create lakes and ponds, lay out a golf course or two—all at a fraction of what land alone would have cost in other parts of the country. Since local wages are generally less than in large cities, quality housing becomes relatively inexpensive.

Two caveats. First: make sure you are going to be satisfied with the physical location of your new home. Most developments we've visited are located several miles from the nearest town. Why? Because that's where the corporation found the cheapest land. This could mean a 20- or 30-mile drive into town to the supermarket or to buy a bit of hardware for the shed you are building.

Second: beware of glib promises and super-salesmanship. When a retirement project is in its initial phase, there will be a beautiful to-scale plan of the development showing the future shopping mall, clubhouses, swimming pools and all the wonderful amenities to come. An enormous supermarket and hardware store are clearly part of the plan. Believe this when you *see* it. Sometimes, when and if the "mall" is completed, the supermarket turns out to be a convenience store. (This doesn't happen as often with the more established developers.)

After you visit a development, check with a real estate office and the newspaper's classified section to see what resales in the development are selling for. If homes are offered at prices drastically below those of the development's sales office, you may have trouble getting your price if you later need to sell out. Also, if you like the development, you could save money by buying a resale instead of a newly-built unit.

An advantage to getting in on the beginning of a retirement complex is that it's easier to become involved socially and to make new friends with neighbors as they move in. You might, however, prefer a well-established neighborhood, where you can join existing clubs and activities instead of having to form them. Another point to keep in mind is that membership fees are involved in planned communities, either yearly or monthly. These fees can be reasonable or considerable, depending on the situation. The rule of thumb is that $100 in monthly fees is roughly equivalent to an additional $10,000 mortgage.

Cost of Living

It goes without saying that finances play an important part in retirement planning. Low taxes and a moderate cost of living go a long way toward making your future affordable. Yet you need to balance the advantages of living in an economical area against the potential lifestyle disadvantages. I have mixed feelings about recommending retirement in some areas—particularly rural Southern communities—to folks from big-city, Yankee backgrounds.

It's nice to enjoy an incredibly low cost of living—with housing at giveaway prices—and neighbors gracious with traditional Southern hospitality. Yet, when you share few common interests with your neighbors, it's easy to feel left out. When almost everyone in the community is in some way involved in agriculture, conversations tend to dwell on the price of corn or the best way to deworm hogs. When your agricultural experience is limited to watering house plants, you find you have few words of wisdom others care to hear. When your accent sounds funny to your neighbors, when your tastes in movies, politics and food are different or when you drive the wrong model pickup, you could feel like an alien.

Happily, situations like this are changing as more and more retirees from all over the nation are moving into small-town U.S.A. We've discovered several wonderfully compatible areas in the South, and we're reporting on them in this edition. However, it behooves you to look beyond the cost-of-living charts and real estate averages.

Bargain Opportunities!

Local boosters too often place undue emphasis on low cost of living and cheap real estate as prime attractions of their area. True, these items go hand in hand; that is, when you find low-cost housing, you'll also find economical living costs in general. In our travels, we've encountered real estate markets where $19,000 will buy a three-bedroom home; where carpenters will remodel for $5.00 an hour, where haircuts are still $3.50 and permanent waves $14.75. However, as I continually stress, *inexpensive* living isn't necessarily the same as *quality* living. Some low-cost areas are exceptional bargains, combining a high quality of life with welcoming neighbors and affordable living costs. Yet other low-cost areas are intensely dreary and boring, places you'd visit only at gunpoint.

Why is the cost of living and housing so much less in some localities? Basically, you'll find two reasons for cheap real estate and low rents. The most common reason is: it's an undesirable place to live. These towns steadily lose population because they have absolutely nothing going for them—no jobs, no charm. Homes sell for rock-bottom prices because eager sellers outnumber reluctant buyers. Unless you are sincerely dedicated to boredom, bad weather and cable TV, these are not places you would seek out for retirement.

The second situation deals with an unforeseen, disastrous business slump or trend that causes the job market to disintegrate. In this event, people don't necessarily *want* to leave and seek work elsewhere, they

22

have to. Homes go on the real estate market at giveaway prices. There's no other choice.

Although situations like this are personal tragedies for displaced families, it opens windows of opportunity for retired folks. Since working for a living and a regular weekly paycheck aren't essential for most retired couples, bargain real estate is theirs for a fraction of what similar housing would cost elsewhere. As younger folks with growing children move away, over-60 people move in and raise the ratio between retired and working people to impressive levels. The over-60 crowd becomes a majority and wields appreciable influence over local government and political processes.

We've visited a few of these towns and reported on them in earlier editions, places like the towns of Ajo and Bisbee in Arizona, where mines closed, and Colorado's Grand Junction, whose economy toppled when the oil shale industry collapsed. As you might imagine, opportunities like these don't last forever. As retirees move in and snap up the bargains, prices naturally rise. Yet they rarely rise to the level they were at before the problem occurred.

Military Base Closings

The newest bonanza for retirees: the closing and cutting back of a number of Army, Navy and Air Force facilities. The closings were planned to do minimal local damage, but it's impossible to transfer thousands of military personnel and leave thousands of civilian workers jobless without some disruption.

A case in point is Fort Ord, near Monterey, California. When its closure is final, 14,000 military personnel will have gone elsewhere. This will affect 17,000 families, a considerable percentage of the county's population. Naturally, real estate brokers will be flooded with homes, creating a buyer's market. Apartment rents will drop. Job competition will become sharper. To make matters somewhat worse, the military administrators are offering to rent base housing to city and county employees at low rates, further depressing the rental market.

Before you pack your furniture and go speeding off to Monterey, Pebble Beach or Carmel, realize that reduced prices here are bargains only when compared to original prices, which started off at a stratispherical level in the first place. When prices drop in an already expensive neighborhood, they have a long way to fall before they become as cheap as in Ajo, Arizona, where prices were reasonable even before the mine closing. Lower prices in this case simply mean that some folks who couldn't quite afford to buy into Monterey before can now do so. The situation won't last forever; the state has plans for converting the base into a university campus which will eventually have as many employees and students as Fort Ord's previous population. At some point the housing market will surely return to its normal, ridiculously high level.

Below is a list of bases slated for closure by 1997. Not all base closures will have a detrimental effect. For example, when the Air Force pulls its squadrons out of the base near Knob Noster, Missouri, a wing of Stealth bombers will move in. The local chamber of commerce informed me that they expect more personnel there than *before* the base "closure." This will require some individual research, to see whether the areas will fit into your retirement place profile, and whether the closure is for real or merely a cosmetic change.

ARMY BASE CLOSURES:

Fort Benjamin Harrison, IN	Fort Devens, MA
Ford Ord, CA	Sacramento Army Depot, CA

NAVY BASE CLOSURES:

Chase Field Naval Air Station, TX	Construction Battalion Center, RI
Treasure Island Naval Station, CA	Marine Corps Air Station, Tustin, CA
Moffett Field, Mountain View, CA	Long Beach Naval Station, CA
Philadelphia Naval Shipyard, PA	Puget Sound Naval St., Sand Point, WA

AIR FORCE BASE CLOSURES:

Bergstrom AFB, Austin, TX	Carswell AFB, Ft. Worth, TX
Castle AFB, CA	Baker AFB, AR
England AFB, Alexandria, LA	Grissom AFB, IN
Loring AFB, ME	Lowry AFB, CO
Myrtle Beach AFB, SC	Rickenbacker Air Guard Base, OH
Williams AFB, Tucson, AZ	Wurtsmith AFB, MI

Working During Retirement

Somehow, the question of working seems out of place in a book on retirement. If you merely change jobs, or quit your job to go into business for yourself, how can you be *retired*? Yet the sad truth is, many retirees need part-time work to supplement retirement income. They face a dilemma. To earn decent wages, they must live in a high-cost area where salaries are high, as opposed to moving to a low-cost area where they are forced to compete with other retirees and students for scarce part-time jobs, at substandard wages.

The fact is, most places we consider to be practical retirement areas do not offer high wages and good employment opportunities. Why? Because the most desirable places to live almost *always* have a surplus of people eager to live there, who are willing to work for less in order to enjoy the higher quality of life. This results in a soft job market—bad for wage earners, good for non-working retirees. For instance, at the moment I write these words, a man with a graduate degree in science is painting our house rather than move to another part of the country where he had been offered a high-paying teaching position! If you need part-time work to supplement your retirement, the best place to find it is probably right where you live now. You have contacts there and won't be competing with strangers for jobs.

An additional complication in finding part-time jobs arises when retiring in a place favored by military retirees. Because of military cutbacks and forced early retirements, those retiring from the service tend to be young, often in their forties. Energetic and eager for a second career, these younger retirees compete fiercely for jobs, both part-time and full-time. Their spouses, accustomed to working part-time during their frequent moves from military base to military base, are also skilled at ferreting out available work. Older workers, strangers to the area, will face stiff competition for scarce jobs.

The chapter on RV retirement has more information on part-time work, should you definitely feel that's what you want to do. Although the focus is on RV travelers, the same principles and job opportunities can apply to any retiree.

Many people just *think* they need part-time jobs. The real problem is that they've always worked and are horrified at the prospect of suddenly not having anything meaningful to do. The curse of the work ethic is all too real; after all those years of toil, folks tend to feel guilty and decadent when they no longer leap out of bed at 6:30 a.m. and scurry off to a job. Too often, those who don't really need the income end up working just for the sake of working.

This work ethic is understandable, and it is difficult to shake. Our recommendation is to get into volunteer pursuits should you not find enough to do around the house. As a volunteer, you will not only be doing meaningful work, but you'll meet others in the community, widen your network of friends and lay the groundwork for later years when you may need volunteers to help *you*. A special bonus is that your services will be sincerely appreciated and valued more highly than if you were to work in a fast-food restaurant or some other high-competition, low-pay job, trying to please an employer you don't like in the first place.

Let's take the case of Katharine, a retired librarian who lived in a nice apartment in Monterey, California. Her rent was $700 a month. A part-time job in a bookstore paid $6.00 an hour ($400 a month clear) for working 20 hours a week. When she moved to a small town in coastal Oregon, she found an equally nice apartment for $300 a month. This one had a view of the Pacific Ocean. Part-time jobs there pay minimum wage, but part-time jobs were all filled. However, Katharine discovered that the $400 she saved in rent made up for the $400 she had been earning at her bookstore job. In other words, she had been working half a day, five days a week just to pay higher rent. Now she devotes her time to art classes and satisfying volunteer work in the community.

Taxes

Property taxes vary from state to state and locality to locality, with Arkansas and Alabama taking less than Arizona or California. But choosing retirement in Alabama over Arizona simply to save a few dollars a year would be foolish unless Alabama has everything you want in the way of retirement and Arizona lacks something. Taxes are just one of many retirement components. Just because a state has no individual income taxes or sales tax doesn't mean the total tax burden will be slight. They have ways of making up the difference. When there is no income tax, sales taxes and property taxes are often boosted. If there isn't a sales tax, the difference comes from higher tax rates in some other area.

If you are like most retirees, your income will be lower; a lot of it will come from tax-deductible pensions and Social Security, so state income taxes won't be all that serious. On the other hand, if you're in a high tax bracket, clearly, elevated tax rates could be significant, and you might consider one of the states that taxes income lightly or not at all. Those without individual income taxes are Alaska, Florida, Nevada, South Dakota, Texas, Washington and Wyoming.

But beware! Retirees who draw pensions or annuities don't necessarily escape taxes by moving to one of these states. Thirteen states have what are known as "Source Tax" laws. This means pensions which have been earned in one of these states are considered taxable, no matter where you live! The idea is that this is deferred compensation that you earned while working in that state and that you're now collecting, so you owe taxes on it *there!* Furthermore, the pension is taxable at the rate of the source state, which could be higher than the income tax where you now live! If you retire to Georgia, you'll not only pay taxes on the pension to your previous state, but to Georgia as well.

Example: a California retiree, unaware of the law, moved to Washington state, which happens not to have a state income tax. Then, 15 years later he received a California tax bill for $26,000! California attached his pension checks for payment. He had no idea his pension was taxable.

Three states vigorously enforce this law at the moment: California, New York and Vermont. But the others could crank up their computers and go after you at any time. The other states with source tax laws are: Arizona, Colorado, Georgia, Kansas, Kentucky, Louisiana, Minnesota, North Dakota, Ohio and Oregon.

The good news is, Washington and Nevada passed laws prohibiting other states from seizing assets within those states to satisfy a tax thirst. Recently, Arizona, Colorado, Florida, Hawaii, Louisiana and New Mexico also passed similar laws. (Even though some of these states have source laws themselves!) But the bad news is, if you own property in, say, California, the state can (and will) seize your property; or if your pension check comes from a state, county or city government, it can be attached. Another problem: even though you live in one of the states that won't permit tax liens, the state trying to collect can go to a collection agency with its bill. That won't get them any money, but it could wreck your credit rating.

Check to see how your state enforces this law. You might consider joining a very active organization which is fighting these laws by pressing for national legislation outlawing source taxes: RESIST of America, 2440 Ash Canyon Rd. Carson City, NV 89703. It's an active group that is having some successes. Write for more information.

Another thing to consider: most states insist that you pay taxes on income currently earned in that state—whether you live there or not—on income like rents, real estate sales, royalties and the like. You'll have to file a non-resident tax form. In some states those non-resident taxes are *not* deductible from your new home state's assessments.

Some states allow you to deduct federal taxes from your income: Alabama, Arizona, Iowa, Kansas, Kentucky, Louisiana, Missouri, Montana, North Dakota, Oklahoma, Oregon and Utah. Most states consider Social Security as exempt, but the following states *will* tax at least a portion of your benefits: Colorado, Connecticut, Iowa, Kansas, Minnesota, Missouri, Montana, Nebraska, New Mexico, North Dakota, Rhode Island, Utah, Vermont, West Virginia and Wisconsin. However, many grant pension exclusions, so that only high-income taxpayers are affected. Colorado, for example grants a $20,000 exclusion for combined Social Security benefits and pension before it starts taxing.*

Finally, a few states also levy an "intangibles" tax on stock and bond holdings; we've noted those that do and don't in each state's tax chart.

State Sales Taxes   Sales taxes are creeping up around the country as states try to scrounge funds for keeping the ship afloat. Rates vary from 8.5% in some states to no tax at all in Delaware, Montana, New Hampshire and Oregon. Example: a $15,000 automobile will cost $1,125 more in Texas than in Oregon. The balancing factor is that in Oregon you pay state income tax, and in Texas you do not. One couple we interviewed in Vancouver, Washington, reported that since they live in Washington, they pay no state income tax, and when they shop across the river in Oregon, they pay no sales tax!

Inheritance Taxes   Because the federal government doesn't tax the first $600,000 of your estate, and almost nothing of that which goes to your spouse, the majority of readers of this book won't worry about inheritance taxes. Most states take their share out of what the federal government taxes. (This is called a "pickup tax" for some reason.) But a few others will tax the estate on top of the federal take. If you are in the happy position of having to worry about this, you might check with a tax consultant or lawyer.

Relative Tax Burdens   According to the Advisory Commission of Intergovernmental Relations, the tax burdens of the states discussed in this book are ranked as follows (from lowest to highest):

1. Alabama	9. Mississippi	17. Nevada
2. Arkansas	10. South Carolina	18. Virginia
3. Utah	11. Louisiana	19. Oregon
4. Washington	12. North Carolina	20. California
5. Tennessee	13. Florida	21. Colorado
6. Oklahoma	14. New Mexico	22. Arizona
7. Kentucky	15. Missouri	23. Hawaii
8. Texas	16. Georgia	

Choosing Your Climate

All your working life you've heroically put up with whatever inconveniences, insults and misery your local weather dumped on you. The good

* Tax information from *Significant Features of Fiscal Federalism,* Advisory Commission of Intergovernmental Relations, Feb. 1993.

news is, when you retire, you no longer have to take it; you can look for a perfect climate and live happily ever after. The bad news is, there is no perfect climate.

Folks in Maine love their summers, but say it's too cold in the winter. Their friends in Miami love Florida winters, but complain because summers are hot and muggy. Newcomers to Hawaii say they miss the changes in season. Parts of California have what I consider the best overall climate—sunny, relatively bug-free and comfortable, with low humidity most of the year—yet folks here bitch about winter days below 50 degrees and winter rains that keep them from walks along the beach or sunning beside the pool. (My friends in Michigan think we Californians are weather wimps!)

Even though you can't find the *perfect* climate, you certainly can find one that suits you best. And, chances are that you will find one far superior to the weather you've had to put up with all those working years. This is one of the exciting features about retirement: for the first time in your life, work doesn't dictate where you must live. You now have a *choice* in the matter!

Another advantage of retirement: you needn't lock yourself into one weather pattern. You can choose any *combination* of climates that fits your new lifestyle. Many people keep their home towns as base camps, enjoying wonderful springs and summers there, and then head south to Florida, Texas or Arizona and enjoy another summer. Mexico or Costa Rica for the cold months are entirely practical, as we will discuss later in this book. It takes a little gumption to get started "following the sun," but hundreds of thousands do just that, and they love it! We will also point out how to do it on a bare-bones budget.

Why Not My State?

After publication of a previous retirement guide called *Retirement Choices*, we received letters from readers demanding to know why we hadn't included their home states: Iowa or Indiana, for example. "What do you have against my state?" they inquire. "It's a wonderful place to retire." Other letters complained that we hadn't covered places such as Kalispell, Montana, which often receives retirement writers' praise.

Aside from the obvious explanation that it would be impossible to cover all communities in one book, there are other reasons for limiting coverage. Let's take Kalispell as an example. I've been there in the summer and can vouch for the fact that it's a delightful town in an exceptionally beautiful part of the country. Nearby Glacier National Park and the "Big Sky" Montana country make it a wonderful place to visit and to live. Kalispell itself, however, is not much different from many other pleasant Montana towns. Most folks who were born and raised in Kalispell will surely retire there when they leave the work/marketplace. If statistics hold true, 75 percent will not move away from their home town, just as 75 percent of the retirees in Pittsburgh, Omaha and Milwaukee probably will never move away from their towns.

However, I feel that it is irresponsible to encourage someone from Pittsburgh, Omaha or Milwaukee to leave one cold climate to move to an even colder, bitterly cold climate just for the sake of a few glorious summer months. A major reason folks want to retire someplace other than the northern states is to escape winter's snow and ice. If you're going to move, why not choose someplace comfortable? For those who love snow, surely the 40 to 45 total inches per season in Pittsburgh or Omaha should suffice. But in places like Kalispell, winter effectively begins in October with a three-foot snow pack that stays until April.

From my point of view, it's far better to retire in your home town or move to a pleasantly warm winter climate and then make summer visits to Kalispell and Glacier National Park. I seriously doubt that many Montana retirees eagerly put chains on their cars and cruise through the snowbound, below-zero environs of Glacier Park during winter.

True, some folks thrive on cold weather. They love to bundle up and toodle about the countryside in their snowmobiles, to race full-tilt down the ski slopes or to chop holes through thick ice on the lake to drop in fishing lines. But most retired people, after a few days of outdoor fun, will find themselves lying on sofas in front of television sets when it becomes unbearably cold outside. Precious months of their lives are invested in "Family Feud" and "Jeopardy." Their only outdoor activities are shoveling snow off the driveway and trying to get the car started. Indoor exercise consists of opening and closing the refrigerator door. Had they moved to a warmer climate, they could be playing golf, taking brisk walks or doing laps in the swimming pool throughout the winter.

Snow-phobia

I have to admit that after years of working in towns like Detroit, St. Louis and Chicago, I've acquired a definite bias against winter. As I traveled around the country, I preferred working in warmer places: Florida, Alabama, Texas, Arizona and, finally, California.

In all our many interviews and questionnaires that asked people where they would like to retire, we found not one person with lifelong dreams of moving from their home towns to retire in Pittsburgh, Omaha or Milwaukee—not unless there were specific, individual reasons for doing so. In our research, one overwhelming preference came through clearly: those living in cold climates wanted to move someplace mild, if not warm. As you might guess, those from warm climates didn't think that was so important; obviously, they take comfort for granted.

However, I fully realize that everybody isn't trying to escape snow shovels. Actually, we were surprised to see how often our retirement questionnaires failed to place warm winters at the top of the list. Therefore, having expressed my bias against cold weather, I must point out that this edition does look at some communities in colder states. These places are added because certain advantages and amenities, specific to the areas, more than compensate for the harsh weather.

You'll note that many locations discussed have four distinct seasons, complete with snowfall and freezing Januarys. Places like Prescott, Arizona, or Eureka Springs, Arkansas, for example, boast of seasonal change as one of their attractions. However, if you look at the temperature charts with the place descriptions, you'll notice most places we endorse have mild midday winter temperatures. Ideally, during all but a few days of winter you can go outdoors for a walk wearing a sweater or light jacket. Although it may snow, a typical snowfall is but a few inches, making everything pretty, then generally melting away within a day or so. This contrasts with places like Montana, Minnesota or Michigan where snow is measured in feet rather than in inches, turning alternately from salty slush to ice and collecting soot and dirt until the next layer piles up, month after month, keeping people prisoners indoors.

I feel justified in my bias against harsh winters. Medical and health experts agree that inactivity is a threat to retired folks' health. In warm climates you'll tend to go outdoors more often to exercise and enjoy healthful activities, instead of huddling next to the heater and the television set. Swimming, golf, tennis or brisk walks by the river are enjoyable, year-round activities in warmer climates.

Cold Weather vs. Warm Weather Expenses

Besides comfort and health, another reason for choosing a warm-climate retirement involves economics. Extremely cold weather can eat up more of your budget than any other controllable factor. Many people who answered our questionnaires—those living in cold climates—reported that they spend more money on heating oil than they do at the grocery store. According to our survey, the average retired couple spends about

$265 a month on food, but many who live through sub-zero winters pay that much for heating bills. On the other hand, residents of some warmer places report an average of $40 a month for utilities.

An extra wardrobe is required for cold weather, with down jackets, padded boots and long underwear adding to the seasonal expenses. But clothing is not nearly as expensive as cold-weather destruction to your automobile. Batteries deteriorate rapidly in freezing temperatures, and cold-weather starts wear out engine cylinders. Antifreeze and snow tires also batter away at the budget.

The worst part is that an automobile's life expentancy is dramatically shortened where roads must be salted to clear away ice and snow. Salt eats up steel and body sheet metal faster than termites could ever attack a house! It's interesting to note that automobiles over ten years old are rare in areas where salted roads are the norm. Tourists from cold climates are continually amazed at the variety of old, classic cars still in daily use in places like Arizona, California, and other warm, dry climates. Where they come from, older cars have long ago dissolved in the salt solutions that slosh around on cold-weather streets and highways.

Most retired folks drive fewer miles and reasonably expect their autos to last longer. Suppose you drive 10,000 miles each year, and suppose an automobile can reasonably be expected to give 100,000 miles of service. This would mean surviving ten winters. In a warm climate, that's not unreasonable, but cold-weather salt damage and engine wear can totally trash a car long before its warm-weather life expectancy. (The California automobile I drive is a 1967 Volkswagen Bug. Its body is rust-free and solid, even though I almost never park it in the garage.)

When you total all the extra expenses of winter, you'll see that winter is costly as well as uncomfortable. But what about hot summers? Some retirement writers claim that air conditioning cancels out warm-weather heat savings. It can, of course. I know people who illogically keep their homes heated to 75 degrees in the winter and down to 68 in the summer!

However, there is an important difference in principle between winter heating and summer air conditioning. Keeping warm in the winter is a matter of life and death, whereas summer air conditioning is a matter of relative comfort. When the thermometer rises above 90 degrees, yes, the air conditioner feels nice. A pleasant dip in the pool or lounging in a hammock under the oak trees with an iced tea in hand also does the trick. Unless there is some medical condition to the contrary, you seldom *have* to turn on the air conditioner. Think back a few years—when we were children and nobody had air conditioning—we survived just fine, didn't we? Remember when the only air-conditioned building in town was the local movie theater? However, when a sub-zero freeze settles over your shivering home, you don't have the option of lighting the furnace or not. If you don't, you die. It's as simple as that.

If you absolutely can't stand the thought of hot summers, yet still want above-freezing winters, there are places (mostly on the West Coast) where air conditioning would be a waste of money. In the California town I presently call home (one block from the ocean), nobody uses air conditioners. We sleep under blankets year-round. The same conditions apply in most coastal locations in California, Oregon and Washington. But personally, I miss the yearly experience of a real summer! I dearly love backyard barbecues on warm summer evenings.

Finding Your Optimum Climate

We're fortunate in North America, because we have a wider variety of climates to choose from than almost any other country in the world. We can decide how warm our summers should be or how cold we care to be in winter, and then we can find a town or city that matches our ideals.

How do you find an ideal climate? One way is by studying weather charts of towns and cities throughout the United States. Temperature charts are included with the town profiles throughout the book when data is available for that locality. Not all towns supply weather information to the National Oceanic and Atmospheric Administration, which compiles data in its *Comparative Climatic Data for the United States*. Comparing high and low temperatures with relative humidity should give an accurate picture. That seems simple enough, but a few ways of looking at statistics can lead to misleading conclusions.

One misuse of statistics is commonly found in chamber of commerce literature. Their brochures sometimes quote "average temperatures" which tell you little about the climate. If you average July temperatures of a desert town (where it goes over 100 degrees in the afternoon, but drops to 60 at night), you can come up with a pleasant-sounding 80-degree summer temperature. Or, when you average year-round high temperatures, you may find that Illinois has a climate identical to California, according to statistics anyway.

Averaging humidity for all 12 months is also misleading. Humidity varies widely with the season and makes a big difference in how you perceive temperatures. For example: Sacramento, California, has an average relative humidity of about 46 percent. Yet, afternoon measurements in January show 71 percent and only 28 percent in July!

33

Now, just because statistics on average humidity are not very helpful does not mean that you shouldn't pay attention to humidity at all. At 15 percent humidity—typical of many western desert environments—a 90-degree day will be perceived as 86 degrees of relative comfort. However, a 90-degree day in the Midwest, with 75 percent humidity, will make your body think it's 109 degrees! Since damp air holds heat and dry air doesn't, the desert can be hot during the day and then cool rapidly after the sun goes down. That's why many desert towns with afternoon temperatures over 100 degrees will have lows in the 60s for your sleeping comfort.

Winter humidity readings are equally important. A 40-degree evening in Reno at 28 percent humidity can be quite pleasant—a light sweater does nicely—whereas 40 degrees in Florida at 70 percent humidity drives people indoors to turn up the thermostats. Damp air can also bother people with arthritis, rheumatism or chronic bronchitis. On the other hand, extremely dry climates can dry out the skin and nasal passages, sometimes causing nosebleeds and other complications. Low humidity also means fewer bugs, mosquitoes and critters. The common household cockroach is almost non-existent in dry, Western climates.

Personal Safety

Most everyone agrees that crime is the United States' major problem. Too many people live in neighborhoods as virtual prisoners in their own homes. Instead of criminals being behind bars, law-abiding citizens find themselves hiding behind barred windows and chained doors. Meanwhile, the criminals roam freely through the streets.

There is little we, as private citizens, can do about any of this. The only solution for us retirees is to look for safe places to live. Curiously, in neighborhoods not so very far away from high-crime areas, people can leave their doors unlocked and can walk home from a late movie without anxiety. There are still places where things are almost as calm as they used to be when we were children. Remember when kids used to play outside long after dark? Remember when nobody locked doors? In our research, we've come across many locations with almost that same, safe feeling of those good old days. (I say *almost* because conditions have changed, even in the best of places.)

Not long ago my wife and I bought a summer home in a small town in Oregon (less than 100 population). When we inquired about safety there, we discovered some residents never lock their cars and some even leave their keys in the ignition so they won't lose them! On the other hand, other Oregon residents (in a much larger city) also don't lock their cars, but for another reason. Automobile break-ins are so common in their neighborhood that locking the car doors is an invitation for a thief to break the windows to see if something valuable might be inside. Yet, in the better neighborhoods of that same city, things are safe.

Causes of Crime

Why are some neighborhoods safe and others plagued by thefts and burglaries? What are the factors that make for an "old-fashioned" neighborhood? The experts can't answer either question with certainty. There are some clues, however, discovered by criminologists, sociologists and law enforcement specialists that we can pass along in this chapter.

One factor that does *not* seem to determine crime levels is the number of police in a town. In our little Oregon town, we have *no* police force; the nearest police officer is 15 miles away along a narrow, winding road. He seldom visits our town unless specifically summoned. Yet, long-time residents in our community can't recall the last time a house was burglarized. New York City, on the other hand, has more cops than small countries have soldiers; some neighborhoods there have more than a thousand cops per square mile. Doesn't help a bit. The point is, a large number of police officers is a *response* to a high crime rate, not an indication of how safe a place is. Cops don't prevent crime; their job is to apprehend criminals *after* the crime is committed.

Generally, the larger the city, the higher the crime rate. However, even among the larger cities, you'll find areas of relative tranquility, sometimes not too far from the problem areas. These are usually stable, low-turnover neighborhoods where residents know each other and where most people are over 50. (Few teenagers mean low crime rates.)

When you have a large population of young people—particularly males between the ages of 15 and 30—coupled with high unemployment, you have an ideal crime situation. According to the FBI, about four-fifths of all arrests for property crimes or for violent offenses are males age 20 years or younger. That's one reason adult-only communities are safer.

Another point: don't make the mistake of automatically associating unemployment with crime. In some parts of the country with high unemployment, crime rates are *lower* than in areas where jobs are plentiful!

Criminologists point to several factors, such as the time of day or months of the year, when certain offenses are more likely to occur. Winter (except for Christmas holidays) is a slow time for burglars and summer months are busy ones; August is the busiest month of all. Daytime burglaries account for 49 percent of the offenses, 51 percent after dark. Most home burglaries occur during the daylight hours, when people are at work, leaving their homes unoccupied. Houses with non-working residents—such as retirees—with unpredictable schedules are far less likely to be robbed. Burglars prefer houses with nobody home and occupants unlikely to return for a time. (If there's anything a burglar hates, it's having someone look over his shoulder as he works.) Most business burglaries happen at night or on weekends when the offices are closed (otherwise the crime would be theft instead of burglary).

However, some of these facts seem irrelevant. For retirees, the important thing is not *when* burglaries occur but *where* and *how frequently* they happen.

Finding a Crime-Free Area

Unfortunately, there is no such thing as a crime-free area. As long as people live in social groups, there will always be individuals who can't seem to distinguish between their belongings and those of their neighbors. It just stands to reason that the larger the social group, the more deviant individuals it produces. Thus, you find much higher crime rates in Washington, D.C., than in Walla Walla, Washington, and more crimes in New York City, New York, than in New Madrid, Missouri.

The safety ratings in each chapter will give you a start toward locating a low-crime locale. You also might check out a list of potential retirement towns by going to your public library and asking for the FBI's publication, *Crime in the United States—Uniform Crime Reports.* The time you spend analyzing the city, county and state reports will be fascinating. Before writing off a community because of a high number of crimes listed, remember that some offenses, like assault, are often inflated because of special circumstances such as an armed forces training facility nearby (the kids like to brawl when on leave), massive arrests during traditional spring breaks for college students, or an unusually strict enforcement policy by the local police department.

While you're at the library, check the out-of-state newspaper section and check on how crime is reported in the hometown newspaper. As mentioned earlier, this can tell you a lot about crime. For example: not long ago, I noticed an article in the *New York Times* with a headline that read: "Two Shot Dead, Three Wounded After Collision."

The killings occurred in Manhattan after a fender-bender at an intersection. Apparently the problem started when someone in the crowd pointed out that the cars were blocking traffic. This incensed one of the drivers. He whipped out a gun and opened fire on the crowd of bystanders. Two dead, three wounded. If a horrible crime of this magnitude happened in most other civilized nations, headlines would scream the event across front pages in every newspaper in the country. Yet, in New York City, a crime of this consequence rates a one-column story on the corner of page 23!

As a rule, your best bet for finding a low-tension, low-crime area is to choose a small town or suburb. However, not *all* small towns are idyllic islands of honest citizenship and peaceful tranquility. Occasionally you'll run across one that is surprisingly violent and plagued by persistent burglars and robbers. On the other hand, just because a town is peaceful doesn't mean that it is a great place to live. It could also be so boring that burglars and robbers can't stand working there.

You can learn a great deal about a neighborhood by simply driving around and observing. Are the homes neat, with trimmed shrubbery and mowed lawns, or are they shabby, obviously owned by absentee landlords? Are there lots of old junkers parked around the neighborhood, with teenagers trying to get them started? Or do you see folks your own age working in the yard, walking the dog or polishing the car? The best way to ascertain a neighborhood's safety is to simply ask. If folks feel safe living there, they're happy to tell you all about it. If they offer to lend you a weapon to protect yourself, it's not a safe neighborhood.

FBI Crime Reports

In the FBI's *Crime in the United States* the list of criminal offenses is broken down into the types of crime committed: murder, forcible rape, robbery, aggravated assault, burglary, larceny-theft, and automobile theft. In this book, we carefully analyze these statistics and attempt to interpret them from the viewpoint of someone looking for a safe place to retire. Unfortunately, the FBI doesn't publish statistics on places with less than 10,000 population. Furthermore, not all towns submit reports to the FBI. Even worse, police departments commonly juggle figures to make themselves look good.

Funny thing about crime statistics; when you study them closely, something curious happens—some common beliefs seem to shift position. For instance: I had always imagined that the highest rates of burglaries and robberies should occur in the wealthiest neighborhoods. After all, wouldn't they be the most lucrative places for burglars to operate? Certainly, if I were a burglar, I'd seek out affluent families to be my clients. Surprisingly enough, the wealthiest neighborhoods tend to have the *lowest* crime rates! Poor neighborhoods suffer the most break-ins, robberies and assaults.

You'll notice something else about crime rates: the safest places are small towns; the worst crime areas are in large cities. Nothing surprising about that. The problem is, when you lump together crime statistics from a large conglomeration of communities, like Los Angeles, you'll get a foggy picture. According to FBI crime figures, Los Angeles ranks medium in safety, about the same as Tucson, Arizona, or Eureka, California. My personal rating places L.A. much lower on the scale, but this still doesn't give you the complete picture. Because so many neighborhoods are included— safe neighborhoods outnumbering the exceedingly dangerous areas—statistics would prove Los Angeles to be a safe place to live. Not exactly. Example: Hermosa Beach, an affluent suburb in the L.A. metropolitan area, ranks exceptionally high in safety, yet is 20 minutes away from one of the highest crime areas in the country.

Let's analyze the FBI reports and see what they really mean to retired folks. The charts and statistics which follow illustrate the types of crime in an average community and their frequency.

Distribution of Criminal Offenses

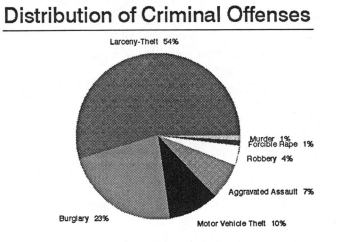

Larceny-Theft 54%

Murder 1%
Forcible Rape 1%

Robbery 4%

Aggravated Assault 7%

Burglary 23%

Motor Vehicle Theft 10%

Aggravated Assault   Most aggravated assault incidents happen when young people get to arguing after a few drinks and start punching each other out. The vast majority of those involved are males under the age of 30. Frequently, drug deals are involved. This is another statistic that doesn't affect the elderly to any great measure.

Sometimes the number of arrests for aggravated assault is an indication of police diligence. They'll arrest brawlers rather than send them home with warnings. In resort areas, the incidence of assault will also be high when crowds of boisterous young college students congregate to celebrate semester break. The other side of the coin is when cops don't bother about barroom fights or neighborhood brawls unless there are injuries. Since most retirees won't be retiring in neighborhoods where assault cases occur, these statistics aren't as crucial. My considered advice is this: avoid getting into fistfights with people under the age of 30, and you'll probably avoid contributing to the statistics.

Burglary The important crimes for most senior citizens are "violent" offenses—crimes such as burglary and robbery. You might ask, "Why include burglary as a violent crime?" Ask anyone whose home has been ransacked and you'll invariably hear something like, "I felt as though I had been raped. The thought that someone could enter my home and do as they please frightens me as much as anything I can think of." Violating the privacy of your home is indeed violence against your person.

Now, the national average of burglaries is close to 13 per thousand people. This is shocking. Some of the sting is taken away when you realize that one-third of the burglaries are against businesses. Consider also, some neighborhoods suffer three to eight times as many burglaries as other, safer places, raising the overall burglary rate. Also, some people are burglarized several times while others, never. A police officer once told me, "When we find a multiple-burglary victim, we immediately look for a male teenage relative—a son, nephew or grandson—who is into drugs and who knows the routine in the family home. When we find this situation, we find our burglar."

The fewest burglaries occur in quiet neighborhoods, where most homes are owner-occupied, and where residents tend to be older. More break-ins occur in areas where a high proportion of tenants are young and transient. Large numbers of neighborhood teenagers is a bad sign.

Robbery This is another common violent crime. Whether the robber uses a gun, a knife or physical threat to take your valuables, the end result is the same: a strike against your self-confidence and your sense of security. Robberies account for only 4 percent of all crimes, yet that 4 percent is important, since more than half the offenses occurred on streets or highways. The other half were against businesses.

There is a definite pattern to robberies. They rarely happen in peaceful, residential neighborhoods. Smaller towns and suburban areas are the safest. Robbery statistics are relevant since they show an area's level of violent crime and a probable linkage to drug addiction. Unlike aggravated assault, robbery victims are not mostly males under 30; they can be any age. The best way to avoid muggings and holdups is to avoid areas where they are likely to occur.

Rape and Murder   Forcible rape and murder rates are very low for senior citizens, even for those living in high-crime areas. Most rape victims, for example, are 40 years or younger.

The most serious crime possible, murder, accounts for only 1 percent of all crimes committed. Again, most murder victims are males, 30 years or younger, with the biggest percentage being 15- to 24-year-old males. Senior citizens are rarely involved. Statistics notwithstanding, this is of small comfort to the families of those murdered. Interesting to note, strangers aren't to blame for the typical murder. Most murders are committed by family members, friends or acquaintances. Only 13 percent of the murders are committed by total strangers, and again, most murder victims are youngsters. Sigh!

Larceny-Theft Crimes . The majority of reported offenses fall into one major category: larceny-theft. Police report twice as many larceny-theft crimes as burglaries, sometimes three times as many. Purse-snatching and pocket-picking—while definitely threats to elderly victims—account for only 2 percent of all larceny-theft crimes. In many low-crime areas, these offenses are almost unheard of. When high rates of purse-snatching—as high as 5 percent in some downtown areas—are mixed with low rates elsewhere, we end up with the 1 percent figure.

The next three crimes—coin machine robbery, shoplifting and non-burglary theft from buildings—account for a whopping 31 percent of all larceny-theft crimes. Personally, I lose very little sleep worrying about coin machine vandalism. Shoplifting is another crime that doesn't affect senior citizens. (Not unless we get caught at it!) Ditto for thefts from public buildings. It's a shame that people steal things, but as long as they aren't stealing from me or my neighbors, I can sleep soundly. The burglary rate in *my* neighborhood is far more important to me than what happens in downtown businesses.

The largest percentage of theft is from automobiles (22 percent). This is the easiest kind of theft to prevent: simply don't leave valuables in your car! It's hard to muster sympathy for someone who loses a purse or wallet because it was left in plain sight in an unlocked automobile.

Another common crime is stealing automobile accessories (hub caps, stereos, etc.), accounting for 16 percent of all thefts. Accessory theft is not preventable, but since you are insured, your losses will be negligible. One way to minimize the risk of having your stereo stolen is to park your car in a low-crime area.

Some thieves specialize in stealing the whole car. Clearly, there is very little you can do to prevent someone from driving away with your wheels. If a professional wants your vehicle, you can bet he will take it. Car theft is big business. Experts will travel to any city, town or neighborhood to select the exact model they are looking for. A good car thief can get into your car and drive it away in less time than you can—and you have the keys! So, don't worry about car theft; just keep your insurance current and don't leave valuables inside.

The "all others" portion of the larceny-theft chart refers to crimes like embezzlement and bad checks. Again, these aren't crimes that need occupy much of our attention or need worry us to any great extent as long as we don't take any bum checks (or write any).

To recap, the vast majority of larceny-theft crimes target businesses or else are covered by auto insurance. Therefore, when analyzing crime rates for residential areas, I feel it's a mistake to give these statistics the same importance as crimes like burglary and robbery. You end up with a distorted picture because a residential area—without stores and businesses to report shoplifting, thefts and coin machine vandalism—appears to have a very low crime rate even though residential burglaries are common. Conversely, a commercial area where shoplifting is prevalent—or where zealous security guards snare 90 percent of the offenders—might show a high rate of crime, even though crimes that threaten retired folks could be low.

Breakdown of Larceny-Theft

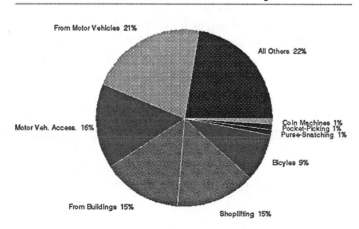

From Motor Vehicles 21%

All Others 22%

Motor Veh. Access. 16%

Coin Machines 1%
Pocket-Picking 1%
Purse-Snatching 1%

Bicyles 9%

From Buildings 15%

Shoplifting 15%

Our Safety Ratings

Along with the descriptions of the towns presented in this book, you will find bar graphs indicating their relative safety. This at-a-glance measurement is based on many hours of testing, comparing and compiling figures supplied by police departments around the country through the FBI. It's important to remember that the graphs are only a means of comparison. I can't emphasize too strongly that cities with exceptionally high crime ratings almost always have enclaves of peace and security in the suburbs.

Also keep in mind that resort towns will naturally show higher crime rates for reasons not related to retiree safety. For example: burglary rates can be exceptionally high in seasonal resort towns or other places where homeowners live elsewhere most of the year, leaving their places as tempting targets for local teenagers. Year-round residents aren't affected by this. In high tourist areas, crime statistics soar because police make more arrests for disorderly behavior, and many crooks specialize in tourists. This makes the town appear to be less safe, which isn't necessarily so. For example, Fort Myers and Cape Coral, Florida, are about equal in size; they sit adjacent to each other, and for all practical purposes can be considered one city. Yet because Cape Coral is primarily residential, its crime rate is exceptionally low, and because Fort Myers attracts many tourists, crime figures are high. We've tried to compensate for such misleading statistics in our graphs.

Some small towns look worse than they really are simply because the cops are gung-ho and arrest anyone who gets slightly out of line, and are quite proud of their arrest records. On the other hand, some police departments are notorious for suppressing crime statistics. This makes them look good and makes it easier to get increases in their budget from the city council. While working with the new FBI statistics, I discovered a community that scored exceptionally "safe" because theft and larceny offenses were way down last year. Now, I know that town; it's a place where I wouldn't walk Main Street without a Doberman at my side (a big, mean one). I can only suspect that thefts are down because there's nothing left to steal! They're out stealing in other neighborhoods.

To reiterate, crime statistics are merely a guide. Don't write off a delightful retirement haven because of some statistics! Go and see for yourself, talk to the local people and get a feeling for what it's like to live there. It may not be that bad.

Chapter 2

Florida: Retirement Tradition

When dreaming of retirement, many people automatically picture Florida. Visions of warm weather, snow-free streets and easy living dance temptingly through their retirement fantasies. Soft, sandy beaches with swaying palm trees and balmy January days complete the vision. Beginning in the 1920s, retirees moved south in such numbers that Florida retirement became almost a cliché.

Recently, some have started to question this traditional Florida dream. Attention-catching, negative publicity recently sent waves of doubt throughout the nation. Magazines, newspapers and television describe Florida as a place of violence, overcrowding and general disrepair. Tourist-robberies, car-jackings and drive-by shootings make Florida sound dangerous. Hurricanes, drugs and illegal immigration would appear to foreclose Florida as a nice place to retire.

Does this mean we should write off Florida as a viable choice? *Not by any means!* From our research, we are convinced that of all the states, Florida still offers the best bargains in quality living and affordable retirement for the average retiree. Regardless of what you see on TV, most Florida communities are as safe as other popular retirement destinations. If this book were to give ratings, many Florida towns would receive ratings far above similar-sized towns elsewhere—both in livability and safety. Even though it isn't for everyone, Florida is still a great place to retire. That is precisely why so many retire here!

Recently I asked a Florida friend from Cape Coral how she felt about her own personal safety and her family's experiences with the crime problem. She replied, "The only crime I see is on television or newspaper front pages. It doesn't bother me, because most violent crimes happen in places I'd never go in the first place. I don't live in a high-crime area, so I feel safe." Crime statistics confirm that many Florida places rank exceptionally high in safety. Cape Coral is a good example; it happens to have one of the state's lowest crime rates, and compares well with other U.S. cities.

Another Florida retiree offered this observation: "The secret to avoiding problems in Florida is to stay away from tourist attractions. Criminals know that tourists have money, and wherever you find tourists and money, that's where criminals go. They don't hang around neighborhoods like mine." I visited this man and his wife in their rural community home in central Florida. It certainly seemed peaceful enough. The view from their living room picture window was across an expanse of wetlands to a distant meadow where three Holstein cows grazed.

Isn't Florida Overcrowded?

Florida is the fourth most populous state in the Union. New residents move here at the rate of 900 a day, most of them retirees. Florida is expected to be third in population by the beginning of the new century, ranking only behind New York and California.

With all those retirees moving in, isn't Florida overcrowded? That depends upon what part of Florida we're talking about. Certainly, some parts of Florida are heavily populated, with high-rise apartments and condos clustered together with nothing but shopping centers and parking lots to break the monotony. Yet, large sections of Florida are sparsely populated. Thousands of square miles scarcely know the presence of humans. Herons, egrets, ducks, storks and wildfowl of all description share vast expanses of land with other wildlife ranging from panthers to rabbits and alligators to turtles. Deer abound in the open countryside and in the state's large system of national forests.

Lightly-populated central Florida features rolling, wooded terrain dotted with small towns and crossroad communities comparable to those in small-town Ohio or Illinois. They are quiet, safe and rural. Were it not for an occasional palm tree, you could easily forget this is Florida. These places are often overlooked in retirees' enthusiasm for living close to beaches and excitement. Surprisingly, most locations in the interior require much less than an hour's drive to a beach. No place in the entire state is more than 70 miles from salt water. Some towns in the very center of the state give you a choice: an hour or so drive in either direction takes you to the Atlantic Ocean or to the Gulf of Mexico. You can spend a day playing in the sand and return home in time for dinner. And the state is well endowed with coastline, 8,426 miles of it!

Florida offers a wide range of choices. You can select the convenience and excitement of a city, or you can choose a small-town atmosphere with slow traffic and rural tranquility. Florida has it all, except perhaps mountain climbing and downhill skiing.

Florida Weather

The near-tropical climate of Florida's peninsula has always been the main attraction for those in the North and Midwest who want something better to do with their winters than shovel snow and stay indoors to watch TV. January afternoon temperatures generally climb into the 60s or low 70s, with nights dropping to the 40s and 50s in some areas. Summers are hot, to be sure, but aren't summers in the Midwest and North scorchers, too? If you insist upon cool summers *and* mild winters, you need to think Pacific Coast—California, Oregon or Washington. But that's in another chapter. In the summer, early morning temperatures are usually in the 70s, giving you plenty of opportunity to exercise outdoors. Summer afternoons are why God gave Florida swimming pools.

Florida's tropical setting is an accident created by a huge flow of warm water—a kind of oceanic river—known as the Gulf Stream. This balmy current sweeps up from the Caribbean, hooks around the Florida Keys and then brushes across Florida's east coast. Its benevolent warmth flows close to shore, bestowing its blessings on the Atlantic coast, until a point near Vero Beach, where it swerves out to sea.

The entire state benefits from the Gulf Stream, but the 80-mile stretch of southeastern coast known as the "Gold Coast" is the biggest beneficiary. Summers here aren't quite as hot because of the ocean's constant temperature and some cloud cover. The best part is winter; this part of Florida is warmer than anywhere else in the continental United States. This dreamy weather explains why you see several million people crowded together along the Gold Coast.

The rest of Florida experiences cooler winters and warmer summers than the Gold Coast, but not remarkably so, because the Gulf Stream—although offshore a distance in the northern parts and across the peninsula from the western shore—still influences the weather. All but Florida's coldest winter days are pleasant enough for golf or bicycling; rarely will you see frost in the morning. January lows average 52 degrees in Fort Myers (on the Gulf Coast side), compared with Miami's 60 degrees. Yet the average January high reaches 75 degrees in Fort Myers and 76 in Miami. Not bad for January!

Further north along the Gulf, winters are cooler. Pensacola sees January highs averaging around 61 degrees and lows around 42. This is balmy to those who are used to below-zero chill factors all winter long. Canadians are known to swim in the Gulf of Mexico throughout the winter (shudder).

Rainfall in Florida is generous. Most of the state rests on porous limestone, covered with layers of sand and clay. This acts like a giant sponge, soaking up the rainfall and providing almost unlimited water supplies, even in times of drought. Water problems will occur, however, near the coast, when seawater seeps in and makes drinking water brackish. This is something you need to check on when buying beach property. Insist on a water quality report before making an offer.

> **FLORIDA TAX PROFILE**
> **Sales tax:** 6% to 7%, food, drugs exempt
> **State income tax:** no
> **Property taxes:** approximately 1.6%
> **Intangibles tax:** yes
> **Social Security taxed:** no
> **Pensions taxed:** no
> **Gasoline tax:** 4¢ to 10¢ per gallon

Thanks to its far-ranging ocean breezes, air pollution is all but non-existent in Florida. Among the ten "cleanest" cities in the United States, three are in Florida: West Palm Beach, Orlando and Jacksonville. The biggest industry here is tourism; tourists don't pollute the air, just the beaches.

Because of Florida's warm winter and balmy spring, many major league baseball teams make their spring training headquarters here. Every year more than a dozen ball clubs call Florida home, and residents all over the state enjoy the spring training games. Many people retire here specifically for that purpose. Among the teams here:

Atlanta Braves—West Palm Beach   Kansas City Royals—Baseball City
Baltimore Orioles—St. Petersburg   Minnesota Twins—Ft. Myers
Boston Red Sox—Ft. Myers   New York Mets—Port St. Lucie
Chicago White Sox—Sarasota   Philadelphia Phillies—Clearwater
Cincinnati Reds—Plant City   Pittsburgh Pirates—Bradenton
Cleveland Indians—Winter Haven   St. Louis Cardinals—St. Petersburg
Detroit Tigers—Lakeland   Texas Rangers—Port Charlotte
Houston Astros—Kissimmee   Toronto Blue Jays—Dunedin

Florida Real Estate

If high-quality, yet inexpensive, real estate is an important consideration, then Florida should rank high, for you'll find the best bargains, dollar for dollar and feature for feature, here of anywhere in the country. True, you can find homes selling for less in Oklahoma or Idaho, but as I continually stress, cheap housing should not govern your retirement choices.

Florida offers virtually any kind of housing imaginable. Condos, townhouses and apartments are common along the coasts, or wherever land costs are high. Mobile homes and manufactured homes (mobile homes on foundations) allow for downscale, economical housing. Traditional subdivisions are common, particularly away from the beaches, as are custom homes. A common type of development is a "retirement community," often reserved for over-55 folks and built around a clubhouse and tennis courts, sometimes with its own private golf course and other facilities.

Coastal Properties

For many folks, tourists and retirees alike, Florida's beaches are what it's all about. Condos rent by the day or week and motels, hotels and glitzy restaurants abound, mostly catering to the needs of vacationers and weekend visitors. Yet, just a few miles away from the beachfront crush—sometimes just a few blocks away—a different world presents itself: the world of residents.

It's entirely possible to live in a quiet, normal neighborhood and then—whenever you choose—slip away to join the hedonistic, suntan-crazy world of the tourist, just a few blocks away. When the sun starts to set, you can walk home to peace and quiet. With beaches on three sides of Florida—east, west and south—no matter where you decide to settle, you can be near the coast.

Not all beachfront real estate is devoted to tourism; most coastal properties are residential. Some of the fanciest housing is found along sandy beaches, screened from the road by thick stands of palms and tropical shrubbery. Some areas are so exclusive that the only research we did was to drive past and sigh enviously. Yet, happily, there are beach areas where houses are definitely affordable.

Golf and Boating Properties

One of Florida's top retirement benefits is year-round outdoor recreation. Not surprisingly, some of the most successful retirement communities here are those focused on exercise and recreation. Thus we find country-club developments featuring Olympic-sized pools, exercise rooms, jogging paths and golf courses as centerpieces. The more desirable homes edge expanses of greens and fairways, giving a wide-open feeling as well as access to the game. In addition to the first tee sitting just a three-iron shot away from your back door, you probably won't have to wait long for a starting time, since residence in the development usually includes membership in the club.

The good part about some golf complexes is that membership is optional, so if you play golf as badly as I do, you don't have to pay for upkeep of the golf course and feel obligated to humiliate yourself on a regular basis. Often, these courses are open to the public, with green fees for non-club members affordable. A typical monthly fee (without golf) might be about $100, for which you receive cable TV, have your lawn mowed and edged, and have membership in the community club complete with tennis courts and swimming pool, social activities, hobbies and dinners. Not only are houses and condominiums commonly bundled with a golf course, but some of the more expensive mobile home communities often feature their own links.

Another Florida innovation is boat-canal living: homes built along a waterway, with sailboats, powerboats and yachts tied up in their backyards. Residents of canal developments enjoy the ocean or gulf in ways that beachside folks can not. Some boating communities are locked-in or gated arrangements, but most are in open neighborhoods. I'm continually surprised that homes backing up to a canal are often priced not much higher than similar places in "dry" neighborhoods.

Developing a boating community isn't as expensive or extravagant as it might seem. Since so much of Florida's real estate is low lying—just a few feet above sea level—a practical way of reclaiming marsh land is to dredge drainage canals and use the dredged material as landfill to raise the level of the land. Since canals must be constructed anyway, boating access is a natural result of the preparation of the land for housing. All that remains is to place a wooden dock at the rear of each home and put up signs pointing the way to the salt water.

Although country club-type golf, tennis and boating communities would appear to be expensive and luxurious, they can be surprisingly affordable. In fact, compared with some parts of the country, these houses can be downright cheap! To be sure, there are monthly maintenance fees, but because the golf courses, swimming pools and tennis courts serve the country club community, the costs and upkeep are spread among hundreds of families.

Ordinary Housing

Regular single-family homes, the kind you'll find in subdivisions and neighborhoods all over America, are priced quite reasonably. In most parts of Florida, two- or three-bedroom homes can usually be found in the low $60,000 range. Although only a small percentage of the housing goes for $50,000 and less, homes in this range can be found. I visited a friend's daughter recently in West Palm Beach, where she lives in a $45,000 home she purchased in the summer of 1993. It was perfectly adequate, not far from the beach and good shopping, and most important, it was what she could afford.

A continual difference of opinion exists between those who insist on retiring in a regular neighborhood, with neighbors of mixed ages and generations, and those who prefer the "same-age community" of the retirement developments. Each has its advantages. The decision largely depends on your particular personality and lifestyle.

Those who make friends easily and tend to jump feet-first into community affairs will choose the mixed-generation neighborhoods. They'll soon know everyone on the block and will build a social life quickly. Other people have individual outside interests such as ocean fishing, college classes or developing a part-time business. They don't need or want organized activities to keep them busy; they already have too much to do. If they want a swimming pool, they'll buy a home with one already installed, and they won't have to share it with others. They don't see any point in paying extra money for something they won't use.

Those who prefer the retirement communities love the idea of entering a neighborhood where everything is in place. Newcomers are immediately part of a social group and automatically invited to join bridge clubs, hobby groups and all sorts of organized activities. They don't have to look for things to do and people to make friends with; this just happens. They won't feel like strangers in a new neighborhood; their neighbors come from somewhere else, too. Back in their home towns, when they were younger, the neighborhood children were the focal point. Parents became friends of their children's friends; social life often focused around school activities. Now, they feel they'd have little in common with younger neighbors in a traditional neighborhood.

To be perfectly honest, my wife and I can't decide which option we prefer. We have no recommendations one way or another.

The Mobile Home Alternative

Those who are able to move to Florida and buy any property they choose with little regard for price are usually those fortunate people who bought a home in the 1950s for the going price, then in the 1990s sold for a 300 percent profit. Perhaps they realized a 1,000 percent profit; that's not unusual. These folks pay cash for their retirement homes and stash the rest of their profits in the bank, the monthly interest helping with expenses.

But we all weren't that lucky or that far-seeing. If you've lived in an apartment or rented a house all these years, you'll probably be renting when you move to Florida. However, there is another option: a mobile home. Although you can pay as much for a Florida mobile home as you would for a conventional home, you can also buy one for the same price as a used car. At that price it won't be elegant, but it will be yours.

Mobile homes are a standard feature in most Florida communities. Unlike some other states, where mobile homes are considered low-cost housing, many parks and developments in Florida are as spiffy (and as expensive) as some upscale traditional home communities. So many families live in mobile homes that owners have become an organized political force in the state. Lobbyists for mobile homeowners' associations continually press for legislation protecting their rights.

Don't get the idea that the cheaper mobile homes are only for the impoverished. Other benefits accrue to this lifestyle besides low-cost living, not the least of which are friendly neighbors and park clubhouse social activities. Also, a great number of retirees who can afford more expensive housing would rather put even more of their home-sale profits into income-producing investments.

Mobile home parks come in all levels of luxury, from the strictly utilitarian, with no amenities except a laundry room, to the ultra-luxurious, complete with 18-hole golf courses, Olympic-sized pools and deluxe country club surroundings. Prices can be remarkably low or exorbitantly high, depending upon the level of park you choose. Most of the better ones also sell new mobile homes and will set one up to your specifications.

Following are several mobile home scenarios we found during our last visit to the state. One was in Florida's interior, northwest of Tampa. We interviewed a couple from Clarksville, Tennessee, who were in the process of purchasing a new 14-foot wide, 70-foot long, two-bedroom, two-bath mobile home. The cost was $17,900, installed on a lot (all hookups, air conditioning, etc., included). They bought their lot for $7,000 in a park with a nine-hole golf course. If the lot hadn't been next to the golf course, it would have cost only $3,000. The monthly membership fee: $75, which includes maintenance of their small lawn.

"We could have bought an acre lot away from town for $10,000," said the wife, "but since we plan on spending most summers in Tennessee, we feel better about having close neighbors to watch our home while we're gone." Her husband said, "We were coming here every winter and spending $900 a month for a small condo, so we decided to get our own place. And for $75 a month, we can afford to let it sit empty while we're traveling."

Another, even less expensive example, is the case of an old friend who lives in Boynton Beach, on the Intracoastal Waterway between Palm Beach and Boca Raton. Ed is a spry 93 years old, very much interested in fishing, betting on dog races and playing the "penny" stock market. His park is definitely an economy affair, packed with trailers 35 feet long and under—mostly one-bedroom—showing unmistakable signs of age.

"Most folks who live here are from Canada," Ed said as he took me on a guided tour of his park. "Most of 'em go home about the first of April." He led the way onto a dock jutting into the Intracoastal waterway, about 150 feet from his trailer door. "Couldn't get any closer to the water, not without owning one of those half-million dollar houses on Palm Beach. This is where I catch fish. I could damn near have a fish dinner every evening if I wanted." He pointed out a well-kept trailer with a For Sale sign in the window. "Canadian lady owns that one," he said, "Wants $3,500 for it. It's bigger than mine, but I'm satisfied where I am."

How much does it cost to live here? "My rent just went up," he replied. "Now I pay $150 a month. With my social security and the money I win at the dog track, I put money in the bank every month." I thought he was joking, but when we went to the track that afternoon, Ed won $86 while I lost 18 bucks.

Over on the Gulf Coast, near Sarasota, we looked at three levels of park luxury in a single afternoon. The first was truly spiffy, with new double-wide, three-bedroom, two-bath units on large lots selling in excess of $65,000. This park had all the amenities, including a golf course, tennis courts and a deluxe clubhouse. Park rent was about $350.

Nearby was a mid-range park, with units grouped around a small lake (no golf course, but some tennis courts and a large swimming pool). Used two-bedroom units were priced at $14,000 to $21,000, with new units starting at $27,000, all double-wide. The landscaping was elegant, and the clubhouse had a social director to organize activities. Park rent was $225 a month. In other, more rural areas, similar parks advertise $150 a month rent, including water, sewer and trash.

The third park was two miles closer to town and was full of older units, many 20 years old. The mobile homes here were spaced closely together, similar to conventional parks found in other parts of the country. The only facility was a laundry room, which served as a place to meet and gossip. According to residents, there was a level of social activity, but organized by residents on an informal basis rather than by the park management. It was quite pleasant and peaceful, with mature trees for shade. A few homes displayed For Sale signs, including a single-wide, two-bedroom place for under $8,000. Park rent was $175 a month.

Most parks we inspected included lawn maintenance in the rent. This makes it nice for those who spend the winter months in an inexpensive mobile home and then leave it for the rest of the year. But it isn't just snowbirds who live in the less-expensive units. The majority in the parks we visited were full-time Florida residents. It was comforting to realize that people of limited means have the opportunity to retire in their own home in Florida so inexpensively.

Many developments sell mobile home lots rather than simply renting them. This is usually a package deal; they sell you a mobile home as well as the land. One park we visited in Brooksville offered a $38,900 package (including taxes and fees) for a good-sized lot and a two-bedroom mobile home with carport, utility room and screened patio. It had a 24-hour guarded gate, a swimming pool and tennis courts. This price seemed in line with others, although we've seen advertisements for mobile homes complete with land for much less. As with any community development, monthly membership and maintenance fees go on top of the original price.

Try Before You Buy

Renting mobile homes is rarely permitted in all but the cheapest parks. However, an interesting concept in mobile home living—one we've seen in a few Florida parks but not elsewhere—is a "try before you buy" plan. A park near the town of Hudson, for example, has a limited number of two-bedroom, furnished mobile homes for lease. Average-looking, well-kept and nicely landscaped—but without a golf course or lake—this park offers trials with a minimum stay of three months, maximum six months. The manager of the park told us, "We don't make money on these leases, but most folks decide to buy after they spend a month or two here, getting acquainted. This is our best sales producer."

For more information about Florida mobile home living, write to the magazine *Mobile Homes and Parks* at 17 Live Oak Avenue, Yalaha, FL 34797. It publishes a directory of mobile home parks that lists all the better places in the state.

You can sometimes try before you buy in some conventional-housing retirement complexes, using their special rental units. They also encourage buyers to purchase homes long *before* retirement. They will then rent your home while you are waiting to retire, and, presumably, the income will defray expenses and loan payments. One developer guaranteed us $7,000-a-year income to put against our loan, should we decide to buy. I look upon these deals with a suspicious eye. It's the old saying: anything that sounds too good to be true, usually is. It could be financially sound, or it could be another high-pressure sales gimmick; we were unable to interview anyone who had experience, good or bad.

Rent or Own?

Apartment rentals offer an interesting alternative. Not everyone is up to buying property. Even though prices are comparatively reasonable in Florida, home-buying still involves a considerable outlay of cash. Investing savings in a home means forgoing the interest or dividends that money would earn if invested in stocks or a money market fund. For example: an $80,000 investment at a 7-percent return would bring in $466 a month. That $466 a month you lose by not investing can rent a nice apartment in Florida. In other words, the money you save by *not* buying a house allows you to live rent-free.

Example: a nice apartment complex in Daytona Beach offers two bedrooms, air conditioning, two swimming pools, lighted tennis courts and 24-hour emergency service, for $450 per month. A one-bedroom place rents for $335. Throughout the state, the local shopping centers usually have free, full-color booklets and brochures listing apartment complexes complete with color photos of the grounds and facilities.

Almost anywhere you'll find an abundance of competing apartments, each trying to offer more than its neighbor to attract tenants. Swimming pools, hot tubs and tennis courts are standard equipment, as are putting greens, exercise rooms and billiards.

Why are apartments so high class and low priced? The answer is overbuilding: too many apartment buildings competing for too few tenants. It's the age-old law of supply and demand in action. You see, during the wild-west heyday of our savings-and-loan rodeo—when the *supply* of depositors' money was as unlimited as the *demands* of promoters—billions of dollars were spent building shopping centers, commercial buildings and apartment buildings. Florida was considered an especially nice place to build. Since the supply of savings-and-loan dollars was virtually unlimited, we now have an overly generous supply of apartment complexes.

Wheeling and Dealing

Florida has long been famous for the land salesman with glib talk, fast pencils and alligator shoes: the epitome of the wheeler-dealer. This tradition originated many years ago, when a tourist from Madrid—a guy named Ponce de Leon—purchased some land from a Seminole real estate salesman. At the time, it seemed like a good deal; after all, the property included a genuine Fountain of Youth. But it turned out the deed was faulty, and poor ol' Ponce ran himself bedraggled trying to locate the parcel on the tract map. Never did find it. The Fountain of Youth is still in escrow.

From that point on, Florida real estate ethics steadily slipped downhill. Promoters eagerly began subdividing swamps and selling lovely underwater lots by mail throughout the country. When they ran out of swamp, they made do with ocean bottom. Oddly enough, some of this property became valuable when the swamps were drained.

Because of a steady flow of buyers moving into the state and competition for their business, real estate people and developers have become masters at creative selling. Few if any of their methods are illegal, but some deals aren't exactly as they appear on the surface. There are so many ingenious ways to sell property, so many variables, that it behooves a buyer to be exceedingly careful. I'm not suggesting that salespeople or developers are dishonest, just that some are more open than others. In fact, it was a real estate salesman who pointed out the conditions described here. If you ask the right questions, you'll have a better chance of making the right decision. Situations like the following sketches are not unique to Florida, just more common.

Homeowners' Associations Homes in retirement developments are commonly packaged with membership in a homeowners' association as a condition of sale. You're obligated to monthly dues and assessments for upkeep of the clubhouse, swimming pools, golf course, and things of that nature. This extra money must be considered when figuring the cost of your home. An additional $100 a month is the equivalent of $10,000 added to the mortgage. It may be well worth the extra money, but you should be reasonably sure it won't increase by another $100 later on.

It's important to know whether the association actually owns the clubhouse and other facilities you're supporting, or whether your association only has a contract or lease with the developer. There's a big difference. If the contract or lease agreement permits the owner to increase fees at will, you have to go along with it. Even worse, if the development is under-financed and/or heavily mortgaged, there's always a danger of bankruptcy. The mortgage-holder who takes over the facility may not be bound to honor the contract with your association, and you'll suddenly find yourself without the clubhouse, golf course and Olympic pool that you thought were yours.

Another thing to find out is whether the association is incorporated and you are a shareholder, or whether it's a partnership and you are a "partner" with a lot more personal liability than you thought. Incorporation limits your liabilities. There's nothing wrong with the above arrangements, as long as you are aware of the conditions and are protected.

Condominium Associations   Condo owners own their individual portions of the development as well as an interest in the facilities and common grounds. The condo owner also has a financial responsibility for maintenance of the grounds, recreation room, clubhouse, swimming pool, common hallways and entryways, as well as the roof and exterior of the condominium. A condominium association is the equivalent of a homeowners' association. The same questions should be asked: "Who owns these common facilities and how are we protected?" After a project is completed, the developer may have little interest in keeping the facilities going. He could sell it to a third party, who may or may not have an obligation to honor the lease arrangement. Have a lawyer check these things out for you before you invest your bundle of cash.

Leaseholds   Mobile homes and modular homes (permanently attached units) are often sold on leased or rented ground. Again, if the development goes into foreclosure, the new owners may not have to honor the lease. If your investment is large, I suggest that you make sure of several things: one, that the lease is renewable in perpetuity; two, that monthly payments cannot go up more than the Consumer Price Index adjustment for inflation; and three, that the lease is transferable, just as a piece of property is transferable.

Less-expensive mobile homes are usually placed on rented, rather than leased land. If someday, down the road, something happens to the park, you won't have as much to lose by moving to another mobile home park. But an expensive development involves large investments in non-movable items such as carports, screened rooms, utility rooms and storage rooms and landscaping.

Another item to consider is how difficult might it be to sell your home, when or if the necessity arises. A home on rented or leased land sometimes finds difficulty getting bank financing; you may have to carry paper in order to sell. With an inexpensive property this may not be a problem, but if you have a large mortgage, you may have to dig into your pocket to pay it off if you can't sell for top dollar. If you are in a limited access park, potential buyers may be stopped from looking. Beware of rental or lease agreements that give the park managers an exclusive right to re-sell or to purchase your property. Don't count on them making any big effort to do so, not if they still have new properties to sell of their own. With an exclusive right to purchase your property, they have a license to take you to the cleaners; they can pay you whatever they please. Perhaps the present management wouldn't do this, but who knows about the future?

Florida law prohibits forced removal of a mobile home for any other reason than unsafe or unsightly conditions. Don't hang your hat on this, however, because for all I know, a home's just being 20 years old could be considered unsightly by some. You might feel more secure if you had something in your lease agreement to protect your home. We all know how age discrimination feels, don't we?

The Bottom Line Don't get so starry-eyed about your lovely new home that you don't ask about the *total* cost. Let's say you've agreed upon a sales price plus the "usual hook-up fees and closing costs," and eagerly sign the papers. Only after it's too late, the sales person explains that "usual hook-up fees" in this case mean an extra $5,000.

"After all, ma'am, you didn't expect that sewer and water connections were free, did you? They cost money. Oh yes, will you be needing electricity? Well, that's expensive, too. By the way, we'll be increasing the association fees once the developer finishes with this project, because he won't be subsidizing your clubhouse any longer. And then there's a few additional closing costs that we forgot to . . ."

The time to cover your backside is *before* you sign the papers! Get it all in writing.

North-Central Florida

Although attractive retirement places can be found all over the state, an area often overlooked for retirement possibilities is Florida's interior. The north-central part of Florida is a different world, as distinct from either coast as you can imagine. This is Florida with a four-season climate. Instead of being ironing board-flat as is most of the state, central Florida sits at a higher elevation on rolling hills covered with dense woodlands, meadows and hundreds of lakes. Forests of oak, pine and maple, flowering dogwood and azalea make this a unique cosmos, a place where palm trees and other tropical flora seem out of place. Yet the fun beaches of either the Gulf or the Atlantic are within easy driving distance. Because of its slightly higher altitude and distance from the water, you'll find a true change of season, with cooler summer nights, even an occasional dusting of snow in the winter.

This part of Florida attracts more retirees from Midwestern and Northern states than from New York and New England, as is the case with Florida's Gold Coast. Residents here tend to duplicate the ambience of their hometowns. By and large, the state's interior is more peaceful, rural and safer; it feels more like home to them than the hectic beachfront zones. Generous lawns and single-family homes make this a re-creation of smalltown America, with a slight Florida flourish—that is, homes come equipped with the pools, sun decks and outdoor rooms so important for Florida outdoor lifestyles. Were it not for an occasional orange grove, many neighborhoods

would look right at home in Peoria or Terre Haute, where their owners came from. Part of this openness is due to lower land costs that encourage large building lots, which are routinely measured in acreage rather than square feet.

The climate is different here, too. In this region, the weather-stabilizing Gulf Stream is far off Florida's coast, headed toward the open Atlantic. Consequently, summers days are hotter and winters are a few degrees colder. Rainfall here is slightly less as well. These temperature differences can be significant when you consider Florida's high humidity. Miami averages 30 days a year above 90 degrees, whereas inland it's more like 100 days over 90 degrees. This is enough to encourage many who retire in central and west coast Florida to return north for the summer.

However, if you are the type who loves warm weather—like me— 90-degree days aren't bad, even with the 75-percent humidity you find in most of Florida. As one person from Rochester, New York, pointed out, "Coping with hot weather is simply a matter of changing my living patterns. Back home in New York, I stayed indoors all winter. I only went outside to go to work or to shovel snow. Here, I stay indoors during the *summer,* yet every morning and evening it's comfortable outdoors for golf or bicycling."

Orlando Area   At one time, I considered Orlando one of Florida's better retirement ideas. That was before it became so busy. In a short time, the city made a remarkable transition from a sleepy crossroad of citrus orchards and cattle ranches into a dynamic city, the fastest-growing in the state. Actually, for such a booming economy, Orlando managed to make this transition fairly painless by diversifying commerce and concentrating on clean, high-tech industry, gaining the nickname, "Silicon Swamp." Another nickname for Orlando is "Hollywood East," because of the film industry's focus on this area. Disney, MGM and Universal Studios invested millions in sound stages, production entities and tourist-attractions; apparently, this is just the beginning. There is much, much more to come!

Orlando's major problem, as far as retirement is concerned, is that it grew too much and too fast. With tourist super-attractions like Disney World and other Hollywood-style promotions, throngs of visitors create enormous traffic jams and encourage the proliferation of fast food joints, souvenir stands, motels and business areas which can be depressing to those who live here year-round. This shouldn't detract from the fact that Orlando has many wonderful services and attractions that are worth a day visit for local residents. The secret to successful retirement living here is to settle *near* Orlando, not *in* Orlando.

The metropolitan area is surrounded by small, pleasant towns that are truly pastoral, yet close enough to downtown Orlando to take advantage of big-city offerings. The countryside is rolling, with orange groves and lemon blossoms to sweeten the air. Over 50 lakes dot the landscape, many with gorgeous, tropical shores edged with cypress, pines and tall palm trees. Fish abound in the lakes, as well as an occasional alligator.

Leesburg/DeLand   The best retirement bets near Orlando are found north of the city in a fan-shaped area starting at Orlando's northern edge. A dozen small towns are scattered throughout this triangle, from De Land on the east to Leesburg on the west, places little-publicized as retirement locations. Most towns are long-settled, with established neighborhoods and mature shade trees along quiet streets, plus great real estate bargains. Shopping facilities are adequate, with Orlando a short drive away for heavy-duty shopping.

Most homes in these smaller towns are located in conventional neighborhoods, and larger retirement developments can be found in the surrounding countryside. We looked at a very impressive retirement complex near the comfortable little city of Leesburg. Since country property is inexpensive in this area, the developer was able to purchase a huge tract of land, a mixture of rolling hills, pastures, small lakes and marshland. Because homes can't be placed on wetlands, much of the land is open, giving most homes unobstructed views and privacy. The facilities (completely owned by the homeowners' association) are top quality, and include an Olympic pool, huge clubhouse, tennis courts and large areas of parkland. The development has no golf course, but you'll find half a dozen links within a 16-mile radius. Excellently designed models sell for $70,000 and up.

ORLANDO AND VICINITY			Rel. Humidity: Jan. 62%, July 64%			
	Jan.	April	July	Oct.	Rain	Snow
Daily Highs	72	84	92	84	48"	—
Daily Lows	49	60	73	65		

Winter Haven   Another possibility that shouldn't be neglected is the area southwest of Orlando and east of Tampa, a group of small communities centered around Winter Haven. Lakeland (pop. 72,000) is the largest and newest of the cities, and Frostproof (pop. 3,000) the smallest and probably the oldest. Winter Haven (pop. 25,000) is the best known, for it's received much positive publicity as a retirement center. Besides being the spring training camp of the Cleveland Indians and the home of Cypress Gardens, a famous tourist attraction, Winter Haven bills itself as the water-skiing capital of the world. For good reason: a series of 18 spring-fed lakes known as Chain O' Lakes, interconnected by navigable canals, provide unlimited opportunities for water skiing, boating, fishing and swimming. Forty percent of the city is covered by lakes or canals, which contributes to a cooling in the summer and warming in the winter.

Winter Haven, FL
AFFORDABILITY
SAFETY

Housing is affordable, with the median price for single-family homes in the $60,000 range. This places Winter Haven as the 40th most economical city in the nation, and maybe the lowest in Florida, real estate-wise. During my last visit, I found several modest houses for under $40,000. Much lakefront is open and park-like, but boat access is almost unlimited. Lakes away from Winter Haven commonly have homes with private docks. Health care is a major industry, with seven hospitals and ten medical centers scattered about the county.

Interstate 4 hustles traffic to Tampa or Orlando for serious shopping in short order, but shopping is more than adequate in Winter Haven and environs, with a large mall just off the interstate that rivals those in larger cities. The area is lucky to have daily Greyhound bus service to Tampa, Orlando, Jacksonville and Miami. Disney World is 35 minutes away, Busch Gardens 60 minutes away and Sea World is 45 minutes away. Granted, these distractions are not nearly as far away as one might wish.

Gainesville   The home of the University of Florida, Gainesville is one of the most culturally stimulating cities in the state. It's interesting how much one university town can resemble another, with the same kinds of businesses, services, students, even similar street names. Large, old homes on tree-shaded streets, some converted to fraternity houses, plus unobtrusive university construction, recall memories of my own college days. The city's official nickname, "The Tree City," is appropriate.

Gainesville, FL

You needn't be a student to participate in the many activities connected with the University. Theater for all tastes is highlighted by the Hippodrome, one of only four state theaters for the performing arts. Miracle on 34th Street is a cultural complex with museums of art and natural history as well as an 1,800-seat performing arts center. The university's ongoing program of public lectures and other cultural events entertains many retirees in the area.

Gainesville was originally planned as a health resort. Described as the "Eden of the South" by its founder, the town was visualized as a community with a "regular body of skilled physicians in attendance." In a way, this dream was fulfilled, since Gainesville is number one when it comes to Florida health care. Four full-service hospitals serve the area, including the University's nationally renowned Shands Hospital, a nonprofit, 548-bed facility.

Nearby wildlife areas provide great pleasure to bird watchers and to those interested in ecology. About 65 percent of the county's 965 square miles is a wilderness of forests and wetlands, dotted with scenic lakes.

Housing costs are affordable, with the median price of a three-bedroom home at $69,000. As in most college towns, rentals are at a premium, except for the summer quarter, when many students leave town. If a town of 90,000 is too large for you, nearby communities of High Springs and Archer are a 15-minute drive away. Housing costs less here and small farms are affordable. An upscale golf-course development, Haile Plantation, offers miles of walking/bicycle trails, tennis courts, swimming pools and other recreational amenities in addition to a new 18-hole golf course. Prices range from $50,000 to over $400,000. This is but one of several such entities.

Besides the 35,000-student university, there's the two-year Santa Fe College with a student body of about 7,500. A walk through its pleasant campus reveals a large percentage of students here with gray hair. Those over 60 years go tuition-free under most circumstances. The extensive curriculum covers classes like dog training, computers and antique collecting. If you're looking for Florida retirement in an intellectual climate, Gainesville is the place to investigate.

For outdoors people, there's plenty to do. A dozen nearby lakes invite anglers, six of them with boat ramps. For golf, Ironwood, an 18-hole, par 72, public golf course, is one of four public or semi-private links. Thirty parks, many with tennis courts, are publicly maintained. And of course either the Gulf or the Atlantic is a short drive away. The closest saltwater fishing is in Cedar Key, a 49-mile drive to the Gulf. Driving time on Interstate 75 is about two hours to Tampa Bay. The University of Florida Gators football team draws fans from all over the nation and creates great excitement with local residents. If indoor shopping is your favorite sport, there's the million-square-foot Oaks mall, an enclosed shopping facility with five department stores and 150 other shops and boutiques.

GAINESVILLE/OCALA			Rel. Humidity: Jan. 61%, July 62%			
	Jan.	April	July	Oct.	Rain	Snow
Daily Highs	66	81	90	81	52"	—
Daily Lows	42	55	71	59		

Ocala Another of Florida's fast-growing areas, Ocala's new population includes large numbers of retirees. About one in four adults is 65 or older. Its quiet, laid-back lifestyle attracts those who hate northern

Ocala, FL

AFFORDABILITY

SAFETY

Low   High

winters yet want to avoid the traffic jams and insanity of the beach cities. The cost of living here is the lowest in Florida, and the average selling price of real estate is the third lowest. New-home subdivisions, as well as conventional homes in comfortable-looking neighborhoods, offer a range of housing choices.

Ocala's business district or downtown is rather orthodox, looking very much like a typical Midwestern agricultural town, with a traditional downtown square. This isn't surprising, since Ocala is an agricultural center. Modern malls and chain stores haven't totally killed the town center as happens in some small cities.

The countryside is checkered with farms, especially horse farms. The area around Ocala is one of the most important thoroughbred-breeding areas in the country. There are even "farm subdivisions," developments where you can buy a few acres, a barn and a house, and do small-scale farming or horse raising as your retirement hobby.

One retiree told us that he chose to live here because Ocala reminded him of the countryside where he grew up in northern Illinois. "The only thing it lacks is the ice and snow in the winter time," he added. When asked about northern Florida summers, he replied, "I don't believe they are any hotter than they were back home. Anyway, whenever we get the notion, the wife and I drive an hour and 20 minutes to Daytona Beach and cool off in the Atlantic Ocean. We can get there by nine in the morning and be home with sunburns by supper time!"

Several inviting mobile-home parks surround Ocala. We inspected one park, just an eight-minute drive from Ocala city limits, that had a country setting worthy of the name, yet with a Florida accent. Shaded by spreading oak trees, the mobile homes rest on large parcels along paved drives that wind through the park. A radio-operated gate keeps out high-pressure salespeople. The park's ample clubhouse hosts senior citizens' activities plus a swimming pool and tennis courts, creating an atmosphere conducive to quiet, slow-paced retirement.

Not only do Ocala's mobile home parks range from ordinary to deluxe, but it's also possible to buy a few acres, or just a lot, and install your own mobile home. Many small farms of 5 to 50 acres dot the countryside, with nothing but a mobile home and a barn on the property.

Atlantic Coast

Palm Coast Let's take a look at one of those multiple-use communities, one with beach, golf, tennis and boating facilities all in one. This is not to be considered an advertisement or an endorsement of this particu-

Palm Coast, FL

AFFORDABILITY

SAFETY

Low   High

lar community, but rather an example of similar communities found all over the state. Some are much more expensive and most are smaller; because this one has changed from a closed development into an actual city of some 21,000 residents, I don't feel as if we are promoting a developer, but rather a bona fide town.

Palm Coast is located halfway between St. Augustine and Daytona Beach—22 miles each way. A private ocean beach club (open to residents) is an easy walk or bike ride across the Intracoastal Waterway bridge. The planned community was developed by ITT Community Development Corporation over a two-decade span and is still underway.

As you exit Interstate 95 to enter the Palm Coast development, you immediately feel as if you have entered a park. The landscaped, four-lane parkway through residential and commercial areas is bordered by lush forests of oak and native palms. Bicycle and jogging paths meander through the landscaped commons and are fully used by Palm Coast residents and visitors.

Great pains were taken to preserve the semi-tropical aspects of the Florida natureland, with its magnificent tall trees, tangled vines and indigenous palm trees. Housing and businesses are skillfully hidden behind the vegetation so that it appears to the casual visitor that most of the developments are natural parklands. The business district and shopping centers are tastefully landscaped and surrounded by a buffer of trees to keep noise and traffic away from residential areas. Of the original 42,000 acres in the development, 5,000 acres are set aside as a nature reserve.

This development wasn't planned solely as a place for retirement. Provisions were made for business parks and light, technology-oriented industry to provide jobs for the residents of Palm Coast. These areas are located near the interstate and screened from the residential areas by nature preserves, yet close enough for workers to walk or ride bicycles to work. The infusion of young couples and children adds a freshness to the face of Palm Coast, taking it out of the category of a retirement center.

Scattered through the complex are four championship golf courses, two of them designed by Arnold Palmer. The community tennis club is one of only four clubs in the country with clay, grass and hard surface within the same complex. Sixteen hard-surface courts draw players of all skill levels. The club is complete with aerobics room, lockers and restaurant.

Boating enthusiasts have their own private marinas at their back doors. The canals vary from 60 to 125 feet wide and are about eight feet deep. Houses here cost considerably more than houses on ordinary streets, but are still surprisingly inexpensive. Not long ago, several canal

63

properties were being offered from $130,000 to $180,000. New model homes start from the low $60,000s to the $150,000 range, condos for much less. Because the development is mature, many older places are now on the market.

All Florida retirement communities are not created equal. Across the Intracoastal Waterway is another development (also by ITT Community Development Corp.) called Hammock Dunes. It also features golf courses and natural Florida landscaping, but on a lavish scale, along five miles of ocean front. An impressive 32,000-square-foot clubhouse overlooks the Atlantic and a spectacular golf course. Prices for homes start at the mid-$200,000 range. Building lots vary from $135,000 to $875,000. "Exclusive" is the appropriate description here.

PALM OOAOT			Rel. Humidity: Jan. 60%, July 65%			
	Jan.	April	July	Oct.	Rain	Snow
Daily Highs	68	80	89	81	48"	—
Daily Lows	47	59	72	65		

Daytona Beach   Daytona Beach is about 65 miles south of St. Augustine and is situated partly on the peninsula and partly on the mainland. Daytona's main tourist section is on the peninsula's ocean side rather than on the mainland. The city population is 65,000, with 100,000 in the metropolitan area. The 23-mile-long white sand beach is perhaps its most famous feature, one of the few places in Florida where autos are permitted to drive along the beach. The only time to drive it is during low or outgoing tide, when it is hardpacked and pavement-like. Many speed records have been posted on this beach. Overnight parking or camping aren't allowed.

Daytona Beach, FL

AFFORDABILITY

SAFETY

Low   High

The famous tourist area—on the peninsula—has a wide promenade, an amusement park and a fishing pier to entertain vacationers. To keep tourism alive during the slow tourist months, automobile and motorcycle racing were instituted. Over the years, these events have gained wide media recognition, bringing racing enthusiasts from all over the nation. During important races, the fans outnumber the residents. This creates welcome revenue for Daytona Beach and the surrounding communities, but also produces some marvelous traffic jams. Local people pay close attention to the schedules and avoid the peninsula during races.

Daytona Beach is one of Florida's nicer-looking Atlantic cities, with graceful buildings on both the peninsula side and on the mainland, where the commercial district is located. As you drive across the connecting causeway, rows of mature tropical trees outline a pleasant view of downtown in the distance.

The Halifax River is part of the Intracoastal Waterway that stretches from the Florida Keys north to Chesapeake Bay. It's wide and sheltered—a perfect place for learning how to handle a sailboat before venturing into open water. Everything from fishing dinghies to freighters uses this channel to follow the coast. You can make it to the Florida Keys with very little exposure to the open ocean. A new development in Daytona Beach is the recently completed Halifax Harbor Marina, which is now the largest marina between Baltimore and Fort Lauderdale.

Rents in the tourist sector vary widely, depending upon the season, the view and access to the beach. When buying something near the beach, always make sure you aren't buying into a party pad. Any complex where most units are rented to tourists by the week is liable to mean trouble. A clean-cut college student can invite the whole fraternity house for an around-the-clock animal party. Retirement-type housing is available on the peninsula, but most retirees prefer to live in the comparative peace and quiet of the mainland.

Some nearby communities worth investigating are Ormond Beach—where the famous daredevils like Barney Oldfield raced automobiles in attempts to break the one-time, 60-mile-an-hour speed barrier—and New Smyrna Beach, which is as far as autos can be driven on the sand. This is where Canaveral National Seashore wildlife preserve begins, the refuge of alligators, turtles, manatees and a marvelous variety of birds.

Where the wildlife preserve ends, the Canaveral Peninsula and the John F. Kennedy Space Center begin. New Smyrna Beach, by the way, is one of the oldest settlements in America. Historians believe Ponce de Leon landed here in 1513.

DAYTONA BEACH				Rel. Humidity: Jan. 59%, July 65%	
	Jan.	April	July	Oct.	Rain	Snow
Daily Highs	68	80	90	81	48"	—
Daily Lows	47	59	73	65		

Cocoa Beach to Melbourne The "Space Coast" derives its name from the John F. Kennedy Space Center on the Canaveral Peninsula. All along this section of coast, from Cocoa Beach down to Melbourne and Melbourne Beach, is an attractive group of towns just made for retirement.

Cocoa Beach's commercial center is much larger than its actual population of 13,000 might indicate. Its downtown streets are lined with flower boxes and oldtime village shops where folks can watch potters at work, as well as leathersmiths making belts and hats, and skilled craftsmen restoring antiques. Cocoa Beach serves as a focal point for nearby cities such as Cocoa, Merritt Island and Rockledge. The Canaveral Pier at Cocoa Beach extends almost 800 feet into the ocean, a great place for fishing, dining and nightlife.

Cocoa Beach is home to many space center workers and military families from nearby Cape Canaveral and Patrick Air Force Base. Cocoa Beach and the nearby towns have attracted a large share of military retirees—folks who liked the area when stationed here.

According to the local chamber of commerce, a good percentage of the population are retirees, and they are very active in politics. The number of services available to senior citizens reflects this. Thirteen apartments and housing complexes are for senior citizens. A good public transportation system is augmented by the free van service for wheelchair-confined residents provided by a local surfing shop.

A community college and a state university are located here, with plenty of activities that involve retired residents. Hospitals are within ten miles and air transportation is 45 miles away.

The area has an interesting mixture of very expensive and very ordinary homes. All in all, prices seemed a bit higher than in other sections of the state, probably because of the nearby air bases and space industries. Even so, plenty of inexpensive homes and condos are on the market. Some developments and mobile home parks near the ocean are having problems with water; be sure to check for drinkability before buying on the beach.

Sitting at the lower end of this famous coast is the largest of the towns, Melbourne, with a population of 60,000. Palm Bay, Merritt Island and Satellite Beach are also part of Melbourne's shopping area. This is a relatively quiet area, at least compared to the hectic, tourist-clogged pace of nearby Orlando.

Melbourne itself is on the mainland; a causeway takes you to the beach town of Indiatlantic. And what a beach it is, with 33 miles of sandy, uncrowded Atlantic shore! At one time this beach was nicknamed the "Treasure Coast"; when a hurricane shipwrecked a fleet of Spanish ships against the shore, millions of Spanish doubloons spilled into the sea. The survivors—some 1,500 men, women and children—spent three years trying to recover the treasure. Today, divers still keep their eyes peeled for coins and bullion.

During the summer, from May until September, loggerhead turtles visit the beaches to dig nests and lay eggs. As many as 12,000 nests are dug each season. Retirees are invited to join the Sea Turtle Preservation Society. The elusive manatee is often sighted around here, as well.

This coast is liberally endowed with attractive apartments, complete with swimming pools, tennis courts and social directors, starting at $450 and going up. Single-family housing and condos are comparably priced. We saw two nice little condos offered for just under $40,000. Mobile home parks are plentiful and well maintained.

COCOA BEACH-MELBOURNE			Rel. Humidity: Jan. 58%, July 65%			
	Jan.	April	July	Oct.	Rain	Snow
Daily Highs	72	81	89	83	51"	—
Daily Lows	52	62	72	67		

Florida's Gold Coast

It all started back in the 1880s when two starry-eyed promoters, John and James Lummus, bought a barren spit of sand that jutted offshore from the southern Florida mainland. Lying in the indigo waters between Biscayne Bay and the Atlantic Ocean, their new purchase inspired a dream. They were convinced they could turn this worthless piece of land into a fabulously productive coconut plantation. They planted thousands of trees and sat back, waiting for them to mature and for tropical winds to shake the harvest to the ground.

However, things didn't work out that way. Blight cut the harvest potential and tree rats harvested more than did the plantation owners. Mosquitoes and other insects drove workers away, and finally the dream died. But the coconut trees survived. Later promoters saw a different promise: tourism and retirement. They called their new development "Miami Beach."

The boom started in the 1920s and spilled from Key Biscayne north to Fort Lauderdale, Pompano Beach, Boca Raton, all the way to Palm Beach and beyond. By the 1930s it was in full swing as a winter retreat and retirement haven. This is Florida's famous Gold Coast. A drive along the coastal highway will explain how it received its name. It certainly took a lot of gold to build it, and more to maintain it.

Individually, the cities from West Palm Beach down to Coral Gables don't appear to be particularly large. Miami has only 350,000 people, Miami Beach about 97,000, West Palm Beach only about 67,000. But, together the more than 40 towns comprise one long, enormous metropolitan area (of about 2.8 million people). These many communities spread along the beach have no chance of having a central focus or a common "downtown" area. Broken into a string of suburbs without an urban area to be suburban to, each has its own shopping center, stores, businesses, and its own small political entity. In this unconsolidated way, Florida's Gold Coast resembles Los Angeles.

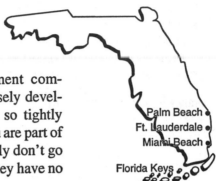

Except for the classy sections along the beaches, most housing is single-family bungalows, low-profile condominiums and expansive apartment complexes. In some of the less intensely developed areas, where things aren't so tightly packed, it's easy to forget that you are part of an urban sprawl. People commonly don't go shopping away from their area; they have no need to.

Along the Gold Coast you'll find the biggest contrasts in all of Florida. From tall forests of condominiums and apartments that remind you of New York's Park Avenue, to rows of tract houses reminiscent of Los Angeles, you'll find almost every imaginable type of housing and neighborhood—all within miles or sometimes yards of each other. Then, just 10 to 20 miles to the west, the land is uninhabited, totally the domain of wildlife.

The Miami Complex   This is the Florida you usually read about in your newspaper's travel section, the Florida you see on television and in movies. For some folks, the thought of living in such a crowded area is a turnoff. But for others, the amenities of a metropolitan area—combined with a mild climate and gorgeous beaches—add up to ideal retirement living. They adore everything about the Gold Coast. They love the convenience of well-stocked shopping centers, good medical facilities and a choice of good restaurants. Folks here enjoy apartment living, having someone else wash windows, mow lawns and trim shrubs. As one lady put it, "We've lived all our lives in or near Manhattan. We couldn't survive in some dinky, one-horse town where they roll up the sidewalks after dark!"

Curiously, in the midst of this densely-packed, tropical replica of Manhattan, distinct concepts of neighborhood and community emerge. We've visited several large condominium developments and are always fascinated by the way folks create their own islands of interests and community. A typical complex, this one in Pompano Beach, has a dozen eight-story buildings set apart in a park-like setting. Each building has complete laundry facilities and an exercise room. Jogging paths, swimming pools and tennis courts are strategically placed about the grounds, and a clubhouse dominates the center.

Miami area, FL

AFFORDABILITY

SAFETY

Low — High

In effect, the development corresponds to a small town, or an intimate neighborhood in a larger city. The condo owners' association substitutes for city politics back home. Residents have a great time voting for officers, running for election, lobbying for pet projects, or trying to recall those who aren't doing their job. "I feel like I have a helluva lot more control and say-so about my neighborhood now, than I ever could hope for back in New York," said one resident who was in the middle of a fight to redecorate the clubhouse and install more outdoor lighting.

Another example is a condo development in Deerfield Beach, a place called Century Village East. It seems to be populated primarily by former New Yorkers, many of whom knew one another back home. Century Village is not only large, but well organized, so much so that it puts out an impressive 48-page newspaper every month to carry news of the development's activities to the 8,000 residential units in the development. Residents have their own shopping center, golf course, even buses and trolleys. They elect members to serve in positions analogous to mayor, city council, etc.

As in any metropolitan area, living in the Gold Coast area has drawbacks. Higher crime rates, traffic jams and crowded stores are pretty much standard. However, the crime picture is somewhat distorted in the Miami area because of vigorous commerce in illegal drugs. Presumably, you are not into drug dealing and won't be participating in car chases, revenge killings and Mafia shoot-outs as featured on television shows. Therefore, statistics on drug busts, drive-by shootings and gang-related activities should not affect you significantly—as long as you stay away from the dangerous neighborhoods. Robberies of tourists usually occur in tourist-clogged areas, places you would avoid under normal circumstances.

One important point: what metropolitan areas lack in peace and quiet, they more than make up for in services and conveniences for retirees. The larger the population, the more and better senior citizen centers, health care facilities, libraries, educational opportunities and other advantages.

GOLD COAST			Rel. Humidity: Jan. 59%, July 63%			
	Jan.	April	July	Oct.	Rain	Snow
Daily Highs	75	82	89	84	60"	—
Daily Lows	56	65	74	70		

Florida Keys, End of the Line   Except for Hawaii, this jumbled string of islands and reefs is the most tropical part of the United States. A highway follows the route of an old railway line, an engineering marvel in itself, 110 miles to the last of the accessible islands, Key West. The highway skips from one coral atoll to another over numerous causeways and bridges, across islands festooned with palm trees, hibiscus and bougainvillea and bearing such romantic names as Key Largo, Islamorada and Matacumbre.

Key West, FL

AFFORDABILITY

SAFETY

Low   High

Substantial numbers of retirees, both snowbirds and regular residents, populate these islands. Boating and fishing are top attractions, with year-round tropical weather the frosting on the cake. When it comes to snorkeling and diving, these islands are a virtual paradise. Folks here boast of the longest living reef in the western hemisphere, crystal-clear waters with visibility up to 100 feet and more than 500 wrecks to explore.

Yachts are "in" throughout the Keys, large ones and small ones. Resident sailors simply cut berths into the coral and limestone backyards of their homes and tie up. Other houses are set back against networks of canals, where their occupants can dock after a day's adventure of fishing or treasure hunting in the warm waters of the Gulf Stream. You'll even find mobile homes with sloops moored at their floating patios.

At one time, Key West developed a reputation as a retreat and retirement spot for writers and artists. Wallace Stevens fell in love with Key West back in 1922, and in his poem, *The Idea of Order in Key West*, he praised it as "a summer without end." Having let the cat out of the bag, Stevens soon found himself in the company of other intellectuals who wanted to participate in this "summer without end." Ernest Hemingway, John Dos Passos and Tennessee Williams all maintained houses in Key West. Some of their homes are now major tourist attractions.

The tradition of an artist colony continues, however in a somewhat diminished form. Key West's become incredibly crowded and overrun with tourists and weekending college students. Finding a parking place becomes a treasure hunt. Key West's tolerant openness to varying lifestyles and its "live and let live" attitude has encouraged the establishment of a considerable gay community. Because it's such a long drive from the mainland, over a snail's pace, two-lane highway, and because housing costs in Key West are hardly bargains, our recommendations lean toward retirement farther up the line, in places like Key Largo or Marathon.

A perpetual problem facing those living on the Keys is the threat of hurricane-driven tides—another reason for living closer to the mainland. Everywhere you look, you'll find some (not all) homes and businesses raised off the ground 10 or 12 feet. Storm tides are the obvious reason; they simply wash underneath the houses without causing much damage. Flood insurance rates are considerably less with this type of construction. That's good. But being up in the air raises the chances of wind damage, so storm insurance is higher. That's bad.

Although somewhat more expensive than the mainland, Keys real estate can be reasonable, considering the unique location and special circumstances. On both Key Largo and Marathon we checked out several homes, some with canals at their backs, where motorboats, launches and yachts were tied to individual docks. Newly constructed three-bedroom places can be found for $90,000; make it $120,000 if you want your own boat dock. You can also pay much, much more, with spiffy places going for over $750,000. Older, fixer-upper homes can sometimes be located for $60,000. (I'm always worried about that term, "fixer-upper.") We looked at a two-bedroom, two-bath mobile home with a dock and huge screened porch that sits out over the water for $90,000.

Florida's West Coast

Like Central Florida, Gulf Coast retirees tend to come from different parts of the country than the northern Atlantic Coast. Instead of drawing its newcomers from New York and New England, a higher percentage of residents immigrate from Midwestern and Northern states. Therefore, it isn't surprising that architecture and lifestyles are more disposed toward Midwestern values. Instead of tall condos and apartments, the preferred style is low-profile, informal and conservative. Single-family homes are the norm, sitting on lots often measured in acres rather than in square feet, with generous areas of lawn and landscaping.

The climate is different here, too. The weather-stabilizing Gulf Stream misses Florida's west coast. The result: summers along the gulf are hotter and winters a few degrees cooler than along the Gold Coast. But the folks who've retired here say it's worth it, and they point out that the relative humidity is lower than on the other coast.

This southwestern part of the state is one of our favorites. From Fort Myers/Cape Coral on down to Naples and Marco Island, you'll find a wide assortment of neighborhoods as inexpensive as any developed part of Florida, or as luxurious as you might wish. Cape Coral's average sales price for existing homes is one of the lowest in the country, and Naples and San Marcos are among the most expensive in Florida. Sanibel Island also ranks up there in expense and carries an added handicap of not having any place to park.

Fort Myers and its sister city of Cape Coral are separated by the Caloosahatchee River. (No, I'm not making that up.) Neighboring Pine Island lies across a saltwater pass from Cape Coral. Fort Myers Beach is also an island, one of a string of them that shelter the coastline all the way south to Naples. In the middle are Bonita Springs and Bonita Beach, two excellent choices for in-between expensive and affordable retirement.

Formerly a cattle-growing area, population growth here is nothing short of phenomenal, an astonishing 600 percent in the last 20 years! Good transportation accounts for some of this growth; Interstate 75 shoots through the area, making it a snap to drive east to the Gold Coast or north to the Tampa Bay area in two and a half hours. Fort Myers also boasts an international airport. Medical care is excellent with the new Gulf Coast Hospital's discounts for senior citizens. A half-dozen other hospitals and several nursing facilities serve the area as well.

This is definitely a winter snowbird haven—the population doubles between the first of November and Easter week. Then, when summer's humidity and over-90-degree weather sets in, the comfort-loving snowbirds fly home to cooler northern climes. But year-round residents protest when I suggest that summer might be harsh. "Check it out; it's just a little bit warmer than Miami Beach," they point out, "and it's a lot safer living around here!"

In addition to the usual saltwater sports associated with Florida's west coast, those with a fondness for gambling will enjoy greyhound racing at the Naples-Fort Myers Greyhound Track. Betting the doggies is fun and not very expensive at two bucks a bet.

Fort Myers/Cape Coral   Discovered early in the century by Henry Ford and Thomas Edison, Fort Myers has been booming since. The city's landscaping is a unique heritage left by Thomas Edison. He loved to experiment with trees and shrubs, particularly palm trees. Older residential areas are full of them, grown tall and mature over the decades since

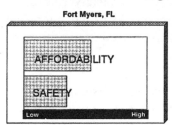
Fort Myers, FL

the great inventor planted them around town. It's claimed that over 70 varieties of palms grace the streets of Fort Myers. Some stand tall and stately, others, short with bottle-like trunks. A few flaunt astonishing leaf patterns that look as if they were created by fashion designers.

The overall theme of this area is one of prosperity, with very few sections of town looking seedy. Well-manicured lawns, flowering bushes and magnolia trees give residential areas of Fort Myers a quiet, homey look. Edison Community College offers a profusion of classes, almost free, in their Lifelong Learning Center. Naturally, landscaping is one of the more popular courses.

Fort Myers and North Fort Myers have a combined population of about 90,000, about the same as sister city, Cape Coral. The island of Fort Myers Beach—population 14,000—fronts the city of Fort Myers and provides open access to the Gulf, making it a popular place for homes with boat docks. The seven-mile-long island is tightly packed with small homes, condos and beachfront properties. It's only about three-quarters of a mile wide. For being close to such a popular beach, prices are affordable, but winter traffic on the island can be horrific and the number of tourists along the beachfront appalling. Be aware that Fort Myers Beach's population *triples* during the winter. A few blocks off the beach, confusion and noise greatly diminish, that's true, but this is a place for the young at heart and possibly the hard of hearing.

Throughout the area is a profusion of condos, some sitting on the edge of their own nine-hole golf courses. Condo styles seem quite practical: mostly two-stories with bedrooms upstairs—no other families living overhead or underfoot. Condominium developers have been generous in providing spacious lawn areas between the condos, so you don't get the cramped, hemmed-in feeling that comes with east Florida multi-story skyscrapers and asphalt parking lots.

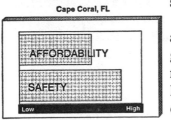

Cape Coral, FL

AFFORDABILITY

SAFETY

Low · High

Mobile home parks are plentiful. Most are beautifully landscaped and offer organized activities in their clubhouses and recreational facilities. Some are downright luxurious, and some are super expensive, others quite affordable.

For quiet, rural island retirement, Pine Island is the place. Seventeen miles long and about two miles wide, this is the largest of the barrier islands in these parts. Its shores are almost completely ringed with mangrove estuaries, many in wildlife preserves. As its name indicates, the island is rustic, covered with pines and offers inexpensive retirement housing. Approximately 8,000 year-round residents are joined by another 4,000 during the winter months.

Pine Island is accessed from Cape Coral via a fishing bridge that crosses over to Matlacha and Little Pine islands. This is known as "Florida's Fishingest Bridge," and at most any time, day or night, you are apt to see fishermen dipping their lines into Matlacha Pass. This area is a throwback to the time when tiny fishing villages were the norm along the southwest coast. The western shore sits in the lee of Captiva Island, which makes the water safe for sailing and peaceful fishing.

FORT MYERS/NAPLES			Rel. Humidity: Jan. 57%, July 60%			
	Jan.	April	July	Oct.	Rain	Snow
Daily Highs	74	85	91	85	54"	—
Daily Lows	53	62	74	68		

Naples/Bonita Springs Those accustomed to going first-class will want to check out Naples and nearby Marco Island. Naples dominates a stretch of public beaches 41 miles long. It's one of the fastest-growing up-scale communities in Florida. One section of Naples, appropriately called Venice, is a modern-day recreation of its Italian namesake, with luxury condos and some of the finest shops and boutiques on Florida's west coast built right down on the water line.

Naples has the reputation of being super-expensive, and it is, if compared with nearby Florida communities. Yet many impressive neighborhoods of lovely landscaping, mature shade trees and upscale housing look like bargains to folks from some parts of the country. A home costing $350,000 here couldn't be duplicated for twice that amount in the spiffy parts of California or New York.

This is the western terminus of the Tamiami Trail, a famous highway that cuts right through the Everglades. In addition to golf and the usual Florida pastimes, swamp buggy racing is popular in the Marco Island-Naples area. Hopped-up swamp machines are run in special events in October to mark the beginning of the Everglades hunting season.

Bonita Springs, about 15 minutes north of Naples and 20 minutes south of Fort Myers, is a mixed affordable/luxury community. The year-round population is around 25,000. Great beaches are about four minutes from town at Bonita Shores, which is a kind of "less expensive Naples." My impression is this beach is patronized more by local folks rather than tourists, which makes it much less zoo-like. The entire area is much more laid-back and quiet than the northern beaches. The water temperature of the Gulf is about 71 degrees in the winter and 84 in the summer, which translates into pleasant swimming.

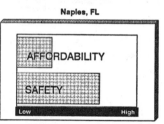

Naples, FL

Many homes are built on canals with open water access, thus making boating and yachting popular pastimes here. The average selling price on these places is about 50 percent higher than homes in conventional neighborhoods. Overall, home prices are higher than Florida averages, with residential sales averaging about $95,000. Affordable housing is available as well, in the range of $55,000 to $65,000 for a three-bedroom, two-bath home.

Port Charlotte/Punta Gorda   Not far north from Fort Myers, on expansive Charlotte Harbor, the cities of Punta Gorda and Port Charlotte display interests different from their neighbors. Beaches aren't the big deal here; instead, residents focus on the miles of man-made canals and waterways that cut through their neighborhoods like boulevards. More than 150 miles of these man-made waterways provide easy access to the gulf for thousands of boating and fishing enthusiasts. As one resident pointed out, "The water is so clean and unpolluted here, we don't hesitate to swim or water ski right here in town." The Myakka River and the harbor make possible some of the best fishing and boating in the state.

Having a boat tied up in the backyard is as common as having an automobile in the garage. Prices on these waterside residences are surprisingly affordable, probably because they are so common, and you'll notice some rather ordinary houses backed up to the waterways with more invested in the sailboats and yachts than in the homes. Boaters are quick to point out, however, that waterways in neighborhoods on the west of the Tamiami Trail—the main highway that bisects Port Charlotte—must pass under low bridges. Only boats with low profiles—motor boats or small sailboats with masts that can be dismantled—can make their way to salt water. So, if you're a fan of tall-masted ships, better look on the saltwater side of the river, otherwise you'll never make it out to open water. Perhaps this is why some neighborhoods on Port Charlotte's west side benefit from such exceptionally low property prices. Everyone wants to be on the "saltwater side."

Port Charlotte/Punta Gorda, FL

Port Charlotte is large, about 95,000 population, but it doesn't give you a city feeling. It spreads out along the Tamiami Trail (Highway 41), with businesses and malls scattered along the highway rather than concentrated in a downtown civic center. Just a block or so off the main thoroughfare, tranquil neighborhoods offer peaceful havens.

Punta Gorda, a smaller place with less than 20,000 inhabitants, sits just across the Peace River from Port Charlotte. It's older, more sedate, and housing can be fairly expensive. This is because most homes are built on one of Punta Gorda's 85 miles of navigable canals, all of which can access the Gulf.

Every February, local people commemorate Ponce de Leon's reputed visit to Charlotte Harbor with a festival, complete with Conquistador costumes. They reenact the Spaniard's historic landing on the shore of Charlotte Harbor in his stubborn search for the Fountain of Youth.

From Port Charlotte, along the 30 miles of highway down to Fort Myers, are some most impressive mobile home developments. Some parks are country clubs in every sense of the term. They aren't cheap, but they are well worth a visit even if you can't afford them—just to see how the other half lives. In some developments you purchase the lot your home sits on, in other places you lease and in still others you rent. Each system has its own advantages and drawbacks, as explained earlier.

PORT CHARLOTTE AREA			Rel. Humidity: Jan. 59%, July 63%			
	Jan.	April	July	Oct.	Rain	Snow
Daily Highs	74	85	91	85	54"	—
Daily Lows	53	62	74	68		

Tampa/St. Petersburg   Separated by Tampa Bay, the twin cities of St. Petersburg and Tampa are connected by three causeways. Interstate 275, the area's main link to southern Florida, crosses the wide mouth of Tampa Bay on yet another long causeway as it heads south to Bradenton. Together, the cities and their suburbs have about 1.6 million people, making it the second largest metropolitan area in Florida. Although many retire here, the best places are nearby.

St. Petersburg (pop. 250,000) is famous for its proclaimed year-round sunshine; the local newspaper has a standing pledge to give away a newspaper every day the sun doesn't peek out at least some. On one visit it was overcast all day. I'm still waiting for my free newspaper. According

Tampa/St. Petersburg, FL

to the U.S. Weather Bureau, the Tampa-St. Petersburg area can expect an average of 127 cloudy days a year and 107 days of rain. This surprised me, especially when I compared these figures to San Francisco, a place famous for foggy and overcast days. Turns out that San Francisco averages 100 cloudy days and only 67 days with rain.

St. Petersburg entered into the retirement business long ago, advertising in newspapers around the country, stressing its great climate and emphasizing the pleasant retirement possibilities here. It worked so well that the city soon became overrun with senior citizens. The city fathers then changed the advertising campaign to attract industry and younger people. The story goes that the city even removed park benches in an effort to discourage senior citizens from "hanging out." Perhaps they were concerned about gangs of geriatric delinquents getting out of hand. That didn't discourage retirees; they kept on coming, probably bringing their own park benches.

The emphasis on retirement here is not necessarily in either St. Petersburg or Tampa, but in surrounding, smaller locations, and using the metropolitan area as a central focus. The nearby towns of Sarasota and Bradenton to the south and Clearwater, Indian Shores, Tarpon Springs and a dozen other communities north of the St. Petersburg are all pleasant places for retirement. Clearwater is famous for its stretch of pure white sand beach. North of Tampa, along Interstate 75, you'll find another series of great prospects, particularly for inexpensive mobile home living, in farming communities with affordable acreages and a down-home country atmosphere, yet minutes from big-city life.

Sarasota is our particular favorite in this area. It has a solidly established artist colony. Painters, musicians and writers populate the town, and among Sarasota's cultural highlights are an opera and a symphony orchestra. We have a friend who lives here, a portrait artist, who has lived in and visited just about every part of the country, including Hawaii, but chooses to live here because of the city's low density and leisurely pace.

Saltwater fishing is one of Tampa Bay's outdoor attractions. Early summer sees fishermen out for silver king tarpon and then kingfish in early fall. By the way, fishing licenses aren't required in Florida for residents over 60. Baseball fans might be interested to know that this coast is the winter home for the St. Louis Cardinals, Baltimore Orioles, Chicago White Sox, Pittsburg Pirates and the Philadelphia Phillies. Another popular sport here is greyhound racing in "St. Pete." Admission is reasonable; the track makes it up on the pari-mutuel (rabbits get in free). For golf addicts, about 70 golf courses dot the surrounding area.

For cultural balance the metropolitan area supports two theater groups, a ballet and an opera company. Nine art museums, including two at the university and the Museum of Fine Arts, complete the schedule. Numerous hospitals and medical specialists ensure good health care.

TAMPA-ST. PETERSBURG			Rel. Humidity: Jan. 59%, July 63%			
	Jan.	April	July	Oct.	Rain	Snow
Daily Highs	70	82	90	84	47"	—
Daily Lows	49	61	74	65		

Sun Coast   North of Tampa-St. Petersburg is another area largely ignored by retirement writers. Local public relations folks call this area Florida's "Sun Coast." In our estimation, this is one of the more practical retirement areas in the state from several angles. Long stretches of Highway 19 are largely underdeveloped, with many patches of affordable and quality housing. As Highway 19 goes north from Clearwater, it passes through several moderately settled areas and finally thins out into open farmland and untouched forest. Parts of it are as rural as you'll find in the state.

New housing developments and liveable mobile home parks spice up pleasant towns such as Hudson, Crystal Springs and Homesassa. We especially liked the name of one town: Weeki Wachee. (As you've probably already guessed, Weeki Wachee is just south of the town of Chassahowitzka and is within easy striking distance of nearby Withlacoochee State Forest.)

Roadside signs and billboards clearly affirm the Sun Coast's dedication to retirement services. Large billboards announce items of interest to senior citizens, services like cataract surgery, arthritis clinics, hearing aides, and cardiac care. A billboard announces a large-print book fair, another advertised supplementary Medicare policies.

From Clearwater north, stores and businesses crowd the main route (U.S. Highway 19) and begin thinning out past New Port Richey. Even though much of this portion of the route sometimes seems to be one long shopping center, just a block off the highway in either direction you will find quiet residential areas.

But then, as you drive further north, population becomes sparse. Abandoned gift shops, motels and restaurants give mute testimony that tourist traffic along this highway has fallen away drastically. My guess is that construction of Interstate 75, which parallels Highway 19, drew the flow of tourist traffic away onto its faster, 65-mile-an-hour route. For those entrepreneurs who hoped to make a killing from selling milkshakes and souvenirs to tourists, this must have been devastating, but for the retiree who hates heavy highway traffic, it is a boon. This is the lightest-traveled highway I've yet to drive in Florida—with divided pavement and few competing autos. The most important roadside signs caution motorists to watch for deer crossing the road.

SUN COAST			Rel. Humidity: Jan. 59%, July 63%			
	Jan.	April	July	Oct.	Rain	Snow
Daily Highs	70	82	90	84	47"	—
Daily Lows	49	61	74	65		

Florida's Panhandle

Starting from Tallahassee, the state's capital, and stretching westward to Pensacola, Florida's Panhandle is different from most of the state. Pure white sand beaches and enterprising resort towns clearly remind you that you're in Florida, but the Panhandle also borrows from nearby Georgia and Alabama. There's a "down-home" atmosphere here; the native accent is Deep South, the thinking is pure country. Many Southerners and Midwesterners feel specially comfortable with this combination of resort-country retirement living. Our research shows many Panhandle locations have personal safety rates similar to those in Alabama and Georgia, which contrasts pleasantly with statistics for the Gold Coast.

It's the Gulf Coast beaches that draw outsiders for vacationing and tempt them to return later for retirement. Seeing the coast requires a drive over peaceful, slow-moving Highway 98. This lone highway follows the coast through many small towns, fishing villages and an occasional town of size. The gulf's gentle waters lay just a few feet from the pavement's edge, and the northern side of the road is bordered by wilderness that sometimes extends 50 miles to the north without human habitation. You can drive for miles seeing nothing but a few cabins or an occasional mobile home set back into a clearing in the pines and moss-draped oaks.

Most towns and villages along the way are fishing centers. Fishermen unload their catches and sell them to wholesale and retail outlets. Tiny restaurants offer steamed crab, fresh oysters, fried mullet and other seafood delicacies—to eat there or to take with you. Trucks line up at a multitude of fish wholesalers to rush the produce of the sea to restaurants all over the South. And, of course, numerous bait shops and boat rentals take care of the amateur fisherman. Ninety percent of Florida's oysters come from this area, particularly around Apalachicola, where 10,000 acres of oyster beds are maintained.

The main tourist and retiree attraction is a 100-mile length of beach that begins at the little town of Mexico Beach and runs westward to Pensacola. Many folks who eventually retire along this coast are those who regularly spent their summer vacations here with their families. They fondly remember summers on the white sand beaches and fishing expeditions far out on the gulf's blue waters.

Apalachicola   The stretch along Highway 98 from Lighthouse Point to Port St. Joe passes through some rather interesting and historical towns; the only one large enough to be called a small city is Apalachicola. Although most of Florida is new, with buildings from the 1920s considered antiques, Apalachicola is a fascinating treasure trove of pre-Civil War memorabilia, a quiet town steeped in the past. Homes built in the 1830s aren't unusual. Stately, two-story, wood-frame or brick mansions and churches imported from New England sit adjacent a business district that looks as if it had been transported from a Mississippi River levee of a hundred years ago.

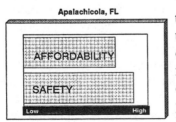

Apalachicola, FL

80

The downtown section slopes gently down to abandoned docks by the Apalachicola River. The old buildings were constructed of handmade brick at least 150 years ago. One gets the feeling that this could be Natchez, Vicksburg or some other Deep South river town. Before the Civil War, this was one of the largest shipping ports on the gulf, surpassed only by Mobile and New Orleans. When war broke out between North and South, the port was used to smuggle in supplies for the Confederates.

The town is full of historic buildings with selling prices the same as ordinary old houses. For anyone who is into restoring old homes, this would be a great place to pick up a piece of history at a bargain price.

Whether Apalachicola or any other place along this stretch of gulf would be a plausible retirement haven depends a lot on your personality. If you like quiet, with not too many tourists messing in your life, and if fishing and seafood are important, you might take a look here.

APALACHICOLA			Rel. Humidity: Jan. 66%, July 71%			
	Jan.	April	July	Oct.	Rain	Snow
Daily Highs	61	75	88	78	55"	—
Daily Lows	45	61	75	62		

Panama City   About 20 miles west of Apalachicola the land ends abruptly at Cape San Blas, and the highway makes a right-angle turn north toward Port St. Joe. From here, all the way to the Alabama state line, two main features characterize this part of Florida's Panhandle: military bases and powder-white beaches.

From Port St. Joe to Pensacola are more than a dozen little towns that cater to tourists and retirees. Often no more than a few blocks wide, the towns string along the highway and beach in a very laid-back manner. Single-family homes, duplexes and small apartments are available for either seasonal or year-round rentals. However, some stretches of high-rise construction would do justice to Florida's Gold Coast. During the winter months these little towns are quiet, but summers make up for this bustle deficit. The largest population center is Panama City (36,662 inhabitants). Like many towns in this area, Panama City has a dual personality. One side is that of a happy summer resort, the other a peaceful winter retreat. From November until March, the beaches are uncrowded and quiet. About the only tourists you'll see are speaking French with a Quebec accent. So many French Canadians congregate here in the winter that one begins to wonder who's tending to business in Montreal. But with warmer weather, French Canadians go home just as Midwesterners arrive for their turn at the beaches.

An offshoot of the Gulf Stream known as the "Yucatan Current" moves close to Panama City. It tends to warm the water in the winter just a tad. This flow also brings nutrient-rich waters from the Caribbean and, with it, schools of sport fish. Fishermen haul in marlin, sailfish, tuna and dolphin, as well as buckets of panfish. A fishing pier extends about 1,600 feet into the gulf for the convenience of anglers. To a certain extent, the Yucatan Current moderates summer weather, but not to any appreciable amount. This doesn't deter the tourists, because as one of the natives pointed out, "It flat cain't get too hot for tourists!"

You needn't live on the beach to enjoy Gulf Coast living. Many folks reside in nearby towns just a 20-minute drive from the sand and surf. Callaway, Springfield, Lynn Haven and others are preferred by many retirees, particularly those who aren't captivated by the busy beach scene.

Part of the dual personality is the question of seasonal apartment and home rentals. In the off-season most rents drop rapidly, just as you would expect, but beach condos vary wildly, depending on season and demand. In general, real estate prices seem to be in line with the rest of Florida, with condos selling from the low $50,000s and houses from the low $60,000s.

The Emerald Coast   Between Panama City and Pensacola stretches a selection of towns ranging from ordinary to luxurious. A particularly interesting area circles a large body of water known as Choctawhatchee Bay. This is the self-styled "Emerald Coast." It includes the town of Navarre and a dozen other little towns, but does not include Seagrove

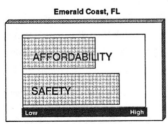

Emerald Coast, FL

Beach. Some places look very comfortable, and living isn't too expensive. Other towns look as if they coddle tourists to the *nth* degree. The skyscraper-type condo towers would look right at home on Miami Beach. Despite the tourist factor, the area enjoys an unusually low crime rate.

Major towns on the bay are Fort Walton Beach and Destin, which seem to blend together into one city with a combined population of around 40,000. Valparaiso is the second city across the bay. Personnel at Elgin Air Force Base account for much of the off-season business activity as well as the high numbers of retired military who live around Choctawhatchee Bay.

The long string of beaches here is famous as having some of the whitest, cleanest and softest sand in the world. According to geologists, the beaches are composed mainly of quartz washed down from the

Appalachians via the Apalachicola River, some 130 miles east of Fort Walton Beach. By the time they get to Fort Walton Beach, the grains have been polished into tiny ovals that cause the sand to squeak when you walk along the dry part of the beach. Local residents are conservation minded and are working hard to prevent erosion. Fishing is said to be wonderful both on the beach side and particularly good in the bay itself. A fishing pier at Navarre Beach, on Santa Rosa Island, is a popular loafing place for local retirees.

Okaloosa Island, where Fort Walton Beach and Destin are located, is one of several barrier islands that protect the mainland. The bay is sheltered and makes for great swimming, boating and picnicking. This is the place to look if you insist on living within blocks of the water. Winter rentals are inexpensive and plentiful during the off-season, but expect to pay your dues during the rest of the year.

For the area's best bargains in housing and rentals, check around Niceville and other communities on the mainland side of the bay. About a 25-mile drive along a divided highway is Crestview, near Interstate 10. Real estate prices here are also favorable for retirees, and the interstate brings Pensacola's hospitals and services within a 45-minute drive.

In these towns away from the beach, houses start selling in the low $60,000 range with several older ones listed for as low as $35,000. A large 1990 mobile home (three-bedroom, two-bath) on a one-acre lot was priced at $29,500. These examples were in Crestview, but prices are similar in most of the surrounding towns. Santa Rosa, a gulf-side resort-like locality, had homes selling in the $80,000 and up bracket. There is at least one golf course complex with homes selling for $500,000 and more, with cheap ones going for $250,000.

EMERALD COAST AREA			Rel. Humidity: Jan. 62%, July 64%			
	Jan.	April	July	Oct.	Rain	Snow
Daily Highs	61	77	90	79	61"	—
Daily Lows	43	59	74	59		

Pensacola   The Spanish recognized Pensacola as an excellent seaport when they settled here in 1559. With both an offshore island and a peninsula barrier against storm-driven tides, the town is quite secure from the scourge of hurricanes.

Pensacola has a checkered history, its political allegiance changing 13 times—among Spain, France, England, the Confederacy and the United States. (Flag-making must have been a bustling cottage industry.)

Its growth from when I worked here in 1952 has been phenomenal, changing from a small town into a modern city of over 60,000.

Its beaches are extensive, with pretty white sand. But they're becoming covered with condos. Summer sees a greater influx of younger people than in other parts of the Panhandle coast. You'll find an emphasis on things like discos and bars that might be downplayed elsewhere. That shouldn't deter retirees, since they'll be living away from the hustle and bustle of the beach scene.

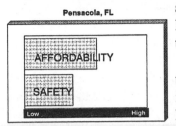

Pensacola, FL

Pensacola is the choice of many military retirees. Elgin Air Force Base, Whiting Field Naval Air Station and the Pensacola Naval Air Academy ring the town. Upon retirement, pilots who've served here naturally recall the attraction of the Panhandle's "Riviera" beaches and the convenience of military medical and PX privileges.

Other Panhandle towns also have military bases. Tyndall Air Force Base, with 6,300 personnel, starts just west of Mexico Beach and extends to Panama City. There's also a Naval Coastal Systems center in Panama City, with about 2,300 personnel. Next is Eglin Air Force Base and finally Pensacola's Naval Air Station. The military presence is significant indeed, with large payrolls supporting the economy because many civilians work on the bases.

Chapter 3

Southeast Coast States

For those who live in the Midwest or on the East Coast, the idea of a West Coast retirement is a pleasant thought, but it's too far away from friends and family. Florida, too, may be out of the question for any number of reasons. The search is then narrowed to an affordable location with a mild, four-season climate that isn't too far to return "home" periodically and where friends and family can reasonably be expected to visit from time to time. Of course, your retirement home should be in an attractive setting where friends and family will look upon visits with joyful anticipation rather than with dread. The southeastern part of the United States—Georgia, the Carolinas and Virginia—fulfills all these requirements for a growing number of retired families.

It's not just Northerners who choose Southeastern states for retirement. From earliest times, Southern colonists who owned plantations in the warm, coastal regions traditionally enjoyed the cool highlands as summer retreats. That Southern tradition continues, augmented by Florida residents who are discovering the high country in the nearby Carolinas and Georgia as sanctuaries from Florida's hot and humid summers.

Part-time Retirees

Mountain sections of Georgia, the Carolinas and Virginia are noted for a growing population of "part-time" retirees from Florida who come here to cool off in the summer. After spending a couple of seasons in the upland hill country, many visitors become *ex*-Florida retirees, choosing to settle here permanently. One North Carolina native said, "Northerners are discovering our part of the country by going to Florida first and then making a second retirement move here."

The coastal Atlantic states offer a rich variety of retirement settings: sandy beaches, rolling green hills, and forested mountains brightened with azaleas, mountain laurel and myrtle trees. From fertile agricultural lands with neat farms and white fences, to rugged mountains where bears and herds of deer roam unmolested by humans, the Atlantic Coast region has it all. The ocean yields harvests of fish, crab and oysters; inland streams offer superb sport opportunities for trout, bass and other game fish. Modern cities with full conveniences and cultural attractions are but short drives from rural villages that are steeped in 19th-century atmosphere and country friendliness.

Any of these ecological worlds are within a few easy driving hours from almost anywhere in this area you might select as a home base. Florida is just next door and accessible for visits any time. Some Southeasterners take advantage of Florida's merciful winters by spending the coldest months there and returning to their mountain homes for the rest of the year.

Southern Hospitality

"Southern hospitality" is an oft-tossed-about phrase, but there's more than a kernel of truth here. It's interesting to note how Southerners interact with one another—as well as with strangers. You'll notice an open friendliness and sharing that differs from the general custom in other parts of the country. For example, when visiting friends or relatives in the South, I am always surprised how often people drop in unannounced for a visit. Sometimes it's a steady procession of acquaintances coming and going all day long. Close friends sometimes don't bother to knock. They'll just open the door and call out, "Anybody home?" They know they're always welcome for a chat. "Just passin' by," they'll explain, "so I thought I'd stop in to say hello." An extra cup of coffee is usually on the kitchen table before they can pull out a chair.

In other parts of the country, this would be unheard of. In my California neighborhood, before you visit someone other than a close friend, you telephone first and see if it's okay to come over. In still other parts of the country, you either wait for an invitation or you suggest meeting for lunch at a nearby restaurant. For some folks, Southern-style hospitality would take some getting used to. Some feel abused if casual acquaintances drop in and expect them to interrupt whatever they're doing to entertain them. Other folks love it.

However, don't expect to move into a Southern neighborhood and immediately become friends with all the other kids on the block. It doesn't work that way in Southern communities any more than it does in your home town. Although small-town Southerners are inclined to be more courteous and considerate than people from other parts of the country, they also tend to restrict their intimate friendships to people who share similar backgrounds and life experiences. Those who didn't grow up in their home town, or who come from an alien part of the world, will always be "outsiders" to some degree. (An alien part of the world is someplace other than the South.)

When asked whether residents of a small North Carolina town were friendly to outsider retirees, the local chamber of commerce representative thought for a moment and then replied, "Well, we tend to be friendly to everyone. But it's the *outsiders* who are most friendly to other outsiders." She added, "Outsiders have to learn to accept mountain people for who we are: sincere, hard-working folks who enjoy a simple life. We hate it when outsiders try to change things." They have a saying here, "You don't push mountain folks; you have to try and lead them."

Geography Lesson

The southeast coast states are divided into three distinct regions. The first is a broad coastal plain that rises from the Atlantic, often in low, marshy ground studded with palmettos and scrub oak. Several hundred miles of beautiful white-sand beaches are convenient for retirees who need to include the seashore in their retirement schemes. Farther inland, fertile fields and comfortable small towns offer a quieter, more introspective lifestyle.

These flat lowlands end at the fall line, where the foothills of the Blue Ridge and Great Smokey mountains begin. Rivers, creeks and streams flowing down from the mountains suddenly change into rapids and low waterfalls at this point, hence the name "fall line." This is the Piedmont or foothill region, a country of rolling hills covered with hardwood forests and dotted with more than 400,000 acres of lakes. Peach orchards, horse farms, neighborly small-town squares and country lanes characterize the Piedmont country.

Finally, we come to the Blue Ridge and Great Smokey highlands, where the Appalachians lift to an elevation of nearly 3,000 feet. This mountain chain runs in a northeast-southwest direction from near the Canadian border to just north of Atlanta. Ancient, eroded mountains, sometimes scarcely touched by civilization, are richly cloaked with hardwoods and flowering trees, pines, beeches, poplars and birch. Crystal-clear rivers and streams cascade through canyons and tumble over waterfalls into deep pools. This is a nature-lover's treat. Over 250 miles of trout streams run through South Carolina, probably at least that many in North Carolina. Northern Georgia also shares in this bounty.

Yet the mountain country isn't so high that it catches harsh winters. Snow is a regular winter visitor, but it seldom sticks around more than a day or two (except for a few higher, skiing areas). Compared with Cleveland or Chicago weather, even the worst days of winter here seem gentle. The mountains have other functions besides being picturesque. They deflect or delay cold air masses approaching from the north and west and thus protect coastal areas from arctic blasts.

North Carolina

We're convinced that some of the most beautiful and scenic places in the world are found in the Blue Ridge and Great Smokey mountains. October, when leaves are turning, is a marvelous time for a visit. Hardwood trees display a full explosion of color, with brilliant reds, yellows, purples and lavenders, and all colors in between to dazzle the eye while evergreens provided a conservative background of green. We've also made the rounds in the spring, when the dogwoods, azaleas and mountain laurel trees were in full bloom. The sight and smell of spring makes one forget winter.

Driving the Blue Ridge Parkway is an experience not soon forgotten. The parkway starts at the small town of Front Royal in northern Virginia and wends its way southwest until it ends at Great Smokey Mountains National Park—partly in Tennessee and partly in North Carolina. This scenic highway winds through beautiful mountain terrain, past wild rivers and thick forests. Hikers and river rafters love this country. Golf is a top sport here, with more than 20 first-quality courses throughout the Great Smokey Mountain area alone.

Unless you are country bred and raised, you'll probably prefer to settle within striking distance of a city. Once in a while you'll get a hankering for a genuine supermarket or a department store. Even the bigger mountain towns—Asheville (62,000), Greenville (59,000) and Hendersonville (44,000) in the southern parts; Bristol (24,000) and Johnson City (41,000) up around the Tennessee border—aren't all that large. Each of these cities is large enough, however, for adequate medical care, heavy shopping and services you might need from time to time.

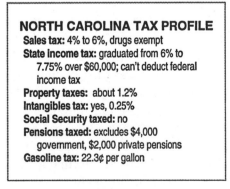

NORTH CAROLINA TAX PROFILE
Sales tax: 4% to 6%, drugs exempt
State income tax: graduated from 6% to 7.75% over $60,000; can't deduct federal income tax
Property taxes: about 1.2%
Intangibles tax: yes, 0.25%
Social Security taxed: no
Pensions taxed: excludes $4,000 government, $2,000 private pensions
Gasoline tax: 22.3¢ per gallon

Asheville Three North Carolina towns: Asheville, Hendersonville and Brevard, form a triangle, about 20 miles apart in the western portion of the state. Asheville, the largest city in western North Carolina, is the region's cultural and commercial center. This country is characterized by prosperous farms and rounded, forest-covered foothills, growing steeper toward the north.

Its natural setting, surrounded by a million acres of national forest, combines with the convenience of city living to make Asheville and environs one of North Carolina's favorite retirement and vacation destinations. Since the turn of the century, famous Americans such as Henry Ford, his pal Thomas Edison, F. Scott Fitzgerald and William Jennings Bryan enjoyed summers here. About 20 percent of today's residents are over 65.

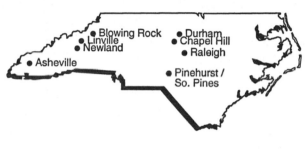

Because of its distance from a truly large metropolitan center, Asheville enjoys many services and amenities not normally found in a small city. No less than 16 shopping centers, four of them indoor malls, ensure wide selections of merchandise. Two interstate highways (I-40 and I-26) intersect in Asheville, as well as the Blue Ridge Parkway and ten other U.S. and state highways. This, plus an airport with daily flights and connections to all major cities, makes Asheville a transportation hub for this area.

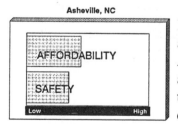

A concentration of hospitals and related facilities firmly establishes the city as a medical center. The claim is that Asheville has more doctors per capita than anywhere else in the world. Whether or not this is accurate, the fact remains that health care here is outstanding.

In addition to a branch of the University of North Carolina, two other four-year colleges and several two-year schools serve the area. Residents, whether connected with the school or not, have access to the cultural events associated with universities. Retirees take advantage of the many non-credit courses offered by the university and community colleges. The unique "College for Seniors" program encourages retirees with special qualifications to join with university faculty in teaching classes to mature adults.

Outdoor recreation here is enhanced by Asheville's nearness to some of the prettiest Appalachian country imaginable. Always within view, the Blue Ridge and Great Smokey mountains soar to heights of 5,000 feet. Hiking, fishing, camping and winter skiing make for year-round outdoor recreation, within walking or driving distance. Several public and private golf courses challenge players with good weather in all but the two coldest months of the year.

According to statistics, Asheville real estate sells at slightly above national averages, however many single-family homes sell for well under, many priced in the $80,000 to $90,000 range, and two-bedroom condos go for between $65,000 and $85,000.

The nearby towns of Hendersonville and Brevard are known for well-groomed residential districts and more than adequate shopping. Both towns routinely receive top recommendations as retirement destinations by retirement writers. Both are comfortable-looking places with picturesque settings (especially the country around Brevard). Unlike Asheville, Brevard is in a dry county, so don't plan on Cabernet Sauvignon with your prime rib; it'll be Pepsi-Cola.

Real estate costs in Brevard are above-average to high, with one nearby private community on the extremely expensive side—many homes are priced well over $500,000. Homes in Brevard enjoy a natural setting of trees and mature shrubs, with 33 percent of the county in the Pisgah National Forest. Since much of the remaining land cannot be developed, land is expensive in comparison to surrounding counties.

ASHEVILLE			Rel. Humidity: Jan. 62%, July 59%			
	Jan.	April	July	Oct.	Rain	Snow
Daily Highs	48	69	84	69	48"	17"
Daily Lows	26	43	62	43		

Blue Ridge Country

The rugged mountain country to the north of Asheville is appropriate for those demanding the best in Appalachian settings. This was Daniel Boone's country. The famous pioneer was born and raised in Boone, one of the major towns in this area.

For over a century wealthy families from all over the nation have traditionally used these mountains as summer hideaways, secluded places where they could slip away for quiet vacations. Industrialists from

Chicago and Pittsburgh, socialites from New York and Boston and southern aristocracy from Charleston, Charlotte and other affluent cities maintained summer retreats deep in the mountains. Places like Linville, Banner Elk and Blowing Rock are places unknown to most of the country, but quite familiar to the wealthy.

The first resorts and retirement homes appeared on the scene in the 1890s, but it wasn't until the advent of the automobile and good roads that retirement began in earnest. Then, anyone who could afford a Chevy could visit and settle in these formerly exclusive areas. And they did. This turned out to be a natural retirement haven, with inexpensive property, a mild climate and gorgeous surroundings.

Today's latest retirement wave began around 20 or 30 years ago when a few developers bought small valleys of wooded land and built golf courses. Golf was the irresistible bait to entice northern buyers to these parts. The ones with money built posh homes, at first for summer get-aways, eventually for retirement.

Blue Ridge Country, NC

AFFORDABILITY

SAFETY

Low   High

Hounds Ear Despite its "down-home" name, Hounds Ear is an example of an expensive development, one of the area's earliest. A developer visualized a golf course there, spreading over a valley floor. After laying out beautiful greens and fairways and an attractive clubhouse, he quickly sold the lots he had developed around the golf course. Buyers demanded more for retirement homes. He began cutting roads through the woods and into the hills that overlooked his valley golf course. As fast as he could lay out a new section of lots, it sold out. Each new house seemed to be more luxurious than the previous one, with some homes valued well into the six-figure mode. We were told that one couple put $500,000 into construction, but before they could finish, someone offered them a million dollars for the house, as is.

Obviously, these places aren't for folks with ordinary pocketbooks. Security guards staff the entrances 24 hours a day, keeping out us uncelestial beings. In fact, one development (Linville Ridge) is said to be so exclusive that one can buy into the development only by invitation! So far, the developers haven't invited me, so I suppose I won't buy. They probably wouldn't let me put it on my credit card, anyway.

However, all isn't for the rich. Enjoying the North Carolina mountains is practical because there are many affordable properties available.

Although these dwellings may not be as costly, the view, the fresh air and the delightful weather do not depend on our bank accounts. There are many small towns (and some not so small) where you can blend into the daily routine living among friendly neighbors. The local folk, who proudly refer to themselves as "mountain people," are famous for their hospitality to "flatlanders." The number of such outsiders from various parts of the country is growing larger every day.

Linville   Inexpensive homes abound in North Carolina towns and villages, as well as a few affordable country club-type resorts. One example is the Linville Land Harbor development. An 18-hole golf course was laid out over an area that was originally a commercial shrub and tree nursery. The bluegrass fairways and bent grass greens are said to be some of the best in the area. A 65-acre lake is stocked with brown and rainbow trout, and a mile of the Linville River's rapids and pools pose a challenge to fly fisherman. A large clubhouse, two tennis courts and an Olympic-sized pool complete the development.

This endeavor, which originally began as an RV park, marketed large-sized lots to vacationers. However, after putting in the resort's amenities, the developer declared bankruptcy. Fortunately, the lot owners were able to buy the property out of bankruptcy and now own the property as joint tenants.

Because the lots were so big, some lot owners decided to build houses while others brought in mobile homes. Some RV owners have built extra rooms beside their cement pads, providing extra sleeping while they are parked plus extra storage while they are gone. Today, instead of a vacation park as originally planned, Land Harbor is an interesting mixture of houses, mobile homes and RVs, with most people living here year-round.

Newland and Blowing Rock   The roads in this area are not for high-speed driving; they meander lazily around hill and dale. Every few miles turns up another surprise, another lovely town for retirement seekers. Each has its own personality and charm. The little town of Newland, for example, is a quiet, country town, unpretentious and economical. A house set back from the road on several acres can be found for less than $80,000 and cozy little homes in a friendly in-town neighborhood for half that amount. The most popular restaurant has an old-fashioned soda fountain and sells a lunch special for under $3.00. A public golf course—just as beautiful as the exclusive, private ones—provides sport for the duffers in the crowd.

A contrasting town is nearby Blowing Rock, which is a tourist-oriented artist colony. Much older than Newland, Blowing Rock features antique, heirloom homes in the style of the last century, exquisite in design and construction. Many nice restaurants, boutiques and antique shops line the main street, and the town of Boone is nearby for heavy-duty shopping. Although Boone has a little over 10,000 population, it seems larger because of its complete business district. Its crime rate is also very low, almost at the top of the national safety survey.

When you ask people why they chose this part of the Blue Ridge Mountains to retire, a major reason (right behind the area's beauty) is the mountain weather. Residents delight in contrasting seasons: mild summers, beautiful springs, honest-to-goodness falls and winters with soft blankets of snow create a wonderland of beauty. Skiing draws visitors from Florida and other parts of the South. Although Floridians visit here in the winter to enjoy winter sports, many mountain retirees head for Florida to *escape* the snow. We interviewed several retired residents who regularly go to Florida from December through March. Some take RVs; others rent condos or houses on the beach. The wealthier folks own a second home in Florida, with Vero Beach a popular destination for a winter reunion with their warm-weather neighbors.

Even though the region is somewhat isolated from Asheville (a long hour's drive away), a surprising array of cultural activities are available to residents. Mayland College, located in Spruce Pine, sponsors extension class programs in many surrounding communities. This program, called Lifelong Learning, is associated with the Elderhostel Institute, which has as its purpose the fostering of continuing education among older people, regardless of their previous academic pursuits. Some classes offered are pottery, studio glass, mountain weaving, jewelry and iron working, and sculpture/bronze casting.

BLUE RIDGE COUNTRY			Rel. Humidity: Jan. 62%, July 64%			
	Jan.	April	July	Oct.	Rain	Snow
Daily Highs	45	68	84	68	49"	18"
Daily Lows	25	41	62	44		

The North Carolina Midlands

Between the flat coastal regions and the Appalachians is a stretch of forested, gently rolling hills. Here you'll find a unique mix of Americana: from Beethoven to Bluegrass, from stock car racing to scholarly research, just about any kind of intellectual and recreational pursuit imaginable.

University Triangle   Unlike some sections of the South, where outsiders are rare curiosities, the area known as the "Triangle" attracts folks with academic interests and technical skills. People from all over North America and from all walks of life are represented. The Triangle consists of the cities of Chapel Hill, Durham and Raleigh. Within these cities are three major universities, plus several other academic institutions that attract intellectuals and technicians from all over the nation. It's said that per capita, more academics, PhD's and scientists live here than in any other part of the country. World-renowned Research Triangle Park employs some of the nation's top scientists and is located within easy driving distance of any of the Triangle cities.

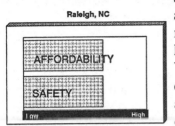
Raleigh, NC

Universities and colleges profoundly influence lifestyles here, with a large percentage of the community either working for or with educational institutions and others benefiting from the many stimulating events connected with academic life. Dramatic performances, lectures, sports and a host of other presentations are open to the public as well as those involved with schools.

The University of North Carolina was chartered in 1789 at Chapel Hill as the nation's first state university, beginning a tradition of education in the Midlands. From one building, 100 students and two professors, the university has grown to 22,000 students and more than 1,800 professors teaching in more than 100 fields.

Durham is the home of Duke University, well known as a center of higher learning and famous for its hospital. The Raleigh-Cary area lists five institutions of higher learning: North Carolina State University, St. Augustine's College, Peace College, St. Mary's College and Wake Technical College. Between Raleigh and Durham you'll find eight two-year colleges and eight four-year colleges and universities, with 64,000 students. Education is big business here.

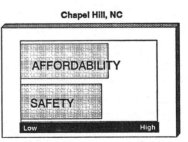
Chapel Hill, NC

Because of the schools and research and related industries, academic and technician wages in the Triangle are higher than in most of the Carolinas. This means higher housing costs and fancier homes in the more elegant sections. Homes in the $200,000-plus price range have no trouble finding buyers. But homes in that price range seem like mansions compared to other parts of the country. We visited a couple who moved to Raleigh from New York City, from a small apartment into a spacious five-bedroom home on two acres of wooded grounds. "Our entire apartment could fit into the dining, living rooms and kitchen," they said. "And never in our wildest dreams could we have afforded to buy an apartment there." Because they bought when interest rates bottomed out, the monthly payment on their $200,000 mansion is one-third what they paid in rent for a tiny apartment.

Even though the cost of living and housing is about 8 percent above national norms, this is the Southeast, a section not famous for excessively high wage scales. Non-academic workers earn typical North Carolina wages, creating a demand for lower cost housing. Therefore, while some subdivisions are priced over $200,000 per home, plenty of quality homes sell for less than $80,000. Some luxury condos start at $100,000; others, perfectly livable, are closer to the $50,000 range.

UNIVERSITY TRIANGLE			Rel. Humidity: Jan. 55%, July 58%			
	Jan.	April	July	Oct.	Rain	Snow
Daily Highs	50	72	88	72	42"	2"
Daily Lows	30	47	67	48		

Pinehurst/Southern Pines   The northern part of North Carolina, in an area known as the "Sandhills," has long been famous for golf—with 30 championship courses within a 16-mile radius. Before they thought about retirement, many people simply thought of Pinehurst and Southern Pines as convenient stopover places on their way to Florida vacations. This was the logical place to break up the trip—about halfway for many Easterners. Why not stay over a day or two and get in a few rounds of golf? As retirement time drew nearer, some folks naturally began thinking more about Pinehurst and less about Florida.

Because the elevation here is higher than most of Florida, summers aren't quite as warm or humid. Furthermore, the 55-degree January days permit plenty of outdoor activities. "Any day it's not raining, I can golf, hike or ride horseback." said a retiree here. "When I lived in Florida, it was too damned muggy in the summer!"

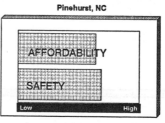

Pinehurst, NC

More than adequate health care is covered by a 397-bed regional hospital with a medical staff of 112 physicians and 1,400 employees, assisted by 500 volunteers. A 24-hour-a-day mobile intensive care unit provides up-to-date life support treatments.

The small-town atmosphere lends itself to a feeling of security, with a lower than average crime rate. Yet because of the large percentage of out-of-state retirees, newcomers don't feel that they stand out as they might in some other small Southern towns.

PINEHURST/SOUTHERN PINES			Rel. Humidity: Jan. 56%, July 59%			
	Jan.	April	July	Oct.	Rain	Snow
Daily Highs	55	68	91	71	41"	2"
Daily Lows	34	51	67	58		

South Carolina

Columbia   Another educational center of the south, Columbia (pop. 110,000) has the University of South Carolina as its focal point of cultural enrichment. A surprising number of Northerners have found this to be a great place for retirement. By the way, Columbia claims to have a higher percentage of retirees living here than anywhere else in the state.

Columbia is situated at the point where the coastal plain meets the beginning of the Piedmont. At the western edge of the city, rolling foothills begin, and at the opposite edge, the country is flat all the way to the ocean. This is a comfortable city, with the vast majority of the housing owner-occupied. The streets are shaded with tall trees, and

SOUTH CAROLINA TAX PROFILE
Sales tax: 5% to 6%, dugs exempt
State income tax: graduated from 2.5% to 7% over $10,600; can't deduct federal income tax
Property taxes: about 2.5%, residents over 65 receive exemptions
Intangibles tax: no
Social Security taxed: no
Pensions taxed: $3,000 exclusion
Gasoline tax: 16¢ per gallon

there's a quiet charm that comes with ordinary people living in ordinary neighborhoods. Yet, Columbia has its sophisticated side as well, with a cosmopolitan feeling that goes with being a university town.

Many "Old South" cities grew haphazardly, with roads and streets going in random directions, without planning of any sort. But Columbia is different. The British needed a capital city for South Carolina, so in 1686 they designed the first planned city in the Colonies. The city's broad boulevards and architectural gems attest to its early beauty. Robert Mills, one of the pioneers of U.S. architecture, designed several buildings here as well as many in Washington, D.C. (One of his more famous works is the Washington Monument.)

The university, with 28,000 students, is a major source of cultural enrichment. Along with a nearby two-year college, the school attracts academics from around the nation, many of whom later join the ranks of Columbia's retired. All South Carolina state colleges and technical institutes waive tuition for residents over 60 years of age (on a space-available basis). Retirees can also take full advantage of this benefit at regional campuses in Beaufort, Lancaster, Allendale, Sumter, Union, Aiken, Conway and Spartanburg. Special low-cost spring and summer residential academic programs are also available for senior citizens.

This is a popular retirement location for many military families because of the town's proximity to Fort Jackson and the obvious advantages of retiring near a military installation. During World War II, thousands of GIs were stationed here, awaiting shipping orders to join their comrades in Europe. Many fondly recall the mild weather and friendly South Carolinans. These memories are bringing the ex-GIs back to Columbia for their retirement careers. These two out-of-state groups, academic and military, contribute toward making the Columbia area heterogeneous, with open, accepting feelings toward newcomers.

We found several retirees who had started out intending to retire elsewhere, but somehow wound up happily retiring in the Carolinas. For example, one retired couple admitted that they had always planned on retirement in Florida. "Every year, as we made our annual trip to Florida, we broke our trip up with a stopover in Columbia," they explained, "and again on the way back. Then, one day, just before retirement, we realized that we really liked Columbia better than Florida!" They decided to rent an apartment, just to "see how Columbia feels." They found low living costs and friendly, cultured neighbors. "We never made it to Florida," they said with satisfied smiles. "We still go there for vacations, though."

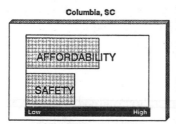

Columbia, SC

I asked him how he felt as a Yankee moving into a Deep South town. Did he find any prejudices? "To tell you the truth, I haven't noticed anything like that," he said. "My neighbors are just as nice as the ones we had back home, but they're definitely more friendly. Other Northerners warned us, 'They'll be neighborly, yes, but they'll never invite you to their daughter's debutante party unless you were born in Columbia.'" He shrugged his shoulders and said, "That's a relief to me, because the last place I'd want to be invited would be to some teenager's debutante party! I'd have to invent an excuse why I couldn't go."

Another advantage they pointed out—aside from the low cost of quality housing—is the excellent medical care available. (As a pharmacist, he was aware of such things.) About 13 hospitals serve the area with over 500 doctors to treat your ills.

COLUMBIA			Rel. Humidity: Jan. 59%, July 58%			
	Jan.	April	July	Oct.	Rain	Snow
Daily Highs	50	72	88	72	43"	5"
Daily Lows	32	50	69	50		

Aiken Here is example of a Piedmont retirement location. Aiken (pop. 21,000) is a genteel, Old-South town sitting in the western corner of South Carolina. Aiken's robust business district makes it look larger than it actually is, because it's the shopping and employment center for a large area. Aiken County has about 115,000 people. The only large industry, the Savannah River Atomic Project, employs a considerable work force, some of whom live in nearby Augusta, Georgia, 17 miles distant.

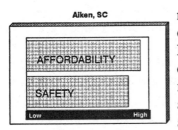
Aiken, SC

Aiken is a good candidate for retirement for a number of reasons, not the least of which is its beautiful, gracious setting. Huge antebellum mansions and cute little cottages are shaded by enormous trees on meticulously landscaped lots. The natives are ingrained with notions of politeness and Southern chivalry, all adding immeasurable charm to the setting. Unlike many Southern cities that suffered damage during the Civil War, Aiken escaped the torch of vengeful Union soldiers. So today, Aiken is a showcase of homes that survived the war, many buildings more than 150 years old.

From its inception, Aiken was known as a health resort. Wealthy people from Charleston and the coastal plantations came here to escape the sultry, lowland summer heat and malaria-bearing mosquitoes. The Civil War and its aftermath of poverty put a temporary halt to Aiken's role as a summer health resort. But by the 1890s, Aiken entered a new golden age when wealthy Northerners, seeking pleasant, quiet places for their winter homes, "discovered" the town.

At an altitude of only 527 feet, the town had a climate mild enough to permit year-round grazing and was a perfect place to raise thorough-bred horses. Soon the ordinary rich, the filthy rich, and the disgustingly filthy rich bought old mansions and built new ones of their own designs. They bought farms for their race horses and enclosed pastures with white fences. They established the Palmetto Golf Club in 1893 and were slicing drives into the lake by the time the first thoroughbred colts were frisking in the meadows.

These activities quickly established Aiken as a rich man's play-ground, mostly a haven for wealthy Yankees from New York and Connecticut. These newcomers brought prosperity to Aiken and, with it, a return to a genteel lifestyle that had disappeared with the Civil War. Aiken's old, aristocratic families quickly accepted the winter residents into local society despite different customs and accents. This established a tradition of openness and hospitality that has characterized Aiken ever since. Today, the super-rich Northerners have gone elsewhere, yet the legacy of hospitality and friendliness remains.

Aiken differs from most Southern towns in that so many outsiders have moved here that distinctions between natives and newcomers have blurred. Townspeople are used to different accents and other lifestyles; a cosmopolitan mix has broken through all but the most inbred social barriers.

Where did these outsiders come from? When the DuPont corporation was building the local atomic power plant, engineers, physicists, techni-cians, bricklayers—you name it—came from all over the country. At the peak more than 13,000 people worked on the project. These newcomers severely strained Aiken's housing market, so DuPont built a large number of single-family dwellings and rented them to employees.

When the energy plant was finally completed, many workers moved elsewhere to new jobs. Although others—many of whom were nearing retirement anyway—elected to stay, DuPont was stuck with hundreds of homes, so the corporation began selling them at fire-sale prices. For a time, $10,000 was the going price for a three-bedroom home. Naturally, this knocked the local real estate market into a spin. But the word slipped out that here was a beautiful little town, with mild winters, friendly people and fantastic real estate prices. A multitude of folks from all over the country began snapping up DuPont's houses. However, be aware that the easy real estate days of a few years ago are over. DuPont's surplus housing is long gone, with newcomers rescuing the market from a downspin.

Aiken isn't all single-family homes, antebellum mansions and honeysuckle. Modern condominiums and apartments compete with mobile home parks for renters. Away from town, you'll find properties where you can set up a mobile home and have an instant farm. Luxury retirement communities—Kalmia Landing and Woodside Plantation—offer country club retirement accommodations and an atmosphere of studied elegance.

Aiken boasts a campus of the University of South Carolina and Aiken Technical College. This means free, or nearly free, courses for senior citizens and entry into the academic community of the town. There's a 190-bed medical facility that, we were told, has an excellent reputation. Military retirees and dependents have VA hospitals in both Columbia and Augusta.

Recreational choices abound; since the weather is generally mild, year-round outdoor activities are possible. Nineteen golf courses within a 20-mile radius of Aiken make this sport convenient; several feature senior citizens clubs. In nearby Augusta, the famous Masters Tournament is played every year. Each autumn on the shores of Lake Hartwell, Clemson University conducts a camping program for senior citizens. Fishing, swimming, even water skiing for all those oldtimers who go for that sort of nonsense, are available at any number of nearby ponds or lakes. Hunting and fishing permits are free to residents over 65.

AIKEN			Rel. Humidity: Jan. 54%, July 54%			
	Jan.	April	July	Oct.	Rain	Snow
Daily Highs	57	77	91	77	43"	1"
Daily Lows	33	49	69	50		

On the Ocean

The Atlantic states —from Virginia to Georgia—share 3,000 miles of low coastal country and wild barrier islands. This extended estuarine shoreline—with beaches, inlets, quiet coves and bays, sounds and lazy saltwater marshes—is an aquatic wonderland. The southeast coast is a haven for countless snow geese, and its pristine beaches serve up rare and elaborate seashells.

Myrtle Beach   The city of Myrtle Beach occupies a lovely stretch of sandy shore near the upper edge of the South Carolina coast. It regularly receives praise from retirement writers as a great place to retire. This is South Carolina's equivalent of Florida Panhandle resorts—tourist-frenzied in the peak season and somewhat relaxed in the winter. Myrtle

Beach's population doubles every summer as the town bustles with holiday sun-and-fun seekers.

It used to be, after Labor Day, the town would drop its frantic, super-hero role and change to its mild-mannered, sleepy identity for the rest of the year. Not any more. An intrusion of country-western entertainment centers—modeled after Branson, Missouri, and Tennessee's Grand Ol' Opry—are making full-tilt tourism a year-round business. This raises the problem of traffic congestion and additional strain on summer-season facilities, already under pressure. With an increased work force and long-term visitors competing for housing, inexpensive housing is out of the picture for some time to come.

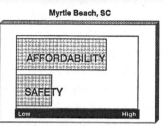

The local chamber of commerce claims that the Grand Strand is only two degrees cooler than the northern Florida coast. However, local residents qualify this by saying, "We do get some right smart cold spells from time to time." According to what I can determine from weather charts, Myrtle Beach has about twice as many frost days as Jacksonville or St. Augustine. Our first visit to Myrtle Beach was during a cold snap, and I remember it vividly. A freezing north wind tortured me as I tried to changed a flat tire with numb, frozen hands (our only flat in more than 30,000 miles of research). However, the next afternoon it warmed up to the point that we could stroll the beach in our shirtsleeves.

MYRTLE BEACH			Rel. Humidity: Jan. 56%, July 53%			
	Jan.	April	July	Oct.	Rain	Snow
Daily Highs	56	74	89	75	53"	2"
Daily Lows	38	52	71	53		

Charleston   Proud of her reputation as the "cultural center of the South," Charleston has scrupulously—almost jealously—maintained this tradition for over three centuries. Like an aristocratic Southern belle who appreciates the finer points of chivalry and good manners, Charleston has rejected the unspeakably common intrusion of colored-glass buildings and towering condominiums. She refuses to replace tradition and history with glitter and quick profits. The result is a treasury of historical architecture and purity unmatched anywhere else in the country. The city is not simply a collection of historical buildings, but a living museum of Old South traditions, cuisine, architecture and gracious manners. Charleston is a way of life.

We fell in love with this city while researching our first retirement book, so it was with complete horror that we watched television coverage of 1989's Hurricane Hugo attacking Charleston. From what TV screens showed, the town was all but destroyed. We watched winds tear away trees and rip roofs from the historic old buildings. We felt as if we were witnessing the destruction of an old friend. It was horrible.

Therefore, when we made our latest visit, we were prepared for the very worst. To our surprise and delight, we could detect no damage to the historic downtown section. Even the trees along Battery Park, which we expected to be bare, stood waving in the breeze just as they had a few years earlier. How could this damage be repaired so quickly?

High winds had scarcely subsided when plucky residents rolled up their sleeves and started to work. They began trimming damaged limbs from trees, repairing slate roofs and straightening the disorder. Charleston citizens are justifiably proud of the recovery. "Within six months," said one, "we had things cleaned up and repaired as good as before."

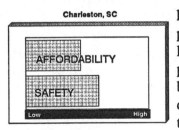

After its settlement in 1670, Charleston quickly became one of the most prosperous cities of the 13 colonies. Charleston was the standard against which people measured other cities in terms of beauty, culture and riches. Planters, acquiring wealth from fantastically productive rice plantations, began designing mansions as lavish as money could provide. They built with such loving attention to detail and such devotion to quality and style that future generations of Charlestonians resisted all temptations to exchange those prizes for new fashions. At least 240 homes are known to have been built before 1840. Seventy-six predate the Revolution, with some dating back to the 1720s! Hundreds more date from the time of the Civil War and the reconstruction era.

Charleston is so steeped in history that a walk through its downtown streets is an adventure in time travel. It's easy to imagine fine carriages jaunting along the cobblestone streets or fashionably dressed women and nattily attired men strolling the sidewalks. A pause in front of a home built in 1720 evokes a feeling of humility as one mentally recreates the setting—almost three centuries past. In California, where I live, any building over 100 years old is considered a priceless antique, so you can see why I felt overwhelmed.

Built on a narrow peninsula, the downtown section isn't very large. The peninsula is so narrow that it's almost an island between two rivers that empty into the ocean at the city's east end. The emphasis is on private homes rather than on commercial activity. The most important enterprise (from my standpoint as a lover of seafood) in this old section is the superb collection of fine restaurants. As major tourist attractions, Charleston's restaurants fully live up to their reputation for excellent seafood and Southern gourmet dishes of all descriptions. (We can never pass through town without a pause for our favorite culinary delight: she-crab soup.)

Charleston living isn't for everyone. It can be terribly formal, paced with the tempo of Southern society, intellectual pursuits and traditional manners. But even if you aren't into buying historic mansions and entering the social whirl, some alternatives might be an adventure for a part-time living arrangement. You can do as the old-time planters did: live in Charleston most of the year and somewhere else for the summer.

Many old mansions were long ago converted to apartments. Rents are uncommonly reasonable, considering the enchanted, historic atmosphere. Carriage houses behind the mansions have been remodeled into studio apartments, some as charming cottages with lofts converted into upstairs bedrooms. The gorgeous flowered landscaping for which Charleston is so famous makes even the most humble carriage house seem elegant. We saw apartments in historic mansions advertised at $500 and under, carriage houses just a little higher.

Should you become ambitious and want to own your own historic mansion, you might be surprised at the prices. I expected prices starting at $500,000, but several were priced under $200,000. I can't vouch for the condition or the amount of restoration needed. Certainly you would have to be prepared to invest a lot of money, but there is a certain satisfaction in restoration, if you can afford it.

All is not lace curtains and fresh paint in old Charleston. As in most cities, the curse of urban blight hovers overhead. Not very far from the prosperous streets I have described are rows of abandoned houses, so old and uncared-for that they look as if they might collapse from age and decay. I wish there were some way to preserve these old mansions just as they are—not restored to modern-day building codes and remodeled to please today's esthetics. Some are three stories high with beautifully crafted balconies and balustrades rising the full facade. Porches, high columns and carved woodwork add to the impression of museum pieces from an irretrievable past. Probably within a decade these will all be gone.

Outside of town several resort-type retirement developments offer Charleston living in country club environments. These are the Elms of Charleston, Ladson and Fairfield Ocean Ridge.

Charleston's Islands   A network of rivers meet at Charleston: the Stono, Ashley, Cooper and Wando rivers make Charleston Harbor and the surrounding coast a virtual cluster of islands. Most are uninhabited, overgrown with thick brush, rising only a few feet above high-tide level.

In our first retirement volume we featured a retired couple who had a wonderful idea: build a house on one of those islands! They purchased an eight-acre island with bridge access and proceeded to clear just enough of the natural vegetation to build their dream place.

That sounded like a great idea. But I had a few questions. "What about high tides?" I asked. "What happens when a hurricane sends in a lot of water?"

"That's why we built the house on pilings," the husband replied. "The first level will be a carport and storage for things that won't be hurt by water. And we're making sure all landscaping is in natural plants that won't be destroyed by a little extra water."

His wife added, "Floods covered this island once in the past ten years. A hurricane backed the river up about three feet over our property. But our house will stand on ten-foot-tall stilts."

This interview took place *before* Hurricane Hugo struck so rudely. As best we can tell, they were correct about their house being safe. It still stands, thanks to the hurricane-proof construction. Actually, few island homes built in the last decade were severely damaged, because stricter building regulations demand hurricane-proof construction. Houses built in the last century also fared well. Those suffering most were built in the 1960s and 1970s, before the strict building codes were law. Sullivan Island suffered the least damage, with homes and trees doing quite well. The Isle of Palms, on the other hand, bore the brunt of the storm and lost many trees and homes. The worst damage was done to the golf course, with the 17th and 18th greens totally destroyed. (As a terrible golfer, I've been known to destroy a few greens myself.)

CHARLESTON			Rel. Humidity: Jan. 62%, July 64%			
	Jan.	April	July	Oct.	Rain	Snow
Daily Highs	61	78	90	77	49"	—
Daily Lows	38	54	71	55		

Hilton Head Island Still in South Carolina, but just 40 miles north of Savannah, Georgia, is luxurious Hilton Head Island. The playground for affluent Savannah citizens, Hilton Head is also a preferred retirement destination for the truly affluent from all over the nation. I include it here

Hilton Head, SC

simply on the off-chance that some rich person accidentally purchased a copy of this book and deserves some consideration. The island is divided into eight developments (called "plantations") centered around active living—golf, tennis, boating or the 12 miles of white, sandy beach.

Golfers love the courses here and the 425 holes of golf spread over 12 locations on Hilton Head and nearby Daufuskie Island. For tennis buffs, there are more than 250 courts ranging from major complexes that host national championships to one or two courts adjoining a condo or apartment complex. Five hundred acres are reserved as a forest preserve with an astonishing 260 species of birds, alligators, deer, raccoon and wild turkey. (A $3.00 gate pass is required to enter. Wild animals enter free of charge.) Hiking, shrimping from the shore, biking and boating fill out the menu of outdoor activities. The list of gourmet restaurants is also impressive. According to the chamber of commerce, about 200 restaurants, cafes and fast-food emporiums serve everything from stand-up pizza and eggrolls to haute cuisine.

Hilton Head Island is a place for those who can afford it, who are willing to pay for a high-quality lifestyle. If you can afford Hilton Head Island, then you might read the chapter in this book on Hawaii.

Georgia

The state of Georgia is trying hard to tempt out-of-state retirees into moving here rather than continuing on to Florida, and a growing number of folks discover that they like the state's varied menu of locations and its sunbelt climate. The largest state east of the Mississippi, Georgia stretches from the golden beaches of the Atlantic to the foothills of the Appalachians. The Blue Ridge Mountains taper off in the northern end of the state, but not before

rewarding the region with rich valleys, forested hills and scenic mountains. Another good prospect for retirement is Georgia's Atlantic coast, characterized by barrier islands with moss-draped oaks and magnificently preserved colonial towns, affordable retirement choices that once were domains of millionaires. To the south is the Plantation Trace with its early spring, delightful small cities and nearness to both the Gulf and Atlantic. Another popular retirement area is around Augusta, which enjoys the benefits of two geographical areas: the Piedmont Plateau and the Atlantic Coastal Plain. This is golf and thoroughbred country.

GEORGIA TAX PROFILE

Sales tax: 4% to 6%, drugs exempt
State income tax: graduated from 1% to 6% over $7,000; can't deduct federal income tax
Property taxes: taxed on 40% of market value minus $2,000 homestead exemption; typically 0.98%, plus variable local taxes
Intangibles tax: yes
Social Security taxed: no
Pensions taxed: excludes first $10,000 for older taxpayers
Gasoline tax: 7.5¢ per gallon, plus 3% sales tax

Valdosta   In their haste to get to Florida, many vacationers zip right past the city of Valdosta (pop. 40,000), never suspecting that a delightful little city sits undiscovered just a short skip away from Interstate 75. Some tourists stay overnight in motels, maybe getting in some shopping at the manufacturers' outlet stores before steering their cars back onto the interstate to resume the high-speed parade to the saltwater beaches a couple of hours down the cement pavement.

Perhaps because Moody Air Force Base is connected with Valdosta, tourists imagine a typical military "gate town" with a major commerce in honky tonks, pawn shops and fast-food mills. I confess to entertaining a vague image like that myself, before actually visiting Valdosta. What I discovered was one of the better retirement areas in this part of the country, one of the pleasant surprises of the research trip.

Valdosta is set in Georgia's "Plantation Trace," a region marked by fertile plains, bountiful woods and hundreds of blue lakes. Steeped in Victorian history and architecture, as well as modern subdivisions, Valdosta stands out as south Georgia's dominant city. Featuring immaculately maintained neighborhoods, shaded by enormous trees and landscaping that emphasizes flowering plants, Valdosta's residential sections are exceptionally inviting. One retiree affirmed that this well-groomed, upscale ambience influenced his decision to choose Valdosta as a place to settle, saying, "You can tell Valdostans respect their town by the way they treat it. It's a joy to live among people like that."

106

To be fair, I'll have to admit that my Valdosta research coincided with the first riotous days of spring in the midst of an outrageous explosion of blossoms splashing color from every tree, bush and garden. It's no coincidence that Valdosta is called "the Azalea City." Yet, the overall quality of these neighborhoods transcends mere flower beds and magnolia trees. In Valdosta, the phrase "quality living" is not a shopworn cliché; it's an apt description.

A glance at cost-of-living charts indicates that Valdosta is just a little under the national averages. This is understandable because of a recession-proof economy based on military and university payrolls, which don't vary a great deal. Home prices, for example are just 7 percent below national average. However, this is another instance where statistics can mislead. Even though the average Valdosta home sells for $96,000, that tells you nothing about the elegance and quality you get for that money. According to real estate people, a medium-priced home is about $62,000 and an expensive one, $116,000. Because of a high turnover of Air Force families (mostly officers) who are transferred in and out for training, there's a wealth of apartment complexes scattered about town—more than 100.

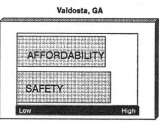

As I visited neighborhoods, noticing beautiful, quality brick homes on half-acre lots, a theme kept recurring: this is a place where a couple cashing in equity in over-priced sections of the country could "move up" and live in a fabulous neighborhood, in a style never dreamed of—and probably bank some of their profits from the sale of their house.

The downtown area, too, shows that Valdosta residents care. An ambitious renovation of an already nice-looking town center is going to make this one of the showplaces of the South. To finance this project, a special sales tax measure passed with an overwhelming margin, a refreshing vote of confidence in Valdosta and its future.

An important consideration for those retiring from other parts of the nation is Valdosta's cosmopolitan retiree community; they come from everywhere! Large numbers of Air Force officers spent training time at Moody Air Force Base. Naturally, when retirement draws near, when military families begin discussing favorite towns, they remember this area with fondness.

The "Azalea City" is a university town, and Valdosta State University's grounds and campus are in keeping with the upscale look of its surroundings. The university offers continuing education, with low-cost fees, in classes ranging from Calligraphy to Tai Chi. Transportation is another strong point here. Strategically located on Interstate 75 and near east-west Interstate 10, Valdosta is just 18 miles from the Florida state line, and an easy drive to Florida beaches. The city is also served by rail and intercity bus service (Greyhound) and has an airport with five daily commercial flights to Atlanta. Why Atlanta? Because in this part of the world, no matter where you are flying, the first leg of your flight goes to Atlanta, the South's all-important air transport hub. Travelers here say: "When you die, you may not know if your destination is Heaven or Hell; but you *do* know you'll be going through Atlanta to get there."

The surrounding countryside's woodlands and numerous lakes make hunters and fishermen happy, particularly the federally-owned Grand Bay Wildlife Area which provides 5,900 acres of hunting preserve. With a wildlife management stamp firmly affixed to their state hunting licenses, sportsmen decimate ducks and geese as they make their way south each fall. It isn't all hunting and fishing at Grand Bay. An archery range draws bow-hunters—1,800 of them in June, 1994—and there are facilities for camping, nature hikes and bird watching. A "canoe trail" leads you through Blackgum Swamp—an array of wetlands that mimics the Okefenokee—with signs that mark the way and explain the natural wonders of this area. For those who don't happen to have a canoe with them, there's a 2,000-foot boardwalk and an observation tower.

The nearby town of Lake Park is a quality example of lakeside living in south Georgia. Homes circle the lake, with an interesting mixture of small, inexpensive houses and large, extravagant places democratically sitting side by side. Moss-draped live oaks and cypress trees shade boat docks and yards that look over the blue water. When a real estate broker quoted home prices, I was astounded at the affordability of Lake Park. (Of course, being from California, *any* real estate looks affordable.) Commercial facilities include a full-fledged medical facility, three shopping malls, several restaurants, and a library.

VALDOSTA			Rel. Humidity: Jan. 59%, July 58%			
	Jan.	April	July	Oct.	Rain	Snow
Daily Highs	70	80	94	83	49"	1"
Daily Lows	45	54	71	59		

Savannah Guarding the South Carolina-Georgia state line is the old port city of Savannah (pop. 148,000). Like Charleston, Savannah also has a wealth of interesting old homes. Although it promotes the image of gracious, old-Southern charm, the city falls short of possessing the magical aura that makes Charleston so special. Many graceful old mansions are for sale at reasonable prices, should anyone have the urge to try a hand at restoration. However, few of them predate the Civil War; General Sherman's troops did their work well in destroying beautiful old antebellum homes here. One fascinating section of Savannah, by the waterfront, has been restored with antique stores, restaurants and bars.

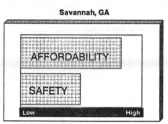

Savannah, GA

Real estate here falls way below the national averages, placing Savannah into the category of truly inexpensive localities. Another place to investigate is the area around Richmond Hill State Park. Also, several islands near Savannah are said to be popular with retirees: Wilmington, Skidaway and Tybee.

SAVANNAH			Rel. Humidity: Jan. 54%, July 58%			
	Jan.	April	July	Oct.	Rain	Snow
Daily Highs	60	78	91	78	49"	—
Daily Lows	38	54	72	56		

Brunswick and the Golden Isles   A hundred years ago—when being a millionaire meant more than having equity in an above-average Connecticut home—millionaires from all over the country converged upon the "Golden Isles" and encouraged their contractors and interior decorators to enter the competition for the fanciest homes possible. The objects of their affection were the islands of St. Simons and Jekyll on the south Georgia coast. Today, if you can afford to live there, you don't need a book about "where to retire."

The mainland base camp and supply for the islands is the conservative old town of Brunswick. Compared to its rich island cousins, Brunswick is a rather ordinary community of about 20,000 inhabitants. But there's a charm about the place that money can't buy.

The town was founded before the Revolution, with the names of streets and squares honoring English nobility of that time, like Prince, Gloucester, Norwich and Newcastle. Property here is reasonable (if not downright cheap), and the homes are well kept. Streets are sheltered by overhanging oak trees hung with Spanish moss—quiet and peaceful. Some antebellum homes, with columns and balconies, grace the side streets, mixed in with more modern cottages. We saw a few mobile home parks, but none had the class of Florida parks. These seem to be more for economical living, without extensive landscaping and organized clubhouse activities. All in all, Brunswick looks like the place to live for those who want to enjoy the fishing, beaches and ambience of nearby Jekyll and St. Simons without paying the higher cost of actually living on the islands.

Development on the islands began in the 1880s when opulent families like the J.P. Morgans, Rockefellers and Goulds formed the "Jekyll Island Club." Only club members were permitted to live on the island, making this one of the most exclusive resorts in the entire world.

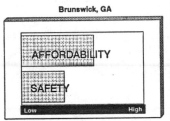

Historians estimate that at one time Jekyll Island Club members represented one-sixth of the world's wealth!

Nearby St. Simons imparts a pleasant small-town atmosphere, even though it's much more upscale than the average small town. An attractive pier and public park abut a low-key downtown—actually, just a collection of tasteful shops. A quiet shopping center hides behind shrubbery on the main road that curves along the beach side of the island. Several miles of fine public beach make excellent places for picnics. Good restaurants aren't scarce, with seafood the most popular fare.

BRUNSWICK/GOLDEN ISLES		Rel. Humidity: Jan. 54%, July 58%				
	Jan.	April	July	Oct.	Rain	Snow
Daily Highs	61	78	91	78	49"	—
Daily Lows	38	54	71	56		

Rabun County "We feel like we're on the edge of heaven here in the Blue Ridge Mountains of northeast Georgia. It has to be one of the most beautiful spots in the country!" Marjorie Seaver, a freelance writer from New Orleans, said this as she and her husband John looked out over the Chattahoochee National Forest from their retirement home which they built on a 2,500-foot ridge. Theirs is one of about 600 homes tucked away in the forest in an area called Sylvan Falls, the vast majority owned by retirees. Not all homes are blessed with such breathtaking views, but each enjoys its own little natural paradise of rustic beauty. On the county's eastern edge, Lake Burton supports a gorgeous lakefront settlement of upscale retirement homes as well as weekend hideaways for affluent Atlanta citizens. The lake is owned by Georgia Power Company, and the lots are leased, rather than sold.

Clayton is the largest town in Rabun county, in fact it's the only settlement worthy of being called much more than a village. For this reason, folks hereabouts don't think in terms of towns; when you ask where they live, they'll reply "Rabun County," rather than mention a specific locality. With only 1,700 inhabitants, Clayton is the commercial center for the county's 11,648 residents; as such, it provides an unusually good selection of shopping, business and medical services. Two hospitals, with 24-hour staffed emergency rooms, deliver a wide range of health care services.

One feature all residents point to proudly is their four-season weather. As local boosters say, "This is where spring spends the summer." Flowering trees in the spring, fall colors and delightful summers keep you aware of the season and comfortable enough to enjoy it. One minus which nobody seems to complain about is an unusually high rainfall: 60 or more inches a year. Gotta admit, it keeps wild rivers roaring and trees green.

Surprisingly, housing costs here range from inexpensive to moderate. This is because land is not as inexpensive as you might expect in a sparsely-settled, forested countryside. It turns out that 63 percent of the county is U.S. Forest Service property and Georgia Power owns another 7 percent; it's a seller's market when it comes to purchasing that building lot. According to the Rabun County chamber of commerce, the median price for a two- or three-bedroom home is $75,000, with condos starting at $60,000. This being a rural setting, condos and apartments aren't overly abundant, so inexpensive rentals are not easy to come by.

Few communities the size of Clayton can support a senior citizens' center, and here is no exception. As an excellent substitute, the chamber of commerce organized a club called the Silver Eagles. About 200 very active members hold regular meetings, elect officers, arrange social activities, tours, and share their expertise

with others in the community. The comaraderie developed among the members is said to be contagious. This is the place for newcomers to come and meet their new neighbors and forge all-important community connections.

Outdoor recreational opportunities are tops in Rabun County, partially because of the lakes, rivers and forest, and partly because so much of the land belongs to the public. The ridgetop Appalachian Trail runs along Rabun County's western border, and the federally protected wild and scenic Chattooga River is on the eastern border. Georgia's only ski lift is located in nearby Sky Valley. Rabun County Country Club has a nine-hole golf course, and Sky Valley has an 18-hole championship layout that's open to the public. As for indoor recreation, Rabun is not a dry county. (Thank-you, Rabun County!)

Clarkesville (pop. 1,400), the county seat of nearby Habersham County, is another town often praised by retirement writers. A tourist brochure claims it is just an hour's drive from Atlanta, but I'd hesitate a long while before getting into a car with anyone who makes the 75-mile drive in an hour! The countryside here is rolling hills rather than low mountains and, while not as picturesque as Clayton, has a rural charm about it.

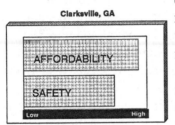

Another interesting town—not far from Clayton—is Dahlonega, the location of the United States' first full-blown gold strike. Gold was discovered here in 1828 and can still be panned today. Dahlonega was booming until gold was discovered in California in 1849. Suddenly the local miners deserted their claims en masse and hot-footed it out west. The restored county courthouse has a gold museum. Trout fishing, canoeing, whitewater rafting and horseback riding are readily available.

RABUN COUNTY			Rel. Humidity: Jan. 54%, July 54%			
	Jan.	April	July	Oct.	Rain	Snow
Daily Highs	52	69	84	69	60"	10"
Daily Lows	32	45	65	46		

Virginia

Previous editions of *Where to Retire* didn't include Virginia as a retirement possibility. But so many readers have inquired about this state that we made a special trip to check it out.

As anyone who has traveled through Virginia can attest, it is a lovely state. The portion around Washington D.C., however, is too heavily settled and business-oriented for our taste in retirement locations. Real estate prices reflect this orientation and so does traffic congestion.

The western portion of Virginia shares in the glory of the Appalachians, and the Blue Ridge Parkway runs diagonally from North Carolina, almost to the upper edge of Virginia. Descriptions of North

Carolina's Smokey Mountains apply here as well, with small towns tucked away between wooded ridges and fast-running rivers.

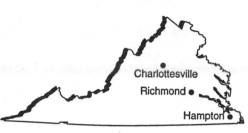

The central portions of Virginia are similar to North Carolina's Midlands, with miles of rolling hills alternating between grassy pastures, woods and well-tended farms. Historic Charlottesville is an excellent example of this country. This was Thomas Jefferson's home, a place he called "the Eden of the United States." It's also the home of the University of Virginia, with its cultural and recreational activities, visiting dance troupes and summer opera festival. Washington D.C. and the Kennedy Center are just an hour away for additional entertainment.

But it's the eastern ("Tidewater") part of Virginia, the area that embraces Chesapeake Bay, that makes Virginia so different from the other Southeastern states. Wonderfully rural and sparsely settled, the land looks as it must have in colonial times. Some farmhouses indeed date from that period and appear to have remains of tobacco barns and old slave quarters falling into disrepair behind the large homes.

We combined our research with a visit to some good friends who live in this region. They live in a tiny crossroads community of about 150 people, an hour commute from Richmond. They dearly love their new home, a 100-year-old farm house sitting on five acres of partly-wooded ground. The couple paid $90,000 for the property, which included a barn, a chicken house and a rabbit hutch. One acre is cultivated as a truck garden, supplying veggies for their kitchen; there's even an asparagus patch.

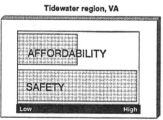

The delightful part about where they live is their access to a nearby tidal inlet of the York River. The walk to the riverbank takes you through a wonderland of wildlife and unspoiled nature, with tidal waters swirling with fish, turtles, and who knows what else, swimming beneath the surface. Ducks, herons and songbirds go about their business uncowed by human presence.

The downside of living in a Chesapeake Bay crossroads community is the total lack of services. Purchasing a can of tomato sauce or a roll of paper towels entails a 20-mile round trip. The nearest doctor is 15 miles away, the same distance as the video-rental store. But as my friend Pam says, "It's worth it. We don't have many neighbors, but the ones we have are quality. They're more than neighbors, they're friends we can count on if we need them. We don't need a big city to be happy."

For saltwater retirement in more populated areas of Virginia, try Hampton or Virginia Beach. Both offer upscale living conditions, with the cultural and social benefits of a larger city. Hampton is top-heavy into education, with the College of William and Mary, Old Dominion University and a satellite campus of George Washington University, all contributing to the cultural and intellectual milieu.

VIRGINIA TAX PROFILE

Sales tax: 3.5% to 4.5%, drugs exempt

State income tax: graduated from 2% to 5.75% over $17,000; can't deduct federal income tax

Property taxes: average 1.2% of assessed value

Intangibles tax: no

Social Security taxed: no

Pensions taxed: excludes $6,000 for people 62-64, $12,000 for 65 and older, minus Social Security and Railroad Retirement Benefits

Gasoline tax: 17.5¢ per gallon, plus sales tax

Chapter 4

The Mid-Southern Hills

If you look at a map of the United States, you'll notice a curious east-west line that cuts the country almost in two. From the point where Nevada, Arizona and Utah intersect, state boundaries form a line that runs eastward until it hits the Atlantic Ocean near Norfolk, Virginia. This line bisects the nation, separating the states of Virginia-North Carolina, Kentucky-Tennessee, Missouri-Arkansas, Kansas-Oklahoma, Colorado-New Mexico and Utah-Arizona. Except for a slight deviation around the southern edge of Missouri, the demarcation is almost perfectly straight.

Why the line runs as it does is something only historians or geographers can explain. A long stretch runs through what I call the "Mid-Southern Hills"—through the heart of the Appalachians, the Tennessee-Kentucky hill country, the Ozark Mountains of Missouri and Arkansas and into Oklahoma's Ozark section. Straddling this line is an interesting swathe of woodlands, hills, plains and mountains, places that offer prime retirement conditions for those who like four seasons, with a woodsy and slow-paced lifestyle. A low cost of living, inexpensive housing and high personal safety are bonuses.

Industry and modern agriculture characterize the country to the north of this strip of semi-wilderness. Below is the Deep South. Life in the Mid-Southern Hills moves at its own pace, always a little out of sync with the rest of the nation. Until World War II, this was one of the most poverty-stricken segments of the nation. Cartoonist Al Capp created his imaginary town of Dogpatch here, the home of indigent Lil' Abner, his family and his girlfriend, Daisy Mae. Although the cartoon strip amused folks who didn't have to live in Dogpatch, real-life circumstances were anything but funny. Roads were often gravel and dirt. Subsistence farmers lived in flimsy shacks as they raised families and tried to coax a living from the rocky soil.

The change in living standards since the war years has been nothing less than miraculous. Change began with the government building dams and water power projects to provide cheap electricity. Manufacturing industries and businesses relocated to take advantage of inexpensive power as well as low labor costs. Local people no longer had to move to the north to find employment.

Fortunately progress didn't destroy the Mid-Southern Hills' natural beauty; it actually improved things. With the dams came lakes, hundreds of them. The combination of Ozark and Appalachian scenery with new lakes—perfect for fishing, boating, water-skiing and just plain looking—created an overnight tourist sensation. Vacationers brought money, and retirees brought even more dollars, which further contributed to economic growth. Today, small farms are more often a hobby or a sideline than a means for survival.

Because of its porous limestone base, the Ozark formation is honeycombed with underground caves, sometimes storing so much water that rivers gush from the cavernous depths as if by magic. One example: in Missouri's Big Spring Park, a full-fledged river surfaces at the rate of 286 million gallons a day! Ozark soil—typically rock-studded, rust-red in color and nutrient-poor—doesn't lend itself easily to plows or farm machinery. For this reason large portions of this country escaped agricultural development; they remain rustic, unspoiled and delightful places for retirement hideaways.

Climate

Every retiree we interview here emphasizes the four-season climate as a major plus. "I like to know what time of year it is," said one lady who had lived in California before retirement. "Here, I get the feeling of seasons. Summer is nice and hot, fall is beautiful and colorful, winter is short and merciful, and then comes spring!" She sighed in ecstasy.

Make no mistake: winter does bring chilly winds; creeks ice over, and your furnace gets a work-out. Still, it doesn't begin to compare with winters farther north. Summers are humid, but not unbearable, with 90-degree highs normal. Enough rain falls in the summer to keep the landscape looking green and fresh, streams flowing and fishing good to excellent year-round.

Politics

Most Mid-Southern Hills retirees come from northern or midwestern states. Besides bringing money, they often bring political know-how and a willingness to participate in local politics. This combination is tipping political scales throughout foothill and mountain communities. Since many retirees are well-to-do, they tend to think conservatively, and as a consequence, traditionally Democratic states such as Arkansas, Kentucky and Tennessee gain more Republican voters daily, much to the delight of Republican party workers. One Republican party official said, "When I started campaigning in north Arkansas in the '60s, it was like pulling teeth to find people to come out and help. This movement of new faces into the state has had a tremendous impact on Arkansas politics. People in the Republican party are no longer considered carpetbaggers."

Regardless of political affiliation, retirees vote in much higher proportions than the younger set, and they tend to get involved in non-partisan issues that affect community and state decision making. This new political power shows up clearly in the state legislature as well as in county and city partisan politics. Politicians are always sensitive to such a large bloc of voters. As an illustration: Arkansas spends more money per capita on services for the elderly than any other state in the nation. As you might imagine, Arkansas senior citizens' organizations are very active and take full advantage of state and federal allocations of funds.

Transportation

As mentioned earlier in this book, many small towns lack intercity bus service and air transportation. This is particularly common in the Mid-Southern area. Without intercity buses or passenger trains, you are totally dependent upon an automobile. The nearest airport could be 75 miles away. When the grandkids come to visit, how do they get to your place from the airport? If you don't drive, and if you're used to public transportation, don't take it for granted when looking for a retirement destination. Make it a point to determine the situation before locking yourself in.

Mobile Homes

Unlike some parts of the country, where mobile homes are restricted to parks or developments, mobile homes here are generally treated the same as conventional housing. This means installing a mobile home on your privately owned land is acceptable. Except for larger towns and certain municipalities with restrictive zoning, mobile homes are often found mixed with conventional homes or on acreage out in the country.

A big advantage of a mobile home is that it is completely self-contained, as far as appliances are concerned, and easy to install. If your property has water, electric and sewer connections, all that's necessary to begin housekeeping is to move the unit onto the property and connect. Constructing a conventional home on the same land requires months of labor by carpenters, plumbers and electricians. Some mighty nice-looking farms nestle in Ozark valleys, complete with barns, chicken houses, woods and pasture, with a cozy mobile home serving as the farmhouse.

Arkansas

Arkansas is a major beneficiary of today's retirement trends. Next to Florida, Arkansas is one of the fastest-growing states in number of new residents over age 65. Throughout the state almost a fifth of the population is over 60, with percentages much higher in popular retirement locations.

Newcomers from Chicago or Indianapolis find it easy to make friends, because they find that many of their neighbors have come from the same part of the country, have similar interests and have common things to talk about. This is convenient, because believe it or not, many Arkansas natives have never even *heard* of the Chicago Cubs, much less spent time discussing their pennant possibilities for the season.

What is the attraction here? Arkansas' mild, four-season climate, low taxes and personal safety. Inexpensive housing and friendly people figure into the picture, but the catalyst for retirees settling in Arkansas is the glorious Ozark environment. These low, ancient, thickly forested mountains symbolize many retirement dreams. The Ozarks represent a rebirth of simplicity, a purging of city life and a new mode of relaxation.

Besides clear-running streams, squeaky-clean air and lakes swarming with fish, many retirement dreams also picture an isolated cabin with a boat dock at the back door and lazy days of casting for bigmouth bass or lake trout. True, the *wife* doesn't always picture things exactly that way, but even non-fishermen enjoy the Ozarks' beautiful surroundings.

The southern part of Arkansas, below the Ozarks, is rarely the choice of folks coming from other states. They prefer the northern half, above Hot Springs and Little Rock. This is important to know. Without a

---

ARKANSAS TAX PROFILE

Sales tax: 5.5%, plus 3.5% on fast food
State Income tax: graduated from 1% on first $3000 income to 7% on $25,000 and over
Property taxes: average 3.9% of assessed value, set at 20% of appraised value
Intangibles tax: no
Social Security taxed: no
Pensions taxed: excludes $6,000 from government and private pensions
Gasoline tax: 18.5¢ per gallon

---

substantial number of out-of-state retirees or other outsiders for neighbors, you could find yourself isolated among folks with whom you have little in common. Not that people would be anything but friendly and neighborly, but unless your cultural background is basically agricultural and small-town, you could have a difficult time adjusting.

Arkansas state policy on college education is to waive general student fees for credit courses to persons age 60 and older on a space available basis. State vocational and technical schools also waive fees.

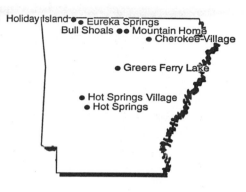

Following are some northern Arkansas towns we've visited and which we feel confident have potential for retirement. All have a significant number of non-natives living there. Some places are small, but none are isolated from medical and other important services. Intercity transportation is sometimes a problem, something you'll have to look at if you don't drive.

Eureka Springs This delightful town in northwest Arkansas started with a retirement boom over a century ago. The word "eureka" means "I've found it," and this is how many visitors felt when they decided to convert their vacation visits into permanent retirement here.

People started coming to Eureka Springs around the turn of the century because of the "magical" healing qualities of the spring waters that gushed out of the canyon's grottoes. Perhaps the mineral water helped, but getting away from the crowds and squalor of the city, breathing the pure mountain air and seeing the lovely Ozark surroundings probably had more than a little to do with the miracle cures.

Of course, the spring waters were known and appreciated by the native Americans, long before the white man muscled into the region. The paleface newcomers began arriving in large numbers in the 1880s, when the Frisco Railroad ran a line into town to carry visitors from Chicago, St. Louis and Kansas City. Several large and luxurious hotels accommodated the crowds. Wealthy families built ambitious Victorian mansions that duplicated their big-city homes. Before long, the town's winding streets were lined with houses, hotels and commercial buildings, many displaying fancy gingerbread styles of that era.

119

During the First World War, folks stopped coming to Eureka Springs. The town's bonanza was put on hold; its popularity declined as new residents moved away or died. Lovely homes were boarded up and forgotten as absentee owners lost interest in the town. The Great Depression was the final blow; Eureka Springs almost became a ghost town. At the time, townsfolk must have viewed this abandonment as extreme misfortune, but today's residents see it as a stroke of luck. Otherwise, Eureka Springs would have suffered from modernization, with the old buildings gradually replaced by modern structures. This temporary loss of popularity created a virtual time capsule of Victorian architecture.

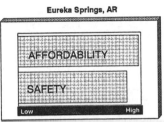

Eureka Springs, AR

Your first glimpse of Eureka Springs is a guaranteed surprise. Solid limestone and brick buildings, wrought-iron fancy work and gracefully styled mansions with winding carriageways make the town a fascinating window into yesterday. Boutiques, restaurants, art galleries and other businesses occupy the downtown's street-level stores with second- and third-floor apartments for those who live downtown.

Majestic residences line the streets that twist and climb the mountainside above the business district. This incredible collection of Victorians rivals and perhaps even surpasses the finest that San Francisco has to offer. Some have fluted columns rising three stories in front of dignified brick facades and wrought-iron balconies—homes that look as if they belong on a *Gone with the Wind* movie set. It's difficult to describe Eureka Springs without slipping into clichés, because the entire town *is* a cliché, a magic peek at yesterday.

The town and environs offer all the amenities retirees seek: good medical facilities, a quaint, artistic cultural atmosphere, friendly neighbors, recreational opportunities and inexpensive real estate. Eureka Springs has become both a retirement mecca and an artist colony.

An interesting aspect of Eureka Springs is that you often can buy a historic Victorian for about what you'd pay for an ordinary tract house in most parts of the country—even less. Several retired couples have converted their spacious old mansions into delightful bed-and-breakfasts. In the old days, not all Victorian homes were mansions, however. Ordinary folks lived in modest-sized houses just as they do today. These places are exceptional bargains, and conventional housing on the town's outskirts is similarly priced well below national averages.

Nearby Beaver Lake is a place for cabins and lakeside homes, without the fancy facilities of a resort or high resort prices. Rogers (pop. 23,000) and Fayetteville (pop. 41,000) are the nearby "big cities" for heavy shopping and serious medical problems. Fayetteville has the advantage of being a college town with all the accompanying cultural and educational benefits. Were Fayetteville a little more picturesque, it would have been featured in this book; but it's well worth looking at, and is recommended for retirement by many writers and authors.

Holiday Island   A half-hour's drive from Eureka Springs takes you to an ambitious golf/country club resort known as Holiday Island. Located on Table Rock Lake, the resort is set on 5,000 acres of natural beauty. The lake is narrow at this point, following the twists and turns of an old riverbed, thus creating a large number of lakefront lots. Two golf courses (one a nine-hole layout), a number of tennis courts, two swimming pools and most of the facilities expected of a resort community are in place. Ninety percent of the residents are from other states, mostly from Illinois, Missouri and Texas.

Houses and condos are reasonably priced, considering the amenities of the development. We looked at one three-bedroom, two-bath place on a big lot for $46,000 (advertised by a private party; it would cost more through the sales office). Condos start at around $44,000. Lots begin at $3,000 (as low as $2,000 from private sellers). Golf seems to be excellent here, so much so that enthusiastic golfers purchase inexpensive lots and pay the $283 annual assessment for unlimited use of the courses. Owners of lots also have the right to stay in the development's campground and use all the facilities.

EUREKA SPRINGS AREA			Rel. Humidity: Jan. 60%, July 54%			
	Jan.	April	July	Oct.	Rain	Snow
Daily Highs	48	73	90	76	44"	6"
Daily Lows	27	49	69	49		

Greers Ferry Lake Area   About 60 miles north of Little Rock, this area is one of Arkansas' retirement success stories. Three towns share in this success: Heber Springs, Greers Ferry and Fairfield Bay. They sit on the shores of a 40,000-acre lake created by an Army Corps of Engineers dam. (One of President Kennedy's last official acts was to dedicate Greers Ferry Dam, on his way to Dallas.)

This 300 miles of wooded shoreline—encompassing a lake filled with bass, stripers, walleye, catfish and lunker-sized trout—soon caught the attention of folks considering an Ozark retirement. Inexpensive property, low taxes, a temperate climate and an almost non-existent crime rate added to the attraction of retirement here. Folks from Chicago and St. Louis paid particular attention, for the lake wasn't so far from their grandchildren and old friends that they couldn't go home for a visit whenever they pleased.

Heber Springs/Greers Ferry, AR

AFFORDABILITY

SAFETY

Low   High

In a matter of 20 years, Heber Springs—the largest of the communities—zoomed from a population of 2,500 to well over 6,000. The vast majority of newcomers were retired couples. Their pension money and savings pumped up bank deposits more than twenty-fold and the extra purchasing power boosted retail sales, created jobs and generated tax money for local improvements. Home building activity continues today, with lovely new neighborhoods materializing in low-density clusters, hidden in wooded, lakeshore settings.

Actually, the area's population increased much more than the figures indicate. Many small neighborhoods are located *outside* town limits, nestled in wooded glades, often invisible from roads and highways. Typically, a development consists of a grouping of from 10 to 50 homes, sometimes with lake views. This arrangement cuts the expense of utility installation as well as construction costs. There could be as many as 150 of these mini-neighborhoods scattered through the forests. Although building lots are usually half an acre or more, the setting creates a sense of closeness among the neighbors. "We never worry about leaving our home vacant during the winter," remarked one resident, "because our friends watch the place for us."

Construction quality is high, most homes are of brick, and low labor costs keep the selling prices affordable for retirees. Properties on the lake are priced higher, but not remarkably so. This is because the Army Corps of Engineers prohibits ownership of land directly on the water beyond a determined high water line. This means no boat docks or direct access, and no immediate advantage to being next to the water. Lakeside homes enjoy the view, but so do places set farther back. Unlimited water access is provided by public docks, ramps and marinas. A unique type of retirement development that appeals to those who fly small planes is Sky Point Estates, where you can build your home next to an airstrip.

For even smaller small-town retirement, Greers Ferry sits invitingly on the other side of the lake. The community provides all the basic services needed for day-to-day living, yet it's so small and uncongested that it doesn't require traffic lights. Greers Ferry has grocery stores, craft shops, and three branch banks. As a consideration for retiree's health care, the community has two full-time doctors and provides free ambulance service to Heber Springs' Cleburne Hospital.

Fairfield Bay, at the far end of the lake, is for those who prefer a more upscale setting, where they can own a home near a golf course. This resort/retirement community features round-the-clock security and all the advantages of an exclusive, gated complex. Its parent company has built several other developments around the country.

One of the advantages of living in the Greers Ferry Lake area is its proximity to Little Rock, an hour's drive away. With a metropolitan area of nearly 250,000, Little Rock provides the health services that smaller towns cannot. Libraries, museums and other cultural attractions fill a void for those who are used to larger cities. Little Rock is also the closest place to stock up on wine and beer to serve your guests, for like most smaller Arkansas areas, this is in a dry county.

Housing prices here have risen along with the improving economy, but prices and quality are remarkably better than where the retirees come from. A typical remark by new residents is, "Our new home is twice the size as the one we sold back home, and it cost half the money." Property taxes come as a pleasant shock when new residents receive tax bills just a fraction of what they paid back home.

GREERS FERRY LAKE AREA			Rel. Humidity: Jan. 63%, July 59%			
	Jan.	April	July	Oct.	Rain	Snow
Daily Highs	50	74	96	75	49"	4"
Daily Lows	29	51	71	50		

Bull Shoals/Mountain Home   In the north-central part of Arkansas, along the Missouri border, a forested area of lakes and rivers has become a miniature melting pot, with retirees moving here from all over the country. Even traditional retirement areas like California and Florida are represented by former residents taking advantage of an exceptionally low crime rate, inexpensive living and gorgeous scenery.

Surrounded on three sides by water, Bull Shoals and Lakeview sit on the shore of a lake that stretches for almost 100 miles. Its deep, blue waters are legend among bass fishermen, and the rivers and streams feeding the lake are considered premier spots for rainbow trout fishing, which in the spring and summer is done at night under lights. There are no closed seasons here; you can fish year-round. Sports aren't restricted to fishing or hunting; several challenging golf courses in the area will test your skills, whether pro or duffer.

The lake's shore is off-limit to construction up to the high-water mark, but the public has free access to both lake rivers. This restriction protects the lake's pristine quality, keeping it from being cluttered with sagging docks and scruffy-looking boats. The shoreline always looks clean and natural. Public marinas will house your boat for less than $400 a year, so you don't have to keep pulling your boat out of the water after every fishing trip.

Mountain Home is 15 miles from Bull Shoals and Lakeview over a highway that winds through picturesque Ozark woods. This small city of about 10,000 is the commercial center for the lake communities and the surrounding county of nearly 30,000 inhabitants. Mountain Home has a real downtown area, including an archetypal, old-fashioned town square. Major shopping and consumer businesses are located on the highway and around the major crossroads. Stores here supply any consumer goods for which anyone could reasonably ask. A community college serves the area, and retiree organizations offer opportunities for volunteer work. A hospital accommodates the area's population and an airport runs shuttle services to the nearest large cities. The Area Agency on Aging operates a local bus service.

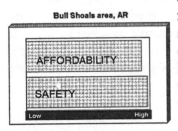

Bull Shoals area, AR

AFFORDABILITY

SAFETY

Low   High

The county in which Mountain Home is located allows the sale of package liquor, and cocktails are permitted to be served in at least one restaurant. Bull Shoals is dry except for one private club.

According to couples who retired in this area, major attractions are mild winters and low living costs. One couple from just north of Chicago said, "We cut our property taxes by $2,000 a year by coming here, and we cut our heating bills by more than half." They explained that they spend less than $100 a month for heat, whereas the colder Lake Michigan winters had whacked $250 out of their monthly budget during the coldest months. The husband said, "The money we save makes the difference between struggling to stay within our budget and having money to spend for luxuries."

Housing is exceptionally inexpensive for a resort area. According to residents, a small house can be rented for $250 to $300 a month, and according to real estate people, two- or three-bedroom places should sell from $38,000 up to $65,000. A three-bedroom, two-bath mobile home on two acres was being offered at $25,000—including a 20-foot by 22-foot garage and a covered, screened deck. The most expensive listing we found was $185,000, but that was for a large brick home on 74 acres.

BULL SHOALS/MTN. HOME			Rel. Humidity: Jan. 60%, July 54%		
	Jan.	April	July	Oct.	Rain	Snow
Daily Highs	46	73	92	74	42"	8"
Daily Lows	25	47	67	48		

Hot Springs   This fascinating little city, situated partially within Hot Springs National Park, is one of the more attractive retirement possibilities in Arkansas. Hot Springs combines the spirit of a 1920s resort with that of a 1990s city. It is as different from the previously described towns as can be, yet its rustic setting in the lower edge of the Ozarks lends Hot Springs some of that scenic magic that comes with Ozark living.

The old part of town sits in a canyon with buildings and homes clinging to the sloping-to-steep sides of the ravine. During the decades before, during, and shortly after World War II, Hot Springs maintained a reputation as a lively nightlife town. Roulette, blackjack and slot machines were as much an attraction as the gushing hot springs. Nightclubs and fancy restaurants flourished in a kind of mid-country Monaco atmosphere. Wealthy and famous citizens rubbed elbows with ordinary workers and the elite of the crime syndicates. Gambling, drinking and dancing the night away preceded health-restoring soakings in the hot springs the next morning. During its heyday, Hot Springs was considered as sumptuous a resort as Las Vegas or Palm Springs is today.

Casino gambling and nightclubs are just memories. The action now is bathing in soothing waters and enjoying the quiet atmosphere of the Ozark Mountains. After gambling was prohibited, the "old town," in the steepest part of the canyon, gradually fell into disrepair. When high rollers stopped visiting, money ceased flowing. Local folks preferred to shop in the malls away from downtown. But a new wave of retirees and a revival of tourist interest in the hot springs stirred a renewal of the downtown. Once-abandoned buildings now sport fine restaurants, art galleries and quality shopping. The motif is turn-of-the-century, with antique globe street lamps, Victorian trim, even horse-drawn carriages for sightseeing. A new breed of visitors come to Hot Springs today, bringing retirement money instead of gambling money, and they tend to stay permanently.

Residential areas are located on higher levels where the land is rolling and hilly, but not steep. A good thing, too, because the canyon is subject to flash floods. Not long ago, newspapers reported that a six-foot wall of water crashed its way down the main business street, flooding stores and wreaking havoc. Hot Springs businesspeople are used to this. After cleaning out the mud, bath houses, boutiques and restaurants opened for business with little delay.

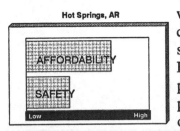

Hot Springs, AR

AFFORDABILITY

SAFETY

Low   High

Volcanic springs pour steaming hot water from grottoes and crevices in the canyon floor. Neither drought nor rainy seasons affect the water's copious flow. For generations, the elderly and infirm praised the waters' healing and revivifying powers. The young and healthy (unaware of what revivification entails) simply enjoyed sitting in the hot water and relaxing. The bonus for all is the fresh mountain air and the smell of pines and sassafras trees. The bewitched waters are reputed to heal everything from rheumatism to dandruff.

Residential neighborhoods fall into two distinct categories: Victorian and modern. The older sections have ample yards and large homes—often with enormous lawns and large shade trees. Other neighborhoods are more modern, with conventional bungalows, duplexes and low-profile apartment buildings. There are several new, quality senior citizens' developments and some excellent mobile home parks, and homes sell for below national average. The local newspaper lists two- and three-bedroom homes for $70,000 and up and lakefront houses for as low as $100,000.

There appear to be more apartments than usual for a town of this size, probably because of the seasonal tourist invasions which encourage temporary housing. Since the demise of gambling and the subsequent tourist scarcity, apartment owners have been forced to become competitive with rents.

Hot Springs Village Fifteen miles from the city is one of the more impressive retirement complexes in Arkansas: Hot Springs Village, one of those Florida-style, self-contained and guarded enclaves. The assurances and dreams of the promoters have been realized here; the promised improvements are in place, including a shopping center that would do justice to a good-sized town.

Property is not inexpensive, at least not for Arkansas, but it is certainly first class and returns full value for the money. Condo prices start in the low $60,000 range, three-bedroom homes at $80,000. These compare favorably with similar developments we've investigated in Florida, Arizona and California.

Situated on 21,000 acres of rolling-to-steep Ozark foothill wilderness, the property is covered with hardwood forest—oaks, hickories and a scattering of evergreens. Roughly one-third of the property has been converted into lakes and golf courses. There are four 72-par golf courses and one par-62 layout, each with its own clubhouse, restaurant and pro shop, each a separate "country club." Another third of the land is devoted to homesites, and the remaining third is in natural forest.

Hot Springs Village is not exclusively a retirement complex; people who work in the nearby city of Hot Springs also buy houses here. But since there are no schools (residents voted down a school tax to avoid having schools), families with younger children rarely purchase property. According to the salespeople, the majority of the residents come from large Midwestern cities in Illinois, Missouri and Kansas.

HOT SPRINGS AREA			Rel. Humidity: Jan. 60%, July 55%			
	Jan.	April	July	Oct.	Rain	Snow
Daily Highs	52	75	93	77	55"	3"
Daily Lows	31	52	71	53		

Cherokee Village   We heard that the same corporation that developed Hot Springs Village built Cherokee Village, an earlier complex in northeast Arkansas. It was one of the earliest projects of this kind, a sort of prototype for other developers to study and follow. We wanted to see what one of these places looks like after the property has been sold and the promoters have made their profit. We detoured out of our way to have a look, and we were pleased that we did.

Cherokee Village sits about two miles off the main highway. When it was built it was a bit isolated, but over the years individual homes and small subdivisions grew closer and closer; now it's difficult to discern the original Cherokee Village limits.

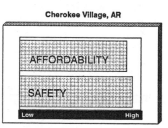
Cherokee Village, AR

The security guard posts are gone; access is now free. Homes have held up well, as neighborhoods aged gracefully, with tall shade trees, rose bushes and hedges imparting a comfortable look. Property values, although low compared to many areas of the country, also have held up well, for local workers consider Cherokee Village a prime place to live and raise children.

Missouri

Of course, Ozark hills and forests do not stop at the Arkansas border. They extend into Oklahoma on the west and about halfway up the state of Missouri before fading into plains and prairie country. Although the Ozarks bestow beauty in a non-discriminatory manner upon all three states, Missouri's share is the largest, with 33,000 square miles of low mountains, verdant valleys and rolling plateaus. The Missouri River marks the northern boundary of the Ozark range, Springfield the western edge, and the mountains taper out before they reach the Mississippi River on the east. Even in the midst of the mountains, plateaus can stretch for miles, with flat-to-rolling country reminiscent of the prairie to the north and west.

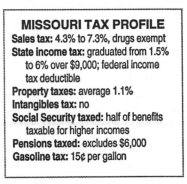

MISSOURI TAX PROFILE
Sales tax: 4.3% to 7.3%, drugs exempt
State income tax: graduated from 1.5% to 6% over $9,000; federal income tax deductible
Property taxes: average 1.1%
Intangibles tax: no
Social Security taxed: half of benefits taxable for higher incomes
Pensions taxed: excludes $6,000
Gasoline tax: 15¢ per gallon

One of the more scenic areas is the 86,000-acre Current and Jacks Fork River country, set aside as the Ozark National Scenic Riverways. I cherish fond childhood memories of camping along the Current River and watching my father fly-fish for trout. Memories like this are probably why men dream of retiring in a fisherman's paradise like the Ozarks. (Perhaps a woman's memory of her mother cleaning fish influences her to dream of other locations.)

Most Missouri Ozark rivers have been impounded by dams, forming long chains of lakes. They sprawl and twist through wooded valleys, covering a great part of both Missouri and Arkansas with water surface. The largest lakes are the Lake of the Ozarks—in the middle of the Missouri mountain range—and the Table Rock-Bull Shoals-Lake Taneycomo complex on the Missouri-Arkansas state line.

Lake of the Ozarks/Osage Beach This lake, largest in the Ozarks, originated with the construction of Bagnell Dam across the Osage River in the 1930s. Ninety-four miles long, the lake boasts over a thousand miles of shoreline for fishing and recreation. Ozark forests climb from the water's edge, up and over low mountains, as far as the eye can see.

Years ago, before World War II, most outsiders who owned Ozark property expected, and demanded, rustic accommodations. They preferred log cabins for use as summer retreats or as fall hunting lodges. Most cabin owners lived in St. Louis or Kansas City, occasionally coming from large cities as far away as Chicago. City folks prized their backwoods hideaways and wanted to keep things rustic. Ozark natives were few in number and culturally isolated from the outside world. Natives and outsiders had little in common and lived in separate worlds even though they might be next-door neighbors every summer.

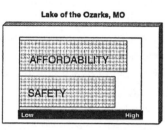

Things have changed around the Lake of the Ozarks. The site of my family's vacation cabin, where we drew buckets of water from a well, cooked freshly caught fish on a wood stove and ate dinner by the orange glow of a kerosene lantern—is now the site of a bustling motel complex replete with a gourmet restaurant and marina. Across the highway is a shopping mall. In contrast to sleepy lake towns in other parts of Missouri and Arkansas, Missouri's Lake of the Ozarks is jumping. Kerosene lamps are out, contemporary living is in.

Osage Beach is the largest town on the Lake of the Ozarks and by far the most commercialized, with shopping malls, classy restaurants and all the other amenities that come with full development. Vacationers, weekenders and retirees come from all over the Midwest. Newcomers spend dollars that attract more businesses and more employees in a circular growth pattern. Instead of a summer resort with businesses that close every winter, Osage Beach has become a year-round city of about 6,000, the commercial center for an unknown number of lakeside residents and cabin owners outside the city limits.

One couple, who retired to Osage Beach from St. Louis, said, "We're used to shopping malls, nice restaurants and big city conveniences. We couldn't stand living in a small, isolated village where we would have to settle for whatever the stores *have* rather than what we *want*. Yet we want to live on a lake and be away from it all." The couple's home is 15 minutes from a shopping mall, but it couldn't be more private. It sits on a large lakefront lot surrounded by a forest of northern red oak, black oak, shagbark hickory and basswood. They can't see a neighbor in any direction. Since this is not an Army Corps of Engineers lake, a private boat slip is permitted at the lake's edge. Roads follow the lake's twisted arms to reach large, luxurious homes, ordinary houses and rustic, unsophisticated cabins, most within easy shopping distance of town.

A few years ago, a financial crisis in St. Louis' largest high-tech manufacturing industry caused a large number of employees—executives and factory workers alike—to seek employment elsewhere. This had a profound effect upon real estate prices around the Lake of the Ozarks. Weekend homes were unceremoniously dumped on the market. Bargains were legion, and the real estate market never fully recovered from the shock.

Of course, lakefront homes can be as expensive as you care to consider. Some areas are quite prestigious, with homes commonly approaching half a million bucks in price. We looked at one (briefly) for $379,000 in Hawk Island Estates that had five bedrooms, four baths, what seemed to be an acre of deck overlooking the water and a four-car garage. In contrast, two-bedroom condos on the water were going for around $40,000, up to $90,000 for deluxe models. Away from the lake prices drop dramatically. Someone who loved country would have loved a place we saw for $50,000: a large, three-bedroom home on 18 wooded acres.

LAKE OF THE OZARKS AREA			Rel. Humidity: Jan. 66%, July 55%			
	Jan.	April	July	Oct.	Rain	Snow
Daily Highs	42	68	90	71	40"	17"
Daily Lows	21	44	66	46		

Columbia   Although not exactly in the Ozarks, just a short drive takes you from the small city of Columbia to the Ozarks' outdoor recreation and rustic mountain scenery. With a population of 70,000, Columbia is large enough to supply all the amenities and conveniences of a modern city, yet not so large that it suffers from the inherent congestion, crime and pollution of the big cities.

As a place to retire, Columbia is popular with folks from large Midwestern cities like St. Louis, Chicago and Kansas City. Just as visiting the Ozarks is convenient from Columbia, so are visits to places like Kansas City or St. Louis. Either city is a two-hour interstate drive, giving Columbia residents access to major league professional sports, stage plays and all the good things offered in a large city. Then they return to the refuge of a safe, quiet, clean home town.

Making the decision to retire in Columbia is made easy by a unique program provided by Columbia's chamber of commerce. Enlisting the aid of retired volunteers, newcomers are given an hour-and-a-half "windshield tour" of the city. The tour visits residential neighborhoods ranging from economical to deluxe. They drive you past the three colleges in town, as well as golf courses and hospitals. You'll see the best shopping areas and visit Columbia's delightful downtown. This way, potential retirees check out neighborhoods, home styles and amenities without being pressured by a real estate agent.

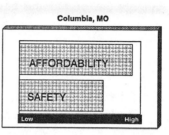

Despite Columbia's upscale appearance, housing costs are 16 percent below national averages. The most popular retiree housing here is split-level ranch, usually brick construction with large lawns. Condominiums are available for those who don't care for mowing lawns. Because of the college population, apartment rentals are often scarce. During the summer, however, temporary housing is easily found for those who want to savor the atmosphere of Columbia as a final test for livability. At least three developments are aimed at the 55 and older market. One development underway will feature golf course living.

The economy here is solidly based on education, with three institutions of higher learning: University of Missouri, Stephens College and Columbia College, the city's major employers. This translates into a high level of prosperity, stability and an almost recession-proof economy. The academic milieu enhances the city's cultural and social life with school activities that spill over into the community. It seems as if something is always happening for the public to participate in—lectures, concerts, sports events or celebrations—some of which are free. The huge university library is open to the public for browsing and research, and although you can't check out books, the staff is very accommodating in helping you locate material. As you might guess, Columbia is a great place for continuing education. Many retirees choose Columbia specifically for that purpose; a myriad of adult education programs reach out to mature residents and encourage them in their quest for lifetime learning.

Education flows through all sectors of the community, even in law enforcement; 90 percent of Columbia police officers are college graduates. That may have something to do with the city's low crime rate: 30 percent below national average.

The university, with its medical school, confers another blessing on the community by leading the way in health care. In addition to the university hospital, seven other hospitals serve the community along with so many health-care personnel that one in five workers in Columbia are employed in health-related occupations. A unique service provided by the university is the Elder Care Center. Its major goal is to keep patients out of nursing homes by providing activities to help them maintain high functional levels. The daily fee is $32, often covered by Medicaid—less than half the usual nursing home costs in the area. University students in physical, occupational and speech therapy benefit from their experience from the center while patients benefit from more robust health and postponement of nursing home care.

Outdoor recreation is more than adequate. Besides two municipal golf courses and two private country clubs, there's the Twin Lakes Recreation Area, complete with boating, fishing and swimming. A relatively new hiking and recreation trail follows the abandoned MKT Railroad line which will eventually connect up with hiking trails that cross the state. This 4.7-mile stretch invites jogging and biking through dense woods, past streambeds, rock cuts, and open space meadows—a small escape to the country, yet just yards removed from the surrounding city. For inclement-weather exercise, the university hospital has organized a "mallwalker's" club. At 6:30 every morning, long before the huge indoor Columbia Mall opens for business, you'll find several hundred walkers working on their stamina and blood pressure. In 30 minutes you can do two full laps, equaling almost two miles of vigorous walking, and you don't get rained on.

Columbia consistently makes *Money Magazine*'s list of top places to live. According to this publication, "Columbia is not just inexpensive," it also is "clean and green," referring to the city's pioneer recycling deposit law, enacted back in 1977. Columbia's dedication to improving its environment is furthered by an ongoing campaign to plant shade trees, called "Tree Power." The city-owned Water and Light Department sponsored this program, providing shade trees free of charge. As a result of this awareness, Columbia neighborhoods show a pride of ownership, neatness and quality seldom surpassed anywhere.

COLUMBIA			Rel. Humidity: Jan. 66%, July 55%			
	Jan.	April	July	Oct.	Rain	Snow
Daily Highs	36	65	89	68	36"	23"
Daily Lows	19	44	67	46		

Oklahoma

When people think of Oklahoma they imagine flat plains extending to the horizon, perhaps rolling hills studded with oil derricks or farm machinery, and cattle fenced in by barbed wire. True, parts of Oklahoma fit this description, for this is a state renowned for cattle, agriculture and petroleum. But, just as New York State isn't all Manhattan, Oklahoma is not all flat farm country.

OKLAHOMA TAX PROFILE
Sales tax: 4.5% to 8.5%, drugs exempt
State income tax: graduated from 0.5% to 7% over $9,950; federal income tax deductible
Property taxes: average 0.8%
Intangibles tax: no
Social Security taxed: no
Pensions taxed: excludes $5,500 government pension; private pensions fully taxable
Gasoline tax:: 16¢ per gallon

Parts of Oklahoma, particularly in the eastern and northern portions, are hilly and heavily forested, the tail end of the Ozark Mountains. Some places are even less populated than the Missouri and Arkansas Ozarks. You can drive for miles with barely a suggestion that anyone might be living behind the solid mask of forest that lines the highways. Several dams take advantage of the deep river valleys to create long, wide lakes that wiggle and squirm across the wooded landscape and through the hills. The largest, Eufala Reservoir, covers more than 100,000 surface acres. At least 18 lakes, most of them built by the Army Corps of Engineers, provide recreation as well as irrigation and power. This huge complex of water storage changed forever the face of a state that once was in danger of drying up and blowing away during the 1930s.

The desolation of Oklahoma's Dust Bowl, drought and depression is a well-known piece of history. Those dismal times are far behind as Oklahoma becomes a center for aerospace and aviation industries. The latest agricultural technology, conservation and flood control protect the land from a repeat of the 1930s disaster. Wonder of wonders: a deep river channel— utilizing a system of dams and locks— links Tulsa with the Gulf of Mexico, making it an important seaport!

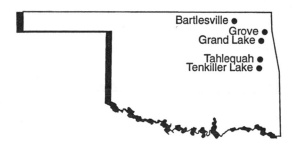

Bartlesville ●
Grove ●
Grand Lake ●
Tahlequah ●
Tenkiller Lake ●

John Steinbeck's famous book, *The Grapes of Wrath*, dramatizes the desperate condition of life in Oklahoma during the Dust Bowl era. The book chronicles a dream of a good life in California and the Joad family's struggle to get there. (Of course, that was before California suffered from graffiti, drive-by shootings and Madonna.)

Today, the children of those refugees who emigrated to California 50 to 60 years ago are old enough to retire. After suffering the hardships of freeway traffic, high taxes and idiotic politicians, the Joad family dreams of a good life somewhere else. This time it's Oklahoma. Over the years, they've kept touch with relatives and friends who didn't leave Oklahoma; visits between the two states were common. So it seems natural that the second generation, now affluent, is making the reverse trek from the West Coast's "land of milk and honey" to down-to-earth Oklahoma. Few have even a hint of an Oklahoma accent; they have no "country" mannerisms about them. Some don't even have relatives or family friends drawing them back here, yet Californians turn out to be Oklahoma's strongest boosters.

Grand Lake o' the Cherokees   A series of lakes run halfway down the state near the Missouri and Arkansas border. Each lake supports small towns which can be practical for retirement. One of the more popular areas is in the state's northeast corner, named after its largest lake, the Grand Lake o' the Cherokees. Sometimes it's called the Pensacola Dam Project or simply Grand Lake. The contraction "o" does not mean *of,* but *over,* to commemorate the Cherokee burial grounds that lie at the bottom of the lake. Sixty-six miles long, with 1,300 miles of shoreline and 60,000 surface acres of water, this is one of the Ozarks' largest bodies of water. Unlike many reservoirs created by the government, workers cleared trees and stumps before impoundment, greatly improving both navigation and esthetics. The countryside around these lakes is not as rugged as the true Ozark mountains to the east or to the south in the Tenkiller Lake area, but the charm of the Ozark foothills is still evident.

The lake's wide stretches of water encourage sailboats, even full-fledged yachts capable of cruising in all kinds of weather. Some marinas specialize in sailboat moorings. Fishing is great; bass are so abundant that there's no size limit. Countless coves throughout the many crooks and branches of the lake make great places for picnics, should you become tired of torturing worms by sticking them with fishhooks. The rivers that run into the lake are famous for canoeing, an important tourist activity, with "canoe trails" as part of the Oklahoma park system.

The Grand Lake area supports more population than most Ozark waterways, with houses all along the lakeshore. Also, unlike many man-made lakes in the Mid-Southern areas, lakefront ownership is not restricted, private docks are allowed. In addition to simple fishing piers, some folks build flat docks, like floating patios; other boat docks are covered and enclosed, sort of floating cabins.

For years these lakes were considered the playground of Oklahoma oil patriarchs and big-city vacationers. They have long been popular weekend retreats for residents of northern Oklahoma, Missouri, Kansas, and Arkansas. Lately, however, the area is gaining prominence as a retirement destination.

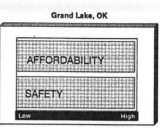

Grand Lake even has a country club-type development. The 600-acre Coves of Bird Island (actually a peninsula) has a golf course, clubhouse, restaurant and about 150 homes, mostly owned by retirees. The usual swimming pools, tennis courts and 24-hour security are provided, a plus for those who like to leave their homes and travel. Prices start at $65,000. Don't expect to see mobile homes or trailers here; they're not permitted. Residents do their shopping in nearby Grove or in Langley.

A number of little towns sit on the shore of Grand Lake, the largest being Grove, with a population of almost 5,000. About twice that number living nearby consider Grove to be their home town as well. Without large industry to provide employment, most folks either work in service jobs or are retired. An estimated 30 percent of the total population are retired—a very high percentage. Heavy shopping is available in Joplin (Missouri), a 45-minute drive, or 75 miles away in Tulsa. Grove is fortunate to have its own hospital. Another hospital is located in Vinita, a half-hour drive away.

Several properties were listed for over $300,000, but they were top quality, with four or more bedrooms and deluxe docks with multiple slips. Most lakefront property starts in the low $100,000 range, although we noticed some smaller homes on the lake selling for as low as $80,000. Homes within walking distance of the lakes can be had for $60,000 and sometimes even below this amount. Mobile homes are common housing alternatives—exceptionally nice ones going for $30,000 to $40,000. Farther away from the lake prices drop considerably, with many homes priced at $40,000 or under and prices for mobile homes dropping to as low as $10,000 including a lot.

Tenkiller Lake Further south, about halfway down the chain of lakes, is an exceptionally pretty place known as Tenkiller Lake. A few years ago, Tenkiller was rated one of the best places in the country for retirement by a popular retirement guide. We were intrigued by this recommendation, because we weren't aware of any thriving retirement community in that region. So we went to visit and see for ourselves.

Tenkiller Lake is a long and convoluted reservoir created by an Army Corps of Engineers dam across the Illinois River. With steep valleys, limestone bluffs and forested slopes dipping beneath the water, the old riverbed filled to the brim makes this one of the prettiest of all the Ozark lakes. It's said to be the clearest lake in the state, and this is easy to accept as more than just local pride; the water is as blue as an April sky.

Tenkiller Lake, OK

AFFORDABILITY

SAFETY

Low   High

As we drove along the highway around the lake, we enjoyed glimpses of the azure water and breathed deeply of clean air sweetened by pine needles and soft breezes. Because it was autumn, tourist traffic was light—we practically had the highway to ourselves—and we enjoyed poking along at our own speed, taking in the sights.

We kept looking for retirement complexes and retired folks to interview. We wanted to ask someone where people retired here, but we saw no one to ask. Then we encountered a huge roadside sign that proudly proclaimed Tenkiller's number-four rating as a retirement location—but still we saw no people. We looked at the map once more, looking for the town of Tenkiller, but discovered that there is no such place. Tenkiller is the name of the lake. The nearest town of any size is Tahlequah, a good 20-minute drive from Tenkiller Lake. Well, yes, there is a place called Cookson, a few miles from the lake, but it's mostly a general store and a trailer park.

We were feeling discouraged with Tenkiller as a retirement area until we encountered a group of retired couples having Sunday breakfast at a little cafe in the crossroads community of Keys. Apparently, this weekly brunch-meeting is a tradition with neighbors who live around the Tenkiller Lake area. "Tell us where all the retirees live," we pleaded. "We've been looking for hours, and you are the first retirees we've met!"

The couples' enthusiasm for their retirement homes soon cleared away our disappointment. It turns out that families here make their homes on gravel side roads that snake back through the woods toward the lake.

Since the banks of the lake are usually steep and because ownership to the water line is prohibited, buildings are set back and above the water, with views. One after another, the couples testified as to their happiness at living here. One member of the breakfast party was a single lady, a school teacher from Chicago who hadn't yet retired. "I come here as often as I can," she explained, "and I love working on my place to get it in shape for that magic day when I won't have to return to the classroom."

One couple invited us to see their home, which was hidden away in the woods with a view of the lake. As we drove the four miles of gravel road to their place, we noticed a scattering of houses set back from the road on heavily wooded, multi-acre lots. Our newfound friends' residence was an attractive four-bedroom, two-bath brick home sitting on the edge of ten acres of forest,. with a view of Tenkiller lake in the background. They estimated their property's value at around $45,000. That's equivalent to the value of a driveway and front lawn of the average Pebble Beach home. At that point, we began to understand why folks love this lakeview paradise.

Still, we have mixed feelings about retirement in an area like this. On one hand, living costs are probably as low as you'll find anywhere in the country, and scenic values equally high. But Tenkiller Lake is for those who need no other company than an occasional small-mouth bass or a band of bluejays. Clearly it isn't appropriate for someone with medical problems. In case of emergency you either use a CB radio or else mail the doctor a postcard and hope for a speedy reply.

Tahlequah (pronounced TAH-luh-quaw) is the largest community in the area, with a population of about 9,500. Tahlequah has a fascinating history. Indians who were evicted from the Southeast in the early 1800s—after their tragic and deadly trek known as the "Trail of Tears"—chose this location as the capital of their newly

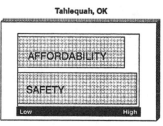

Tahlequah, OK

created "Indian Territory." Unfortunately, the Indian's euphoria over having their own territory didn't last too long. Politicians in Washington decided to revamp the treaty—unilaterally, of course—and opened the territory to all comers with a spectacular land rush.

Tahlequah is a pleasant town, with old-fashioned brick buildings in its downtown, quiet residential neighborhoods, and exceptionally low-cost housing. This is an amiable compromise between isolated Ozark hills and large city conveniences.

The local hospital is adequate, but the Indian Hospital in Tahlequah is said to be excellent. Presumably, this hospital is reserved for native Americans; however, a blonde waitress in a Tahlequah diner informed us that since she has 1/32nd Indian blood, she is accepted at the hospital. When I puzzled over how someone goes about proving 1/32nd blood relationships, the waitress explained that her great-great-grandmother had a child by an Indian. (That would be the waitress's great-grandmother.) When I asked what tribe, the waitress protested, "It wasn't a *tribe!* Just one, solitary, wandering Indian!"

After apologizing for insulting her great-great-grandmother's honor, I was still left with the puzzle of how one proves Indian ancestry.

Bartlesville   Not everyone is enamoured of the idea of living in Ozark small towns, and many retirees rank hunting and fishing low on their must-have list. Bartlesville is our idea of Oklahoma small-city living, a place consistently given high marks for quality of life by national publications. Located in the gently rolling grasslands of northern Oklahoma, Bartlesville is just 45 minutes from Tulsa International Airport and a short drive to Ozark lake environs.

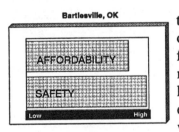
Bartlesville, OK

The city is small enough (pop. 34,000) that newcomers can make friends throughout the community, yet Bartlesville is sufficiently ample in size to afford amenities missing from more rustic sections of Oklahoma. In fact, the showcase entertainment events that Bartlesville stages each year would do honors to a much larger city. Its famous community center, designed by Frank Lloyd Wright, hosts the internationally-acclaimed OK Mozart Festival. This occasion lasts ten days in mid-June, hosting guest artists from all over the world. The entire populace is invited to participate.

Bartlesville Community Center is not one of those public buildings that sits idle between big-time events. Over 200 community service groups stage art shows, performances, exhibitions, festivals and parties. My wife and I attended a wedding dinner there—a fabulous evening! The 75-piece Bartlesville Symphony is recognized as one of the best in the country. The Bartlesville Civic Ballet offers a mixed palette of music and dance, and the Theater Guild presents year-round entertainment. This is hardly what one would expect to find in small-town Oklahoma!

Bartlesville's overall cost of living is 7 percent below average. Housing costs fall 15 percent below national averages, making quality living in a nice neighborhood affordable. Two-bedroom home rentals start at $300 a month. Five apartment complexes offer a choice of lifestyles ranging in price from 30% of net income to $2000 a month. Another point in Bartlesville's favor is its low crime rate. It ranks 26th in our personal safety analysis.

BARTLESVILLE			Rel. Humidity: Jan. 59%, July 53%			
	Jan.	April	July	Oct.	Rain	Snow
Daily Highs	46	72	93	75	38"	9"
Daily Lows	24	49	72	50		

Kentucky

The Mississippi River marks Kentucky's western border and the deep valleys and rugged gorges of the Appalachians, the eastern. Between you'll find a wide selection of countrysides from which to choose: from gently rolling farming country to magnificent panoramas of the Blue Ridge Mountains; from quiet, rural crossroad communities to sophisticated cities and university towns. The first region west of the Allegheny Mountains settled by American pioneers, Kentucky epitomizes America's rugged frontier heritage. This is the country of Daniel Boone, the Hatfields and McCoys and good ol' mountain music. Today it's much more than that. With up-to-date services, neighborly people and modern shopping everywhere, Kentucky is a great choice for retirement.

Modern-day transportation, with paved highways crisscrossing the state, has opened the back country to the world. A robust economic development since the end of World War II boosted most rural areas out of Al Capp's "Dogpatch" past. No longer are large parts of the state isolated and populated with illiterate mountaineers and moonshiners. Kentucky today is too open for that. This opening of the state also created retirement opportunities that didn't exist previously. But the entire state certainly hasn't become a carbon copy of middle America. Many charming areas back in the hills are almost as rustic and unspoiled as ever. And since many Kentucky counties have opted for prohibition, you can bet some of those piney hills contain moonshiners, as well.

KENTUCKY TAX PROFILE

Sales tax: 6%, food, drugs exempt

State income tax: graduated from 2% to 6% over $8,000; can't deduct federal income tax

Property taxes: average 1%

Intangibles tax: yes

Social Security taxed: no

Pensions taxed: private pensions taxable

Gasoline tax: 15¢ per gallon

Kentucky is particularly attractive for Midwestern and Northern retirees who see advantages in retiring close to their prior homes, in inexpensive, low-crime surroundings. The relatively mild, four-season weather easily satisfies requirements for those who insist on colorful autumns, invigorating winters and glorious springs.

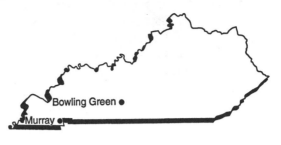

Bowling Green   About an hour's drive north of Nashville (65 miles by Interstate 65) and the Nashville International Airport is the delightful little city of Bowling Green. Because of its central location (within one day's drive of three-fourths of the U.S. population), this is becoming a popular retirement location for fugitives from crowded Northern cities. The interstate, a major north/south artery, facilitates transportation and makes it easy for the grandchildren to visit.

Originally, the town was called "The Barrens," after the Barren River that runs through the site, but in 1797 it was renamed something a bit more descriptive of the area: Bowling Green. The second name derived from the habit of court officials and visiting attorneys amusing themselves between trials by bowling on the lawn beside the old courthouse. The surrounding countryside is as green as its name—lush, with rolling meadows surrounded by white fences, with thoroughbred horses munch-

ing away at the Kentucky bluegrass. Bowling Green looks exactly as one imagines Kentucky should look.

Due to its location, Bowling Green serves as a regional hub for retail shopping and medical services. And, because this is the only place between Louisville and Nashville where alcohol is served, Bowling Green's higher-quality restaurants attract folks from miles around for celebrating that special occasion. According to a recent survey, Bowling Green has more restaurants per capita than any other U.S. city except San Francisco.

Another factor in maintaining an upscale atmosphere is the presence of Western Kentucky University, with 15,000 students adding intellectual warmth. The university maintains a symphony orchestra and two theater groups, and it hosts frequent visits from touring artists and entertainers. Other cultural offerings are presented by the Capitol Arts Center and the Public Theatre of Kentucky.

Participation in university affairs is made easy by Kentucky's policy of senior citizen scholarships which pay the full cost of tuition. This is true for both full-time and part-time students and applies toward either graduate or undergraduate courses. Numerous continuing education programs are also offered, ranging from "History of American Presidents," to motorcycle training.

A popular local attraction, about 30 miles away, is world-famous Mammoth Cave National Park, with 52,000 acres of beautiful hardwood forest and more than 300 miles of mapped passageways in the caverns. The area also supports five golf courses, 59 tennis courts, 27 public parks and two country clubs. As is the case anywhere in Kentucky or Tennessee, excellent hunting and fishing are nearby.

Although Bowling Green is a fine example of a larger Kentucky town, it's not big enough to suffer from big-city problems. Crime rates here are low, pollution is almost non-existent and the cost of living is almost 10 percent below national average. Housing and utility costs are exceptionally low, with homes selling for 17 percent below average and utilities at an astounding 27 percent less than national averages.

Building costs for a high-quality home in a nice neighborhood run about $50 per square foot. Homes just a few years old are going for bargain prices—about 20 percent below national average—for example, a brick, three-bedroom place with large lot and detached garage typically sells for $80,000.

BOWLING GREEN			Rel. Humidity: Jan. 64%, July 58%			
	Jan.	April	July	Oct.	Rain	Snow
Daily Highs	41	68	88	69	43"	14"
Daily Lows	24	46	67	46		

Murray   This is a small city that consistently garners recommendations from retirement writers as a good place to relocate. It's also an excellent example of how good things happen to a community when retirees move in. A few years ago Murray received a rash of national publicity when a popular retirement guide designated the town as the year's "top-rated" retirement location. This created an enormous amount of interest among folks planning retirement; before long, 250 couples made the move to Murray.

As you might expect, this had a snowball effect on the area's economy. The real estate market zoomed out of the doldrums and, before long, exhausted its inventory. Building construction increased to keep pace. At last report, five new housing developments were underway. In short, retiree immigration has proven to be an economic bonanza. Another positive side effect: these extra retirees were enough to push the city into enlarging the senior citizens' center and adding more services. The staff at the local center, by the way, is dedicated and enthusiastic about plans for the facility's future.

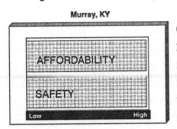

Murray, KY

What were the bad effects? Apparently none. According to the FBI's last report, Murray came in very high in personal safety, with a record indicating that most criminals in Murray must have retired or moved away. The cost of living may have gone up slightly, but it started at such a low level that the increase is hardly significant. Real estate prices went up some, of course—but again, they started from a rock-bottom level. People moving into the Mid-South from most parts of the country feel like bandits as they sign the escrow papers.

One of the volunteer workers at the Senior Center had retired from California and told of a special California Club composed of others like her who had also chosen Kentucky for retirement. It turns out that a colleague of mine, who had lived in California for the past two decades, recently retired in Murray. When I asked why, he and his wife explained that with children living in St. Louis and Nashville, they were within a few hours' drive of either place. They also liked fishing in the nearby lake. What were the drawbacks? They had to admit that snow and ice took some getting used to, but since they were originally from Canada, no problem there. The lack of good restaurants (this being a dry county) was the only other thing they missed from their California experience.

My friends were particularly pleased with the cultural activities sponsored by the university. Summer dramatic performances are presented in a city park, and concerts and lectures at the school keep them from boredom. The university makes a special effort to reach out to senior citizens and involve them in its curriculum.

What does Murray, Kentucky, have going for it that makes it the "best place" in the country to retire? Well, we've already covered most points: low crime and inexpensive real estate, nearby outdoor recreation, and a university. But many, if not most, towns throughout the Mid-South can boast similar advantages. Since I don't believe there is any "best place," all I will admit is that Murray is one of the best places to retire in Kentucky. But is it any better than Bowling Green, which offers much the same attractions? That's something everyone has to judge personally.

MURRAY			Rel. Humidity: Jan. 68%, July 58%			
	Jan.	April	July	Oct.	Rain	Snow
Daily Highs	42	68	88	71	47"	12"
Daily Lows	25	48	69	47		

Tennessee

Tennessee is somewhat of a mirror image of Kentucky to the north and Arkansas on the west. Eastward, the land slopes gradually upward until the foothills finally become the Appalachian Mountains. They grow ever more rugged, reaching their highest peaks in eastern Tennessee, near the state's border with the Carolinas.

Near the Mississippi River, plains of fertile bottom lands alternate with dense hardwood forests. King Cotton once ruled this domain, a land steeped in the genteel traditions of the Old South. Flat-to-rolling land covers much of the eastern portions of Tennessee: rich agricultural fields hedged with rows of trees, neat and prosperous-looking farmhouses, barns and silos. Most smaller towns here look pretty much like any in Middle America. Memphis and Nashville are the large cities.

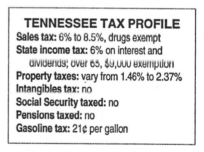

TENNESSEE TAX PROFILE
Sales tax: 6% to 8.5%, drugs exempt
State income tax: 6% on interest and dividends; over 65, $9,000 exemption
Property taxes: vary from 1.46% to 2.37%
Intangibles tax: no
Social Security taxed: no
Pensions taxed: no
Gasoline tax: 21¢ per gallon

As you move eastward you come upon Tennessee's heartland, a region of gently rolling hills and bluegrass meadows. Continuing east, the landscape grows more scenic with every mile. Before long you find yourselves in foothill country and finally in Tennessee's high country, rugged, tree-shrouded mountains that cross into the Carolinas and the Blue Ridge Mountains.

Clarksville Located on the northern border, next to Kentucky, Clarksville sits conveniently on an interstate highway that whisks you to the big city of Nashville in less than 45 minutes. This is one of our favorite Mid-Southern Hills locations. Clarksville combines an atmosphere of small-town living with city and urban conveniences.

Don't misunderstand, Clarksville is no small town. An estimated 76,000 population places it into the realm of a city, yet it somehow manages to maintain the flavor of small-town life. This a place where friends are constantly honking greetings to each other as they drive around town. Yet, shopping malls and complexes are as large and complete as you could hope for in a much bigger city.

For those who cannot live without hauling fish out of the water or killing ducks, this is a great place to 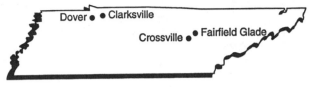 be, with all the conveniences of a city plus great hunting and fishing nearby. The Land Between the Lakes recreational area is 35 miles away, with 170,000 acres of public lands for hiking, camping, fishing and scheduled hunting. The peaceful Cumberland River flows through Clarksville; pleasure boats cruise where huge paddle-wheelers once carried tobacco and cotton for European ports. A half-hour drive from pleasant residential neighborhoods can take you to thick forests or rich farms and bluegrass meadows where horse breeding is a major industry. This is where the Tennessee Walking Horse breed was developed.

For big-city life, nearby Nashville offers fine restaurants, historical museums and its famous Grand Ol' Opry. Seems as if every country and western star from Minnie Pearl to Conway Twitty has a museum dedicated to them. But to me, the most interesting museum is the home of President Andrew Jackson, where his original log cabin homestead still

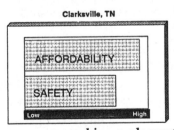

stands behind the stately Hermitage, the Greek Revival mansion he built during his more successful career.

A condition that makes Clarksville different from many Mid-Southern Hills towns is the large number of out-of-state folks who retire here. This happens whenever you combine a pleasant area with a large military base like Fort Campbell, which straddles the Tennessee-Kentucky state line adjacent to Clarksville. The base covers 105,000 acres, mostly in Tennessee, but since the post office is in Kentucky, that state claims Fort Campbell as its own. Military retirees enjoy base PX privileges and medical benefits. The fort, almost a city in itself, has a population of 38,000, with a PX as large as a shopping center, plus seven on-post schools for military dependents.

The early-day prosperity of the tobacco plantations shows clearly in the beautiful antebellum mansions in town. Set back from the street among magnificent oaks and magnolia trees, surrounded by acres of lawn, these old homes are among the best preserved in the South. This notion of large lawns carries over into modern housing. Big lots are in. Even humble, two-bedroom homes sit on enormous lots with awesome expanses of lawn—awesome because of the amount of energy spent in keeping the grass mowed. Yet folks tell you with straight faces, "I really enjoy yard work. Cutting grass is relaxing." Yes, of course it is. That's why rich people are so tense; they hire someone else to cut the grass.

Our previous research showed Clarksville to be one of the housing bargains of the nation. Median sales prices are still about 19 percent below national average. But conditions change here, depending upon what happens at Fort Campbell. When world conditions are peaceful, Fort Campbell operates with full staff and demand for housing is up. But when some military problems arise somewhere in the world, troops here are the first to go. When this happens, vacancies become easy to find and For Sale signs sprout on lawns.

Clarksville offers a large range of activities. Austin Peay State University is located here, complete with an active theater department that produces five shows a season ranging from comedy to serious theater, and even musicals. A jazz festival is held in March, and a spring opera in May. Guest artist recitals are offered throughout the year, with free admission. Fort Campbell has an entertainment services office, and it produces seven theatrical productions a year, open to the public.

Thirty miles to the west of Clarksville is the little town of Dover. This is the gateway to the Land Between the Lakes, a 170,000-acre wilderness area that stretches over a narrow peninsula, 40 miles between Kentucky Lake and Lake Barkley. Almost 90 percent of this area is unspoiled forest, with just a few scattered farms and some facilities for boat launching, hunting and fishing. Some retirees from Clarksville have moved into Dover, attracted by exceptionally low housing costs, peaceful living and proximity to hunting and fishing in the Land Between the Lakes. Dover is an interesting town, but verges on being provincial, with fewer outsiders in residence. To retire here happily, you'll have to love small-town living.

CLARKSVILLE			Rel. Humidity: Jan. 64%, July 61%			
	Jan.	April	July	Oct.	Rain	Snow
Daily Highs	46	71	90	72	48"	11"
Daily Lows	28	48	69	48		

Crossville East from Nashville along Interstate 40 or southeast on Interstate 24 brings you to the foothills of the Blue Ridge Mountains and the town of Crossville. While doing research in Crossville, we noticed that it looked somehow different from similar Tennessee towns. Much of the downtown construction seemed to be fairly recent, with fewer old buildings than one might expect. Farms surrounding the town lacked older-looking houses and barns, the kind built before the Civil War. When we asked about it, a young lady who worked in a local business disagreed that the buildings are new, saying, "No sir, Crossville is a very old town. Almost nothing hereabouts is new." When we asked, "How old?" She replied, "Well, I understand that many buildings here date back to the days of the Franklin D. Roosevelt Administration." We had to agree that was indeed a long time ago.

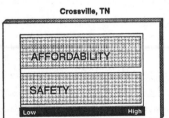

It turns out that until depression days, Crossville was pretty much woods and empty countryside. Despite rich soil and abundant rainfall, the district had been all but ignored. FDR's New Deal administration, searching for worthwhile projects to bootstrap the country out of the depression, seized upon a plan to develop the Crossville region as a model agricultural center. Government workers cleared forests, and homesteaders were given loans and seed money to get started. The plan evidently worked, because this is a very prosperous area today. Cheap electricity from the Tennessee Valley Authority Project lured industry into the area, adding jobs and even more prosperity.

As do most larger-sized towns in the South, Crossville enjoys friendly neighbors and inexpensive housing. The level of services for senior citizens is as good as anywhere in the state, with enthusiastic and imaginative folks running programs.

The town is dry, with residents routinely making the trek to Knoxville for booze—a 70-mile drive each way. When I expressed dismay that drunks should be free-wheeling down the interstate for their supplies, residents cheerfully assured me that bootleggers are plentiful in Crossville. "Why, you can buy anything you want, right here!" This weird custom of a community supporting prohibition and bootleggers at the same time never fails to puzzle me.

Property is quite affordable in Crossville and environs. In 1994, three-bedroom home median prices were under $83,000, with many selling for $65,000 or even less. Homes in town are usually on large lots with plenty of mature shade trees. On the town's outskirts, larger lots are the rule, with small farms commonly used as retirement homes.

Fairfield Glade   When retirement writers speak of Crossville, chances are they have one of the special country club developments in mind. There are several. Fairfield Glade is the oldest and the largest in the area, possibly the largest in the entire state. It's about 15 miles from Crossville and has been under development for two decades. Its year-round population is between 4,500 and 5,000, but thousands more enjoy the facilities on a vacation and part-time retirement basis. The corporation that put the package together has lots of experience—they have similar operations throughout the retirement areas of the nation.

Over the years, Fairfield Glade has matured gracefully. It has changed from a glitzy promotion into a series of stable, pleasant neighborhoods scattered throughout the 12,000 acres. Eleven lakes and four championship golf courses with all the adjuncts—such as tennis, swimming pools and restaurants—uphold the original country club tradition.

Unlike some developments, however, all promised facilities seem to have materialized. A large gymnasium offers everything from basketball to billiards to bicycle rentals. A riding stable presents complete equestrian facilities and miles of hiking and riding trails. Finally, there is a fully functional shopping mall (20,000 square feet under one roof) and a range of good-quality restaurants. Of course, the better establishments serve cocktails to members of Fairfield Glade. A bus service takes residents into Crossville.

Homes surrounding this lake/golf course complex are well built, attractively priced and architecturally pleasing. Acres of wooded and green space separates the various tracts. The closer to the golf course the more expensive the homes; some are really luxurious. Prices range from the mid-$100,000s, those with lake views from the $80,000s. We saw one for $229,000 that was a veritable mansion.

Some of the really older homes in Fairfield Glade sell from $40,000, but those were built for summer resort occupancy years ago and do not have the class of some of the newer ones. Around $60,000 to $70,000 is the normal range for nice three-bedroom homes on attractively landscaped lots. Condos are also available, most of them with lake views, starting from $35,000 on up to $100,000.

Thunder Hollow   Closer to Crossville, just a few miles from the downtown section, is the retirement development of Thunder Hollow. It spreads over 1,200 acres of prime land around a lake and a golf course.

Apparently this one also started as a time-share resort, but retirement homes have become the style. The tennis and clubhouse facilities are excellent.

Thunder Hollow is newer and more convenient to town. Homes are priced comparably to those in Fairfield Glen, and its natural setting is just as beautiful. An interesting feature is the Cumberland County Playhouse, located just outside Thunder Hollow's main gate. Dramas, musicals and ballets draw visitors from all over the nation.

Nearby is another retirement development, a no-frill place called the Orchards. In recognition of retirees' propensity for recreational vehicle travel, they build carports high enough to accommodate RVs. The Crossville area attracts retirees from Indiana, Ohio and Illinois, but the hottest place of origin is Michigan, particularly from the Detroit area, which is an especially popular place to be *from*.

CROSSVILLE AREA			Rel. Humidity: Jan. 62%, July 60%			
	Jan.	April	July	Oct.	Rain	Snow
Daily Highs	47	71	87	70	47"	12"
Daily Lows	29	48	68	48		

Chapter 5

Gulf Coast States

Five states curve around the Gulf of Mexico's 2,000 miles of northern shoreline, to form a sort of private sea. Western Florida and the Panhandle account for more than a third of the gulf's coastline; the other states are Alabama, Mississippi, Louisiana and Texas. Long strands of sparkling beaches—often unmarked by human footprints—alternate with miles and miles of saltwater marsh, the home of egrets, herons, roseate spoonbills and dozens of other shorebird species. Wildlife sanctuaries abound. Fishing ports, sheltered bays and natural harbors protected by offshore islands make saltwater sports convenient and productive. Gulf waters teem with life: shrimp, pompano, flounder, speckled trout, plus weird specimens like blowfish, rays and robbinfish. No telling what might attack your bait.

Sometimes a highway will run along the coast, just a few yards from the water. Other places are accessible only by boat or swamp buggy. Some towns are tourist oriented, with large throngs of summer vacationers crowding the beaches. Other towns are quiet and reserved primarily for the enjoyment of residents. Not everyone chooses to live by the beach; more find their retirement inland, where other, non-marine attractions entice them to live.

The cost of living in these states is as favorable as you'll find anywhere in the nation, and personal safety in the smaller towns is also gratifying. Some parts of the Gulf Coast states offer the most inexpensive housing we've ever seen. Wages are lower, too, to match the living costs. These economic benefits are offset somewhat by above average utility costs in some locales.

Large, modern cities provide cultural and medical facilities prized by retirees. Quaint towns with friendly neighbors make transitions into retirement easy. Gracious old Southern mansions, moss-draped bayous, and Southern hospitality are all part of the stage setting. To all of this add a four-season climate that varies from semi-tropical to mildly temperate, and you have a formula that spells successful retirement.

Alabama

This is possibly the nation's most active state in seeking out retirees and creating a welcoming environment for them. Over the past 15 years, Alabama's share of retirement immigrants climbed from 20th in the country to fifth. Part of this is due to a state-funded program called "Alabama Advantage for Retirees" which works intensively at getting the news out about retirement opportunities within the state. Many Alabama communities participate in this program and deserve special mention as retirement destinations.

An excellent example of Alabama's ongoing campaign to draw more retirees and tourists is an ambitious program of developing a chain of championship golf courses. The idea: catch the attention of tourists on their way to Florida, delay them for a while in Alabama while they play golf, and later on they'll remember Alabama as a place to have fun and possibly a great spot to retire. One state-sponsored scheme to entice tourists and retirees is a chain of golf courses known as the Robert Trent Jones Golf Trail. Seven locations stretch from the foothills of the Appalachians all the way to the Gulf of Mexico, with each stop on the Golf Trail a unique challenge. The concept is to provide the kind of championship courses normally found only at private clubs, yet at affordable daily greens fees, which range from $15 to $35. Beautifully designed clubhouses rival those found at expensive private clubs. Each Golf Trail has something for every level of golfer, usually two par 72 courses, and for the occasional golfer, a par-three layout.

ALABAMA TAX PROFILE

Sales tax: 4% to 9%, drugs exempt
State income tax: graduated, 2% to 5% over $3,000; federal income tax deductible
Property taxes: probably lowest in nation, average 0.3%
Intangibles tax: no
Social Security taxed: no
Pensions taxed: private employer pensions fully taxed
Gasoline tax: 16¢ per gallon, plus possible local taxes

Alabama's convenient location midway between the northern states and Florida, its mild winter climate and crime rates 20% lower than the national average are important to many potential retirees, but there's much more. Among other enticements, Alabama combines quality living with one of the country's most favorable living costs. Tax burdens are lowest in the nation. For example, the property tax on a $100,000 home (way above the median sales price here) assesses out at about $300— often less, depending on the community. No, that isn't $300 each *quarter*; it's $300 for the *year*!

Real estate is among the most affordable in the nation, with average new and resale home prices under $70,000. Other economic advantages for retirees include most pensions being exempt from taxes, plus free fishing and hunting licenses for residents 65 years of age and older. Alabama's colleges and universities offer free or reduced tuition to residents 60 or over. Some private schools offer tuition discounts, special classes, and access to recreation and cultural programs for retirees.

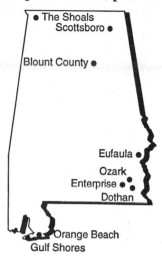

But Alabama's more than just a low-cost place to live, it's a state of multiple lifestyle choices and retirement opportunities. As more and more "outsiders" take up residence, the population becomes more cosmopolitan, making transition into the community easier.

Gulf Shores/Orange Beach   Because of the rude manner in which Florida's Panhandle elbows Alabama aside to hog the Gulf of Mexico shoreline, you wouldn't expect Alabama to have any beach at all. Look at a map and you'll see what I mean. Florida's Panhandle runs from the Georgia state line almost to Mobile in the west. However, visitors are flabbergasted at the quality and beauty of Alabama's 32-mile beach that fronts the gulf between Pensacola and Mobile. It clearly matches anything Florida has to offer. And, it's peaceful and relatively uncrowded.

Mobile—Alabama's only large Gulf Coast location—like most large cities, is best considered as a commercial center, a place for serious shopping and entertainment, with ideal retirement away from the metropolitan area. Traditional candidates for nearby retirement are Fairhope and Daphne. But because the city of Mobile is only about 15 miles distant, these towns here have become "bedroom communities" for those working in the city. As such, property has become more costly and the percentage of retirees has fallen off in recent years.

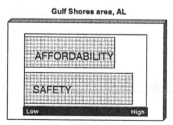

Gulf Shores area, AL

On the other hand, the two small towns that comprise Alabama's Gulf Coast "Riviera" are fast becoming a choice destination for retirees, particularly with golf nuts and fishermen. Traditionally a roost for

151

thousands of "snowbirds" each winter season, Gulf Shores (pop. 5,000) and Orange Beach (pop. 3,000) entice winter visitors to become permanent residents when they retire. White sand beaches that stretch for 32 miles, great fishing and friendly neighbors are persuasive arguments that help retirees make up their mind about Alabama's Gulf Coast. Luxury retirement villages are making an appearance to accommodate newcomers.

World-class saltwater fishing is a strong drawing card. The largest boat charter fleet on the Gulf Coast is located in Orange Beach, and seven golf courses are within a 20-minute drive. Since one of the attractions here is golf, there's an emphasis on golf communities. As one resident put it, "We're becoming a mini-Myrtle Beach, minus the traffic, noise and flash." One development, an upscale place called Craft Farm, offers patio garden homes and condos from $115,000 to $150,000. According to the *Alabama Advantage Retiree Guide*, near the beach, a two-bedroom home will range in price from $45,000 to $75,000, and apartments rent from $225 to $450.

An interesting diversity of retirees gives Gulf Shores and Orange Beach a cosmopolitan flavor not common in smaller resort towns. Because retirees come from all parts of the country, they bring a rich mixture of interests and talents. Year-round residents love to participate in art shows, theater, concerts and other cultural pursuits. Winter tourists bring a blessing to Gulf Coast businesses: this means seasonal part-time jobs are available for those who want them.

Even though the population is small, health care is adequate. Because of the number of elderly tourists each season, this area has an unusual number of paramedics, perhaps the highest per-capita in the nation. A hospital is located in nearby Foley, just five miles from Gulf Shores. Foley, by the way, is a popular place because of its manufacturer's outlet stores, the "shop-till-you-drop" genre. For big-ticket items, Pensacola is just a 30-mile drive, and Mobile is about an hour away.

GULF SHORES/ORANGE BCH.			Rel. Humidity: Jan. 59%, July 60%			
	Jan.	April	July	Oct.	Rain	Snow
Daily Highs	61	78	91	79	64"	—
Daily Lows	41	58	73	56		

Dothan   Before we discovered some of Alabama's better retirement locations, we kept hearing about a town called Dothan (pronounced *DOE-than*). Readers would ask, "Why don't you mention *Dothan* in your books?" We checked our Alabama road map and were puzzled why a place in the corner of southeast Alabama should have something special going for it. We received so many inquiries, we decided to take a look for ourselves. We're glad we did.

Dothan (pop. 54,000) and neighboring communities combine a pleasant Alabama location with an unusually diverse retiree population. Folks come from all over the world to settle here. This is partly due to nearby Fort Rucker, home of the world's largest international helicopter training center; military families from around the world remember Dothan when making retirement plans. Post Exchange privileges and access to military medical services make it a natural.

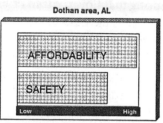

But there's another interesting source of Dothan's unique diversity: a growing colony of civilian retirees from the Panama Canal Zone. Between 100 and 120 families have moved to Dothan to begin (or resume) their retirement careers. With the Canal due to be transferred to Panama in a few years, more families will be on the way.

How did such an unlikely place as southeast Alabama become a mecca for folks who lived most of their lives in tropical Panama? It started some years back when one Canal Zone employee convinced his wife to retire in his home state of Alabama instead of staying in Panama, as most others did. When they returned for visits, they talked so much about the charms and advantages of Dothan that others began visiting and eventually moving here. The treaty between Panama and the United States, which returned control over the canal to Panama, really started the ball rolling. With an unclear future ahead and no roots any place outside Panama, many decided to look more closely into Dothan.

The city and its businesses sensed a trend and, in an effort to draw as many retirees into the community as possible, sponsored emissaries to Panama to spread the word about the advantages of moving to Dothan. Obviously, it worked.

One lady said, "We have two excellent hospitals here and any kind of business we need. We are only 90 minutes from Florida beaches. Another 90 minutes takes us to Tallahassee or Montgomery, and four hours to Atlanta or Mobile." When asked how the local people accept outsiders, she replied, "All I know is that the mayor of Dothan keeps saying to our Panamanian Club, 'Bring us some more of those Panamanians'!"

However, the influx of retirees here is more than just an accident. The biggest draw is the high quality of life, which is reflected in the lovely neighborhoods throughout the area. Quiet, tree-shaded streets with large lawns and elegant homes reflect well-kept neighborhoods and pride of ownership. The flowering trees in the spring and colorful leaves in the fall make changes of season a delight here. Visitors come every spring to follow the trail of pink along the Azalea-Dogwood Trail event.

As is the case in most of Alabama, housing is very affordable, with homes ranging from $30,000 to more than $500,000, with average sales at 20 percent below national averages. The cost of living is 10 percent below average. Real estate taxes are almost ridiculous. Example: taxes on an owner-occupied home valued at $65,000 amount to $152.50 a year, but if the occupant is over 65 years of age, taxes drop to $136.25.

The rental market is favorable here, with more than 2,000 units available in private apartment complexes. This is partly due to the large number of military personnel who require temporary housing and create high turnovers. Rents range from $250 to $400 a month. The Dothan Housing Authority manages or subsidizes rents on over 1,200 housing units and manages Vaughn Towers, a 120-unit, senior citizen high-rise.

For a town its size, Dothan has a surprising inventory of cultural events, including a symphony, ballet, community theater, and so forth. Wallace College offers a free tuition program for citizens 60 years or older who meet the admissions standards. Through the college's community services program, citizens, regardless of academic background, can take a wide variety of courses. Troy State University offers one course tuition-free to adults who have been out of school for at least 3 years and qualify for admission to the university.

Health care is more than adequate, with three fine hospitals and two immediate care facilities serving the area. A Medicaid Waiver program provides clients with homemaker services, personal care, sitters, and adult day care.

The Dothan area supports the usual outdoor recreational opportunities, including hunting, fishing and golf. Golfers are pleased that one of the new Robert Trent Jones 36-hole golf courses is located here in Dothan. When I asked my chamber of commerce guide what her husband does, she replied, "He plays golf nine days a week." The city sponsors 37 public tennis courts and many parks.

Enterprise and Ozark Everything said about Dothan can be repeated about Enterprise (pop. 21,000) and Ozark (pop. 13,000). Of course, they are smaller, and those who appreciate small-town values will adore these places. In fact Enterprise is so proud of being small that one of their annual events is the "world's smallest St. Patrick's Day Parade." Parade officials elect a "designated Leprechaun" to march—only one marcher to a parade, please, because more than one might permit some other town to stage a smaller procession and steal Enterprise's thunder! The parade's elected Grand Marshal is always in absentia; because obviously, if he attended the event, there would be more than one marcher. (I was told that my name might be put into nomination for Grand Marshal some day, since I live in California and wouldn't be likely to show up.) When the long-anticipated Saint Patrick's Day arrives, celebrants rendezvous at Tops Restaurant and drink Irish coffee while they wait for the designated Leprechaun to finish the journey. Since the parade route stretches only from Ouida Street to Tops's back door—a distance of approximately 50 feet—the wait isn't overwhelming. But the celebration is.

Both Ozark and Enterprise attract military retirees because of nearby Ft. Rucker and its health care facilities. A top-notch hospital for civilians is also located here. Two nearby community colleges provide tuition-free classes for senior citizens. Like most Alabama towns, personal safety is very high here.

Why retire here? One retiree from Ozark put it this way: "This area is the best of all worlds. We live far enough south to avoid winter cold, far enough away from the ocean to escape destructive humidity. We enjoy a small town atmosphere, yet we're close to the Gulf Coast and great fishing. We're only minutes from Dothan, one and a half hours to Montgomery, and four hours' drive to Atlanta."

Ozark retirees appreciate the fact that they can drive all over the charming city with no traffic jams and few stoplights. A relatively inexpensive, full-service country club with a challenging 18-hole golf course is only two miles from the courthouse square in the center of town.

Eufaula Not far north of Dothan, Eufaula is another place favored by military retirees as well as others seeking Southern retirement in a mild climate. Both Ft. Benning and Ft. Rucker, with their hospitals, PX's and clubs, are an hour's drive away. Its position on the 45,000-acre Lake Eufaula makes it a great place for fishermen—with over 50 tournaments every year—and hunters find the surrounding woods and fields perfect for deer and wild turkey.

Eufaula's lovely antebellum mansions escaped damage during the Civil War and today lend charm to the town and its azalea- and dogwood-lined streets. The town's main residential street, wide and shaded by enormous trees, is a delightful picturebook of Southern architecture. We

155

visited there in the springtime and can still visualize the flowers and smell the freshness of sprouting leaves.

A modern hospital takes care of health needs, and three golf courses should help you cure your backswing. Housing, as usual in Alabama, is low-cost, averaging $75,000 for three-bedroom places. Antebellum mansions sell here for the price of tract homes where I'm from.

DOTHAN AREA			Rel. Humidity: Jan. 60%, July 61%			
	Jan.	April	July	Oct.	Rain	Snow
Daily Highs	57	77	91	77	49"	—
Daily Lows	36	53	72	53		

Blount County   George and Joan laughed as they recalled their children's reaction when they learned their parents were moving from Ohio to a remote, rustic area of Alabama. "They stared at us in disbelief. After a moment of silence, our daughter said, 'You're going into a Witness Protection Program, aren't you?'"

But when the children visited their parents in their new home, they fell in love with the setting. Positioned on five acres of wooded, hilly land, their two-story home enjoys an expansive view of Inland Lake and their own boat dock. "In Ohio, taxes on our house—the same size as this one—were $3,500. Here, we pay $192." Then he added, "That's not a month, but a year." They wouldn't say what they paid for their property, but said that most lakefront homes here are valued between $55,000 and $80,000, with a few exceptional ones in higher brackets.

I found this situation interesting since George and Joan are about the only non-Alabama retired folks on the lake. Curious as to their relationship with the community, I posed the question I always ask of Yankees who move into small Southern communities: "How were you received by your neighbors?" By way of reply, George pointed out that he and Joan had received more invitations to join churches, social groups and clubs than they could possibly accept, and someone suggested that he run for County Supervisor. "We've made more friends here in two years than in 15 years living in Ohio."

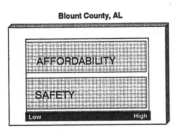
Blount County, AL

Birmingham is only about 35 miles away—good thing, too, because this is the closest place to stock up on wine and liquors. Blount County is dry, although Mayor Pat Bellew of Oneonta says folks are considering a change. Oneonta, by the way, is one of several small towns here that warrant investigation by those interested in this rural section of Alabama for retirement.

Please, don't everyone start off for Inland Lake. It's a tiny community and can't stand the pressure of a land rush. This is simply an example, one of many unheralded retirement havens tucked away in Alabama awaiting your discovery. This is also an example of how "outsiders" can make friends and create an interesting retirement without needing a support group of others like themselves.

BLOUNT COUNTY			Rel. Humidity: Jan. 61%, July 60%			
	Jan.	April	July	Oct.	Rain	Snow
Daily Highs	52	75	91	74	52"	2"
Daily Lows	33	51	70	51		

Scottsboro   Sitting up in Alabama's northeast corner, Scottsboro is a picture-book version of a retirement town. An antique courthouse and old-fashioned town square, tree-graced neighborhoods of substantial brick homes, reasonable housing and lakes galore all contribute to making this a pleasant community for retirement. For those who enjoy fishing, boating and other water sports, Scottsboro sits on one of the Southeast's largest lake complexes (Guntersville Lake), with over a thousand miles of shoreline, just in the county. Even though its population is only about 15,000, it is far enough away from the nearest large city to have ample shopping and facilities. Huntsville is 45 minutes away by car, Chattanooga an hour, and it's three hours to Atlanta or Nashville.

Scottsboro is a city that believes in parks. Goosepond Colony, the largest of 21 parks and recreational areas in the county, is a complete recreational facility and is city-owned and operated. Sitting on the edge of a gorgeous lake, Goosepond Colony boasts an 18-hole championship golf course, a lakeside restaurant, rental cottages, meeting rooms, marinas, plus camping and picnic facilities. (I stayed in one of these "cottages"; it had three bedrooms, four baths and a panoramic view of the lake and mountains.)

Why should Scottsboro be described here, instead of one of a dozen other beautiful, economical, lakefront retirement areas that crowd northern Alabama? It was difficult to make this decision, but I submit two justifications. The first is the cosmopolitan makeup of Scottsboro's population. It seems that several years ago, Revere Corporation moved its plant down here from someplace in the North, transplanting hundreds of employees along with its manufacturing facilities. For some reason or another things didn't work out, and when Revere moved away, many employees liked Scottsboro so much, they refused to transfer away. They either took early retirement or found other jobs. Later on, other Northern companies selected Scottsboro as a place to move their operations and brought along their employees, too. The result: a pleasant mixture of Northern and Southern neighbors.

My second reason is the community's dedication to betterment of their surroundings and quality of life. A case in point: an ultra-modern community recreation center, which serves a wide spectrum of citizens, from pre-school to elderly. Its construction came at a time when voters around the country were refusing to pass school bonds or fund libraries, yet Scottsboro voters didn't hesitate to allocate money for this impressive recreational and cultural facility. It comes complete with an Olympic pool that doubles as a training center for students as well for senior citizen water aerobics, a gymnasium, an indoor walking track, racquetball courts, handball and a game room, plus meeting rooms and hobby shops. Another expensive project underway: an already substantial-looking hospital is undergoing an $11 million expansion, which will make Scottsboro a leading medical center of the region.

An example of an event that reinforces small-city feeling: at a monthly happening called the "First Monday Trade Day," the courthouse lawn fills with residents selling arts and crafts, antiques, flea market items, locally-grown produce—anything that can be traded or sold. The first Monday in every September, the event grows so large they have to move it to a park. This tradition dates from 1868, when circuit court was held once a month.

This is an area that makes the most of its blend of mountains, forests and lakes. Residential areas show taste and charm in this setting. Real estate selling at 22 percent below national average also makes retirement here affordable. Personal safety here is exceptionally high, ranking in the top 15 percent in the nation.

SCOTTSBORO			Rel. Humidity: Jan. 65%, July 59%			
	Jan.	April	July	Oct.	Rain	Snow
Daily Highs	49	73	89	73	54"	3"
Daily Lows	31	50	69	49		

The Shoals   Alabama's northwestern section has many other attractive possibilities for retirement, many places matching Scottsboro's advantages. One area, known as the "Shoals," consists of four cities: Florence, Tuscumbia, Sheffield and Muscle Shoals, all situated on or near Wilson Lake. Local fishermen claim to enjoy the best fishing in Alabama on this part of the Tennessee River lake system. (However, every place I visited in the state makes the same claim. I'd like to believe they are all correct.)

Florence is the largest of these towns, and it is appreciated throughout the region for its four major hospitals that specialize in high-tech care services, some specifically designed for mature adults. A branch of the University of Alabama and a community college offer continuing education classes for a lifetime of learning. Home prices range from $30,000 to $250,000, most selling well below the national average. Lakeside homes are affordable as well as popular with retirees who enjoy the abundant opportunities for water sports here.

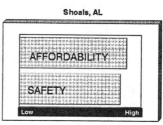

Shoals, AL

Still on the Tennessee River, 42 miles to the east, is the city of Decatur. With several Fortune 500 companies located here, workers and retirees from Northern states are well represented. Since Huntsville is just 20 miles away, Decatur residents have good choices in shopping. Housing costs are slightly higher here than in the Shoals area, but still way below national averages. It can't be stressed to heavily: this is the place for those who dream of a fishing retirement. It may not be the place for a spouse who hates to clean fish, however.

THE SHOALS			Rel. Humidity: Jan. 65%, July 59%			
	Jan.	April	July	Oct.	Rain	Snow
Daily Highs	50	73	89	73	55"	4"
Daily Lows	32	51	69	49		

Mississippi

Like Alabama, Mississippi has been shouldered out of most Gulf Coast beach real estate. In this case Louisiana grabs the waterfront territory, but like Alabama, Mississippi's 30 miles or so of sandy beaches make up in quality for what they've missed in quantity. The portion between Ocean Springs west to Bay St. Louis is the major retirement area in Mississippi. Except for Oxford and Natchez, we've done little research on the rest of the state since it doesn't attract many out-of-state retirees.

MISSISSIPPI TAX PROFILE

Sales tax: 7%, drugs exempt

State income tax: graduated from 3% to 5% over $10,000; can't deduct federal income tax

Property taxes: average 1%, but for over age 65, homestead exemption could be as much as $700

Intangibles tax: no

Social Security taxed: no

Pensions taxed: no

Gasoline tax: 18¢ per gallon, plus local taxes of from 2¢ to 3¢ per gallon

This, however, is changing; several towns, including Madison and Clinton, are entering the retirement sweepstakes race.

For those interested in continuing education, Mississippi waives tuition to residents 55 and older for one credit class per semester and allows unlimited auditing, on a space-available basis. Another interesting development for retirees is that the state recently exempted pensions from any source, from state taxation.

Gulfport-Biloxi   Long a favored retirement destination for military personnel, the area around Gulfport and Biloxi manages to combine a summer carnival atmosphere with sedate, Old-Southern values. The total population here is around 90,000, and the two cities are so closely connected that it's impossible to tell where one ends and another begins.

Years ago, when I first visited the Gulfport-Biloxi area, it was one of the prettiest seascapes I'd ever seen. Vast stretches of sugary beach, with gentle waves lapping at the sand, complemented a lovely beachfront road arched over by branches of majestic oak and magnolia trees. Large, formal estates surveyed the scene with Southern majesty. Here was—and is—the mansion where Jefferson Davis chose to live out his days, writing memoirs of his days of glory as president of the Confederacy.

But nothing ever remains the same, not even in Mississippi. That scenic road—at the expense of many oak and magnolia trees—changed into a cement boulevard with traffic whizzing along all four lanes. Many panoramic views are now obscured by restaurants, souvenir shops and condos. The quiet peacefulness of this

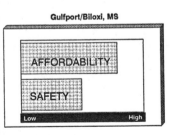

Gulfport/Biloxi, MS

AFFORDABILITY

SAFETY

Low   High

part of the coast retreated before an intense onslaught of tourism. Those who remember back 30 years will feel disappointed at today's Gulfport-Biloxi—but others, with no memories with which to compare, find the excitement and sparkle a delightful experience.

The biggest change of all is casino gambling, complete with several glittering, Las Vegas-style casinos, open 24 hours, seven days a week, with slot machines, roulette, blackjack, the whole kit-and-kaboodle. This provides tourists from surrounding states an additional excuse to congregate here, sunning on the beaches by day and shouting at the dice by night. In the winter, regular tourists are replaced by snowbird tourists, a large percentage of them Canadians, who don't mind the cooler water and occasional nippy days.

Don't let gambling prevent you from considering Mississippi's Gulf Coast, because the way things are going, gaming palaces, riverboat casinos and even ocean-going gaming ships are popping up all over the coast, Mississippi River towns and Florida ports. You're not going to avoid them. Gambling's effect on the local economy brings a mixed bag of assets and deficits. On the one hand, gambling has created more than 5,000 jobs in the Gulfport-Biloxi area (including much part-time work for retirees) and has warmed the hearts of many local businesses. On the other hand, that old-fashioned, Southern charm and honeysuckle neighborliness wears thin when trampled by herds of tourist-gamblers, traffic congestion and inevitable increases in crime levels.

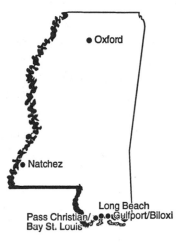

Housing prices used to drop drastically every winter after students went back in school and tourists went home to their jobs. That's still the case, but gambling is putting more year-round pressures on housing. The lavish mansions for which the Gulf Coast is so famous still grace the shore, away from the congested business centers. A block or so away from the beach, the homes become rather ordinary, mostly single-family bungalows in pleasant, comfortable and mature neighborhoods. Homes in these older sections of town are still affordable. Newer sections on the outskirts offer excellent choices of new brick homes starting around $70,000. Condos and apartments are also available in the newer sections.

Many military couples choose to retire here because of convenient medical and PX privileges at Kessler Air Force Base. Most of these military retirees, at one time or another, were stationed in the area and developed a fondness for the beaches and the climate.

Long Beach The best bets for retirement around here are towns *near* Gulfport-Biloxi. When most people talk of retirement on the Mississippi coast, they really mean the towns of Long Beach, Pass Christian and Bay St. Louis. With the convenience of good hospitals and other emergency facilities in nearby Gulfport-Biloxi, many retirees look to the reasonably priced housing and pleasant neighborhoods away from the hustle, bustle and tourist world. A bonus is exceptionally low crime rates in these towns; according to FBI statistics, among the lowest in the country.

The quiet and peaceful atmosphere is one of the first qualities that local residents proudly point out. "Gulfport-Biloxi is too crowded and too honky-tonk," said several retirees in Pass Christian. "Here, we have 26 miles of quiet beach, all to ourselves."

Long Beach (pop. 22,000) is a former farming community to the west of Gulfport, whose quiet residential areas attract retirees who enjoy the quality neighborhoods. You'll find an interesting mixture of homes here, varying from extraordinarily inexpensive to amazingly extravagant. One home, facing the beach, carried a price tag of $350,000—which sounded overpriced for the area, until we looked it over. It was a *Gone with the Wind*-type home: three stories, rooms with 10-foot ceilings, four bedrooms, four baths, fireplaces scattered throughout the place and a swimming pool. Even the garage had two stories and its own bath. Then the price seemed reasonable, but who could afford the servants? In contrast, we looked at a three-bedroom brick home on an acre of ground for $58,000 and an acceptable three-bedroom frame house for $39,000.

Old homes are treated like valuable jewels, continually polished and restored to yesterday's splendor. The city of Long Beach has strict local ordinances against cutting Live Oaks or Magnolia trees without permission of the planning commission, as well as approval of city officials.

Pass Christian Pass Christian (pop. 6,500) is the elegant member of the retirement trio. Long a vacation center for wealthy New Orleans residents, Pass Christian is rich in history and past opulence. At one time steamboats regularly made the 55-mile voyage from New Orleans, bringing high-society families to their second homes. The original families are gone, but their homes remain, as do the gracious lifestyles of the last century. Mansions with manicured lawns line the beachfront and invitations for afternoon tea indicate social standing. But all is not tea and crumpets; there is another side to Pass Christian, just as there is to most gracious Southern towns. Fishermen, craftspeople, artists and laborers make up the community's backbone. Their houses are smaller and located on streets away from the beach.

Twenty-two percent of the residents here are retired. Those with plenty of money live in the mansions and others live in modest cottages, because they don't have money or don't care to put money into extravagant housing.

The town had its beginnings when a Frenchman from New Orleans named Nicholas Christianne settled here in 1745. The pass refers to the deep channel that passes through the oyster reefs, and the town became referred to as "the pass of Christianne." The French pronunciation was retained, becoming Pass Christián. Its seafaring tradition continues to the present day, with shrimping, oystering and fishing the major occupations and a colorful element of the economic life. The Pass Christian Yacht Club dates back to 1849 and is the second oldest yacht club in the country.

In addition to fishing and boating, golf and tennis are popular. Twenty-two golf courses between Gulfport-Biloxi and Bay St. Louis encourage play. The beach is prominent in local recreational possibilities, with seven of the 26 miles of Mississippi beach available for Pass Christian residents' enjoyment.

Bay St. Louis   Called "The Bay" by local residents, Bay St. Louis (pop. 8,500) is even older than neighboring Pass Christian. It was founded in 1699 by the French and named after their king. Its historical downtown, with palm-lined streets, Victorian mansions and an old Catholic seminary, contrast with modern shopping and commercial centers.

During Hurricane Camile and the accompanying tidal wave, Bay St. Louis (as well as much of the coast) suffered considerable damage to its waterfront properties, which accounts for much modernized construction. It didn't take long to rebuild and repair. Many beach homes are new, as are beachfront commercial properties. Housing is as inexpensive here as can be found. We've seen two bedroom homes listed for $28,000 and an older, three-bedroom place on three acres for $42,000. As you can imagine, these won't be in elegant neighborhoods, but they are affordable to say the least.

One of the appealing aspects of living here—or anywhere in Mississippi, for that matter—is tax rates. The per capita tax burden in Mississippi is said to be only 57 percent of the national average. This is based on taxes from personal income, retail sales, residential property, gasoline and auto registration. Compare this with taxes in Illinois of 98 percent, Wisconsin, 132 percent and Michigan, 124 percent of the national per capita average.

MISSISSIPPI GULF COAST				Rel. Humidity: Jan. 62%, July 64%	
	Jan.	April	July	Oct.	Rain	Snow
Daily Highs	61	77	90	79	61"	—
Daily Lows	43	59	74	60		

Oxford Were I to rank places as to the "best town for retirement," Oxford, Mississippi, would surely rank in the top ten. I confess that as an author, I could be biased by a certain mystical literary connection between Oxford and the outside world. Oxford has captivated and developed writers from its very beginning as a university town, even before William Faulkner, who made his home base here, and continues today with several best-selling authors choosing to bask in Oxford's nourishing literary climate.

In some rural, small-city settings, high cultural events are destruction derbies or greased-pig contests. Not Oxford. Its calendar brims with activities appropriate to the town's academic orientation. A well-known example is Oxford's springtime "Conference on the Book." The 1994 event was chaired by Stephen King and John Grisham (who also lives here). Of course, artistic endeavors aren't exclusively literary. Sculptors, painters and ceramists are well represented, as are photographers, potters and weavers.

Oxford's downtown square is a picture-book version of how a Southern university town's center should look. A 117-year-old courthouse with massive columns and centuries-old oak trees dominates the scene, complete with the obligatory statue of a Confederate soldier standing guard, facing south of course. (Faulkner once commented, "No wonder we lost the war; our soldiers always face south, but the Yankees were coming from the north!") Other attractions: a department store dating from 1839, a wonderful art gallery, and enough shops and boutiques to make daily shopping a pleasure. The square also supports several good-to-excellent little restaurants. You could easily find yourself dining at a table next to a best-selling author like Richard Ford or Larry Brown, who also make Oxford their home. (As a matter of fact, I had lunch at a table next to John Grisham one day; but since he didn't appear to recognize me, I didn't want to embarrass him by saying hello.)

Across from the Confederate Soldier is a well-known Oxford tradition, the Square Book Store, which features a second-floor veranda that looks out over the square, where friends meet to sip cappuccino and talk about books. The 25,000-volume collection on many esoteric subjects makes you aware that the owner operates the bookstore with a respect for books rather than an eye on quick turnover and high profits. On the staircase, you'll find stacks of autographed copies of books by local authors. A favorite happening is the Square Book Store's presentations by well-known authors who discuss their works and philosophical approaches in their literary accomplishments.

Oxford is a great place for those interested in continuing education or for literary junkies like me, but it's much more than that. Oxford is a perfect location for those who enjoy Southern hospitality (in a setting where many residents come from the North), those who prefer a small city (population 11,000) with an exceptionally low crime rate, and finally, where cosmopolitan, upscale living can be enjoyed at affordable prices. Its small town warmth is apparent as people who've never seen you before say "good morning" as they pass on the downtown square.

One retiree, who came here after try-ing Florida for retirement, said, "Everyone in Florida seemed to come from someplace else. I wanted to find a *real* town, a place where I could interact with people *from* that town. That's when I started thinking about Oxford."

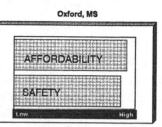

A common supposition is that outsiders may not be accepted in a small Southern town. How do locals accept "outsiders"? There may be parts of Mississippi where Yankees would be considered freaks, but Oxford is too sophisticated for that. In fact, when I was introduced to one of the city councilmen—also a professor at the university—I remarked on his non-Southern accent. He explained that he came here from Illinois to get his Ph.D. in Pharmacology. He found the people of Oxford so friendly, and the town so delightful, that he remained to teach and later became active in local politics.

I interviewed another retiree, a lady from Idaho whose husband is a retired attorney. She said, "It was wonderful how quickly we made friends without work connections or children in school. Our friends predicted that we would never be completely accepted. But the opposite was true. I'm presently serving on the arts council, as a volunteer at the Cedar Oaks museum and other groups, and am chairman of a committee. I'm so busy, I've had to turn down invitations to join groups. One group I belong to buys season tickets to the symphony in Memphis, and once a month we all travel there. Next month we're going to Jackson for a ballet."

Of course, all activities here aren't cultural. Sports fans not only have plenty of bass and crappie fishing at nearby Sardis lake, but also the excitement of basketball and football as the Ole Miss Rebels host nationally ranked powerhouses. A new retirement complex features golf as one of its central attractions.

Homes in town are affordable, with a nice three-bedroom home costing about $70,000. The same amount will purchase an older, Southern-style home on an expansive lot with large trees. A hundred acres of woodlands can be had for $25,000 or less. Small farms are favorites with retirees and can be found just a few minutes away from the city limits.

It's no secret that, throughout the nation, university towns tend to be politically liberal. Student concerns over issues like ecology, civil rights and social justice quite naturally spill over into the community at large. Oxford is no exception. While surrounding towns remain staunchly old-fashioned and mentally rigid, Oxford is an island of liberal, open-minded tolerance—politically and socially. And, despite the bad press Oxford received during the Civil Rights struggles of the 60s (some of it deserved and some not), race relations here appear to be as relaxed and congenial as any place I've ever seen in the United States.

It isn't fair to make this assertion on the basis of a few days' visit, so I discussed this with a prominent African-American social activist who lives in Oxford. Now a successful businessman and member of the state board of education, as a child he was one of those frightened kids we saw on TV, being escorted to school by armed National Guardsmen. He said simply, "That was then. Tell your readers I say, 'Come see us now.'" As much as anything else, that made me like Oxford.

OXFORD			Rel. Humidity: Jan. 59%, July 55%			
	Jan.	April	July	Oct.	Rain	Snow
Daily Highs	51	75	93	76	56"	2"
Daily Lows	31	50	69	49		

Natchez The absolute epitome of Old South living can be found in Natchez. Founded in 1716 and the home of Spanish governors and French plantation owners, the town grew into a prosperous cotton-raising and exporting city. Before the Civil War, when cotton was king, Natchez became one of the wealthiest cities of the South. When war broke out, Natchez fell under a long siege by federal gunboats. Because the town sits on a bluff overlooking the Mississippi and the artillery shells came from below, many magnificent old mansions escaped the destructive fate of other Southern towns.

Natchez, MS

AFFORDABILITY

SAFETY

Low   High

After the war, its economy devastated, Natchez fell into a sleepy period of doldrums. This had the further effect of preserving the antebellum homes from the destruction of modernization and urban renewal. Today, the city is a virtual museum of Southern aristocratic architecture. Approximately 500 historic homes grace the quiet streets of modern-day Natchez. Every spring and fall, antebellum homes open to the public. It is said to take at least three days to see them all because they can be visited only on schedules.

Natchez is a quiet town, with peaceful and well cared-for neighborhoods. Newer subdivisions and apartments are found on the fringes of town. The surrounding countryside is thickly forested with acre-sized lots carved into the woods. We felt very comfortable here and consider Natchez to be a logical place for retirement for someone who is looking for that particular type of ambience. Even if not your choice for retirement, it's well worth a visit to delight in Natchez's antebellum glory.

NATCHEZ			Rel. Humidity: Jan. 62%, July 64%			
	Jan.	April	July	Oct.	Rain	Snow
Daily Highs	61	79	91	80	55"	—
Daily Lows	40	58	73	56		

Louisiana

If you're looking for Gulf Coast beach property in Louisiana, you are out of luck. Except for a short stretch of sand in the western part of the state—humorously referred to as the Cajun Riviera—most of coastal Louisiana is swamps, mud flats and bayous. People in Texas claim they

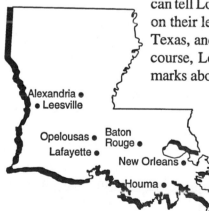

can tell Louisianans by the high-water marks on their legs. Beaches start when you get to Texas, and Texans feel smug about that. Of course, Lousianans enjoy making snide remarks about Texans, so they're even.

Our interviews with folks who've retired in Louisiana from outside the state are invariably enthusiastic about their new homes. This reinforces our overall favorable impression of Louisiana as a retirement possibility.

That's partly understandable, because of our prior connections with this state. My wife (born and raised in Denver) went to high school and college in Baton Rouge, and I was born in New Orleans, although I left at such an early age that I recall little. But later, as an adult, I returned to the city to take a job on the *New Orleans Item,* a now-defunct newspaper that somehow captured the spirit of the town. When I remember New Orleans, visions of the mysterious French Quarter swirl through my mind, conjuring kitchen aromas from fantastic restaurants and an overwhelming sense of history on every street corner. In my opinion, New Orleans, along with San Francisco, are the United States' most unique cities and rank worldwide with places like Paris, Vienna or Buenos Aires.

LOUISIANA TAX PROFILE

Sales tax: 4% to 10%, drugs, some food exempt

State income tax: graduated from 2% to 6% over $50,000; federal income tax deductible

Property taxes: average of 1.15% of market value

Intangibles tax: no

Social Security taxed: no

Pensions taxed: private pensions taxable, $6,000 exemption

Gasoline tax: 20¢ per gallon, plus sales tax

Another ingredient that colors our perception of Louisiana: we have good friends living there, folks we enjoy visiting. That always makes a place seem warmer and more pleasant. Yet, we're convinced that people here are more open and accepting of outsiders than in many other Deep South locations we've researched.

Cajun Food

As always, I do my best research on a full and happy tummy, therefore research in Louisiana is always a happy and productive endeavor. Every time I visit I put on weight from all the delicious tidbits to be sampled. We are exceptionally fortunate to have friends in the heart of Cajun country, friends who also happen to be superb cooks. They treat us to Louisiana-French delicacies such as gumbo (with something called *filé*), homemade sausages (called *boudín*), crawfish and rice dishes (called *estoufé*) and a special desert (called *apple pie and ice cream*).

Louisiana has long been famous for its food, both home cooked and restaurant prepared. Its reputation for fine cuisine goes back two centuries when French settlers adapted continental haute cuisine to available ingredients in this part of the Americas. For a while Spain ruled Lousiana; Spanish cooks added their own unique touches to traditional recipes. French cooking strategies were bolstered in 1755 when a large number of French citizens abandoned their homes in Acadia, Nova Scotia, to immigrate to Louisiana. These Acadians (hence the term 'Cajuns) fled from Canada rather than submit to unjust British rule and suffer from horribly unimaginative English cooking.

Low-Cost Housing

Throughout Louisiana and neighboring Texas, real estate sells at bargain rates and rentals are very affordable. This phenomenon was caused by a sudden drop in oil prices a few years back, sending the local petroleum industry into a tailspin from which it's never fully recovered.

Another factor keeping prices down is the over-building of apartments and condominiums during the easy-money policy of the savings and loan industry. With easy access to insured, non-repayable loans, contractors, promoters and wheeler-dealers went on a construction spree to end all sprees. While we taxpayers are picking up the pieces, some beneficiaries are those retirees looking for inexpensive housing. Of course, the main beneficiaries are those big-spenders who took multi-million-dollar loans and then shrugged them off when the money was spent.

New Orleans My earlier book, *Retirement Choices,* tentatively endorsed New Orleans as a retirement possibility. The caveat was a high crime rate. Over the intervening years, the rate hasn't improved significantly. All I can say is that New Orleans is considerably safer than New York City, if that's any consolation.

The wild Mardi Gras season is partially responsible for the crime statistics. Tourists, sometimes of unsavory character, converge upon New Orleans in an orgy of total abandon. During the weeks around Mardi Gras, arrest figures shoot sky-high. This distorts the city's crime statistics to a certain extent; nevertheless, like most cities today, in New Orleans crime is a fact of life. Even folks who live in the more peaceful sections of town take precautions. Some make it a point to stay away from the French Quarter during Mardi Gras, when tourists start playing looneytoons.

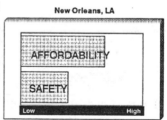

New Orleans, LA

In a way, New Orleans residents are like those New Yorkers who adore living in Manhattan. They ignore statistics and wouldn't dream of living somewhere more secure, but boring. New Orleans—exotic, steeped in history and wrought-iron antiqueness—is anything but boring. But you can enjoy all of this by living *near* rather than *in* New Orleans.

The outskirts of the city and the suburbs offer the safest and the most-satisfying living conditions. Many people choose to drive across the causeways to Lake Pontchatrain's north shore to the suburbs of Slidell, Mandeville, Covington or Hammond. LaPlace, on the southwest

169

edge of the lake, is another possibility for retirement. We drove through those areas on the outskirts—some about 20 minutes from downtown—and looked at a few homes for sale. They were certainly affordable, and we agreed that we wouldn't feel at all out of step living here. Although out of our price range, we had fun looking at a lovely, 150-year-old antebellum home, surrounded by oaks on 104 rolling acres outside Hammond. It was restored and had five bedrooms and three baths. The price? About the same as a two-bedroom cottage on a 25-foot by 75-foot lot in our home town in California: $275,000.

Incidentally, almost anything you buy or rent in the Louisiana will include air conditioning. Summers here demand it. Cockroaches are also included at no extra charge. This Mississippi-River country—with its exceptional humidity—is very healthy for all types of household bugs; they thrive and reproduce marvelously, without any encouragement on the part of homeowners.

Houma   Crime in large cities like New Orleans is always high. When you leave the city, crime rates drop dramatically, no matter what part of the country. Small cities such as Houma (pop. 37,500), about 75 miles southwest of New Orleans, generally report unusually low incidences of crime. When we visited Houma a few years ago, it was ranked tenth in the nation in safety, according to FBI statistics. Today it's dropped a few

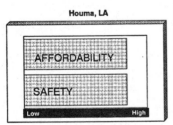
Houma, LA

places, but that doesn't mean much. In a smaller city like Houma, a few isolated problems or a visiting burglar can magnify crime statistics, making it appear as if a crime wave had struck.

The Louisiana countryside not only is quiet and peaceful, but also enjoys one of the lowest costs of living in the United States. According to retired folks who filled out our questionnaires, apartments and houses can be rented for as low as $175 a month in places like Houma, Thibodaux or Lafayette.

As we drove from New Orleans, along a wide road flanking a bayou, we passed numerous roadside stands and restaurants serving barbecued ribs, catfish and boiled crawfish. When we arrived in Houma, our appetites for seafood had built pressures that could drive a locomotive.

The first stop in researching a town is usually the chamber of commerce office. After conducting our business, we asked the clerk's recommendation for a nice restaurant. She frowned momentarily, as though afraid we might not like her suggestions, and then replied, "Well, sir, there are half a dozen nice restaurants in Houma. But I'm afraid they are mostly all seafood restaurants."

"Perfect! Which one is the best?"

"Sir, there just aren't any bad seafood restaurants in Houma!"

We selected a restaurant at random and had to agree with her. The fried catfish and crawfish bisque were marvelous—as good as at any high-priced New Orleans restaurant, perhaps better. A platter of steamed crabs was thrown in, just something left over from last night's dinner special. The bill for two, including wine, was around $12. I believe I could like Houma even if there were muggers on every street corner—as long as they didn't block the restaurant doors. Its residential streets and homes are comfortable looking: neatly mowed lawns, children roller skating on sidewalks and neighbors talking over backyard fences. If that's what you are looking for, you might investigate any number of towns like this, within striking distance of New Orleans, but far enough away not to be struck back.

NEW ORLEANS AREA			Rel. Humidity: Jan. 66%, July 66%			
	Jan.	April	July	Oct.	Rain	Snow
Daily Highs	62	79	91	79	59"	—
Daily Lows	43	59	73	59		

Baton Rouge   As you might expect, Louisiana's state capital—Baton Rouge (pop. 225,000)—is a handsome city. With neat, prosperous-looking neighborhoods, attractive subdivisions, and one of the prettiest university campuses in the country, Baton Rouge fulfills the image of a state capital. Its distinctive blend of French, Creole, Cajun and Old South traditions makes it as much a part of Louisiana as the great river on which it thrives.

Until the real estate market pushed up prices, Baton Rouge had one of the lowest costs of living of any city of its size in the country. Living costs are still almost 7 percent below average, so Baton Rouge remains an affordable retirement option. But it's the quality of the setting that makes it a bargain.

We have friends who live here, in a magnificent brick home set back on an enormous tree-shaded piece of ground. It looks like the estate of some wealthy industrialist, a gorgeous place just a mile from the university campus. Even though we suspected that Baton Rouge home prices were low, we were shocked when we discovered how much our friends had paid for the property. Suffice it to say it sounded like a gift.

171

A very interesting architectural style, popular in this section of the state, lends character to the residential neighborhoods. Based on centuries-old French and Acadian styles, these single-story homes have high, broad roofs with gables peeking out from upstairs rooms in what normally would be an attic. Often they feature Acadian wrap-around porches—very practical for shading the windows from the sun's rays.

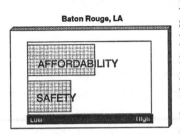

Baton Rouge, LA

Homes of substantial brick construction seem to be the preferred custom. We looked at townhouses, one elegant-looking two-bedroom, two-story plan for $38,500, and not too far away was a three-bedroom, one-and-a-half-bath home for only $32,900. When you get into prices over $80,000, you are talking luxury!

Most university towns have lots to offer retirees. Baton Rouge's Louisiana State University (LSU) is no exception. Its cultural offerings and its enrichment of the intellectual aspect of the community are quite important, but additionally, the school attracts scholars, professors and university employees from all over the country. The narrow, conservative atmosphere of many Southern cities is absent in Baton Rouge. Students, faculty, support personnel and families of these outside people nourish fresh views and lifestyles throughout the community.

My distinct impression is that most residents do *not* use the thick Southern accent one expects from such a deeply Southern location. This shouldn't be surprising, since so many people come from places where Midwestern accents are the norm. I attribute the university's influence for this leveling of accents. Among the natives, a slight Cajun twist of pronunciation is common, but this is totally different from a conventional Southern accent.

The university touches the community in other ways, culturally as well as educationally. A slogan here is "Art is the Heart of Baton Rouge." Using the talent in theater, music and fine arts that LSU attracts, the community has organized some commendable programs. Every year a ten-block stretch of downtown is blocked off so people can see potters at their wheels, musicians entertaining and artists at their easels. Mimes entertain the crowds, and craftspeople of all kinds sell their wares. Two ballet groups bring stars from major companies to work with local students; the Baton Rouge Opera is in its eighth season. Two light opera companies, a symphony orchestra and a professional theater company round out the cultural offerings. The city is quite proud of its historic past and is taking vigorous steps to preserve and restore two downtown neighborhoods, historic Beauregard Town and Spanish Town.

The community offers a wide variety of services for senior citizens. The Baton Rouge Council on Aging coordinates the Retired Senior Volunteer Program (R.S.V.P.), three senior centers, a Meals on Wheels program and free, short-term home care for elderly persons who are temporarily disabled or recently discharged from the hospital. Other services are legal aid, health services, consumer information and a foster grandparent program. Although only about 10 percent of the population in Baton Rouge is over 60, the community obviously intends to take care of its retired.

As a retirement location, Baton Rouge has a lot going for it. It's a cosmopolitan community, and it's centrally located. It's just 70 miles by interstate to New Orleans for those extra-special nights on the town or for the hilarity of Mardi Gras. You can reach the beaches at Pass Christian in two hours by car. Fifty miles to the north is historic Natchez, with its last-century atmosphere.

BATON ROUGE			Rel. Humidity: Jan. 65%, July 62%			
	Jan.	April	July	Oct.	Rain	Snow
Daily Highs	61	79	91	80	55"	—
Daily Lows	41	58	73	56		

Cajun Country/Opelousas/Lafayette   Baton Rouge is not really in the heart of the famous Cajun and Bayou country. It is off to one side, barely touching the border of Cajun-land. West and south lies the true Cajun Country. Occupying about a third of the state's land area, this is the most famous part of Louisiana. At one time, Cajuns were noted for their closed society. As a defense mechanism, they jealously maintained their French language and their private way of living, excluding outsiders—referred to as *les Americaines*—from their lives. World War II, the Korean War and Vietnam forced many Cajuns to join the outside world. Television, radio and other electronic gadgets added to the momentum of change during the last half of this century.

Today some Cajun French can still be heard as it was spoken by the original settlers more than two centuries ago. Cajun music—played on the fiddle, accordion and triangle—is still featured at dances. However, it is usually only old-timers who regularly speak French; the younger generation understands the language and still can converse if need be, but prefers to use English.

The countryside around Baton Rouge is among the prettiest and most historic in the state. Gracious old plantation homes with huge porticoes, wrought-iron balconies and lead-sheathed roofs sit half-hidden by enormous trees, just as they have for almost two centuries. The surrounding countryside is dotted with delightful little towns, some dating from the 1700s. Their streets meander about the town (evidence of early settlement, before the age of planning commissions), past shuttered houses, ancient trees and mature camelia bushes.

Louisiana-French society is much more open today, with retirees from out of state finding interesting retirement in small-town Cajun Country. This is particularly true of those who love hunting and fishing. For over two centuries, people living in these isolated, heavily wooded areas have hunted, not for sport but to put meat on the table. Extensive networks of bayous, rivers and streams provided fresh fish to supplement the diet, with hunting and fishing an integral part of every Cajun family's life. From almost any rural home, it is rarely more than a few minutes by foot or pickup to a camp (a favorite hunting or fishing spot). Duck hunting is one of the favorite and most productive sports, placing roast duck and venison on many menus.

The northern part of Cajun Country, also known as Opelousas Country, actually predated the coming of the Acadians. Bayous and rich farmlands attracted French settlers in 1720. They had been living here for a generation before their French cousins from Nova Scotia moved in with them. Opelousas (pop. 20,000) is the third-oldest city in Louisiana and is famous for Jim Bowie's residence and for having produced many fine Creole and Cajun chefs. The towns of Marksville, Bunkie, Simmesport, Bordelonville and others are wonderfully steeped in history, yet lie quietly and unpretentiously, places for peaceful retirement living.

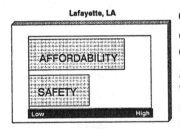
Lafayette, LA

We can't conclude our discussion of Cajun Country without including the city of Lafayette (pop. 86,000), often called the Capital City of Acadiana. Of all the retiree groups who filled out our questionnaires, those from Lafayette were the most enthusiastic. With a full range of activities and services, they unhesitatingly recommended retirement here. The local community college—affectionately known as Gumbo U.—along with a branch of Louisiana State University and an excellent adult education program, provides cultural backup, with comparatively low costs of medical care a bonus. The majority of respondents listed low health care costs as their highest concern. They also reported that housing and rentals are very reasonable.

Lafayette and the surrounding Cajun heartland offers horse racing, boat tours of the Atchafalaya Basin Swamp, plenty of golf and tennis facilities plus active senior citizens' organizations. Nearby Abbeville is known for excellent duck and goose hunting and hosts a duck festival every Labor Day. Festivals are big here, with one taking place nearly every weekend. There's a crawfish festival in Breaux Bridge, a French music festival in Abbeville, a rice festival in Crowley, even a Boudin Festival. (Boudin is a special Cajun sausage.)

Alexandria   This is a central Louisiana city (on the other side of Cajun Country) that deserves to be mentioned as a retirement possibility. It is a clean, neat city with a blending of older homes and modern development. Because the town was burned to the ground in 1864 by federal troops, none of the residential sections are as old or as picturesque as places like Natchez. But they are pleasant and well built in the style of the late 1800s. This gives Alexandria a different look: not quite modern, yet not really old. The city fathers are actively working toward improvements in all facets of the city's character. Attracting retirees is one of their goals. Their efforts seem to be paying off, at least as far as military retirees go.

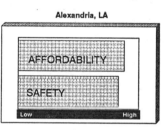

Alexandria, LA

Back in the days of World War II, generals Eisenhower, Patton and Clark used the Alexandria area to train some seven million soldiers. As these troops became ready for overseas duty, they also became acquainted with the attractive town and the many lakes, national forests and state parks in the vicinity. Many, now of retirement age, have returned, bringing the military's usual culturally mixed population. (Were it not for this mixture of Northerners and Southerners, perhaps we wouldn't have looked at Alexandria so favorably.)

As we expected, housing is very reasonable, with some nice places selling for $50,000 and under and older homes for around $30,000. Several homes were offered for low down payments; one older place was $900 down and $215 payments on a new FHA loan. By the way, there is an interesting construction style used by older homes both in town and in the surrounding countryside. They are built off the ground on brick pilings to a height of a couple of feet. One explanation given was that the air beneath the house kept the floors dry and bug free.

Leesville   Another town near a military installation (Fort Polk), Lees-ville is one of the most attractive towns we've seen anywhere. When we came upon it—purely by accident—we were surprised to see it pop up from out of nowhere after 50 miles of very sparsely settled countryside (much of it forested). It seemed as if each home was individually designed, constructed of brick and set on enormous lawns. The older part of town is more conventional, with the traditional white frame homes and large—but not extravagant—lawns and shade trees. Here again, military retirement could be easing the way for conventional retirees. We have no idea how many are retired here, but if there aren't a lot, there ought to be.

Chapter 6

Texas, the B-i-i-g State

You don't have to be told that Texas is one enormous state. Give a Texan half a chance and he'll tell you all about it. Don't give him a chance and he'll tell you anyway. The truth is, Texas is almost as large as Texans claim, and that's pretty darn big. It's bigger than any country in Europe except for Russia, and ten times larger than many European countries. Not only is Texas spacious, but it boasts of some of the prettiest scenery you can imagine—as well as some of the most boring. This wide range of climate, scenery and elevations presents a broad menu of retirement options, something for almost every taste.

Texas's range of climates varies wildly. The subtropical southern tip of the state never sees snow and thinks any temperature below 60 degrees is downright chilly. At the other extreme, the high plains of the northern Panhandle region can be one of the coldest conceivable places in the winter, yet it can also be one of the hottest places this side of Death Valley in the summer. The Gulf Coast is as humid as Florida, and west Texas is dry as the proverbial bone. You'll encounter large cities and small villages and medium-sized places perfect for retirement. Landscapes vary from plains to deserts to seashores to mountains. Variety is the spice of Texas retirement choices!

Texas Gulf Coast

With more than 600 miles of the Texas coast facing the Gulf of Mexico, one would expect beachfront developments galore. The fact is, most of the Texas waterfront is uninhabited. Furthermore, almost all the main-land faces not the gulf, but offshore islands and narrow peninsulas that effectively shut off the open gulf waters. For the most part, these islands are long and narrow, composed of sand dunes and unexplored beaches. Much of the actual coast is little changed from the days in the early 1800s when the French pirate Jean Lafitte used the islands as a base.

Long stretches of these islands, as well as parts of the mainland, are designated as wildlife refuges. Whooping cranes and Kemp's Ridley sea turtles are making a comeback after what once seemed almost certain extinction. Turtle eggs from Mexico planted on the Padre Islands about 20 years ago are beginning to show wonderful results. The hatchlings from the experiment have grown into adult turtles and are returning to their beach of origin to nest in a protected environment. When the new batches of eggs hatch and the baby turtles start for the sea, they are qickly captured and cared for in special pens until they're old enough to have a good chance for survival.

TEXAS TAX PROFILE
Sales tax: 6.25% to 8.25%, food, drugs exempt
State income tax: no
Property taxes: about 2.2%
Intangibles tax: no
Social Security taxed: no
Pensions taxed: no
Gasoline tax: 20¢ per gallon

This is a fisherman's paradise. Both the channel and gulf sides of the long islands teem with fish. From beaches and piers you can expect to catch redfish, speckled and sand trout, flounder, sheepshead, skipjack, croakers and drum. Group boats offer bay and deep-sea fishing, with charter cruisers available for individual or small-party sport. The offshore game includes tarpon, sailfish, kingfish, marlin, mackerel, pompano, ling cod, bonito and red snapper, among others. By far, fishing is the major sport attraction for retirees who have chosen the Texas Gulf Coast for their home.

Galveston   On the entire Texas coast only one city actually faces the open gulf: Galveston. With a population of almost 60,000, it occupies one of those long islands and is reached via a lengthy causeway across Galveston Bay. Except for this 32-mile stretch of beach—not all of which is developed—there is little residential construction on the gulf, just a tiny portion around Corpus Christi and farther south on South Padre Island.

Many years ago Galveston was one of our favorite weekend resorts; we visited as often as we could, swimming in the surf, crabbing off the jetties and driving along the beach with the waves playing at our car wheels. Upon returning, after an interval of almost 30 years, we expected change. To our surprise, we discovered that Galveston had changed very little.

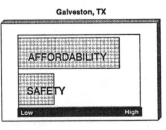

Galveston, TX

AFFORDABILITY

SAFETY

Low   High

This shouldn't have been so surprising, because limited space on Galveston island long ago filled to capacity with homes and businesses. The only new construction possible is replacing old buildings with new, something the local people are reluctant to permit. The old downtown section, instead of being replaced by slick new glass-and-steel monsters, has been preserved and restored to a charming, turn-of-the-century state. Old brick and cast-iron fronts with wrought-iron balconies give the area a New Orleans French Quarter feeling. One street has been turned into a pedestrian mall, complete with restaurants, smart shops and park benches for sunning and people-watching.

True, along the beachfront some older homes and buildings slowly give way to newer, more profitable construction focused on tourist dollars. But change is slow in coming. Most of the town is still the same: old fashioned and comparatively inexpensive. Surf fishermen can try their luck almost anywhere along the beach. There are free municipal jetties and rock groin piers at regular intervals. If you fail to catch anything, markets sell the freshest catch found anywhere—right out of the gulf into your frying pan.

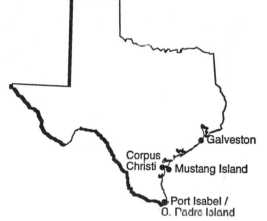

Galveston has few high-rise buildings, either on the beach or in town. Fascinating Victorian homes—some in a poor state of repair, most in fine shape, some positively gorgeous—grace quiet, tree-lined streets away from the bustle of the seashore. When you leave the honky-tonk atmosphere of Seawall Boulevard, it is hard to believe you are in one of the major tourist attractions on the Texas coast—it is too residential and calm.

People who don't live here think of Galveston as a weekend or vacation hot-spot, a convention site, a place to go and blow off steam. However, there is a surprising intellectual air about Galveston. The University of Texas medical school is in downtown Galveston, as well as a branch of Texas A&M and a community college. These are serious students, some interested in art and literature to the exclusion of fishing (heaven forbid).

In the old days, we could drive for at least 20 miles on hard-packed sand, but today the beach is no longer open to automobile traffic. There are plenty of access points, however, where fishermen can surf cast, and

179

there are piers for easier fishing. I fondly remember blissful days and large catches of blue crab, later made into a seafood gumbo at the home of a displaced Cajun who lived in Houston.

Today, the beach outside town is no longer deserted and wild, but is often lined with ugly, unpainted summer homes that are built on 15-foot stilts to avoid high waves during hurricane weather. (All along the Gulf Coast, from Key West to the tip of Texas, you find this stilt construction. Insurance companies insist on new buildings having stilts; it cuts their losses considerably.) Some owners successfully disguise the stilts by screening the lower portions of their houses, turning them into garages and storage spaces. This disguise makes the houses look like attractive two-story homes. But others don't bother, making stretches of beach look as if they had been invaded by spindly-legged monsters. Since the beach area is pure tourist and most popular during the spring and summer, it turns into a ghostly place in winter. Few homes are lived in year-round.

GALVESTON			Rel. Humidity: Jan. 77%, July 70%			
	Jan.	April	July	Oct.	Rain	Snow
Daily Highs	59	73	87	78	40"	—
Daily Lows	48	65	79	68		

Corpus Christi   The only other major city on the Texas coast is Corpus Christi, a fast-growing metropolis of 264,000 inhabitants. It's actually not on the gulf, but on a large bay, sheltered from open water by 30-mile-long Mustang Island. A major deepwater port, Corpus is large enough to mask the tourist crowds in all but the most hectic times (college semester breaks). For the most part, it looks like an ordinary, contemporary city—pleasant and unusually neat. It even has a modern, high-rise downtown. A seawall runs along the downtown area, with stairs that lead down to the water and a yacht basin. Palm-lined boulevards and cosmopolitan hotels and office buildings complete the picture.

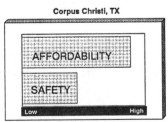
Corpus Christi, TX

Unlike Galveston, which sits exposed to the whims of hurricane-driven tides, Corpus Christi enjoys the protection of offshore islands. Therefore, construction doesn't have to take into consideration the constant threat of flood; the town has a relaxed look about it.

Medical services are excellent here, with 11 hospitals plus the military medical facilities serving the naval air station. (Numerous retired military families live here.) Educational and cultural needs are met by a two-year college as well as a state university. A new aquarium is becoming one of the major tourist attractions, with its 132,000-gallon deepwater exhibit.

Since the Corpus Christi area offers the only beach access along many miles of coastline, it has become quite popular as a resort. Not only are there beaches along the bay, but there are 110 miles of sand and surf on the islands that shelter the mainland. Corpus has become almost as famous as Fort Lauderdale, Florida, for its assemblage of frolicking college students during semester break. As many as 100,000 tourists—an uncounted number of them college students—flock to Corpus Christi and Mustang Island to celebrate every spring.

Because of these sporadic visits by enthusiastic, youthful celebrants, local crime statistics can become exaggerated. The police are kept busy arresting drunks, breaking up fistfights and stopping exuberant youngsters from destroying motel rooms. These offenses show up in the FBI's crime reports even though they are crimes that don't really affect ordinary residents or retirees, who neither live in nor frequent the tourist areas during the wild days.

CORPUS CHRISTI			Rel. Humidity: Jan. 68%, July 57%			
	Jan.	April	July	Oct.	Rain	Snow
Daily Highs	66	82	94	84	30"	—
Daily Lows	46	64	76	64		

Mustang Island So many families from San Antonio and Austin traditionally vacation and maintain summer homes across the Laguna Madre, on Mustang Island, that it is referred to as an annex of San Antonio. There is only one town on the island: Port Aransas, a small community with a year-round population of about 2,000. Summer tourism doubles and triples this figure.

Since the island is unprotected from open water and the possibility of hurricane-driven tides, many homes stand high on the familiar pilings and stilts of Gulf Coast construction. We did our research there in the winter and saw Port Aransas at its quietest time of year. Real estate activity was also at its lowest ebb, with properties rather inexpensive. Several were marked down into the low-$30,000 range. These were three-bedroom affairs, not elegant, of course, but liveable. Others were offered for even less money, but they had a kind of temporary air about them. They looked as if their owners were hesitant to put much maintenance into them, just in case a hurricane might make it a waste of time.

Mustang Islanders brag about their low crime rate. "With only two ways off the island," they point out, "either by ferry to the mainland or by the bridge to Corpus at the other end of the island, no one expects to commit a serious crime and make a getaway." When a crime is committed, the police immediately shut down the ferry and place a roadblock at the bridge. Our own trip by ferry involved an annoying hour of waiting in line for our turn at boarding. I can just imagine how annoyed and nervous I would have been had I been driving a getaway car with the police chasing after me.

Islanders also love to brag about the fishing, claiming that Mustang Island is a place "where the fish bite every day." This is fortunate for the retiree who loves to fish, because there is very little else to do on Mustang or North Padre Island. Boats are available for rent, and deep-sea charters take you out for the big ones. Many people use the conventional rod and reel, but sail fishing is becoming popular. This is done by attaching a trolling line to a sail that moves with the wind, said to be very effective and requiring no work on the part of the fisherman.

When you leave Port Aransas, the island becomes very sparsely populated on the drive south. Long stretches of dunes and beach line the gulf side, with lagoons and marsh facing the mainland. Except for a few tourist condos and some dispersed private homes, the lower part of the island is the domain of sea turtles and birds. If you keep driving south you find yourself on North Padre Island, where the road abruptly ends, with no more pavement for another 80 miles.

South Padre Island   From time to time travel writers describe the coast between Corpus Christi and the tip of Texas—where it touches the Mexican border—as Texas's Riviera. Nothing could be further from the truth; this is one of the most deserted and unpopulated places in the United States. But, that's its charm. Except for one solitary highway approaching the shore, Texas maps show a blank: no roads, no towns, nothing but beach wilderness. A Texas Riviera, it is not.

Pavement penetrates North Padre Island for five miles; from then on you're looking at untouched dunes and deserted beaches for 75 glorious miles. Picnicking, camping and driving are permitted on the seashore, except for a five-mile stretch reserved for pedestrians. Four-wheel drives are almost essential here, but they can't be used anywhere except on the beach. (No dune-running, please.) No bridge connects North Padre Island with South Padre Island. When the island terminates, that's it. The wilderness area continues on this neighboring island for many more miles until a highway heads south to the town of South Padre Island.

Approximately the same latitude as Miami Beach, the southern tip of South Padre Island has always stirred the imagination of developers and promoters as the next tourist and retirement bonanza. So far, their optimism has been higher than their successes. To be sure, a wealth of condos, hotels and rental units compete for space with restaurants and souvenir shops, but the expected mass immigration just hasn't happened yet. Not long ago, luxury condos that had been built to sell for $400,000 were going at auction for $70,000 and less. This has changed, of course, with the real estate market leveling out. Real estate brokers say there are still bargains on the market, but few distress sales at this time. Nice condos start at around $50,000, and they can be listed with rental specialists to be rented out while you are traveling elsewhere.

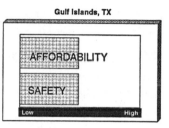

Although the town of South Padre Island looks like a city when first viewed from the causeway that crosses the Laguna Madre from Port Isabel, only about 1,200 residents live here year-round. That figure increases impressively during the season, because over 3,000 condo units are rented out to tourists and visitors, and even in the off-season, a good percentage of the rentals are occupied. During the winter these can be rented for $450, increasing to $800 and up for the summer. Unlike nearby Lower Rio Grande Valley, the peak season is summer, rather than winter. At the crescendo of the tourist crush, during spring semester break, an unbelievable number squeeze into town. Fortunately, miles and miles of camping on the beaches handle the overflow.

The developed portion of the island covers six miles of the southernmost tip, with the remaining 34 miles in deserted dunes and beaches inhabited by RVs, campers and fishermen. The beaches seem endless and gently sloping—great for swimming and surf fishing. By the way, driving the beach is permitted (four-wheel drive recommended) as far as Mansfield Pass. This artificial ship channel created two islands out of one. Local people will argue that an artificial channel doesn't make two islands out of one, but in 1964 the state of Texas officially pronounced it to be two islands, so that settles that. All along the beach fishermen camp and cast bait into the surf for some really great sport fishing.

The Laguna Madre—those bay waters between the mainland and South Padre Island—is said to be jumping with fish such as sand trout, flounder, sheepshead, redfish and croakers. In the town of South Padre

Island and also in Port Isabel you can find charter fishing for sailfish, marlin, tarpon, kingfish and pompano. For those who don't fish, there is plenty to do in the built-up, modern town. Several commercial RV parks accommodate visitors and there is a county park, Isla Blanca, where you can park your rig while you beachcomb for lost pirate treasures.

Since South Padre Island lies at the most southern latitude of anywhere in the continental United States except for the Florida Keys, you might expect it to have a Florida-like climate, particularly since it enjoys a lower summer humidity. But, because the Gulf Stream, the secret to Miami Beach's climate, misses the Texas coast, summers are hotter here and winters cooler. This is more than compensated by the calm and peaceful atmosphere (except during semester break).

Port Isabel   On the mainland across a short causeway is Port Isabel (pop. 5,000). Most retirees choose to live here and make the 2.6-mile drive across the causeway to enjoy South Padre Island without paying premium prices for property. Rents are much less, and year-round accommodations can be found as low as $350 a month. Another advantage to living in Port Isabel is that the island acts as a barrier against storm-driven seas. Stilt construction isn't necessary.

Like all South Texas towns that attract "Winter Texans," Port Isabel's population rises in proportion to the thermometers' fall in the colder sections of the United States and Canada. RV parks begin filling the last of October and stay packed until spring thaw lures the snowbirds back home. Because this is a year-round resort area, several large parks don't empty as they do in the purely winter resort areas. Those with self-contained rigs often prefer to boondock on the island beaches since they don't need electric or water hookups. Just north of town, and for miles up the coast, pristine beaches, all but deserted, invite campers and RV boondockers, offering good surf fishing and quiet times for reading or just sitting and contemplating whitecaps on the gulf's blue waters.

In addition to the climate and beach location, local people point out the low crime rate, lack of rush-hour traffic and serene living as reasons for retirement here. For traffic jams, people need to travel elsewhere.

S. PADRE ISLAND/PORT ISABEL Rel. Humidity: Jan. 68%, July 55%					
	Jan.	April	July	Oct.	Rain	Snow
Daily Highs	69	82	90	82	28"	—
Daily Lows	52	67	75	66		

184

The Rio Grande Valley

After flowing 2,000 miles through Colorado, New Mexico and Texas, the state's most famous river—the Rio Grande—finally empties into the Gulf of Mexico just below South Padre Island. This, the lower Rio Grande Valley, is the domain of motorhomes, trailers and campers—and the yearly destination of the "Winter Texans," those warmth-loving folks who follow the sun south when arctic winds start blowing up north. Their winter target is a 90-mile stretch of valley starting at the Gulf of Mexico and westward to Rio Grande City. RV travelers and snowbirds from the United States and Canada who make the

yearly migration call this place the "Poor Man's Florida." In many ways, this part of Texas does resemble Florida. Lines of palm trees, fragrant citrus blossoms, bougainvillea and other flowering shrubs provide a distinctly tropical flavor. However, temperatures can drop, suddenly and dramatically.

The lower Rio Grande Valley would seem to be an unlikely place to become a popular retirement location because of its stifling summer heat. Many feel that it's all but unlivable from June through August. As evidence, witness the massive exodus of retirees every spring—not to return until summer has faded into late fall. In the coolest part of a summer evening, the temperature here rarely falls below 75 degrees, while it generally climbs into the high 90s during the day. Because of humidity, evaporative coolers are worthless; you must depend on refrigeration units. Yet, despite the hot summers, many retirees are choosing to adopt full-time retirement along the Rio Grande. For them, the pleasant winters make it all worthwhile, and they avoid the hassle of moving twice each year.

Retirement Tradition

Winter is why folks come to the lower Rio Grande Valley. With seemingly endless sunshine, palm trees and other tropical plants gracing the city streets, the ambience is unmistakably subtropical. Balmy breezes from the Gulf of Mexico caress the countryside, perfuming the air with the scent of orange and grapefruit blossoms. Meanwhile, back on the ranch, winds are whipping snow drifts and dropping the chill factor to sub-zero records.

Although most retirees here start off as part-timers, or "Winter Texans," more and more are making their stays permanent and becoming "Year-round Texans." According to the U.S. government, the number of Social Security checks being sent to the lower Rio Grande Valley is up by 16 percent over a three-year period. RV and mobile home parks report twice as many spaces being occupied year-round as ten years ago.

South Texas winter retirement isn't a new concept, not by any means. Midwestern farmers have known about it for years. When snow and ice gripped their fields with bitter winter cold, they arranged for someone to feed the cows and hogs, hooked a house trailer behind the old pickup and headed for the Rio Grande for a winter of leisure and sunshine. Orange groves, palm trees and 80-degree afternoons made for pleasant living while winter paralyzed farming country back home.

The bonus: lower Rio Grande living was (and is) cheap. Local people used to joke that "farmers come down here with a five-dollar bill and a pair of overalls, and don't change either one the whole winter." You don't hear that joke nowadays. Winter retirement means big cash business in South Texas. Social Security, pension checks and millions of outside dollars—American and Canadian—pump well over half a billion dollars into what could otherwise be a sagging economy. Alongside main highways, roadside signs proclaim, "We Love Winter Texans!"

Farmers are no longer a majority today; retirees come from all walks of life and all parts of the continent. More come each year, mostly in RVs. A few years ago, 50,000 snowbirds wintering in the Brownsville-Harlingen-McAllen area was considered a record. But today the number tops 300,000! Don't worry, there's always room for one more. More than 500 RV parks compete for snowbird tenants, some parks have several hundred spaces each. In the town of Mission—just southwest of McAllen—fewer than 100 RV parks accommodate more than 10,000 RVs. Yet the year-round population of Mission is only 25,000!

This floating population has become a political force to reckon with. Because Texas requires only a 30-day residence to become a legal voter, a significant number of folks register to vote as soon as they finish hooking up electricity and water to the motorhome. These enthusiastic voters become involved in brisk political campaigning, providing swing votes to elect local officials and pass ordinances that affect their Winter Texan communities. You can be sure local politicians and city officials are responsive to the wishes of the Winter Texans. They aren't just retirees, they are *voting* retirees!

Organized Activities

RV parks of all descriptions abound, with variety to suit everyone's taste. Some are extremely plush, others plain. The fancy resorts routinely offer refinements like Olympic-sized swimming pools, indoor shuffleboard, tennis, dance halls, libraries, pool rooms, sewing rooms and other special halls for recreation and socializing. Even bare-bones parks usually have a rec hall to go with laundry facilities.

Like all RV facilities that cater to seasonal guests, these south Texas parks compete with each other by offering social activities and other amenities. They hold pancake breakfasts, ice-cream socials, square dances and other events to get people mingling and having a good time. If the Winter Texans enjoy spending the season in one park, they are likely to return to the same park next winter. In addition, most visitors come from the Midwest, an area well known for amiability and informality. They quickly form social groups based on individual interests, activities like bridge clubs, bicycling groups and adult education classes.

Learning Spanish is a popular pastime, since Mexico is just across the river. People go in groups and have fun bargaining for treasures and practicing their new language skills. They travel by car, go in RV caravans, by charted bus or airplanes. A high percentage of tourists you'll meet in Mexico, particularly in the northern part, are winter residents of the Rio Grande Valley on excursion. In the summer, when the sun turns Texas sidewalks into griddles, many permanent valley residents seek relief in the cool mountain towns of Mexico. Saltillo, Guanajuato and San Miguel de Allende are favorite summer destinations, where thousands of North Americans convene to rent affordable apartments or small houses, and renew friendships from the last season.

Restaurants in Mexico serve dishes that are unavailable in the United States. Wild game often appears on menus, items such as venison, dove, wild pig and quail. Merchants in Mexico also benefit from this transfusion of greenbacks; retirees are viewed with gratitude and good will. Local police are instructed to be protective of the Winter Texans.

Mexican businesses and city officials want nothing to discourage them from returning with more dollars!

Border Towns

Border towns are famous for being dreary places, with rundown shacks, high unemployment and boarded-up storefronts. This picture was particularly true after the collapse of the Mexican economy and the demise of the Texas oil industry in the 1980s. When Mexico devalued the peso, merchandise on our side of the border became too expensive for Mexican consumers; they no longer crossed over to shop in U.S. stores. For a time, this was economically disastrous for American businesses that depend on cross-border commerce to stay healthy. Commerce has improved lately, since the Mexican government is holding on to the dollar peso ratio. Once again prices on our side are more favorable for Mexicans, and shoppers are again patronizing U.S. stores. For many border areas, it's an up-again, down-again proposition.

However, the lower Rio Grande Valley's economy generally escapes these cyclical economic hardships. Businesses buzz with activity; restaurants and stores teem with customers. Everyone agrees that this prosperity is largely due to Winter Texans' cash. One bank reports that 20 percent of its deposit growth for the last six years is snowbird money. Another bank admits that one-third of its deposits come from transplanted and temporary Texans. The city of McAllen (one of the border towns) estimates that 25 percent of its winter sales-tax revenue comes from visitors. One bank flies a Canadian flag alongside an American flag to acknowledge the importance of the growing number of northern neighbors who winter here.

A final benefit of living here, one that is constantly pointed out by local boosters, is the low crime rate. Robberies, for example, are less than one-fourth the national average. As a temporary retirement area, we highly recommend the lower Rio Grande Valley. For those who can stand the heat, this is an excellent place for year-round retirement.

Brownsville   This is Texas' southernmost city. Its history began in 1846 when General Zachary Taylor established a military base—calling it Fort Brown—to back up our claim that the Rio Grande should have been the western boundary of Texas. However, Mexico took offense at this, insisting that the agreed-upon boundary was the Pecos River, *not* the Rio Grande River. This misunderstanding touched off the U.S.-Mexican War of 1846-1848. Once the war was underway, our diplomats realized that logically, neither the Pecos *nor* the Rio Grande should mark the western edge of the United States. What else could it be but the Pacific Ocean? Stands to reason. After our troops captured Mexico City and explained the revised negotiating position (at gunpoint), Mexican diplomats reluctantly recognized the logic of our argument. Thus we ended up with not only the Rio Grande but also the states of California, New Mexico, Arizona, Nevada, Utah and parts of Colorado and Wyoming.

Today, Brownsville is the Rio Grande Valley's largest city, with a population of around 105,000. Zachary Taylor's military outpost is now the site of the Texas Southmost College. Some of Fort Brown's facilities are in use today as school administration buildings. In addition to the college, the community is served by two excellent hospitals and several senior nursing homes.

The cost of living here is favorable despite unusually high utility rates. Low housing prices account for the difference, with sales figures fully 25 percent below national averages. That's partly because the floating retiree population returns home every summer—they don't buy

houses and settle down for the entire year along the Rio Grande Valley. Supermarket prices are generally moderate, especially for locally grown produce, since this area is the country's top producer of winter vegetables. Year-round apartment and home rentals are inexpensive, although those rented just for the winter are predictably pricey.

Wages are low, as in most border areas, due in part to the availability of eager workers from Mexico who are willing to cross the river and do a hard day's work for minimal wages. Job competition means lower wages, lower costs of goods and services, and a lower cost of living for visitors. Even so, the large influx of winter visitors creates a cornucopia of seasonal jobs for retirees. Employers like to hire employees they won't have to lay off when the season ends; they'll be leaving anyway.

Just across the river is the Mexican city of Matamoros, a favorite shopping target for Winter Texans staying in and around Brownsville. Nightclubs, restaurants, gift shops and stores of all descriptions compete for the Yankee dollar, although lately prices on the Mexican side have been creeping toward Texas price levels. You'll hear praise for Matamoros dentists, whose work is said to be both inexpensive and high quality. Of course, the usual across-the-border doctors and medical clinics administer unorthodox treatment for diseases such as cancer and arthritis. Although the American Medical Association insists that unapproved remedies are worthless, many patients disagree. One man explained, "My doctor back home claims these Mexican clinics can't help my arthritis. Says I'm wasting my money. But he admits there's nothing *he* can do about arthritis, either. So, for a few dollars, I'm betting that the other doctor's wrong. I can't afford *not* to make the bet."

Another benefit of living along the international border is inexpensive prescription drugs purchased in Mexican *farmacias*. In Mexico—as in most foreign countries—many essential medications do not require prescriptions. Even though manufactured by the same drug companies that distribute in the United States and Canada, prices are significantly lower in Mexico. Just one example: a 30-day supply of Enderal—a common medication for hypertension and heart irregularities—costs about a third to a half of what you would pay on the American side of the border. The Mexican government successfully controls drug prices and carefully monitors the sale of medications to prevent unfair profit-taking. (Is there a lesson here for our government?)

Only a 22-mile drive from Brownsville is South Padre Island, the 34-mile barrier island discussed previously. Gulf fishing, boating and beachcombing are popular pastimes here and are very accessible to Brownsville residents.

Mission   "Home of Winter Texans" is one of the ways Mission advertises itself, but the town can't seem to make up its mind, because it also claims the title of "Home of the Grapefruit." It's said that Texas' first citrus orchard started here when mission priests planted trees in 1824 (hence the name "Mission"). The area is indeed famous for its groves of Texas Ruby Red grapefruit. In addition to the sweet aroma of citrus blossoms in December, residents enjoy a particularly colorful Christmas because of the abundance of poinsettias throughout town. The joyful theme of "Tropical Christmas" is celebrated with profuse displays of these colorful plants in public buildings, parks and private homes.

The Mexican city of Reynosa sits across the river from Mission. A popular shopping place for valley residents, Reynosa offers much the same attractions as Matamoros. Some excellent restaurants here serve cuisine unobtainable in the United States, wild game, for example. As is the case in all the border towns, tourist cards or passports aren't required for visits of less than 72 hours unless you travel to the interior of Mexico.

Harlingen   About 30 miles from Brownsville, Harlingen is somewhat smaller, with a population of about 45,000. Like the rest of the Rio Grande Valley, Harlingen's population climbs dramatically during the winter. This city stands out because of its local beautification campaigns and recycling efforts, and thanks to the hard work of its citizensHarlingen won the All-America City award by the National Civic League. Also, a recent survey by *Money Magazine* ranked the city the 20th best place to live in the United States.

This is an area of truck farms, orange groves and more of the prized Texas Ruby Red grapefruit. With a year-round growing season, one crop or another is ready to be harvested at any given time of the year. Harlingen's appearance is similar to that of Mission, with palm trees, colorful bougainvillea and poinsettias brightening the warm Christmas season.

Overall, Harlingen is a nice place for winter retirement even though it requires a longer drive for shopping in Mexico. A compensating attraction is a large greyhound racing park. (Dogs, not buses.) The city also boasts of four PGA championship golf courses plus a 27-hole municipal course and several par three layouts.

When comparing lower Rio Grande Valley housing and year-round rentals, Harlingen turns out to be the most economical of the towns mentioned here. Housing costs are among the lowest in the country. Efficiency apartments were being advertised from $240 and homes from $500 in 1994.

LOWER RIO GRANDE VALLEY			Rel. Humidity: Jan. 68%, July 55%			
	Jan.	April	July	Oct.	Rain	Snow
Daily Highs	70	83	93	84	26"	—
Daily Lows	51	67	76	66		

El Paso Just over four centuries ago, the first Europeans pushed their way north from Mexico and found an easy crossing, or pass, across the Rio Grande into what is now Texas' upper Rio Grande Valley. Early Spanish explorers named the crossing *El Paso del Norte*. When Mexico relinquished claim to the crossing, the U.S. Army established a post here to protect American settlers from marauding Comanches and to oversee the growing business of international trade between Mexico and the United States. Over the ensuing years, El Paso grew from a dusty cow town into a modern city of over 500,000, the largest city on the American side of the 1,933-mile U.S.-Mexico border.

That first military post established a continuing tradition of military presence in El Paso. Fort Bliss, in northeast El Paso, is the home of the U.S. Army Air Defense Center and contributes a huge payroll to keep the economy level. Military families and civilian support personnel live in all sections of the city and make the population very "middle America." When retirement time rolls around, military personnel quite naturally think of El Paso as one of their retirement possibilities. They remember the cleanliness and neighborliness of the city, as well as the affordable real estate. Of course, being military, post exchange privileges and medical facilities for retirees influence their final decisions.

El Paso has several good things going for it. First, the climate is mild, with summers far cooler than those of the lower Rio Grande Valley. You can usually get out in July or August and play a game of golf without risking sunstroke. Lower humidity and a 3,700-foot elevation makes a world of difference.

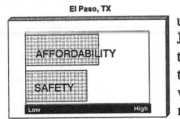

El Paso, TX

Another attraction for retirees is Ciudad Juarez, just across the Rio Grande. Juarez is more than just another border town like Reynosa or Matamoros; it is truly a city. It's even larger than El Paso, with an estimated population nearing a million inhabitants. Juarez's downtown section, situated close to the border, is a bit grungy, with honkytonks, bars, an occasional good restaurant and the inevitable curio and souvenir shops. But when you get away from the old downtown section you'll find modern areas, with broad boulevards, nice restaurants and nice clothing stores. Plus, depending upon the state of the economy, shopping in Juarez can be an experience in bargaining. Some commodities are always cheaper across the border, particularly items like booze, instant coffee and some grocery items. Many retirees make weekly forays across the border to take advantage of bargains. Produce sells at giveaway prices; unfortunately, you can't carry veggies across the border.

El Paso has a delightful way of blending Mexican and Anglo cultures, something that doesn't happen in the lower Rio Grande Valley. Instead of rigid social lines separating Anglo-Saxons and Hispanics, keeping a gulf between U.S. and Mexico—you'll find a congenial mixture of Texas and Chihuahua. Radio and TV announcers on both sides of the border often jump between Spanish and English, never missing a beat. Restaurant menus on both sides of the border do much the same. El Paso restaurants typically offer dishes like pozole or chiles rellenos, and Juarez restaurants are famous for steak-and-lobster dinners and Chinese food. Years ago, when I worked for the *El Paso Times,* my favorite lunch-break restaurant served a great chicken-fried steak. But instead of gravy on the steak, it came with chile con queso sauce!

American modern and old Mexican charm blend to give El Paso a distinctive character. The downtown's wide streets branch out in all directions, and Interstate 10 moves traffic quickly and efficiently through the center of the city. Commercial buildings are modern and crisp, avoiding the garishness and mirrored walls that seem to be in vogue. As you move toward the outskirts of the city, you can't help but be impressed with El Paso's neatness and cleanliness. Most single-family neighborhoods favor brick construction, one-story homes and neatly trimmed landscaping. Housing costs are 11 percent below national averages.

In El Paso's newer sections, away from downtown, you'll find a proliferation of apartment buildings. Like many Texas cities that participated in the savings-and-loan jubilee, condo and apartment construction has been overly enthusiastic, resulting in an over-supply. You'll often spy billboards shouting out special deals to entice renters. Some apartments offer the first month's rent free, or free utilities for the first year, maybe color televisions to bring you into the fold. The best part is the advertised monthly rates: affordable.

When asked, "Why retire in El Paso?" answers include mild weather and healthy, year-round outdoor activities. Besides golf, tennis and jogging, less vigorous, spectator sports include bullfights and horse racing across the river in Mexico. I asked an old friend why he and his wife chose El Paso over other towns where he'd worked, places like San Francisco or Fort Lauderdale, or why they hadn't moved back to their home town in Connecticut.

He smiled wryly as he looked around the spacious, almost-new apartment. "You know what a place like this would cost us in Connecticut?" Before I had a chance to guess, he went on, saying, "At least $750 a month, that's what. A big chunk of my Social Security check would go to make the rent. We'd have to dig into savings every month to buy food. We wouldn't be able to enjoy life if we had to live like paupers."

His wife nodded agreement. "The secret to low-cost retirement is cutting back on housing," she emphasized. "Our rent and utilities here come to about $450 a month. That extra $300 covers groceries and other bills. Actually, we have no problem getting by on our Social Security checks."

EL PASO			Rel. Humidity: Jan. 35%, July 29%			
	Jan.	April	July	Oct.	Rain	Snow
Daily Highs	58	79	95	78	8"	6"
Daily Lows	31	49	70	49		

Central Texas

San Antonio It's difficult to think of San Antonio (pop. 935,000) as being in the south-central part of Texas, because it looks like west Texas to me. Only 28 inches of rain falls on San Antonio, compared to Houston's 45 inches or Port Arthur's 52 inches per year. Dry range country with thorny bushes starts not far from the city limits. Certainly, from here westward, we are looking at the kind of country one expects from the western United States, with brush, cactus and sandy soil. If the "West" doesn't start in San Antonio, then where?

When white men first came here, a Coahuilecan Indian village occupied the bank of a beautiful river, where present-day, downtown San Antonio is located. The river, life-giving and crystal-clear, was shaded by large poplar trees ("alamo" trees in Spanish). The Indians called the river "Yanaguana," or "refreshing waters."

Today, this river is a symbol of San Antonio's fight against urban decay. The downtown river project is a textbook example of how to remedy central core blight. The city completely transformed the river— which was little more than a weed-choked garbage dump a few years ago—and turned it into an elegant shopping and restaurant area. Soaring cypress and cottonwood trees grace the river banks, shading shops, restaurants and hotels. Tourists and residents alike enjoy strolls, boat rides and nightlife along the river banks. The project has revitalized San Antonio's entire downtown section. The Coahuilecan Indians would be proud of the way their river has returned to its "refreshing waters" status.

San Antonio's weather is a plus retirees constantly brag about. Summers are warm, with highs typically in the low 90s. Yet summer evenings are delightful, with temperatures dropping into the high 60s or low 70s; just right for shirt-sleeve evenings and for sleeping without the annoyance of air conditioning. The humidity is moderate, so swamp coolers work efficiently and refrigerated air conditioning isn't absolutely necessary. In the winter, temperatures rarely drop below 40 degrees at night, and afternoons are almost always in the mid-60s, even in the coldest months. For all practical purposes, there is no winter. Snow? Almost none; every three or four years San Antonio catches enough snow to measure, although in 1985 it snowed 13 inches! Rain? Just enough to keep lawns and shrubbery green.

San Antonio, like Austin to the north, enjoys a low cost of living, almost 12 percent below national averages. San Antonio ranks lowest of the top 25 U.S. metropolitan areas—low-cost utilities and real estate are partly responsible for this happy condition. Residential areas flourish on the fringes of the city, with new subdivisions popping up everywhere. The central area and older sections have the biggest bargains in real estate, sometimes in the low $30,000s, yet don't make decisions on price alone; some areas are clearly not suitable for the majority of retirees. Most newcomers prefer to live in the outer ring of newer subdivisions, near one of several large shopping centers. These areas have comfortably high levels of personal safety, as opposed to the inevitable higher crime rate found closer to a city's center. Most San Antonio homes fall in the price range of $40,000 to $70,000, with an average size of 1,400 square feet. Townhouses, for maintenance-free living, price at around $30,000.

Apartments and condo units are overbuilt, with rentals appropriately reasonable. One reason for the abundance of rentals is the enormous military population that is constantly on the move. A few years ago, developers sized up this market and decided to increase the number of rentals. With abundant savings-and-loan money available, apartments and condos sprouted far quicker than tenants.

Medical care here is awesome. The University of Texas Health Science Center is located here, with schools in medicine, dentistry and nursing and research programs in cancer, cardiology and other problems endemic to elderly. This is one of only six sites in the nation that is approved for patients to try experimental

San Antonio, TX

AFFORDABILITY

SAFETY

Low   High

new cancer drugs. The South Texas Medical Center, a 700-acre medical complex, encompasses eight major hospitals, clinics, laboratories, and a cancer research and therapy center. Also there's the world-renowned burn unit at Brooke Army Medical Center at Fort Sam Houston, which receives burn victims from all over the world.

Since its beginning as a Spanish presidio almost three centuries ago, San Antonio has maintained a military tradition. Four air force bases circle the city: Brooks, Kelly Field, Lackland and Randolph, plus Fort Sam Houston, an army post. Brooks Air Force Base is famous in military circles for having one of the finest medical facilities in the country. This alone is an attraction for military retirees and would bring them here even if San Antonio weren't such a nice place to live. Our understanding is that almost 70,000 service personnel and families live in the San Antonio area and at least twice that many retirees. This may well be the largest population of ex-military in the country.

Almost every good-sized town has its share of retirement complexes and life-care communities. But San Antonio also has them for military only. These are non-profit organizations and do not receive direct government funding. We visited one on the western edge of San Antonio, called Air Force Village. Conveniently located across the highway from Brooks Air Force Hospital, this facility provides quality apartments or cottages for a pleasant, life-long environment. Residents—who must be retired air force officers—buy into the complex with a "founder's fee," which starts at $40,280 for a one-bedroom, one-bath unit, up to $83,600 for a deluxe two-bedroom, two-bath, 1,100-square-foot apartment. Then, with a $488 to $1,014 fee (depending on the size of the quarters), the resident is entitled to maid service, physician visits, transportation, all utilities and meals. If it's needed, home health care and food delivery to the apartment are provided, as well as 24-hour nursing home care. It's a once-in-a-lifetime deal.

SAN ANTONIO			Rel. Humidity: Jan. 59%, July 52%			
	Jan.	April	July	Oct.	Rain	Snow
Daily Highs	62	80	95	82	28"	—
Daily Lows	39	59	74	59		

Fredericksburg Seventy-five miles to the north of San Antonio, the town of Fredericksburg (pop. 9,600) nestles in a scenic area of limestone hills covered by junipers and low-growing oak trees. An hour-and-a-half drive to San Antonio—a little further to Austin—takes you to large-city shopping alternatives. Considered one of Texas's most attractive small towns, Fredericksburg was settled by German farmers who moved here when Texas was still a part of Mexico. The pioneers did their best to replicate a Black Forest village, and modern-day residents are determined to preserve and restore their heritage. They've done a good job; tourists come from all over to enjoy the town. A pioneer museum, in an 1849 stone house, displays early-day memorabilia.

An interesting tradition here is the "Fredericksburg Easter Fires." Each year on Easter eve, campfires glow on the hills around the town. The tradition began when Indians camped on the hills overlooking the village, observing carefully as the newcomers constructed their strange village. The Indian's campfires cast ominous glows in the dark. To allay the children's concern, a pioneer mother explained that the campfires belonged to the Easter Rabbit who was busy boiling Easter eggs. That didn't explain why the Easter Bunnies were equipped with tomahawks.

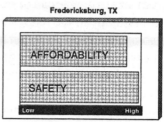
Fredericksburg, TX
AFFORDABILITY
SAFETY
Low   High

When asked about the local weather, one person replied, "Well, we have two definite months of summer and two months of winter, but the rest is all spring and fall. Snow? Almost never!"

Kerrville   Not far away, the small city of Kerrville, with a population of almost 19,000, is one of Fredericksburg's major shopping destinations. Kerrville shares in this part of Texas' panoramic views and rolling hill country, as well as affordable retirement conditions. Its picturesque location has attracted many resident artists who display their works in local galleries and boutiques. Kerrville is quickly acquiring a reputation as an artist colony. One of its museums, the Cowboy Artists of America, may be the nation's only museum that features strictly Western artists.

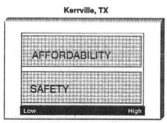
Kerrville, TX
AFFORDABILITY
SAFETY
Low   High

Artistry isn't restricted to visual arts; there are also outdoor theater productions and a performing arts group that brings concerts and other live shows.

Camp Verde, 11 miles south of Kerrville, was the eastern terminus of a camel route that stretched all the way to Yuma, Arizona. This was part of an experiment in overland transportation, an idea whose time has never come.

Austin   Eighty miles north of San Antonio on Interstate 35 is Texas' capital city. Austin's population of 470,000 makes it about half the size of San Antonio, but equally charming. Its downtown centers around an ornate state capitol building and its extensive grounds. More hilly than most Texas cities, Austin is pleasantly landscaped. Modern buildings intersperse with older ones to make an interestingly informal downtown.

Unlike San Antonio, which developed from a haphazard grouping of trails converging at a river crossing, Austin began as a carefully planned city designed to be the state's capital. The downtown is laid out in an easy-to-follow grid, instead of random happenstance.

Austin is becoming widely known as a country music center, second only to Nashville. Not only country and western music, but everything from jazz to reggae can be heard in the clubs around the city, particularly on Sixth Street, the renovated 19th-century historic district. The city is also proud of its reputation as a cultural center in arts other than music. Museums, theaters and art galleries are well attended throughout the city. A symphony, ballet and lyric opera complement the cultural offerings. Medical services are more than adequate, with a dozen hospitals and numerous specialists in attendance.

Austin is a city of universities and colleges. It has a community college, several church schools and the University of Texas at Austin, the largest in the state system. Adult education classes are widely available. Almost 20 golf courses are open to the public, plus another 15 private clubs, the mild climate permitting fairway use throughout the year.

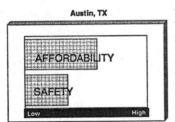

Austin, TX

AFFORDABILITY

SAFETY

Low   High

Real estate costs are similar to San Antonio's, with many pleasant-looking neighborhoods on the fringes of the city. For a time, HUD repossessions dropped prices to a giveaway level, with new, four-bedroom homes going for $57,000, a five-year-old, three-bedroom home for $35,000, and an older two-bedroom, two-bath house for only $27,000. Homes are advertised for nothing down in an effort to secure buyers. These distress sales forced conventional sellers to drop their prices to be competitive. This depressed market recovered to a great extent, but the aftermath still keeps prices in a buyer's market.

Austin is unique in having many retirement communities, at least eight newer ones, most in the north and northwestern edges of the city. They offer retirees a range from luxurious to economical. The services range from full care, with personal care apartments and nursing care units, to ordinary apartment-type living.

As far as we could tell, a place called Hidden Hills was the most expensive. Although not a retirement community per se, its location on Lake Travis and its 18-hole golf course designed by Arnold Palmer has attracted many retirees. (There's good ol' Arnold, with yet another golf course!) Two-bedroom cottages start at $150,000, and some homes are priced at over a million bucks. For this you get high security with guarded gates and in-home security systems linked to the guard station.

A strictly retirement luxury development is located in Lakeway, at the end of World of Tennis Boulevard. (That street name has to tell us something about the place.) Here you must buy in, with a starting price of $97,000 for a small apartment to $200,000 for a home. Then there is a monthly fee of $615 to $890 for single occupancy. For this you get housekeeping, food service, transportation, maintenance and a comprehensive continuum of health care, with nursing care and a medical clinic. Facilities include golf, tennis, swimming, and everything from a beauty salon to a travel agency on the premises.

The lower end of the scale is Heritage Plaza, which is a 90-unit apartment complex that requires no entrance or endowment fee. Apartments begin at $395 a month, which includes planned activities, weekly grocery transportation, a nursing clinic and the supervision of a social worker. For $670 a month they throw in a daily noon meal, housekeeping, laundry and utilities. One-bedroom cottages begin at $435 for single occupancy and $710 monthly for all services. Camlu Apartments is another inexpensive place, with two-bedroom units beginning at $775 a month with paid utilities, daily meals, weekly maid service and shopping transportation.

Highland Lakes   Austin's outdoor recreation centers around the Highland Lakes area, commonly known as the Hill Country. This has long been considered one of the better retirement areas in the state. With 150 miles of water wonderland, a series of lakes stair-step down toward Austin. The lakes area offers abundant fishing and boating as well as wonderful scenery for retirement living. Buchanan Dam (pop. 3,800) is a small resort and retirement community that grew at the construction site of the lake by the same name. This is the largest of the lakes and also the highest. The altitude is 1,025 feet—about 500 feet higher than Austin—high enough to be cooler in the summer, but not so high as to have heavy winter snows. Roads circle the lake, giving access to retirement homes, RV parks and rental properties.

Another retirement possibility, Marble Falls (pop. 4,235) takes its name from the dam that created this particular lake. Sheer bluffs of limestone, granite and marble encompass the lake at this point. Hunting, fishing and camping are popular activities. White-tail deer and wild turkey are said to be plentiful. Nearby Granite Mountain is the source of the distinctive pink and red granite used to construct the state capitol building in downtown Austin. Other lakes in the area are Travis, Austin Town Lake, Canyon Lake and Lake Georgetown.

Georgetown (pop. 12,382) is the largest of the Hill Country retirement towns, about 30 miles from downtown Austin on the interstate. Within commuting distance from the city, Georgetown has many expensive homes along lovely, tree-lined streets. It has an old, historic square with antique stores and boutiques.

Real estate in the Highland Lakes area is affected by the Austin market. At the time of our latest research trip, homes on and near the lakes were selling in roughly the same price ranges as similar places in Austin. On the lakes, as you might expect, prices have held up quite well. As far as we are aware, the lakes are Army Corps of Engineers projects and are subject to the same rules as elsewhere, that is, no docks or ownership on the waterline.

Wimberley Strategically located between Austin and San Antonio, not far off Interstate 35, Wimberley is another excellent retirement choice. The population here is a little over 8,000, large enough for essential services, but it enjoys a small-town atmosphere, with low crime and friendly neighbors. Because it's only 12 miles to San Marcos, that's where most heavy-duty shopping is done, or 45 miles to Austin, about

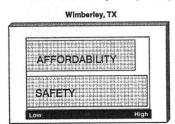

Wimberley, TX

an hour. San Marcos is also the nearest place to purchase bottles of wine or liquor, however local restaurants do serve wines and cocktails by the drink.

Although there is no Greyhound bus service, the county sponsors a service called CARTS, which takes disabled and senior citizens to medical appointments, and even into Austin for shopping and special medical needs. A volunteer ambulance group takes emergency cases to the hospital in nearby San Marcos.

San Marcos is also the location of Southwest Texas State University. The school's music department gives concerts in Wimberley several times a year. Other local events are an annual Crawfish Boil and the Lions Club Market Day, which is held every Saturday from April to December, with 400 booths offering everything from arts and crafts to antiques. Many offer goodies from the back of their trucks or auto trunks.

Wimberley sits at an altitude of 1,100 feet—twice as high as Austin—and therefore enjoys slightly cooler summers and a few inches more rainfall. Like other towns in this part of the country, snow is a rarity. Many of the buildings here are of native stone. In the past two years approximately 200 families have moved in, with 65 percent of the newcomers retirees. Homeowners choose among properties on rivers, hills, on city-size lots or acreages, with homes selling for slightly under national averages. Nearby Woodcreek is a planned community with an 18-hole golf course, tennis courts, clubhouse and other amenities; small homes start at $85,000. Rentals are almost impossible to find, since there are no apartments, just single-family homes. However, there are 29 overnighters and bed and breakfasts in the area, with accommodations ranging from a place with an indoor swimming pool to a log cabin.

A summer community tradition is an outdoor movie theater (bring your own chairs). The Blanco River, lined with huge old cedars and oak trees, passes one edge of town and intersects with Cypress Creek on the other. The rivers are crossed by one-lane bridges, which residents refuse to widen because that would mean cutting some beautiful Cypress trees. The Blanco River's turquoise waters are excellent for swimming, tubing, fishing, and canoeing.

AUSTIN AREA			Rel. Humidity: Jan. 62%, July 64%			
	Jan.	April	July	Oct.	Rain	Snow
Daily Highs	59	79	95	81	32"	1"
Daily Lows	39	58	74	59		

Nacogdoches This town may be located in central Texas as far as its north-south positioning goes, but really Nacogdoches is east Texas in spirit and environment. Here you'll find towering pines, rolling hills, vast blue lakes, cypress swamps and Spanish moss, as well as majestic plantation homes reminiscent of old Natchez and New Orleans. That shouldn't be surprising, since this was the first area of Texas to be settled by pioneers from Tennessee and Louisiana. Their new homes were duplicates of those they left behind. Since few Civil War battles were fought in Texas, war's destruction passed them by, leaving many old historical buildings intact for today's enjoyment.

The oldest town of all is probably Nacogdoches (pop. 28,744), for it was an Indian settlement for centuries before the earliest Spanish explorers passed by. DeSoto's troops stopped here in 1541 and were received hospitably by the city fathers of that time. Today's North Street is claimed to be the oldest public thorough-

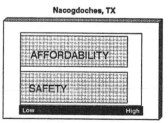

Nacogdoches, TX

fare in the United States, since it was a major route connecting the Indian community of Nacogdoches with other Indian towns to the north. LaSalle's expedition passed over that road in 1687, and Spanish friars established a mission here in 1716. An old Spanish stone fort still stands, now the campus of Stephen F. Austin State University.

The university has 12,000 students and contributes to the city's cultural atmosphere. Many retirees take advantage of the school's program of speakers, concerts and drama presentations. Also important to retirees are two excellent hospitals and a senior citizens' treatment center.

Housing is downright affordable. Because of an expected expansion of the university, optimistic builders overbuilt. Two-bedroom apartments can be found for under $300 a month and houses for just a little more. Three-bedroom houses were going for as low as $45,000. A retirement complex called Pine Lake Estates offered units from $337 a month, with a lot of services thrown in.

The weather is typical Deep South: hot, muggy summers and mild winters. But one retiree said, "Great weather the rest of the year makes up for summer. We have flowers blooming until late November." This part of the country catches about 43 inches of rain a year, enough to keep things pretty without making it too soggy.

A couple of years ago, Nacogdoches was named one of the top ten cities in the United States in which to live by *U.S. News and World Report,* so we had to visit to see if we agreed. We did. Something about this section of Texas feels right for retirement. Nacogdoches in particular seems to be vigorous, prosperous and modern, with none of the run-down qualities that characterize some sleepy Texas towns.

The city seems to have just about everything a person would need, except nearness to a big city. Dallas is a three-and-a-half-hour drive, and Houston is two and a half hours to the south. Add another hour to get to Galveston's beaches.

NACOGDOCHES			Rel. Humidity: Jan. 63%, July 57%			
	Jan.	April	July	Oct.	Rain	Snow
Daily Highs	62	79	94	82	43"	—
Daily Lows	41	58	72	57		

Chapter 7

Western Mountains and Deserts

From New Mexico to eastern California, from the Mexican border to Colorado, the Southwest is a geological and scenic wonderland. Distinctive, dramatic arrangements of earth, water and sky blend together, creating landscapes of unforgettable beauty. Sprawling, forest-covered plateaus scarred by awesome canyons contrast with endless expanses of sand, cactus and sagebrush; great man-made lakes sparkle like aquamarine jewels in stark red settings. Badlands, with enormous monoliths, arches and chiseled buttes, imitate mythical cities while snowcapped peaks preside over all. This is what draws retirees to the Southwest (in addition to snow-free winters).

It isn't all unspoiled natural paradise, because modern cosmopolitan cities rise over the shards of ancient Indian ruins and old ghost towns. In many areas, Anglo, Spanish and native American cultures blend to create a spicy potpourri of something distinctly Southwestern. Huge retirement developments with golf courses and Olympic-sized swimming pools (that look as if they've been magically transported from Florida) compete with small, comfortable localities of a few hundred homes.

The word "desert" incorrectly conjures images of Sahara-like sand dunes and desolate sweeps of barren land. True, North American deserts *can* be like that, but rarely are. Over eons, plants and animals have adapted to living in dry country—even in places with four or five inches of rain per year. Trees and bushes survive on little water, flourishing miraculously in a dry desert or mountain environment. The first spring storm makes the desert bloom with an unforgettable explosion of colorful flowers and a profusion of green, all of which disappear when the plants withdraw into their water-conserving mode for the summer. Some plants have developed tough skins that prevent precious water from evaporating and thus stay green year-round.

Animals, too, have adapted. An amazing variety of reptiles, mammals and birds do perfectly fine in the desert. Some survive the fierce summers by conserving body energy during the heat of the day, then foraging and exercising in the cooler hours of the morning and evening. Other species developed patterns of migration, spending summers in northern or coastal areas where the weather is cool and damp, and then wintering in the pleasant warmth of the desert.

Therefore, it should come as no surprise that the famous species *snowbirdus americanus* has also adapted to dry mountain and desert living. Some have adapted to full-time living in the desert, conserving body energy in air-conditioned homes and autos and by foraging at shopping malls or playing golf in the cooler hours of the morning and evening. Midday is for naps. Instead of developing tough skins that prevent precious water from evaporating, these creatures develop sun-tanned skins and sip cool drinks. Evaporation be damned!

Arizona and New Mexico are favorite winter destinations, although a growing number of retirees choose to live there year-round. Two things you can count on: summer heat and abundant winter sunshine. Phoenix averages 295 days a year of sunny or partly sunny days. Winters are gloriously warm, but daily *summer* temperatures average over 100 degrees! We can't have everything. Fortunately, relative humidity in Phoenix is as low as you can hope to find. This low humidity is why places like Phoenix and Las Vegas are adding permanent residents like crazy, while parts of the Rio Grande Valley double the population in winter, only to lose it again in the summer.

Relative humidity is the key to desert and dry mountain environments. Humidity affects temperature by making it *appear* to be warmer or colder than it really is. Studies show that a 95-degree day in a place like Las Vegas (at 20 percent humidity) is perceived by the body as fairly comfortable. Yet a 95-degree day in Florida (at 75 percent humidity) would be *perceived* as 115 degrees! No wonder people sit in front of their air conditioners in Florida!

The Southwest mountain and desert country was made expressly for snowbirds. When the first days of fall turn frosty in their home towns, they pack up their golf clubs, tennis racquets and suntan oil and head for the Southwest. Many mobile home parks in places like Yuma, Arizona, report that 90 percent of their residents arrive in October and November and are gone by April.

The mobile home makes a perfect winter retreat for the snowbird, inexpensive to buy and park. In hot areas, most parks reduce rents during the summer, making it convenient and affordable to leave your winter retreat sitting empty until next season. With low-maintenance desert landscaping, homes can be shut up for several months without the yard becoming shaggy. Cactus seldom requires mowing; rocks need little water.

All desert retirees, however, are not wanderers. Of those folks who buy conventional homes in places like Phoenix and Las Vegas, only about 5 percent regularly travel to cooler climes for the summer.

Arizona

This is a state with scenic variety: evergreen-covered mountains; peaks with a foot of winter snow; deserts with forests of cactus; mineral-rich, shaded valleys; gently or rapidly flowing, year-round streams and rivers; and America's greatest natural wonder, the Grand Canyon. This is also a state with human variety: one-seventh of the United States native American population resides here, as do generous portions of Spanish speakers and newcomers from across the United States and Canada. Add to this the benefits of mild winters and a strong senior citizen political presence and support structure, and you have a state where retirement is a growth industry.

ARIZONA TAX PROFILE
Sales tax: 5% to 7%, food, drugs exempt
State income tax: graduated from 3.8% to 7% over $150,000
Property taxes: range between 0.8% to 1%
Intangibles tax: no
Social Security taxed: no
Pensions taxed: private employer pensions fully taxed; governmental pensions receive $2,500 exemption; allows personal tax credits
Gasoline tax: 18¢ per gallon

Southern Arizona: Sonoran Desert Living

Arizona's southern towns are strongly flavored by both their social and geographical surroundings. First off, towns here are often just across the border from Mexico. This means that the charm of the Spanish lifestyle is evident in local architecture, food, and language. This nearness to Mexico also allows for easy cross-the-border daytrips for shopping and touring (see the Rio Grande Valley section of the Texas chapter for more details). Secondly, the local Sonoran desert environment provides a mix of classic vistas of desert valleys and mountains with scenes of extensive irrigated croplands, one of the region's major industries.

Bisbee   When I first wrote about Bisbee, the town had just suffered a financial disaster. At one time homes sold, completely furnished, for as little as $500. If nobody had the $500, homes were sometimes abandoned without even bothering to lock the doors. By the time we visited, things had taken a turn for the better, with retirees coming in to buy the cheap real estate and to rebuild the town. Bisbee made a dramatic switch from an abandoned mining town to its newer role as a retirement "discovery."

Revisiting a few years later, we found even more retirees had selected Bisbee for permanent homes. This increase in retiree population encouraged even more activity in services and organizations serving retired people. Of course, this wave of bargain-hunting home-buyers pushed selling prices up. But since prices started at an incredibly low level, real estate is still an excellent buy.

More than just a place of bargain housing, Bisbee's colorful history matches its picturesque desert-mountain setting. Tucked away in a canyon in the southeastern part of Arizona, only a few miles from the Mexican border, its narrow, winding streets present a classic style of mining towns of the late 19th century. The buildings are a mixture of authentic Victorian and western mining camp, with brick and clapboard construction dating from the 1890s and even earlier. Because of its steep hills and ornate Victorian construction, people often describe the town as having a certain San Francisco atmosphere—without the cable cars, of course.

Once a wild, wide-open city of 20,000 miners, merchants and adventurers intent upon making their fortunes, Bisbee's pace today is slow and quiet. Since the town is off the standard tourist track, relatively few visitors disturb the ghosts of yesteryear. A stroll through Bisbee's narrow streets is like stepping into the past. Night sounds are muted, and after midnight the streets are all but deserted. Yet, it's far from a ghost town. Retirees express great satisfaction with Bisbee's balance between leisure and recreation.

What happened to change Bisbee? Disaster struck quite suddenly, beginning in 1975, when Phelps-Dodge, the mining company that sustained Bisbee's economy, ceased operations. Panic struck the hearts of the canyon's households. Families began leaving in droves—sometimes abandoning their houses and furniture. If Bisbee hadn't been the county seat, disaster would have been total.

This collapse happened near the end of the "flower child" movement of the '60s and '70s. Word circulated through the underground that

Bisbee was a great place to "be." Young adventurers, intellectuals, artists and a few loafers floated into town on a wave of fading idealism. Some bought furnished homes from $500 to $5,000; others squatted in vacant houses.

When retirees heard about these bargains, a new wave of emigration to Bisbee began, yet some of the first wave didn't want to leave. These "kids" are now in their 40s and 50s, with graying hair, moving inevitably toward senior citizen status. Fortunately for Bisbee, those who stayed were loaded with talent: artists, writers and intellectuals. Enough creative people stayed to give Bisbee the reputation and flavor of an artist colony. Today's population has stabilized at just over 8,000.

Be aware that the days of bargain homes are long gone. Of course, fixer-uppers can still be found, and satisfactory housing can easily be had for under $50,000. Remember that the really old, historic places can require a lot of remodeling to bring up to acceptable standards. Yet, for many people, renovating and rejuvenating an old house is enjoyable, a chance to allow artistic and creative abilities to run rampant. And, at the price you pay for an old home, you can afford to be creative!

A community college located a few miles east of town offers numerous activities for senior citizens. Several excellent restaurants, with authentic period settings, do good business. Bisbee even has a nine-hole golf course. Regretfully, I didn't see the golf course, and I often wish I had. I just can't imagine where they would find enough level ground, or enough grass, for even one green!

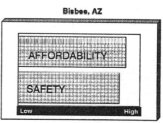

Bisbee, AZ

Medical facilities are impressive for a small town: a 49-bed hospital with eight full-time doctors and an ambulance service. Other medical professionals include five dentists, two optometrists, a chiropractor, and an osteopath. The town has a daily newspaper to keep up with local and national happenings.

The climate is excellent, with enough altitude to keep the summers pleasant, plus low humidity to make the winters brisk, but not bitter. During our January visit the thermometer dropped into the 40s one night, yet we walked around town in light sweaters, feeling perfectly comfortable. Many summer residents come here from Phoenix and Tucson, fleeing the baking, 100-plus degree, July-August season. One reason for the cooler summer temperatures is that the steep canyon walls cast early shadows across the town to block the afternoon heat of the desert sun. A sign painted prominently on one of the downtown business buildings proclaims that Bisbee has the best climate in the world.

BISBEE			Rel. Humidity: Jan. 32%, July 28%			
	Jan.	April	July	Oct.	Rain	Snow
Daily Highs	60	80	96	82	4"	2"
Daily Lows	37	47	71	57		

Ajo   About 100 miles west of Tucson and 100 miles south of Phoenix is another Phelps-Dodge mining town: Ajo. Once a prosperous community of skilled miners and workers employed in the huge open-pit copper mine, the town boasted a population of more than 10,000 people. Its history dates to 1854 with the discovery of copper ore, but it didn't really boom until new recovery methods were adopted after the turn of the century.

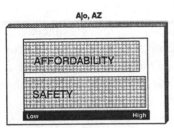

Suddenly, in 1984, the bubble burst—just as it did earlier in Bisbee. The mining company announced the closing of its mines and smelter operations. Caught without regular paychecks, the townspeople wasted no time in packing their belongings and leaving for greener pastures. The bustling town dwindled to a skeleton of its former self, down to 2,800 residents.

Since most houses in town belonged to the mining company, used as employee housing, there wasn't a mass abandonment of dwellings as happened in Bisbee. But the company homes went on the real estate market as low as $13,000 for a two-bedroom home. Privately owned properties also went for giveaway prices. A real estate broker said, "At one time we had 600 houses for sale. However, now all company-owned homes have been sold."

Even though distress sales have subsided and there aren't as many homes for sale today, Ajo's real estate market never fully recovered. Prices are still rock bottom. As of spring 1994, several homes were offered for less than $30,000, and $40,000 would buy a substantial residence. Since retirees purchased most of these homes, the town has embarked upon a new career—as a retirement center. Today, the population is reaching 8,000, about half retirees. "The nice thing about Ajo," said a retired couple, "is that we have a mixture of young and old. We have about 600 children in our school, and many young adults to balance out the social scene."

An oasis in the vast Sonora desert, Ajo sits near the edge of the 300,000-acre Organ Pipe National Monument. The town centers around a pleasant garden plaza, with huge palm trees planted in 1917 when the copper company rebuilt the town. (Originally, Ajo was located elsewhere, but when copper was discovered underneath the town, the mining company promptly moved everything.)

Residents keep in touch with the world via cable TV (with about ten channels), a weekly newspaper and daily delivery of the Phoenix and Tucson papers. An interesting transportation development is La Tortuga Transit, a rural transportation bus project that connects the town with Tucson and points in between. A community health center is open daily from 8 to 5, with a doctor on call around the clock. Helicopter service is available for emergency hospitalization in either Phoenix or Tucson.

The weather is typical of the Arizona desert. The local chamber of commerce describes Ajo as "the place where summer spends the winter" or "the town where warm winters and friendly smiles await you." The chamber of commerce also claims that Ajo is noted for having the best climate in the country, with warm winters and continuous sunshine that other parts of Arizona cannot equal. Notice that the emphasis is on the *winter* climate. Since I've never been there in the summer, I can only go by statistics, but these tell us that it gets hot there.

AJO					Rel. Humidity: Jan. 32%, July 28%	
	Jan.	April	July	Oct.	Rain	Snow
Daily Highs	66	82	100	86	6"	2"
Daily Lows	40	50	74	56		

Tucson Sitting in a high-desert valley surrounded by mountains, Tucson's elevation of 2,375 feet guarantees an agreeable year-round climate. Its dry air and rich desert vegetation qualify it as one of the nation's finest winter resorts. Its 420,000 inhabitants make Tucson a moderately large city, and it is still growing. The fastest-increasing age group here is the over-60 crowd, which used to account for 20 percent of the population but is now pushing 30 percent. Since it's the over-60 group who are most likely to vote, it's no surprise that senior citizens get fair treatment in this city. The well-appointed Tucson Senior Citizens' Center clearly shows the attention that city politicians show retired people.

The University of Arizona, located in Tucson, greatly enriches the community's educational, cultural and recreational life. Classes, lectures, plays and concerts are an ongoing boon to retirees. The state's only opera company is based in Tucson, and a light opera company stages Broadway musicals.

Another favorable aspect of Tucson retirement is a below-average housing market. Buyers have a wide selection of neighborhoods ranging from inexpensive to out-of-touch-with reality. The warm and pleasant winters don't demand much in the way of heating costs, but this will be offset by air conditioning in the summer.

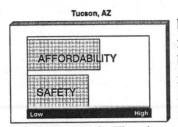

Tucson, AZ

Tucson is also a popular place for mobile home living. The newspaper's classified section usually has listings from mobile home parks advertising spaces for rent, something rare in many metropolitan areas. A space in one of Tucson's adult mobile home parks can be found for as low as $125 a month. The nicer ones charge more, with $180 considered a fairly high rent. Compare this with $350 to $400 in some cities and you'll understand what a bargain mobile home living is in Tucson.

With so many mobile home parks to choose from, you would be well advised to do some shopping. Some parks are primarily for working people, and their interests and social lives are intertwined with friends who live somewhere else. Other parks have mostly retired folks, where you'll find plenty of activities and neighborly retirees. Visiting a park residents' meeting or attending one of the bingo sessions can tell you worlds about who your new neighbors might be.

Tucson is also known for its organized retirement and adults-only complexes. With beautifully designed homes, extensive sports centers, shopping and medical facilities, these complexes are small cities in themselves. One adult community, Saddle Brooke, calls itself the "youngest adult community" because it sets its lower age limit at 45 years of age instead of the usual 55. Housing prices in these adult communities range from $70,000 to $170,000. Typically, these complexes feature 18-hole golf courses, shuffleboard, bocci and tennis courts, cardrooms, jogging tracks, exercise rooms and, of course, the ubiquitous swimming pools.

Smaller, apartment-type retirement quarters are available in and around Tucson. They range from places where renters must be "active" to those offering "senior care" concepts, a euphemism for "nursing home." You'll also find the growing concept of life care centers, in which apartments are provided for those who are still active, then rooms with housekeeping care, and eventually nursing care for those who need it.

The Armory Park Senior Citizens Recreation Center (in downtown Tucson) is a model of its kind. Senior citizens take an energetic part in running the center and have no trouble getting all the volunteer help they need. At any one time several hundred volunteers are on call as they try to use everyone's special skills. For example: retired accountants and tax practitioners give free income tax assistance. Others teach handicrafts such as jewelry making, crocheting and painting. A senior citizens' housing authority high rise is across the street from the center and another is planned, making it convenient for everyone to participate.

TUCSON/GREEN VALLEY			Rel. Humidity: Jan. 32%, July 28%			
	Jan.	April	July	Oct.	Rain	Snow
Daily Highs	65	81	98	82	12"	2"
Daily Lows	38	50	71	56		

Green Valley   Located 25 miles south of Tucson on Interstate 19 and 40 miles north of Mexico, Green Valley is an adult, unincorporated retirement community. It sits at an altitude of 2,900 feet at the foot of the Santa Rita Mountains (an Apache hangout in the olden days). Green River has over 18,000 residents, a high percentage of them retired, living in an area eight miles long and two miles wide, divided by the Interstate.

Complete facilities include a huge shopping center, which has a bowling alley. Three 18-hole public courses and two private courses, plus a couple of private nine-hole courses, satisfy that urge for hunting lost golf balls some retirees cannot shake. The rec center for Green Valley is quite comprehensive, with facilities for arts and crafts, sewing, lapidary and photography. A swimming pool, jacuzzi, sauna and exercise room complete the recreational picture.

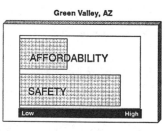
Green Valley, AZ

Green Valley has two highly rated nursing homes and a 24-hour emergency clinic, plus two private clinics and a 60-bed health care center. Tucson hospitals are 20 miles away. There is also a volunteer organization called Friends In Deed (F.I.D.), which assists seniors in sharing their lifetime experiences and skills with one another.

According to the chamber of commerce, sale prices of homes in the past few months were from $30,000 to $300,000. Rentals for unfurnished apartments start at $325 on an annual basis and $900 and up for furnished units on a seasonal contract. Two full-service retirement/apartment complexes are available.

Central Arizona: Between Phoenix and Flagstaff

In between the urban centers of Phoenix and (much smaller) Flagstaff, you'll find small towns and high-altitude resorts and recreation areas where winter skiing, summer fishing, and year-round access to the outdoors is available. This forested, mountainous region is a classic Arizona retirement area, and it's home to the majority of the state's residents, yet once you get off the main highways, you'll be as struck by the lovely, undeveloped landscape as we were.

• Flagstaff
• Sedona
• Prescott
• Payson
• Wickenburg
• Sun City

Sun City   We have investigated large, commercially developed retirement complexes all over the country, but the biggest we've seen is Sun City, near Phoenix. This one goes on and on, with more than 50,000 residents, the vast majority retired!

The homes in this particular development started at about $80,000 and some topped $250,000. Most prospective buyers drove expensive automobiles and looked quite affluent. Many were from parts of the country where a $100,000 home would be a steal. According to a salesman, many buyers come from Florida, having given up on retirement that includes hordes of insects and rainy days. However, we didn't know whether to accept his word, because almost everywhere in the country we went, salespeople kept telling us that a big percentage of their clients came from Florida. On the other hand, in Florida, salespeople claimed their buyers were coming from Arizona!

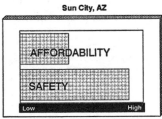

After just one tour through the model homes, one feels tempted to buy immediately. The architecture is bold and imaginative (to match the payments), the furniture is top quality and luxurious. It's terribly easy to stand in the middle of one of these well-lighted and superbly furnished units and imagine how happy you might feel living there.

Although we have reservations against single-generation living, the sales staff presented arguments in favor of it. One of the advantages to buying into a planned community rather than an ordinary neighborhood, they pointed out, is you know that everyone in the development is about your age, and you have a good chance to meet people who need to make friends as badly as you do.

Here you are assured that you won't be bothered by children or teenagers; the community insists upon restrictions against them. You must be over 50 with no dependent children to buy into the development. To further ensure against children, the residents continually vote against property taxes for schools. The result is no children and no schools—only adults. We were told that this has cut teenage vandalism and crime to almost nothing.

The major facilities at Sun City and Sun City West are 11 golf courses (four of them 18-hole layouts), a 40-acre recreation center, the 7,169-seat Sundome Center, a library, seven medical complexes, restaurants, banks and seven other local recreation centers.

PHOENIX/SUN CITY AREA			Rel. Humidity: Jan. 32%, July 20%			
	Jan.	April	July	Oct.	Rain	Snow
Daily Highs	65	83	105	88	7"	—
Daily Lows	39	53	80	59		

Wickenburg   About an hour's drive northwest from Phoenix, the town of Wickenburg is attracting retirees who don't want to accept the neatly arranged, orderly and secure life of Sun City or the bustle of traffic-bound Phoenix. In small-town Wickenburg, they savor the tang of the Old West. The town has been famous for years for its guest ranches (they used to call 'em dude ranches), which go way beyond being simply ranches. They come complete with amenities such as swimming pools, tennis courts, and sometimes a golf course. Although guest ranches are still popular with tourists, the retirement emphasis is on small-acreage places where you can keep and ride your own horses.

Wickenburg has a population of 6,000 and is the shopping center for 20,000 in the area. Health care is adequate, with a 34-bed hospital and many doctors in private practice. Fifty minutes of driving takes you to excellent Sun City hospitals, which specialize in and cater to problems of the elderly.

Land here is abundant and inexpensive, so lots are typically sold by the acre. You may keep horses in your yard if you care to; the local horse population is considerable. You can saddle up and go for a ride through open desert and brush country in almost any direction you care to ride. Since almost all of the surrounding land is owned by the federal Bureau of Land Management (BLM) nobody can interfere with your rides. You don't know how to ride horseback? No problem, local saddle clubs with friendly members will help you get started. The clubs organize numerous social activities centered around horseback riding, from afternoon rides for beginners to the grueling Desert Caballeros Ride for seasoned horsemen, who come from all over the country to participate.

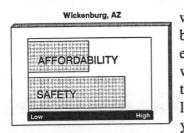

This area is highly mineralized and was the site of a considerable gold rush back in the late 1800s. Several rich mines encircled the town, with millions of dollars worth of the glittering mineral taken from the ground. Although most of the richest locations have been worked out over the years, enough remains to keep the local people busy prospecting and panning for the gold that the old-timers may have missed. Not only gold: other valuable minerals such as silver, copper, turquoise, mercury, nickel and tungsten crop up within a 25-mile radius of Wickenburg. The town celebrates its Wild West past every February with Gold Rush Days, a weekend of rodeos, gold panning and dressing up in period costumes.

Wickenburg has several mobile home parks, with many living units used only part of the year, their owners choosing to live elsewhere during the hot summer months. At one time it was possible to buy a lot and install a mobile home, but nowadays this is frowned upon by the city council.

It does get hot in the summertime, with July and August posting highs of 100 degrees and above. But like most Arizona desert country, low humidity takes much of the sting from the high temperatures. Winter nights can be cold, with frost common, but day temperatures are quite pleasant, with shirt-sleeve weather being the noonday norm, and January highs averaging 63 degrees at midday.

WICKENBURG			Rel. Humidity: Jan. 32%, July 20%			
	Jan.	April	July	Oct.	Rain	Snow
Daily Highs	63	79	103	82	11"	2"
Daily Lows	30	48	70	52		

Sedona   Getting to Sedona from Flagstaff requires a slow, 27-mile drive down the Oak Creek Canyon road, one of the more scenic roads in North America. The pavement winds and twists through thick pine forests and gnarled oaks, with distant glimpses of deep gorges and arroyos embellished with enormous natural stone sculptures. Then, without warning, the view changes to a broad canyon, dramatically carved from colossal red sandstone walls. Fantastic shapes of spires, chimneys and buttes never fail to bring sighs of amazement.

When you reach Sedona, the canyon broadens and drops into a wide amphitheater overshadowed by enormous red, pink and orange rock formations. The rich greens of Arizona cypress, junipers and Piñon pines contrast dramatically with the red background framed by the deep blue Arizona sky—a sight not easily forgotten.

Even though this view of Sedona contained some of the most exciting scenery we had ever seen, there was something curiously familiar about it all. It was as if we had been there before! A strange feeling of *déjà vu* kept nagging at us. (As opposed to our occasional feeling of *vùjá de*: that strange feeling that we've never been here before and hope to God we never come back.)

Suddenly it hit us! We've seen this exact scenery in innumerable Western movies. Countless bands of Indians attacked wagon trains as they lumbered past the red rock formations. Stagecoaches surrendered so many strongboxes full of treasure that we half expected to see a posse arrive at any moment. We could almost smell the buttered popcorn from the concession stand.

Hollywood discovered Sedona and Oak Creek Canyon in the 1920s, beginning a relationship continuing to this day. With all this astounding scenery, it is quite understandable. Actually, it was Zane Grey who discovered Sedona artistically; he fell in love with the place, inspiring his popular novel, *Call of the Canyon*. When Hollywood was ready to film it, Grey insisted that it be shot on location. Since that time hundreds of films and TV commercials have used the dramatic rock formations as a backdrop. A local group, called the Sedona Film Commission, is engaged in promoting the area for more films.

Hollywood artists and technicians came so often that many decided to relocate; some still call Sedona home. This "Red Rock Country" has long attracted artists of all dimensions, who draw inspiration from the country's fantastic vistas.

The number of retirees who select Sedona as their home base is truly impressive. The head of the senior citizens' center estimates that around *40 percent* of the population are retired. "This makes for an interesting mix of retired folks, artists, New Age devotees and business people," he said.

Until recently the town was unincorporated, divided by county lines and governed by differing county ordinances. When Sedona officially became a separate town, a new energy of politics enlivened the community, with vigorous exchanges of opinion and political alignments. "We all have at least one thing in common," said the senior citizens' president, "we are all lovers of the outdoors." Living in Sedona, you couldn't be otherwise.

The town has around 8,100 residents, although the business district and facilities make the town seem much larger. Tourism is big there, and tourist money supports an unusually wide range of restaurants (35 of 'em), plus two nine-hole and two 18-hole golf courses, as well as five tennis club resorts. These are facilities that wouldn't be there were it not for tourist dollars.

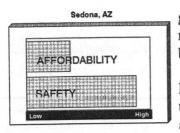

Sedona, AZ

AFFORDABILITY

SAFETY

Low   High

Sedona surely is a place to cultivate latent talents or to appreciate the artistic talents of others. Sedona has between 200 and 300 resident artists, which accounts for the 35 art galleries and an exceptionally active community art center. Two theater groups present year-round performances, plus several ad hoc performances by a senior citizen center group. Another theater group presents outdoor performances on summer evenings.

A local arts and cultural commission tries to focus the efforts of all talented people in the community into interesting, year-round projects. The Theater and Music wing of the Artists and Craftsmen Guild presents programs ranging from jazz to the classics, and the arts center holds monthly art exhibitions to augment the many art galleries in town. Other highlights of the seasons are the two-day Hopi Artists Gathering, a sculpture show, the Native American Arts and Crafts Fair and the Sedona Chamber Music Festival. Each fall, internationally renowned musicians gather to present a day of musical celebration called "Jazz on the Rocks."

Camping, fishing and hiking are exceptionally popular and accessible, because 77 percent of the countryside is government forest service land—open to everyone. The wilderness begins at the edge of town.

A new medical facility is under construction, but until it's completed, the closest ones are in nearby Cottonwood and Flagstaff, 27 miles to the north (on the slow winding road). But the area does have paramedics, ambulances, an out-patient health care center, and a medical evacuation helicopter. Also, an adequate number of doctors, dentists and optometrists take care of residents.

Sedona has grown rapidly in recent years, with retirees and artists forming the bulk of new residents. As a result, property prices have kept pace with growth. This is not a place to look for bargain-basement real estate; views like this do not come dirt-cheap. Some are expensive showplaces, constructed to take full advantage of the natural beauty of the panorama, but you'll also find less costly homes that do quite the same. Manufactured homes start at $45,000 and go up to $130,000; conventional homes on quarter-acre lots start at $125,000. One prestigious development asks $315,000 for its entry-level homes, $900,000 for its top-of-the-line places, with building lots starting at $160,000.

Expect to pay from $800- to $1,200-a-month rent for a house and $500 for an apartment. In nearby Cottonwood, prices are considerably less, with apartments going for $370 for a furnished two-bedroom with a pool.

Since growth has been recent, most construction is new and well maintained. People there understand the beauty and practicality of natural landscaping to blend their homes into Sedona's beauty. (By that I mean the desert landscaping eliminates mowing lawns.)

The altitude at Sedona is 4,300 feet—that's 3,200 feet higher than Phoenix, only two hours away by car, and 2,700 feet lower than Flagstaff, which is less than an hour away. This altitude means warmer winters than Flagstaff and cooler summers than Phoenix. (Some guidebooks list Sedona as being at a 4,400-foot altitude. Since the town slopes downward, it all depends upon where you measure.)

SEDONA				Rel. Humidity: Jan. 59%, July 39%		
	Jan.	April	July	Oct.	Rain	Snow
Daily Highs	55	72	95	78	17"	9"
Daily Lows	30	42	65	49		

Prescott   Sedona's rival in Arizona mountain retirement is Prescott, a few miles to the southwest. Its setting is as spectacular as Sedona's but with a different flavor. Instead of desert scrub, cactus and dramatic red rock formations, Prescott is surrounded by jagged peaks, sometimes snow-covered, and a forest of ponderosa pines (reputedly the largest in the world) overlooks the city. Prescott's movie-set panorama not only equals Sedona's, but its residents claim the weather is better; the four seasons are more sharply delineated. The elevation here is

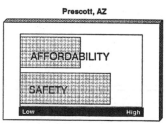

about 1,000 feet higher, which means cooler summers, with daily highs rarely climbing out of the 80s and dropping to the 60s every evening. On the other hand, winters are colder, with several snowfalls every year.

Our last visit to Prescott was in January, two days after a three-inch snow. The sky was brilliant, most of the snow gone after two 60-degree afternoons, although it still looked pretty covering the ground among the ponderosa pines. We found housing prices somewhat lower than Sedona, with an abundance of rentals for those who want to try the area for a few months before making any decisions. This is an older town—founded back in the 1860s—and it has neighborhoods of Victorians and many areas of modest, smaller homes. Since the surrounding area is uneven, most homes are custom, with few tract models constructed. For exceptional bargains in housing, nearby Chino Valley is the place to look.

Prescott likes to think of itself as a small town, but it's actually a good-sized place—30,000 local population, 70,000 in the shopping area. As such, it's able to provide a multitude of services for its citizens, including a museum, a concert hall, and a 110,000-volume library that would be the envy of many larger cities. Yavapai College, a two-year institution, offers a non-credit "retirement college" with 900 students over the age of 62. There are also a liberal arts college and an aeronautical university in the area. Health care is above average here, with nearly 100 physicians and surgeons and a 129-bed hospital. Several golf courses are part of the recreational scheme, along with hiking, camping, fishing and horse trails. Should you be unable to control the urge, 7,600-foot Granite Mountain offers exciting rock-climbing opportunities.

PRESCOTT			Rel. Humidity: Jan. 59%, July 40%			
	Jan.	April	July	Oct.	Rain	Snow
Daily Highs	51	68	90	74	13"	16"
Daily Lows	24	36	61	42		

Payson A third candidate for Arizona mountain retirement is Payson, to the east of Sedona and Prescott. Sitting at about the same altitude as Prescott, at 5,200 feet, Payson shares the same four-season climate. It also is bordered by the Tonto National Forest with its ponderosa pine wonderland. Summers are pleasant, as you might expect in a high altitude; winters are mild enough for hiking, fishing or horseback riding, with occasional snows for cross-country ski treks. The town of Payson is more heavily wooded than its competitors to the west.

Retirees here have plenty of kids their own age to play with. Almost 60 percent of the population is over 55 years of age. The chamber of commerce utilizes retirees, with 29 volunteers working in the chamber office. "We couldn't operate without 'em," said the local chamber manager. Because of the older population here, the local hospital is in the process of enlarging and becoming a cancer treatment center for northern Arizona.

This is the place for outdoor sports, with the spectacular Mogollon Rim just a few miles to the north, where hunting, fishing, hiking and sightseeing are legend. For indoor sports, a nearby gambling casino, operated by the local Indian tribe, brings revenues to the community as well as affording entertainment at the casino's 476 slot machines. A bus service connects the area with Phoenix, some 94 miles to the south.

PAYSON			Rel. Humidity: Jan. 59%, July 39%			
	Jan.	April	July	Oct.	Rain	Snow
Daily Highs	59	78	95	80	13"	30"
Daily Lows	26	40	66	45		

Flagstaff   North of Sedona, and close enough to be a strong cultural influence, is the city of Flagstaff. At 7,000 feet altitude, it receives full mountain winters, averaging 97 inches of snow. Because of the high altitude and sunny days, the melt-off is said to be rapid. Summer highs seldom top 80 degrees, while nearby Phoenix cooks at over 100 degrees. Summer evenings are always cool, with low humidity taking the bite out of a brisk winter. Housing costs are higher than normal, but some terrific buys can be found out in the country, nestled in pine forests.

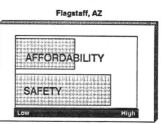
Flagstaff, AZ

Flagstaff is a beautiful, modern city with lots of tall pines and the San Francisco Peaks rising 12,670 feet to provide a breathtaking backdrop. For the outdoor sportsman, fishing and hunting opportunities are without equal. A mid-sized university and a symphony orchestra contribute to a cultural ambience under leadership of the Flagstaff Arts Council and its comprehensive performing arts program.

FLAGSTAFF			Rel. Humidity: Jan. 59%, July 39%			
	Jan.	April	July	Oct.	Rain	Snow
Daily Highs	42	57	82	64	21"	97"
Daily Lows	15	26	50	30		

Western Arizona: Colorado River Retirement

After the wild Colorado River exits from the Grand Canyon, it heads south toward Mexico and the Sea of Cortez. Along the way, the Colorado is captured by a series of dams that provide peaceful lakes, contrasting nicely with the desert hills and shaded canyons that enclose the river.

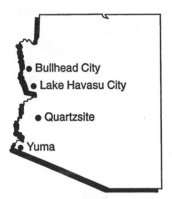

Along this stretch of waterway—from the Arizona town of Parker on the south to the Nevada town of Laughlin on the north— growing numbers of retirees and snowbirds settle in every winter. The numbers increase every year, with more and more buying homes and staying year-round. Places like Bullhead City and Lake Havasu have grown from small clusters of trailers and fishing shacks—with catfish and mallards as the only major attractions—into virtual cities with all the facilities needed for comfortable retirement.

Lake Havasu City This all started when Robert P. McCulloch was flying over the area in search of a place to test his motors and spotted an abandoned army air corps landing strip, which is now the airport of Lake Havasu City. In August 1963, McCulloch purchased 16,630 acres of virgin territory on the Arizona side of the lake and began designing a city. At first the idea of relocating in an isolated desert town seemed outlandish, but gradually the notion took hold and folks began buying lots and building winter homes.

From these unpretentious beginnings, Lake Havasu City has boomed to a city of over 20,000 full-time residents. Houses and condos, trailers and mobile homes, businesses and services of all descriptions appeared

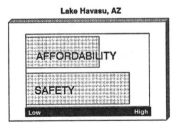

as if by magic. An estimated 6,000 to 8,000 winter residents swell the population and add to the general prosperity.

Despite all this growth, housing costs are generally lower than in other metropolitan areas of Arizona and markedly lower than comparable housing in southern California. According to the Lake Havasu Board of Realtors, single-family detached homes range in price from $45,000 to $400,000 (for golf course sites), with an average selling price of $65,000. Townhouses and condominiums are available from $35,000. Apartments and home rentals are plentiful and available from $275 to $700 per month. Residential lots average around $9,000.

Because of the high number of retirees, the Lake Havasu area enjoys a more complete health care system than ordinarily found in communities of similar size. A 99-bed acute-care hospital staffed with 35 physicians and a 120-bed nursing center serve the community. The hospital is in the process of expanding by 50 percent.

Mobile home and RV parks dot the riverbanks, each with its own boat loading ramp and nearby bait shop. By the way, boating and fishing aren't the only sports enjoyed in Lake Havasu. Several golf courses and at least one bowling alley will keep you active. A bustling senior center provides a dial-a-ride service in addition to the customary bridge games, arts and nutrition facilities. A community college offers fee discounts to senior citizens, and some activities are coordinated with Arizona State University, including drama performances, concerts and lectures.

LAKE HAVASU CITY			Rel. Humidity: Jan. 28%, July 22%			
	Jan.	April	July	Oct.	Rain	Snow
Daily Highs	68	85	104	90	3"	—
Daily Lows	42	55	79	62		

Bullhead City Sitting across the river from each other, Bullhead City and Laughlin, Nevada, are an odd-couple combination of quiet residential and high-life gambling personalities. Both places are booming—Bullhead City's population was about 27,000 at last count. New businesses open yearly, ensuring adequate shopping for the area.

Laughlin is the southernmost point in Nevada where you can gamble, and an enormous percentage of the patrons are retirees. They come with canes, wheelchairs and even walkers, all determined to make a killing. The casinos long ago discovered that putting slot machines and senior citizens together can be a lucrative proposition.

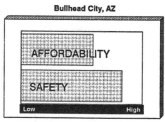
Bullhead City, AZ

Until the casinos began riding high, Bullhead City was a sleepy fishing village, not much more than a scattering of winter retirement places and fishing marinas. But with Laughlin constantly needing more employees for motels and casinos, Bullhead City's growth kept pace as workers and retirees increased their numbers. Today, Bullhead City is in the process of becoming a *real* city and a viable retirement choice. Communication with the outside world is facilitated by an airport on the Arizona side, which permits commercial jetliners to land.

Because Bullhead City grew haphazardly as opposed to Lake Havasu City's carefully planned growth, it has less order. Yet, for the retirement community, that seems to be okay. A new extended-care facility for senior citizens operates in conjunction with Bullhead Community Hospital and is located across the street from the hospital. Four golf courses serve the area.

Yuma Yuma, the last of the Colorado River towns, anchors Arizona's southwest corner, where the mighty Colorado crosses into Mexico on its way to the Sea of Cortez. At this point, the river loses some of its majesty. Much of its flow has been siphoned off along the way to irrigate truck farms, supply drinking water to dozens of communities and make ice cubes for gambling casinos. A sleepy little desert town just a few years ago, Yuma's development can be described as explosive. Since 1980, its population increased by 30% to today's 57,000.

Only the center part, or "old town," shows evidence of its age and historic past. Everything else looks brand new. Originally described as "the great crossing place of a very wide and treacherous river," this was a trading center for early-day adventurers and settlers.

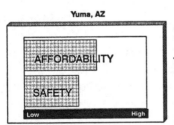

Because of its low desert altitude (only 138 feet), summers here are exceptionally hot. Throughout the year, residents expect just a little more than three inches of rain. Make no mistake, this is desert!

Yuma's winter population triples, as snowbirds from all over the country descend upon the area, bringing motor-homes, trailers and campers. But like the Rio Grande Valley area, Yuma convinces many snowbirds to nest for year-round retirement. Housing costs are exceptionally low, and the cost of living is below average. Median home prices are 18 percent below average, balanced by utility costs 18 percent above average. In 1994, there were in excess of 700 dwellings on the market with prices starting at $35,000 and a median price of $69,000.

Many retirees take advantage of nearby Mexico for inexpensive prescription drugs, dental care and experimental medications not yet approved in the United States (although most have been in Europe). A Marine Corps base is located in the city limits, sharing its runways with private and commercial aircraft. Residents are treated to an interesting display of Marine fighter jets and airliners alternating on take-offs. This base provides PX, commissary and medical care for military retirees.

For gaming activity, Yuma Greyhound Park presents live dog racing and pari-mutuel betting on horses as well as greyhounds. Then there's the Cocopah Gaming Center, a tribal casino south of Yuma on Highway 95. For the academically inclined, a state college, a state university and two private colleges fill the need.

YUMA				Rel. Humidity: Jan. 28%, July 22%		
	Jan.	April	July	Oct.	Rain	Snow
Daily Highs	69	85	107	91	3"	—
Daily Lows	43	56	80	62		

Quartzsite If you don't believe the RV craze has been taken over by retirees, just visit Quartzsite, Arizona, in the winter. This interesting snowbird location, 35 miles south of the Colorado River town of Parker, is inundated by incredible numbers of RV enthusiasts escaping cold and snow. Thousands of RVs congregate, forming a new community each winter. About one million people, mostly retired, will visit Quartzsite during the winter season. When spring rolls around they move on, leaving the desert landscape once again empty and forlorn.

South of town is a place called La Posa Recreation Area, a government-supervised, long-term camping area. Approximately 11,000 acres of public land here have been made available for RVs. Campsites are undeveloped and unmarked; you pick your own location among the sagebrush and mesquite. The setting is beautiful and quiet, and the fees are right: no charge for a 14-day period or $50 for the entire season from October 1 until May 31. At other times the camping is free.

Nevada

Ghost Towns and Prospecting

Ghost towns are interesting relics of Nevada's past. A favorite pastime among Nevada retirees is exploring these historic sites and the nearby mines that once supported the towns. These are fun places to search for old purple-glass bottles and other treasures discarded by yesterday's miners. Some ghost towns are marked by shells of buildings, roofless and disintegrating with time. Others are found only by studying maps and looking for old dumps and traces of

NEVADA TAX PROFILE
Sales tax: 6.5% to 7%, food, drugs exempt
State income tax: no
Property taxes: about 1% of appraised value
Intangibles tax: no
Social Security taxed: no
Pensions taxed: no
Gasoline tax: 23.5¢ per gallon

foundations. The dumps, incidentally, are the best places to find old bottles and artifacts.

Many retirees go one step further and enjoy prospecting and mineral collecting. This is not only fun, it is healthy outdoor recreation that doesn't require special athletic skills. Because the desert and mountain terrain is usually free of vegetation, prospecting is an easy matter. Classes in mineralogy are available in Reno's adult education programs and at the local university, to prepare you for some serious rock hunting and prospecting.

Don't think prospecting for valuable minerals is just a dreamy fantasy. It's still possible to strike it rich. Most western silver mines were abandoned back in the 1930s when silver dropped to 25 cents an ounce, and gold mines were closed during World War II on orders of the federal government. After the war, mining activity never regained its momentum; gold and silver mines were left to revert to nature. With today's higher prices, prospects once passed over because of low values could now be valuable. A case in point: my brother, an amateur prospector on a weekend outing, stumbled across a lead-silver outcropping in Death Valley that turned out to be the state's largest silver producer for the 16 years it yielded ore.

Gamblers Beware!

A word of caution: if you have a tendency to go overboard on gambling and to succumb to the fever of chance, then forget Nevada. Go around it, fly over it or go the opposite direction. The round-the-clock excitement

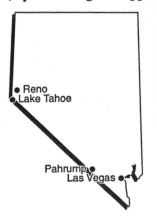

is just too much for some folks. They end up throwing their household money on the tables in increasing amounts in a desperate attempt to recoup their losses. But the odd thing is, when they do hit a lucky streak and win a bundle, the fever won't let them quit. They'll play until they are broke again.

Gambling fever is curious in that many people don't suspect they have a problem until they are exposed to the lure of bouncing dice and whirling slot machines. Nevada banks and finance companies are reluctant to grant loans to newcomers until they've weathered a few months of Las Vegas "conditions." I've seen people who have never gambled in their lives fall apart the moment they hit Nevada.

On the other hand, the majority of Nevada residents handle gambling quite well. Many never even bother to put a nickel in the machines; others take advantage of all the freebies and bargains that the clubs offer to lure customers into the casinos. A common way to handle this is to put aside a certain amount of money that won't dent the budget and spend it on splurges once in a while. One couple said, "We put aside $20 apiece for dinner and some small-time gambling. Our favorite casino serves a great prime rib dinner for $6.95, and the lounge show is free. We have a couple of drinks and put the rest in the nickel poker machines. We never win, but we always have a good time." The other side of the poker chip is the Los Angeles couple who drove to Las Vegas in a $12,000 Chevrolet and went home in a $300,000 Greyhound bus. Now, that's luck.

Las Vegas   Sadly known as "Lost Wages" by chumps who've thrown the rent money across the gambling tables, Las Vegas is gaining a national reputation as much more than a gambling center. Today it is a virtual boomtown. About 60,000 new residents a year arrive—a large percentage retirees—making this one of the fastest growing cities in the country. To accommodate newcomers, about 12,000 houses sprout up annually.

Because of this vigorous growth, retirees easily find part-time— more than just minimum-wage—jobs. Casinos, restaurants and other tourist businesses need part-time help, but the incoming industries and businesses siphon new residents from the labor pool, offering them full-time jobs. The area leads the nation in employment growth with a rate of 9 percent.

As in Reno, casinos give special consideration to hiring senior citizens. The percentage of older employees is impressive. Well, except for the cocktail waitresses, that is, who tend to be young and bosomy. This is certainly age discrimination, but then, you wouldn't care to run around half-naked, delivering booze to a bunch of gamblers anyway, now would you? Personally, I look terrible in one of those frilly tutus, even worse in sequins.

As you might suspect, housing activity has kept up with this influx of newcomers, in fact, it has more than kept up. From its inception, Las Vegas has tended to over-build; optimistic developers keep supply ahead of demand, keeping housing costs under control. Apartments are plentiful, with high vacancy rates. In short, Las Vegas housing isn't inexpensive, but neither is it prohibitive.

Many people who normally might choose Phoenix for retirement are trying Las Vegas instead. When asked why, they gave various reasons, but no state income tax and proximity to southern California headed the list. (Las Vegas is a 5-1/2-hour drive to Los Angeles, compared to Phoenix's 7-1/2 hours. Before long, a privately financed super-train will link Las Vegas and southern California, moving millions of visitors at a fantastic 250 miles per hour!) Other taxes in the state are low, because about 50 percent of all state tax revenues come from the resort, tourism and casino industry. Because of this easy income, Nevada doesn't need corporate-income or personal-income taxes, and its property taxes are among the lowest in the West.

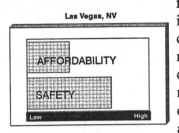

All those questioned about their choice of Las Vegas as a retirement destination included weather in one form or another. Make no mistake, summers in Las Vegas are hot, yet those who retire there maintain that they love it that way.

Because of low humidity and absence of freezing weather, mobile homes are quite practical. Inexpensive evaporative coolers do a fine job during the warm months. Mobile home parks present a wide choice of options, from inexpensive to super-luxurious. During the winter, RV parks fill with cold-weather fugitives, who, as expected, depart for cooler climes come the summer. But, unlike some desert cities, retirees in Las Vegas form a steady, year-round population as opposed to the floating, second-home group found around Lake Havasu.

Las Vegas has several active senior citizens' groups as well as the usual volunteer organizations like R.S.V.P. Local newspapers run regular features covering activities for retirees. Because this is a city instead of a town, senior citizens' centers aren't small and intimate, but they offer a wide range of activities to keep active folks busy and happy.

Surprisingly, Las Vegas' level of medical care is only adequate instead of superb, as is the case in Phoenix or Los Angeles. Las Vegas has a couple of good-sized hospitals, but personally, I would travel to Phoenix for a serious problem. I believe the quality of doctors and hospitals leaves much to be desired. Others who live there agree.

LAS VEGAS/PAHRUMP			Rel. Humidity: Jan. 31%, July 15%			
	Jan.	April	July	Oct.	Rain	Snow
Daily Highs	56	77	104	82	4"	1"
Daily Lows	33	50	76	54		

Pahrump A fast-growing star in Nevada's retirement communities is Pahrump, about 60 miles southwest of Las Vegas. The commercial sector of Pahrump is a loosely scattered clump of businesses spaced widely apart. A casual observer would scarcely guess that a large community of homes, covering perhaps 25 square miles, consider themselves to be part of Pahrump. Two gambling casinos—one large, one catering to locals—provide nightlife for those not willing to travel to Las Vegas.

The closest there is to a town center is what might be called a shopping center, but very small, with a supermarket and some assorted businesses. There are no sidewalks or fire hydrants or other items normally found in a town. It seems as if Pahrump residents want to be isolated, for their homes are located far apart, often on 10- to 20-acre lots, and far off the main highway. Pahrump straddles the county line of Nye and Clark counties. You know when you cross into Nye County, because the architecture styles change. It seems that Nye County has no strict building codes, so homeowners can build any way they please. It makes for some interesting buildings.

Reno Although Las Vegas and Lake Tahoe try to be as formal and glitzy as possible, places like Reno tend to be more informal and relaxed. Except in some of the newer Reno hotel-casinos, neckties and cocktail dresses are rare; western wear—cowboy hats, ornate boots and string ties—are seen about as frequently. This is changing in Reno, to some extent, since the Las Vegas-Atlantic City gambling corporations are attempting to duplicate their luck in Reno. New elaborate and classy casinos are sprouting like magic, but I suspect this will have little effect upon the Reno of the non-tourist.

Reno is an old town, with a deliberately preserved old-West atmosphere. This is a town proud of its rowdy gold- and silver-mining past, a picturesque setting with a backdrop of snow-fringed peaks looming in the distance. Originally, Reno's major business was supplying the booming mining camps that flourished nearby. About the time the mines played out, a new industry arose in the form of quickie divorces. Reno divorces were considered the only practical way to go for an uncomplicated marriage dissolution. As other states liberalized their divorce laws, legalized gambling became the leading industry. Ironically, today Reno has become a quick marriage center, with wedding chapels scattered around town like fast-food restaurants. Today, marriages in Reno outnumber divorces by a ten-to-one ratio.

Although Las Vegas construction imitates southern California modern style—stucco, sprawling ranch houses and tile roofs—Reno prefers old-fashioned houses built of honest red brick. The older neighborhoods are of solidly built, no-nonsense homes—a settled, mature city. Las Vegas is an eastern-style glamour girl, adorned with mink and diamond bracelets; Reno is pure Western, a cowboy with a string tie and blue jeans.

Yet Reno offers 24-hour entertainment and glitter. Folks here are proud of Reno's self-bestowed title of The Biggest Little City in the World. But, there's something hometown about the downtown gaming tables that escapes Lake Tahoe, Las Vegas and Laughlin. This hometown feeling was deliberately cultivated when gambling was legalized during the depression days. Harold Smith, founder of *Harold's Club*, decided to go after local money instead of depending upon tourists. He instituted the practice of giving free drinks and double odds on crap tables. He cashed paychecks without charge and tried to make people feel at home. Harold's Club also started the practice of preferential hiring of local people and senior citizens. Retirees work at everything from dealing blackjack to making change.

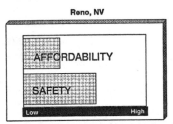

Reno, NV

As a retirement center, Reno is one of our favorites. Because of the large number of retirees, the level of services for senior citizens is exceptionally high. Retiree clubs and organizations are unusually active. Thirteen apartment complexes specialize in assisted housing for the elderly, handicapped and disabled, plus three, large, full-service retirement facilities. Private programs such as Meals on Wheels and Care and Share are active, as are several run by the government. There's a senior citizens' employment service, and a senior citizens' law center provides free assistance with wills, Social Security, leases and things of that nature.

The cost of living is not cheap, but compared to many urban locations, it is reasonable. With the adjoining city of Sparks, the population is about 180,000, making it a good-sized city. The Reno area has all the facilities necessary for good retirement: hospitals, colleges, cultural events and community services.

Some choose Reno retirement for excitement, but most like its extraordinary climate. The 4,440-foot altitude and very low humidity keep the weather pleasant year-round despite its apparent low temperatures. For those who cannot stand hot summer weather, Reno is perfect. Expect to enjoy about 300 sunny days a year in Reno. Even though July and August midday temperatures usually approach 90 degrees by midafternoon, you will sleep under an electric blanket every night; the thermometer always drops into the 40s. Even in the middle of winter the high temperatures are about the same as summer lows!

A light jacket or sweater feels warm in this dry climate, even when the temperature is below freezing. I am always surprised to walk out of a casino in my shirt-sleeves, feeling perfectly comfortable, and then notice a thermometer announcing that it is 38 degrees! Air conditioning is unknown in residential properties, and low electricity rates keep winter heating bills within a reasonable range.

RENO	Jan.	April	July	Oct.	Rel. Humidity: Jan. 51%, July 19%	
					Rain	Snow
Daily Highs	45	63	91	70	7"	24"
Daily Lows	20	29	48	31		

Lake Tahoe   A short drive from Reno up a wide, four-lane highway is a beautiful, bustling area in a forested lake setting that many consider a prime retirement place. This is Lake Tahoe, a sprawling community that straddles the line between Nevada and California. Well-known for luxurious hotels and gambling casinos, Lake Tahoe is also celebrated for beauty; it sits next to one of the most gorgeous lakes in the world. Mark Twain had this to say about Lake Tahoe, in his book *Roughing It:*

> Three months of camp life on Lake Tahoe would restore an Egyptian mummy to his pristine vigor and give him an appetite like an alligator. I do not mean the oldest and driest mummies, of course, but the fresher ones. The air up there in the clouds is very pure and fine, bracing and delicious. And why shouldn't it be? It is the same the angels breathe. Lake Tahoe must surely be the fairest picture the whole earth affords.

Snow is an important part of Tahoe's winter. If there isn't at least a six-foot pack on the ski slopes, skiers feel cheated. From anywhere in town it is a matter of minutes to a ski lift, a joy to those who enjoy the sport. The snow typically falls in isolated, heavy storms that dump up to three feet in one night; then the weather turns sunny for days or weeks until the next snow. From my perspective, the best thing about Lake Tahoe snow is that it takes only a 20-minute drive to be out of it. You can be skiing at Incline Village in the morning and wandering through Carson City in shirt-sleeves that same evening.

Lake Tahoe, NV

AFFORDABILITY

SAFETY

Low   High

Why would folks consider retiring there? "Living here is like being on permanent vacation," says a friend of mine who owns a lakefront cottage near North Shore. Like many residents, he bought his home several years ago, in anticipation of retirement. He rented out his place by the day or week at premium rates to regular visitors—vacationers, skiers and gamblers—and by the time he was ready to retire, a good portion of his retirement home had been paid off. The deductions and depreciation as a rental also helped ease his tax burdens. Long-term rentals, however, are usually available at rates one would expect to pay in most California urban areas. That can be expensive and worth it only if you cannot consider living anywhere else because you love Lake Tahoe so much. Many people living there feel just that way.

New Mexico

Las Cruces   Las Cruces, the largest town in southern New Mexico, is 45 minutes away from El Paso via Interstate 10. Like some other cities along the Rio Grande, Las Cruces is rapidly attracting retirees. Even though the town is small compared to nearby El Paso (62,000 inhabitants), it offers plenty of amenities for its senior citizens. New Mexico State University is located there, complete with a theater and even a symphony orchestra. Community participation in the university's cultural and entertainment events is a definite plus. Shopping is more than adequate, with El Paso nearby for anything not available in Las Cruces. Medical care here is exceptional, with one of the best-equipped hospitals in the state, the 286-bed Memorial Medical Center.

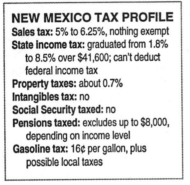

NEW MEXICO TAX PROFILE
Sales tax: 5% to 6.25%, nothing exempt
State income tax: graduated from 1.8% to 8.5% over $41,600; can't deduct federal income tax
Property taxes: about 0.7%
Intangibles tax: no
Social Security taxed: no
Pensions taxed: excludes up to $8,000, depending on income level
Gasoline tax: 16¢ per gallon, plus possible local taxes

Nestled in the fertile Mesilla Valley, which draws irrigation water from the Rio Grande, the city is in the center of a prosperous farming district, producing cotton, pecans and chili peppers. Mountains rising to over 9,000 feet surround Las Cruces and block some of the northern winter winds to produce a mild, low-humidity winter. Summers are warm, similar to El Paso weather, although the large amount of irrigation raises the summer humidity somewhat. Its mild weather permits fishing year-round in nearby Elephant Butte and Caballo reservoirs. Las Cruces has two public golf courses and a private country club. Eighteen lighted tennis courts make for comfortable play on hot summer evenings.

Las Cruces is an unusually attractive setting with a distinctive, old-West, pueblo character. Apparently city planners try to channel architecture toward the pueblo style of Santa Fe, with soft, earthen tones. Yet Las Cruces has avoided a regimented, stiff adherence to this style, permitting pastels and bright colors to intersperse with the muted earthen tones. We looked at a display of exceptionally imaginative homes of elegant, old-West style. They were set on low-maintenance landscaped lots that incorporated natural shrubs and cactus. We guessed the price at $250,000 and were surprised to learn the asking price was just over $100,000. A buyers' market prevails.

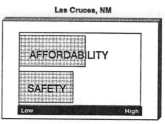

Rents appear reasonable, with an abundance of apartments advertised from $400 a month, and three-bedroom houses starting at $600. Mobile home parks seem to have been overbuilt, with monthly rentals between $125 and $200. Mobile homes for sale are also heavily advertised at seemingly bargain prices. Housing prices are slightly below national median, and utilities are 11 percent below normal.

LAS CRUCES				Rel. Humidity: Jan. 28%, July 22%		
	Jan.	April	July	Oct.	Rain	Snow
Daily Highs	59	79	96	76	9"	3"
Daily Lows	27	42	63	44		

Truth or Consequences   Moving on up the Rio Grande about 70 miles is a nice little town with a silly name. One edge of Truth or Consequences (pop. 6,000) is bordered by dramatic mud and sandstone bluffs, a sort of New Mexico Badlands. Nearby is a good fishing lake formed 70 years ago by damming the Rio Grande. Unexpected in the middle of the desert, the lake provides welcome water-sports recreation.

The original name for Truth or Consequences was Hot Springs, named for the steaming volcanic water that runs beneath the town. Residents tap this water for heating their homes and filling hot tubs. How did the town change names? It happened back in the heyday of Ralph Edward's popular radio show, "Truth or Consequences." (Remember?) At that time, Hot Springs was a little place, little more than a collection of buildings around the hot springs complex. Looking for a way to get publicity and a shot in the arm for the economy, Hot Springs' city fathers decided to make a deal with Ralph Edwards. They offered to change the name of the town if he would come there to broadcast a show.

The deal was consummated at what was probably the height of the town's silly season. But it worked. Newspapers and magazines all over the nation boosted the event with invaluable publicity. Everyone tuned into the radio show that night. (I know I did.) Changing its name literally put the town on the map. From that time on, road maps listed the town of Truth or Consequences, and tourists detoured to see the place. The additional commerce enabled local business to expand until the stores now offer everything one might need without making a trip into Las Cruces or Albuquerque.

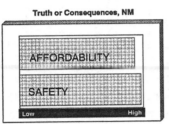

Truth or Consequences, NM

AFFORDABILITY

SAFETY

Low   High

It isn't surprising that many retirees made the detour and discovered a pleasant community with a comfortable, small-town atmosphere. Since almost everyone in town comes from somewhere else, they show an unusual openness to strangers. There are no FBI crime statistics available for the area, but my guess would be that personal safety is excellent. At the recreation center for seniors there are dances nearly every night in addition to the usual shuffleboard, cards, dominoes. The pace here is slow; because there is only one stoplight in town, traffic is easy to manage. Truth or Consequences' positioning on Interstate 25 makes the 73-mile drive to Las Cruces and Interstate 10 an easy chore. There is Greyhound service.

Most housing is single-family homes, modest and affordable. According to the local newspaper classifieds, rents and home prices are quite low. Mobile homes are a popular form of housing, with numerous parks around town as well as units on privately owned lots. This is permitted and is less expensive than constructing a house from scratch.

Because Truth or Consequences sits at a higher elevation than most New Mexico and west Texas desert country, summers are quite pleasant. It occasionally snows in the winter, but local boosters claim this is "very unusual." They point out the mild weather as one of the advantages of retirement, along with active senior citizens' centers and clubs and lake fishing. Golf is played year-round as well as tennis, bicycling and other outdoor activities.

TRUTH OR CONSEQUENCES				Rel. Humidity: Jan. 39%, July 26%	
	Jan.	April	July	Oct.	Rain	Snow
Daily Highs	48	71	94	73	8"	13"
Daily Lows	23	41	65	44		

Albuquerque High in the desert, sitting on the east bank of the Rio Grande at an altitude of over 5,000 feet, Albuquerque is a fast-growing retirement area. Its combination of altitude, dry air and mild temperatures is exactly what many people look for in a place to live. The thermometer rarely hits 100 degrees and almost never sees zero. With 30 percent afternoon humidity, the weather seems even milder than charts might indicate. July's (the hottest month) average highs of 90 degrees always drop into the 60s at night.

Rainfall is a scant eight inches per year, which means lots of brilliant, sunny weather. And the best part is that the winter months of December and January are the sunniest. It's a two-season year, with about 11 inches of snow expected every winter. It doesn't stick around for long, though, because winter days usually hit 50 degrees by noon. Muggy days and long, drizzling spells are just about unknown in Albuquerque. Summers can become quite dry, however, causing the mighty Rio Grande to dwindle to a muddy trickle. Once, when Will Rogers was giving a talk in Albuquerque, he cajoled: "Why, you folks ought to be out there right now irrigating that river to keep it from blowing away!"

Albuquerque's biggest drawback is that its name is difficult to spell. The problem with spelling started in 1706 when the Spanish Duke of Alburquerque decided that this spot, where the old Camino Real crossed the Rio Grande, would be a great place to have a town named after him. But when they put up the city limits sign, somebody left an *r* out of his name. And schoolkids have had trouble spelling it ever since. Sure seems like there should be at least one *k* somewhere in Albuquerque.

The city has taken pains to preserve its historic sector. Preservation was possible partly because the coming of the railroad in 1880 moved the "downtown" away from the original plaza, thus sparing it from development. Today the area, now known as Old Town, offers fine restaurants and shops, and maintains the historic flavor of the Old West. Venerable adobe buildings and museums cluster around the Duke of Alburquerque's village.

The downtown section is clean, modern and prosperous looking. Everything seems polished and tastefully designed. A pedestrian mall completes the picture of a pleasant city center. The rest of the metropolitan area is also quite pleasant, with many homes designed in an adobe style and lots of huge shade trees in the older areas of town.

The metropolitan hub of New Mexico, Albuquerque is also a high-technology center of the Southwest. As such, it attracts people from all over the country to work and live there. The University of New Mexico (25,000 enrollment) accounts for much of the rich cultural offerings of the city. There's a full calendar of lectures, concerts, drama and sporting events, as well as numerous classes of interest to senior citizens.

Almost any direction from the city leads to interesting day trips to cultural and scenic marvels. The snowcapped, 10,000-foot Sandia Mountains tower on the east and a chain of extinct volcanoes on the west. The Turquoise Trail (Highway 22) to the north takes you through the old mining towns of Golden, Madrid and Cerillos. To the south on Mission Trail (Highway 14) are the Indian pueblos of Gran Quivira, Abo and Quarai. Several Zuñi pueblos are within easy visiting distance; Mescalero and Jicarilla Apache and Navajo reservations are not far away.

Skiing is great, with over 11 facilities within striking distance. Sandia Peak (15 miles northeast of Albuquerque) has lifts that rise over 10,000 feet. Hunting, fishing, prospecting and rock-hunting are all great outdoor pastimes. But all outdoor activities don't require going into the

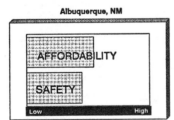

Albuquerque, NM

wilderness. Horse-racing fans will find seven race tracks, with the season starting in January at Downs at Albuquerque.

In Albuquerque, over 70 percent of the dwellings are single-family homes. Albuquerque housing prices are about 5 percent over the national average. At the time of our last visit, we could have purchased a satisfactory three-bedroom home for less than $80,000. Older ones are advertised sometimes as low as $45,000. Mobile home park and apartment rents are moderate.

A particularly beautiful residential area is out of town, near the Sandia Peak Tramway, the longest continuous aerial tramway in the world. The houses are constructed with nature in mind, each designed to fit in with the gnarled juniper trees, rocks and boulders, and look as if they grew naturally rather than being built by humans. There's also a great view of the city. Prices aren't cheap, starting above $100,000, but worth it.

Several retirement complexes compete for senior citizen occupancy. They seem like pretty good deals. We looked at one that offered one-bedroom or studio units with weekly maid and linen service as well as three meals a day in the dining room at surprisingly reasonable rates. It was located in a nice section of town, near shopping.

ALBUQUERQUE				Rel. Humidity: Jan. 40%, July 27%		
	Jan.	April	July	Oct.	Rain	Snow
Daily Highs	47	71	93	72	8"	11"
Daily Lows	22	39	65	43		

Santa Fe Fifty-nine miles northeast of Albuquerque, the town of Santa Fe sits like an antique jewel in the picturesque Sangre de Cristo mountains, perched at an altitude of 7,000 feet. A sense of history pervades the streets and byways of this oldest capital city in the United States. Settled in the year 1610, Santa Fe was a bustling town and commercial center ten years before the Pilgrims set foot on Plymouth Rock! Santa Fe has been a capital city for over 375 years.

Here, you'll find the oldest private house in the United States and the oldest public building in the country, the Palace of the Governors. This building became General Kearney's headquarters in 1846, when his troops captured Santa Fe during the Mexican-American War. Incidentally, this was the first foreign capital ever captured by U.S. armed forces.

Santa Fe is not only a town steeped in history and culture, but its residents work hard at keeping it that way. Strict building codes insist that all new construction be of adobe or adobe-looking material; all exteriors must be earth tones. This preserves the distinctive Spanish pueblo style for which Santa Fe is famous. Occasionally, one sees a home that was built in the days before zoning codes, and the blue or white building sticks out like the proverbial sore thumb. At first the shades of sand, brown and tan can seem a bit somber, but after a while, one grows to appreciate the way they complement the setting.

Along with tourism and retirement, artistic endeavors are one of Santa Fe's prime industries. Art impacts the everyday life of Santa Fe residents, with hundreds of painters, artists and craftspeople doing their thing, and almost 200 galleries exhibiting their treasures. The old plaza in the heart of the city is usually lined with street artisans displaying jewelry, paintings, leather goods and all kinds of quality artwork. Local native Americans bring intricate silver and turquoise jewelry to sell in the plaza. A highly regarded opera company performs in a unique outdoor theater. Fortunately, Santa Fe's weather seldom interferes with the performances; rainfall is only about 15 inches a year. A year-round calendar of events includes concerts by the Orchestra of Santa Fe, the Chorus of Santa Fe, the Desert Chorale, the Santa Fe Symphony, as well

235

as native American fiestas, festivals and celebrations. Numerous theater and drama presentations come from the New Mexico Repertory Theatre, the British American Theatre Institute, the Armory for the Arts, the Santuario de Guadalupe, the Community Theatre and the Greer Garson Theater. There's even a rodeo every summer. Of course, the thoroughbreds race at famous Santa Fe Downs from May to Labor Day.

"When I get up in the morning, I know there's going to be sun," said a man who retired in Santa Fe after living most of his life in northern Illinois. "It makes a big difference in my life." Santa Fe is almost tied with Albuquerque for percentage of sunshine; almost 300 days a year are guaranteed to be at least partly sunny. Santa Fe gets more rain, though, and there's three times as much snow, about 33 inches annually. This keeps Santa Fe greener. You'll find a true four-season year with very pleasant summers. Be prepared to wear a sweater on summer evenings—the temperature typically drops to below 50 degrees at night.

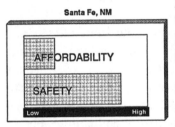

Folks who can afford to buy a second house anywhere they care to, tend to buy one here. That should tell us something about Santa Fe's quality. The problem is that Santa Fe has such a reputation as a retirement and artist center that outsiders have bid up real estate to an unusual level. "It's getting so we natives can't afford to live here anymore," lamented one hometown resident. Yet, housing is curiously mixed in price. Generally, it's more expensive than Albuquerque, particularly for nicer housing. But there are also some inexpensive places. Economical housing sells for over $100,000 per unit, with the median price of a city home at $128,000. Several high-end developments are under way, at least one with its private golf course. A couple of attractive, full-care retirement residences are located in Santa Fe, one without any endowment or entrance fees; but there could be a waiting list. An active senior citizen program, Open Hands, offers services and an opportunity to volunteer for satisfying and worthwhile community projects.

SANTA FE/TAOS			Rel. Humidity: Jan. 42%, July 32%			
	Jan.	April	July	Oct.	Rain	Snow
Daily Highs	40	60	78	62	15"	33"
Daily Lows	19	35	57	39		

Taos Farther up the road from Santa Fe, in the heart of the Sangre de Cristo Mountains, is the delightful town of Taos. A bustling village, quiet retreat, art colony, ski resort—these are but a few of Taos' many faces. Its 55 art galleries and numerous art programs hint at the large number of artists in residence. One drawback could be cold winters. The dryness takes the bitterness from the cold, however. Summers are cool, with air conditioners unheard of.

Compared to Santa Fe, housing is less costly, and the lifestyle is a bit more casual. Taos seems to be more for seriously artistic folks rather than for wealthy summer residents. However, don't expect to find rock-bottom prices there, because Taos is a popular place. Few real estate listings are under $95,000, with $150,000 and up more common. There are retirement complexes here: one, Plaza de Retiro, is located just three blocks from historic Taos Plaza, within walking distance of shopping, churches, restaurants and other facilities. It sits on six acres, with many facilities: a dining room, a library and activities rooms, plus a ten-bed licensed health care facility.

Carlsbad Tucked away in the southeastern corner of New Mexico, Carlsbad (pop. 30,000) sits at an altitude of 3,200 feet and enjoys a mild, four-season climate. With only 12 inches of rain a year, the residents enjoy an average 340 days of sunshine, warm days and cool nights, which add up to a glorious climate for retirement living. The Pecos River runs through town and forms a nearby lake for boating and fishing the year-round. Two golf courses offer fairways with 18 holes each, and there are nine lighted tennis courts and a 24-lane bowling alley.

The local chamber of commerce actively solicits retirees and works hard to bring its story to the retiring public. With low housing costs (the chamber claims that rents start at $200 a month) and taxes ranking at the bottom of the scale, Carlsbad could be a possibility for those who don't need a big city nearby. For its size, Carlsbad has impressive services, with an active Senior Recreation Center. There is a good-sized medical center (134 beds) and a branch of the University of New Mexico. Two full-

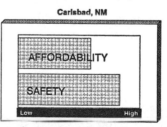

Carlsbad, NM

AFFORDABILITY

SAFETY

Low   High

service retirement centers are church-operated, one by Methodists and another by the Church of Christ. There is no bus service, but taxis give seniors a discount. The major problem for me is Carlsbad's distance from the nearest big towns, El Paso and Albuquerque. That may not be a problem for others.

Colorado

When you think of deserts and mountains, the state of Colorado has to figure big. With the most impressive mountains on the continent, the highways that cross them are so high that some folks have trouble breathing; several passes climb over 10,000 feet. When they do catch their breath, the mountain scenery immediately takes it away again. From legendary old mining towns to ultra-modern cities, from farmlands to forests, Colorado has a lot to offer the retiree. Many part-time retirees love the state for its wonderfully refreshing summers, and full time retirees like the reasonable housing and mild winters of some areas.

> **COLORADO TAX PROFILE**
> **Sales tax:** 3% to 7.5%, food, drugs exempt
> **State income tax:** 5% of federal taxable income; can't deduct federal income tax
> **Property taxes:** average 1% of purchase price
> **Intangibles tax:** no
> **Social Security taxed:** half of benefits are taxable for higher incomes
> **Pensions taxed:** excludes first $20,000; double deduction for taxpayers over 65
> **Gasoline tax:** 22¢ per gallon

Grand Junction   Earlier, we discussed economic disasters that turned out to be bonanzas for retirees. Here's another story. During the late 1970s, encouraged and subsidized by the government, oil companies began experimenting with the enormous oil shale deposits of Colorado and Wyoming. Thousands of workers flocked there to help develop this potentially valuable natural resource.

Grand Junction participated in this welcome economic boom. New houses and apartments went up like mushrooms after a rainstorm. All this new building still wasn't enough, so Exxon, one of the larger companies, was forced to enter the construction business to provide housing for its employees. Among other things, Exxon developed a flat mountaintop, a place called Battlement Mesa, into a spiffy housing development. The company constructed 684 residences, complete with a multi-million-dollar recreation center.

Suddenly, the bubble collapsed. On Sunday, May 2, 1982, Exxon announced that it was closing its $5-billion Colony Oil Shale Project. Slumping oil prices had made it too expensive to squeeze petroleum from the shale. Grand Junction remembers this date as Black Sunday.

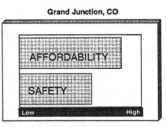

Grand Junction, CO

By the end of a year, almost 8,000 workers lost their jobs. Almost as quickly as they came, they began leaving. Knowing they hadn't even a prayer to make payments, many simply walked away from their homes. They couldn't even *give* the properties away because they owed more money on the mortgages than the market value. The few buyers who were in the market waited for foreclosure and then bought from the banks at bargain prices. As in Bisbee and Ajo, the workers who lost their jobs suffered, both financially and from their shattered plans for the future.

The businesspeople who survived realized that the solution to the problem lay in attracting industry with a stable financial base, something not subject to boom or bust like petroleum. Economic incentives, such as free land for new and expanding industries, were offered. At the same time, they began concentrating on a special business, one that's clean, doesn't pollute the air, and brings in an obvious source of steady income: the retirement industry! Exxon began to market its deluxe Battlement Mesa complex as a retirement community. Nearby towns, such as Parachute, Palisade, Fruita and Clifton, joined in the movement to attract retirees.

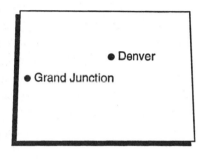

Their efforts were successful. Gradually, the economy recovered, due in large measure to retiree money. Surplus homes were eventually purchased, and the population began rising once more. According to a real estate broker, about 50 percent of today's buyers are retirees from out of state. Although the bargain-basement housing market is no longer available, homes are still plentiful and inexpensive.

Grand Junction would be a nice place to retire regardless of housing bargains. This is the largest city in western Colorado, located in a broad valley in high plateau country west of the Rocky Mountains. Its name came from its location near the junction of the Colorado and Gunnison rivers (the Colorado was originally called the *Grand* River). Grand Junction is the center of an urban area of some 82,000 people, although the town itself has a comfortable population of 33,000. Shopping malls, a senior citizens' center and excellent health care are among the attractions. An abundance of sunshine and a mild winter that permits golf and tennis to be year-round sports adds to its desirability for retirement.

GRAND JUNCTION			Rel. Humidity: Jan. 62%, July 22%			
	Jan.	April	July	Oct.	Rain	Snow
Daily Highs	36	65	94	69	8"	25"
Daily Lows	15	38	64	41		

Denver   The largest city for many miles, Denver is a very interesting place from the perspective of a retiree. At first glance it would seem to be a horrible place to winter, what with a yearly snowfall of 60 inches! But that's only part of the story. Yes, it can snow a foot or more overnight, but within a couple of days, it's all gone, and you'll be basking in 65-degree sunshine! Even the coldest months average 43 degrees every afternoon. Snow doesn't have a chance to stick around. Furthermore, the dryness of the air makes you think it is far warmer than it really is.

Denver is a clean place, with pleasant, tree-shaded residential areas and loads of inexpensive apartment buildings. Most homes are built of brick, especially older ones. According to a common story, an early-day mayor owned a brick factory, so he passed laws that all homes must be constructed of brick. Maybe it's not true, but the brick construction does add a special touch to Denver's architectural flavor.

The most impressive thing about the city is its real estate prices. For a while the daily newspapers ran a 16-page supplement every Sunday full of HUD repossessions. Condos were offered at $15,000, three-bed-

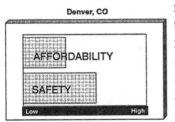

Denver, CO

room brick homes for $40,000. This was the most depressed big-city market we found anywhere in the country. The reasons appear to be twofold: first, the oil shale boom had inflated new construction, and second, the savings-and-loan industry (industry or racket?) had been disbursing construction loans and financing homes, apartments, office buildings, for anyone who asked. Hold out your hand and they would fill it with money. Then, when the petroleum companies suddenly pulled out of the shale exploration business and fired most of their employees, the boom turned into a disheartening fizzle.

During our latest visit, we saw considerable improvement, with most HUD property sold, although the market hadn't fully recovered. Property still sells below what it might bring in other cities of Denver's caliber. A drawback here (as in many urban areas) is the high number of youth gang-related shootings. While this kind of crime rarely affects seniors, the State of Colorado and Denver's police are working on the problem.

DENVER			Rel. Humidity: Jan. 49%, July 34%			
	Jan.	April	July	Oct.	Rain	Snow
Daily Highs	43	61	88	67	15"	60"
Daily Lows	16	34	59	37		

Utah

Of all the states, Utah is the most desert-like, with seemingly endless stretches of barren land. Sometimes alkaline flats stretch as far as the eye can see; occasionally, the landscape is crusted with pavement-like salt surface. The Great Salt Lake, actually an inland sea, has water so loaded with salt that most ocean fish would die if they tried swimming there.

UTAH TAX PROFILE
Sales tax: 5% to 6.25%, drugs exempt
State income tax: graduated from 2.55% to 7.2% over $3,750; federal income tax partially deductible
Property taxes: average 0.8% of market value
Intangibles tax: no
Social Security taxed: half of benefits taxable for higher incomes
Pensions taxed: excludes up to $7,500, depending on income level
Gasoline tax: 19.5¢ per gallon

In contrast, the state boasts the most spectacular mountain scenery in the country, perhaps in the world. Southern Utah, with Zion and Bryce Canyon national parks to take your breath away, competes with Capitol Reef and the Canyonlands areas for sheer desert and mountain beauty.

Although these areas are beautiful beyond description, most are *not* places I would consider for retirement! In the first place, most are in isolated areas with a just a few scattered farms and an occasional rural village. Second, small-town Utah, for those of you who are not Mormons, can be a lonely place indeed. In fact, my main reservation against Utah as a place to retire is its closely knit society that centers around religion. Among themselves, the people are wonderfully warm and loving, with deep concern for one another's welfare. But even converted Mormons tell me of discrimination because they were not born into the church. As an indication of how religion permeates life, 90 percent of the state's politicians are active members of the Mormon church.

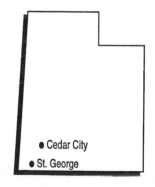

● Cedar City

● St. George

Having said this and emphasizing that this is strictly my opinion, I can also say that many non-Mormons tell me that they haven't found religion much of an obstacle. "It's only a problem if you let it be a problem," said one newcomer to St. George. Most larger towns are pleasant-looking and have affordable property. Salt Lake City is an exceptionally clean and prosperous city. We have friends who live there (Mormons, of course) and who swear by its four-season climate and invigorating, clean air.

Cedar City/St. George Two other places often recommended for retirement are in the southwestern portion of Utah: Cedar City and St. George. We know Cedar City to a certain extent since, until recently, we owned a partnership in an apartment-motel there. Property and rentals are reasonable and plentiful in Cedar City. Adding to the quality of life are the university, the four-season climate and skiing in the winter. Of special note is the excellent safety factor: this area scores high in personal safety on our crime charts.

Cedar City, UT

AFFORDABILITY

SAFETY

Low   High

St. George—a few miles to the south, on the edge of Zion National Park—is by far the more picturesque town, with stark red cliffs sometimes looming vertically from resident's backyards. St. George's dramatic backdrop of mountain scenery is its strongest suit. Its beauty and relatively mild winters draw many more outsiders than some other Utah communities. This is important for non-Mormons, because outsiders dilute the religious majority.

Settled in 1861 by 309 Mormon families, St. George was transformed from a forbidding alkali flat into a livable town in the space of a decade. Some original homes survive and are treated with reverence by local residents. Included is Brigham Young's house where he spent a few of his last years. Streets are wide and tree-lined, and homes are as neat and orderly as Brigham Young would have wished.

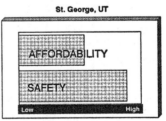

St. George, UT

AFFORDABILITY

SAFETY

Low   High

St. George housing is more costly than in nearby towns, slightly above national averages, but it's still looked upon as a bargain by retirees coming from more expensive, high-rent districts. Nearby Washington offers bargain prices for cost-conscious folks. In the southern section of St. George are the Bloomington and Bloomington Hills developments, with exceptionally well-designed homes, reminiscent of those in Arizona's Sun City complexes. Prices are comparable. The rental market is tough here, with few vacancies and high rents.

CEDAR CITY/ST. GEORGE				Rel. Humidity: Jan. 31%, July 15%	
	Jan.	April	July	Oct.	Rain	Snow
Daily Highs	54	76	101	80	11"	5"
Daily Lows	26	44	66	45		

Chapter 8

California

There is a definite difference between folks who live on the extreme western part of the nation and those who live in the East, Midwest and South. Personalities and worldviews vary with each section. Sometimes the differences are subtle. The reasons for the differences are partly historical and partly environmental.

Folks who live in the southern portions of the United States are, by tradition, rural and outdoor-oriented. Midwesterners share much of the Southern tradition, yet larger cities, larger farms and industrially developed environments, plus a history of Eastern immigration and Eastern ideas, distinguish them from Southerners.

On the other hand, the Eastern mindset is shaped by closely packed cities, little open space and an orientation toward business and industry. In heavily populated areas, the friendliness and hospitality of the South and Midwest just aren't possible.

The West Coast has a comparatively short history, and with the exception of a few native Americans, it is composed principally of "newcomers" from every part of the country and the world. The population is mixed and their personalities are mixed. Southern hospitality mixes with Northeastern reserve, and the love of open spaces mixes with a love of the city. The result is a multifaceted, laid-back lifestyle.

Yes, the West Coast has earned a reputation for being laid back. So, what's wrong with kicking back and enjoying life? I'm convinced you'll live longer and enjoy life more. We have friends in Connecticut who think nothing of commuting an hour and a half each way to work. That's almost two extra working days a week—90 working days a year—staring out a train window! On the other hand, most Californians complain bitterly if their commutes are over 20 minutes (except for Los Angeles, where businesspeople spend their spare time parked on freeways).

Another East-West difference is the attitude toward education. Western community colleges and adult education are accessible and liberally patronized by senior citizens. Many universities waive fees for those over 65, welcoming them and their potential contributions to the system.

A friend who moved west after spending most of his life in New York City once told me,

> A big difference I see between East Coast and West Coast living is a sense of space and belonging. That is, in New York I always felt that I *belonged* to a certain neighborhood, and I felt perfectly comfortable there. When I went elsewhere, I felt almost as if I were intruding—that I didn't *belong*. But in the West, I don't feel this restricted sense of neighborhood. *Everywhere* belongs to me, and I don't feel out of place no matter where I am.

Two factors account for this. One is the historical fact that the West Coast is still in the process of being settled; people have no deeply ingrained sense of neighborhood. Western families tend to live in one house for short intervals, and when they can afford to upgrade their lifestyles, they trade for a more expensive home in another neighborhood. They seldom develop deep roots, binding friendships or loyalty for one locale; the new one is always better than the last.

The second factor is the environmental circumstance of so much open land. Much of it actually belongs to everyone. A huge percentage of western states' lands are in nationally owned forests, deserts and mountain slopes. Unlike the East Coast—where just about every acre is fenced and posted as private property—most Western land is public and open for anyone to enjoy. Almost 50 percent of California and Oregon land belongs to the U.S. government. Nevada is 85 percent federally owned and Arizona, 44 percent. Compare this with only 3.8 percent in New England, the Eastern Seaboard and the Midwestern states.

Openness means more than forests and deserts. The ocean also belongs to the people. Unlike the Atlantic and Gulf shores, where property owners own the beach in front of their homes and can post "No Trespassing" signs, Pacific beaches belong to everyone. By law, property owners must provide public access to their beachfront properties; their ownership extends only to a certain distance above the high tide line. You can stroll along any beach you please, secure in the knowledge that it is as much your property as anyone's.

Weather

Because West Coast weather is mild and generally pleasant year-round, people tend to find outdoor things to do. Most live within a few hours' drive of excellent ski country or uncrowded beaches. They can enjoy snow sports in the afternoon, then drive down the mountain to swim in a pool or relax in a hot tub the same evening. Outdoor living is the hallmark of Westerners.

The West Coast offers the most amazing smorgasbord of retirement choices imaginable. Choose from mountain communities with Alpine winters, deserts that look more like the Sahara than the Sahara, farmlands that remind one of Iowa, rugged coasts as pretty as the Spanish Mediterranean and beaches as smooth as Hawaii's (albeit with colder waters). Within an hour or so of most retirement locations you can be hunting deer, fishing for trout or trolling for salmon. From a rustic cabin, deeply isolated within a redwood forest, you can drive for 30 minutes to an art museum, the theater or an ocean beach. From a city home you can drive 20 minutes to a wild and scenic wilderness. Almost any ecological, environmental or climatic feature can be found on the West Coast.

Yes, some California locations have smog and air pollution, at least as bad as I've seen in many Eastern cities. (L.A. has dramatically cleaned up its act over the last two decades, however.) But most of the state enjoys pristine, clear air.

What about water? Isn't the West always in a drought of some sort? Not really. Some mountain areas in California consistently get so much rain it's ridiculous—over 60 inches a season, and that's nothing compared to parts of Oregon and Washington—while places not far away in the desert are lucky to see a couple of inches all year. But one important similarity is, as a general rule, not much rain ever falls in the summer. In the mountains you might catch some summer rain, and even thunder storms, but elsewhere you can pretty much count on leaving your waterproof hat at home when playing golf, fishing or hiking. This arrangement is perfect for tourists and retirees, but it is a little difficult for farmers—no rain during the growing season, and too much rain when they don't need it. Fortunately, a system of irrigation remedies this situation, permitting California to be one of the most productive of all the farming states. Another nice thing about the weather here is a low relative humidity. This means gentler hot days, more comfortable cool days and far, far fewer bugs such as cockroaches.

Along the ocean, temperatures vary little between winter and summer. It is pleasant year-round from San Diego to Vancouver. Granted, the farther north, the cooler the temperatures, but they remain remarkably stable regardless of the season. This is due to the chain of low, coastal mountains which runs the entire West Coast, from Washington's Puget Sound to San Diego. This ridge separates the coast from the inland valleys and prevents the cool Pacific air from sweeping eastward.

A natural "air conditioning" system occurs when the sun heats up the inland valley air. This warm air rises, creating low pressure that then draws air from the ocean across the coast and over the mountains to cool things off. If it weren't for this occurrence, the coast would be as hot as the interior valleys. In the winter, the air currents are stable and the cooler air stays offshore, allowing both beaches and inland to bask in the sunshine. Often the "heat waves" of the coastal lands occur in November, with 80 degrees common, as opposed to the 70-degree days of August.

Therefore, the coastal towns are for those who don't like air conditioning and also hate freezing weather. Los Angeles is a bit different, since the mountains are farther from the coast and the sun heats the entire coastal plain. However, the ocean breeze performs somewhat the same natural air conditioning function. That's why Los Angeles has such pleasant weather: warm in the winter but rarely extremely hot in the summer. This climate is exactly why so many people live there.

Through the coastal valleys north, across the San Joaquin and Sacramento valleys, through Oregon and Washington, the climate patterns are similar—hot, sunny summers and mild winters. The farther north, the cooler the summer weather and the greater likelihood of a touch of snow in the winter. But all along the coast, rain comes in the winter. This causes a strange switch in seasons. Unlike the green, eastern summers, things turn brown in the summer, sometimes by the first of June, and then brilliant green in November, when the rains begin to fall. This is agricultural land, lush when irrigated. The people living there enjoy a mild climate and snow-free winters.

On the other side of the valleys is yet another range of mountains, high and forbidding. These run almost in an unbroken chain from the Canadian Rockies to the Andes in South America. On the slopes and foothills of these mountains is a third climate system. It was along this uplift, in California's Sierra Nevada range, where the early-day miners found gold and settled during the West's infancy. After a brief flurry of mining activity, the area was almost deserted. Much of it is rolling country, forested with hardwood and pine. Cold-water rivers teaming with trout tumble their way from the mountains on the way to the ocean. Folks who live here like the mild four seasons and the rustic, forest atmosphere plus the knowledge that big-city convenience is a short distance away.

High mountains, deep snow, ski lifts and tall trees characterize the next level of Western living. The high Sierra, with crystal-clear air and brisk mornings, attracts a special breed of retirees. These folks either are not afraid of snow or they are not afraid to admit they hate it and leave every winter; in some places the snow level reaches 12 feet. But summer in the Sierra is beautiful: warm and sunny with cool evenings (and a wood fire). To be perfectly honest, most of these homes are shuttered for the winter while their owners travel in RVs to snow-free climes or move to their alternate digs on the Colorado River or the Pacific shore.

The last type of ecosystem is the desert. This is found in great abundance on the other side of the tall mountains and in both the southern and northernmost sections of the West. In eastern Washington and Oregon, Nevada, Utah, Colorado, California, Arizona and New Mexico, uncountable square miles are desert country. Many people think of desert as searing hot stretches of sand dunes. Some low-altitude desert country can fit that description. But high desert country can be as bitterly cold and uninhabitable as Alaskan tundra, although most falls somewhere between these extremes.

Earthquakes

Shortly after Los Angeles's 1994 Northridge Earthquake, I was traveling through south Georgia on a research trip. The director of a local chamber of commerce—as soon as she found out I'm from California—asked the inevitable question: "Aren't you afraid of earthquakes?" And, typically, she added, "Why, I would be scared to death to live there!"

The truth is, like most Californians, I simply get a mild thrill of excitement whenever the room starts shaking. Why? Because we're used to them and know that the chances of this being the "big one" are extremely remote. After more than 40 years in California, the worst earthquake I've been in did little more than rock the chandeliers. But for sheer terror, I can't imagine anything worse than a tornado. Unlike earthquakes, there's no such thing as a *mild* tornado. Furthermore, killer tornadoes outnumber mild earthquakes a hundred to one.

When I explained this to the Georgia lady, she argued, "But with tornadoes, you get plenty of warning on television. Earthquakes happen without any warning at all."

Now, I have to admit that's quite true. There is absolutely no way to predict an earthquake—although at least twice a year, newspapers quote self-styled experts who predict the "big eight-pointer" is coming within the year. Whenever a newspaper runs short of news, a page editor digs up the latest "expert opinion" to fill empty columns. After the 40 years I've lived here, though, headlines somehow lose their edge.

Anyway, after I'd finished that day's interviews, I returned to my motel room in a driving rainstorm. As I watched the evening news, the storm gained fury. Suddenly, a message flashed across the bottom of the screen! "Tornado Warning for Landfill County!" My heart began pounding furiously.

I snatched up a road map and tried to locate Landfill County. Sweat popped out on my brow, and my hands trembled so that I couldn't read the map. The wind grew even more ferocious. Sleet began pecking at the window panes ominously. I just knew—at any moment, a black twister was going to rip the motel into confetti, shred my body into machaca, and scatter my credit cards to the four winds. (Just my luck, I'd paid for the motel room in advance.) Yet I still couldn't find Landfill County on that blasted map!

In desperation, I tried to remember what you're supposed to do during a tornado. Let's see—hide in the basement? No, motels don't have basements. Stand under a door? No, no—that's for earthquakes. Crawl under the bed? Yukko! Too many ugly dust balls. Then a horrible truth flashed into my mind, accompanied by a flash of lightning outside: the main purpose of a tornado warning is to scare the bejeezels out of you! It worked.

Fortunately, nothing happened to me, my motel or my credit cards that night, but you can be sure that I slept fitfully indeed, cringing with every crash of thunder. Now, an earthquake is a different situation. In 99 out of 100 earthquakes, three seconds of adrenalin rush—and it's over. People don't have time to become frightened. Thank goodness we *don't* get earthquake warnings!

Tragically, the next morning's newscast revealed that a series of tornadoes killed 42 people in Kentucky, Alabama and Georgia. News coverage was brief, since there's nothing unusual about tornado rampages. The important story of the day was whether Arkansas would beat North Carolina. But, if 42 people had been killed in a California earthquake, the networks would have been filled with footage of the damage, interviews with witnesses and hours of rehashing the event.

Unlike tornadoes and hurricanes—which thankfully, California doesn't have—earthquakes kill or injure relatively few people. Property suffers the most damage, with shakers generally trashing construction that wasn't entirely stable in the first place. To sum up, tornadoes have killed 4,625 people since 1917; hurricanes have killed 12,376 since 1900. Yet, the total number of Californians killed by earthquakes in the 20th century is less than 700, and that's including the Big Momma of 1906.

Crime

When I first moved to California I expected to be threatened by bikers in black leather jackets brandishing switchblades. I worried about getting run over by cops and robbers as they routinely chase each other around city streets exchanging gunfire. Television and violent movies prepared me for the worst. Before long I realized that the reason California crime scenes appear so often on TV is because California is where movie and television crews shoot their films. If Omaha were to become the motion picture center of the continent, that's where we'd see criminals. We'd be watching shows like "Streets of Omaha" or "Nebraska Crime Series."

Of course California has crime; there isn't a place in the world that doesn't. What might surprise you is many California towns rank as the safest in the nation. Looking at the FBI crime statistics and comparing town for town, we've found California is just as safe as most other states!

I feel secure in California, not only in smaller towns and cities, but also in big places like Los Angeles and San Francisco where crime rates are obviously high. (Of course, I'm careful about which neighborhoods I visit!) In my years of living in California I've never been robbed, mugged or threatened with a weapon. Well, yes—my wife was involved in a mugging once, but the police made her return my money. (Just joking. My wife would *never* return the money!)

Kooks and Wierdos?

"California, fountainhead of fruitcakes and nuts," was how one Easterner put it when he explained why he had never visited California and had no intention of ever doing so. It's true that the state has been the source of some rather spacey ideas. Back in the 1920s and 1930s, religious cults and movements started here and spread over the country. The 1940s brought us beatniks—mild-mannered intellectuals who sat around coffee houses sipping red wine and reciting bad poetry. They aroused the nation's indignation primarily because beatnik men wore goatees before it was deemed fashionable, and lady beatniks often lived with, rather than married, their lovers—before *that* became fashionable. In the 1960s and 70s, the "love generation" spawned hippies, starting in San Francisco and spreading across the nation.

Eventually these fads, like most fads, faded away. Today, you have the Yuppie movement with an intense pursuit of high-paying jobs, expensive automobiles and designer clothes. (Frankly, I preferred the beatniks.) California is also a major center of computer technology, where the famous Silicon Valley turns out new inventions daily. As a result, the state attracts a steady stream of bright, innovative newcomers.

Californians are not slaves to fad and fashion as people tend to believe. We don't rush out and buy clothes simply because some magazine dictates that this year's fashions must be different. Few restaurants require ties, because California men seldom wear them. Women can wear slacks, blue jeans or fancy dresses for any occasion. On the other hand, when I travel back East I have to remember that folks there dress differently; so I must remember to pack my only suit, some dress shirts, a tie—even socks of matching colors, if I can find them.

Comfort and Affordability

Are there really affordable places in California, without smog and without horrendous traffic? Places with hunting and fishing for the men and quality living for the women? A four-season climate? The unqualified answer: yes!

CALIFORNIA TAX PROFILE
Sales tax: 7.2% to 8.5%, food, drugs exempt
State income tax: graduated from 1% to 11% over $207,200 ($25,000 at 8%); can't deduct federal income tax
Property taxes: vary widely, depending on when home was purchased and locality; typically from 1.5% to 1.75%
Intangibles tax: no
Social Security taxed: no
Pensions taxed: all
Gasoline tax: 18¢ per gallon, plus possible local taxes, and state sales tax

Contrary to popular stereotype, California is not all palm trees, movie stars and surfers. Much of the state, particularly the northern part, is almost Midwestern in character. Small towns set in national forests or in the wine country are pretty much like small towns everywhere when it comes to cost of living and lifestyles. The northern California coast is as different from southern California resort and surfing areas as New England towns are from the Florida beaches.

California's glamorous cities are well-known, places like Santa Barbara, San Diego and San Francisco. We'll discuss them later, of course; it would be neglectful of our duty to do otherwise. But let's first start with some retirement possibilities generally unfamiliar to folks from other states.

California Deserts

Although many commonly think of California as surfing beaches, Hollywood and redwood forests, the majority of California is desert or semi-desert. After all, that most famous of all U.S. deserts, Death Valley, is in California. The great Mojave Desert covers a good portion of southern California and continues up the eastern portion of the state.

Traditionally, California deserts are divided into two classifications: high desert and low desert. As you would expect, the higher country has colder winters and more pleasant summers. However, "colder" winters doesn't mean continual freezing weather; it means that when cold winds blow from the north, it gets cool enough to freeze the hair off a bald mouse. But most of the time, whenever it's sunny, daytime temperatures climb to either shirtsleeve or light sweater weather.

Victorville and Apple Valley are examples of high desert locations that draw retirees. They mostly come from the Los Angeles area, attracted here by the low crime rates, cheap land and wide open spaces. Since few folks outside of California actually retire in high desert country, the discussion here covers mostly low desert towns, although Yucaipa almost falls into the high desert category.

Overall, California desert living may not be as affordable as living in other Western desert states, but for some folks money is less of an issue than locale. And for many retirees, California remains the land of their retirement dreams, no matter the cost.

Palm Springs   When people speak of "Palm Springs" they could mean any of a half-dozen towns scattered along Interstate 10 from Palm Springs to Indian Wells. Playground of millionaires, movie stars and other rich and famous types, Palm Springs is synonymous with "class." Well-known personalities—like Bob Hope, Bing Crosby, Jerry Ford, and a host of others—have made golf fans aware of the great, year-round golf courses. When people with enough money to live anywhere in the world choose the Palm Springs area for their homes, there must be something special going on!

Sheltered in the lee of the rugged San Jacinto Mountains, with abundant water, Palm Springs is verdant and livable year-round. Green landscaping, huge palm trees and manicured golf courses convert the desert into a botanical wonderland. The area supports more golf courses than most cities have supermarkets, 93 in total, although many are private, belonging to residents of the surrounding developments.

251

Winters are as delightful here as summers are hot. As one real estate salesperson put it, "Which is worse, a low-humidity, hot summer—or an icy, freezing winter?" (As I work on my notes, it's the middle of January here in Palm Springs. I am outdoors—barefoot, wearing shorts and no shirt—listening to radio reports of 18-below-zero storms savaging the Midwest and Eastern states, with snow drifts deeper than my pool!)

Instead of snowstorms, Southern California deserts have windstorms. One reason for Palm Springs' popularity is that nearby mountains block most of this wind. The farther south from the interstate, the more protection.

A drive through expensive neighborhoods can be overwhelming: one street after another competing for the title of the fanciest and most opulent. Shopping centers that look as if they were built for sultans or nobility offer any kind of luxury item you can afford (and many that you can't). Clean desert air and a rugged mountain backdrop give Palm Springs an aura of pristine beauty combined with regal affluence.

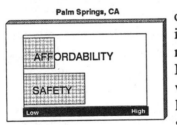

Palm Springs, CA

The curious thing is, although this is one of the more expensive retirement areas in the country, it's not necessarily out of reach for folks with moderate incomes. Most residents are *not* rich; they work for wages and can't afford a super-expensive lifestyle. The main industry is support services: restaurants, stores, hotels, or gardening for wealthy families—jobs of that nature. Wages for grocery clerks or waiters are seldom so high that they drive up the housing market. Palm Springs real estate is an either-or thing: either you can't afford high payments, or you're rich and you don't give a damn!

The fanciest homes are found in adjoining towns, places like Rancho Mirage, Palm Desert or Indian Wells. Yet, interspersed with these exclusive enclaves are affordable neighborhoods for ordinary wage-earners and retirees, often just a few blocks away. Mobile home and RV parks also provide moderate-cost alternatives. Some are elegant, complete with golf privileges; others are more plain, with competitive rates.

On our most recent research trip here, in early 1994, we noticed an unusual number of foreclosure sales and HUD offerings. To our surprise, prices of homes, condos and country-club residences had *dropped* since our previous visit. We looked at a small, two-bedroom condo within walking distance of downtown Palm Springs for $44,000 (a HUD repo). $100,000 would buy a three-bedroom place in a "gated" development (a

24-hour guarded entrance, almost always with pool and tennis, often with golf). How about $130,000 for a luxury place on a private, 18-hole golf course? Even though we visited during the high tourist season, apartment and condo rentals were affordable, with many vacancies.

Why such reasonable prices? Because much of Palm Springs real estate is in second homes owned by Los Angeles residents. Consequently, the market is impacted by L.A.'s sluggish economy. When defense industry jobs dry up, lucrative businesses go sour, and high-paid executives go on unemployment, the first things to go are the yacht and the Palm Springs condo. Also, the series of disasters in L.A.—from fires to the big earthquake of '94—have added to this situation. My guess is, until the economy picks up in Los Angeles, Palm Springs will remain a buyer's market.

To sum up, Palm Springs is without a doubt our favorite desert location in terms of winter weather, luxury and prestige. While it's more expensive than some other places discussed in this book, it's also more affordable than many people think. The key is finding housing that won't break your budget. After that, everything falls into place.

Desert Hot Springs   If the posh atmosphere of Palm Springs is a little intimidating, you'll find a "Poor Man's Palm Springs" just across Interstate 10 about 15 minutes' drive away. This is the town of Desert Hot Springs (pop. 11,000). Its name comes from the hot springs that flow under the town from nearby mountain slopes and are commonly tapped by residents who then enjoy the water in their backyard swimming pools and hot tubs. Much smaller than Palm Springs or any of the ritzy sections on the other side of Interstate 10, Desert Hot Springs has a lot to offer in pleasant, economical desert retirement.

Desert Hot Springs bestows many of Palm Springs' advantages without the higher prices. The fabled restaurants, golf courses, shopping and social life of Palm Springs are just a few minutes away. With an elevation about a thousand feet higher than Palm Springs, Desert Hot Springs enjoys summer temperatures a smidgen lower than communities on the valley floor. Winter days are often

Desert Hot Springs, CA

AFFORDABILITY

SAFETY

Low   High

warmer, due to the mountains which block north winds that occasionally bring cold down from Alaska. The most common weather complaint concerns annoying westerly winds which hit Desert Hot Springs, but circumvent Palm Springs.

Like Palm Springs, a large percentage of the residents live here year-round. Many are retired, but there's also a large balance of younger people who work in Palm Springs but can't afford its prices. The downtown area is low key, as is the rest of the town. For family restaurants, shopping and services, Desert Hot Springs offers anything you need.

Being used to large-city California prices, we thought the rentals and property prices in Desert Hot Springs looked like giveaways. Real estate brokers estimate that you can subtract about $20,000 from Palm Springs prices for similar property in Desert Hot Springs. Mobile homes, in particular, were cheap—some listed for as low as $12,000 for a two-bedroom single-wide. We looked at a manufactured home retirement community, a place called Quail Hollow, and were favorably impressed. Were it not for the fact that the land is leased rather than owned, we would have been tempted to buy.

In our last edition of *Where to Retire,* Desert Hot Springs had a low crime-risk factor, but this year dropped in the ratings. That shows what happens to a small town when a wave of burglaries and car thefts strikes. I feel that this is an anomaly, and things will be better in the next report.

Several new apartment buildings have increased the number of rental units available; since builders were slightly over-optimistic about the rental market, rents are forced to be competitive. Swimming pools and hot springs spas are typically included.

PALM SPRINGS AREA			Rel. Humidity: Jan. 31%, July 15%			
	Jan.	April	July	Oct.	Rain	Snow
Daily Highs	70	86	102	91	3"	—
Daily Lows	39	57	72	58		

Imperial Valley   The Imperial Valley, at the southern end of California, south of the Salton Sea and west of Yuma, sometimes dips below sea level. For those who like desert living, but without the formality of Palm Springs, several other desert locations are worth investigating. Brawley, El Centro and Calexico sit in a straight 25-mile line north from the Mexican border. Here, you'll find a relaxed style of living, with a touch of nearby Mexico's heritage. Spanish is the second language here, rivaling English, especially in the border town of Calexico. You'll have an opportunity to learn the language if you care to.

This is *really* desert country. With less than two inches of rain a year, this area probably soaks up more sunshine than anywhere in the United States. Were it not for irrigation from the Colorado River and from wells, this place would look as barren as Death Valley. But when you add water, the desert blooms into some of the richest farm country imaginable. Winter daytime temperatures average 70 degrees, giving the Imperial Valley a 12-month growing season. Summers are quite hot, with early afternoons best spent in the shade or in an air-cooled shelter with a cold drink grasped firmly in your hand.

Calexico is distinguished by broad streets, many lined with stately date palms, neatly maintained homes and green lawns that mock the desert's stingy natural water supply. Mobile home and RV parks abound. This is a popular snowbird destination, with warm winters and inexpensive living. Other towns nearby, places like Calipatria, Holtville and Westmoreland are not much more than little crossroad-farming communities, places with small grocery stores and hardware supplies for those too busy to run into El Centro or Brawley.

When retirees are asked what they like best about Imperial Valley living, almost all put warm winters at the top of the list. Those who like to hunt pointed out the abundance of ducks, geese and pheasant during the season. Others mentioned the nearby Anza-Borrego Desert State Park, rock and mineral collecting and four-wheel driving through open lands.

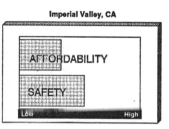

Imperial Valley, CA

Some people live in Calexico because of the availability of medical treatments across the U.S.-Mexican border that are prohibited in the United States. Many patients swear by Mexican arthritis medications, acupuncture treatments, or laetrile injections, although most medical authorities disagree vigorously. But all agree that dental work, including bridges and dentures, in Mexicali is top quality and at prices long forgotten on the U.S. side of the line. Caution is urged, however, to patronize only dentists whose work is recommended by other retirees. Eyeglasses are also a bargain, with identical frames costing a fraction of those in the United States.

Mexicali, on the Mexican side of the line, is a large place, growing constantly and in a constant state of change. A few years ago it was a rather grim place, with cabarets, hookers and rampant vice among its major attractions. But the city has done an amazingly thorough job of cleaning up its act. The downtown area is closely monitored to make sure no hanky-panky goes on. Police are conspicuous by their presence. The city encourages merchants and property owners to keep things neat and clean and to make things attractive for tourists and residents alike.

Yucaipa   About midway between Palm Springs and Los Angeles is another interesting retirement area, one that is neither desert nor temperate. The Yucaipa Valley actually sits on the borderline of three climatic zones. To the south the desert stretches to Palm Springs and on to Mexico. On the eastern and northern edges the mountains rise to over a mile high, up to the ski country of Big Bear and Lake Arrowhead. Finally, to the west, the lower portions of the valley are orchard country, with plums, peaches and grapes growing in a profusion of well-tended orchards. The higher altitudes of the valley are ideal for apples, which love a touch of frost in the fall and winter and nice, warm summers.

With 25 inches of rain a year, the countryside is considerably greener than much of the nearby country I've discussed. The word "Yucaipa" is supposed to have come from a Serrano Indian word meaning "wet, green place." The altitude varies from 2,000 to 5,000 feet, with most people living around the 2,600-foot level. This is an area of small homes on large acreage, usually with a generous amount of the land in orchard or pasture for riding horses.

Despite a population of about 37,000 in Yucaipa and nearby Calimesa, the valley is unincorporated. This means several things that may or may not be beneficial, depending on your point of view. One advantage is you don't pay city taxes, some of which would ordinarily pay for services already provided by county and state governments. For example, Yucaipa has no city police force to duplicate the services of the county sheriff's office, which already patrols the area. There aren't separate city and county library systems or road-building and maintenance departments. The county or state provides these services at a considerable saving of taxpayers' money. Several parks, a community center, tennis courts, swimming pool and services of that nature are county funded.

A disadvantage is the distance of local government and the lack of some personal services that a low tax base can't provide. With a smaller, more accessible city government, senior citizens carry much more weight than when their voices and votes are diluted among an entire county. When the elderly complain about lacking services, the county or state finds it convenient to plead insufficient tax funds or to simply ignore the requests.

Yucaipa's central focus shows a clear emphasis on mobile homes. Almost 60 parks dot the valley, some elegant, some plain. As usual, proliferation of mobile homes and parks means lower prices and reasonable rents. The local newspaper lists more than twice as many ads for mobile homes than houses for sale. Asking prices are exceptionally low, with two-bedroom units starting around $7,000. This wouldn't be in a luxury park, however. With so many choices, you should have no problem finding a mobile home park that suits your wants and needs.

Yucaipa isn't the fanciest retirement area around. It's an earthy, folksy kind of place. Don't expect to find gourmet restaurants or night life. But, since it's less than an hour's drive from Los Angeles and 45 minutes from Palm Springs, you can have the amenities of sophisticated city life when you choose.

YUCAIPA				Rel. Humidity: Jan. 28%, July 22%		
	Jan.	April	July	Oct.	Rain	Snow
Daily Highs	62	85	98	79	6"	—
Daily Lows	44	54	69	60		

Gold Country

In 1847, in a part of Mexico called "Alta California," a group of workers labored to construct a sawmill on a rushing stream that flowed down from the Sierra Nevada range. This was in the north-central part of what was to become California, near what is now Sacramento. As they dug into the river's bank, one man noticed something curious in his shovel's blade. Sparkling metal pebbles mixed with the gravel. Gold!

This event touched off one of the most exciting chapters in United States history. News of the discovery spread; the rush was on. People came by covered wagon and horseback; some sailed around Cape Horn to join in a frenzy of prospecting. Eager miners attacked streams with gold pan and sluice box to fill their pockets with gold nuggets. Gold deposits were so rich that miners called the area the "Mother Lode."

Within a short span of time, rude mining camps became towns and then small cities. Paved streets, brick buildings, theaters and businesses flourished, creating replicas in miniature of Midwestern and Eastern towns of that era.

When gold claims finally played out, gold miners drifted on to other enterprises. Some moved to fertile California valleys to seek fortunes as growers. Others settled in the growing coastal cities. When miners moved away, Mother Lode towns became virtual ghost towns. Luckily, this abandonment preserved many old mining towns in time-capsule form—fascinating pictures of life as it was during California's romantic past. Because of low-cost housing and pleasant environments, these are now great places for retirement.

Gold Country is about as far from the usual California image as you can get. Its collection of old mining towns, with narrow streets and buildings of native stone and brick, harmonize perfectly with the green-clad mountain backdrops. The state jealously preserves the sites as a charming part of California's past, the country of Brett Harte, Mark Twain and John Fremont.

From rolling hills studded with black oaks and manzanita to the majestic peaks of the Sierra Nevada, the Mother Lode encompasses a unique scenic wonderland. Here you find not only a true four-season climate, but variation on the seasons, depending on the altitude you choose. From mild winters and warm summers in Jackson and Angels Camp to deep snow-pack and cool summers in Lake Tahoe, you have a complete selection of climates and seasonal colors. Trout streams are well-stocked, with rare golden trout waiting to be hooked in higher lakes.

The Mother Lode encompasses a 300-mile stretch of rolling-to-rugged country that runs from Downieville in the north down to Coarsegold in the south. It takes in nine counties—Madera, Mariposa, Tuolumne, Calaveras, El Dorado, Placer, Nevada, Sierra and Amador. Then, 100 miles to the northwest, another area of historic gold-mining towns spreads across several more counties—Butte, Siskiyou, Tehama, Shasta, Trinity and Lassen.

By the way, the '49ers didn't get *all* the gold. The left enough to keep hundreds of weekend prospectors and amateur miners working at their dredges and sluice boxes. With most of the countryside designated public land and national forest, you'll have ample opportunity to try your luck if you wish. A favorite family outing is to take a picnic lunch and a couple of gold pans and spend the afternoon working one of the many creeks and streams that traverse hills covered with oak, pine and cedar. Some people do quite well, but you can expect them to be very close-mouthed about *where* they found their private bonanzas. Others are ashamed that they can't locate much gold, and they lie about how much they find. That's what I do.

Amador County   As an example of the Gold Country, let's look in detail at one location in the center of the Mother Lode. Amador County straddles historic Highway 49, which runs along the route of the trail that once connected the busiest of the mining towns from north to south. One of the richest gold-mining districts, Amador County accounted for more than half of all the gold harvested from the Mother Lode. Here are found such fascinating towns as Jackson, Sutter Creek, Volcano, Fiddletown and Plymouth. Drytown, now a wide spot on Highway 49, was once not so small or so dry. At its prime, the mining camp boasted 27 saloons. That was before it drew the attention of indignant prohibitionists, after which it earned the title of Drytown.

Loaded with relics of the past, each of these towns takes pride in maintaining and restoring its historic old buildings. Jackson, the largest town in the county, is an intriguing mixture of old and new, with the downtown preserved in the tradition of the gold rush days. Brick and stone buildings line narrow streets, adorned with iron shutters and wrought-iron balconies in the style of the mid-1800s. Yet, the newer outskirts have modern ranch-style homes as California-looking as you might expect to find anywhere. Like other Mother Lode towns, Jackson is proud of its restored old brick and Victorian frame houses, with all modern conveniences added. Housing costs are below national average, and far, far below what you would pay in the larger California cities. Because of very mild winters, mobile homes are practical. You may choose from five mobile home parks in the county.

Highway 88, the trans-Sierra route, cuts through Jackson on its way east across the mountains at Carson Pass and down into Nevada. Highway 88 was once designated as the country's most scenic highway by *Parade* magazine. It winds through Pine Grove and Volcano, past Inspiration Point, Maiden's Grave and Tragedy Springs, just to name a few historical sights along the way. This route was once called the Carson Emigrant Trail because of its popularity with gold-seeking settlers.

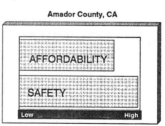

In western, more mountainous locations, climate varies with altitude, and the altitude varies wildly in Amador County. Lower elevations start at 200 feet and climb all the way to over 9,000 feet. Magnificent views of snow-covered peaks, mountain lakes and meadows are everywhere. With low summer humidity, even the warmest days are comfortable. Winters are short and mild (January highs average 56 degrees), and the area enjoys a true spring and colorful fall season.

When I asked Marcia Oxford of the Amador County Chamber of Commerce why she thinks retirees are moving there, she replied: "It *must* be attractive here; almost 50 percent of our population consists of retirees. Because of the geographical diversity, people can live in the rolling foothills, in the pines and evergreens or higher in the snow country. We enjoy four distinct seasons, the air is clean, and there's a wonderful, warm small-town care and friendliness that we all enjoy."

Grass Valley/Nevada City   Other popular retirement towns are found to the north of Jackson, places like Grass Valley and Nevada City, which are a bit more sophisticated and offer a more cosmopolitan charm than Jackson. The area teems with a sense of history and abundant natural beauty. Gold Rush architecture with white church steeples and Victorian buildings are shaded by century-old sugar maples and liquidambars which early settlers brought with them from the New England states. Thousands of miners came here in the 1800's—one of California's richest gold-producing regions—and today, retirees are finding their personal bonanzas in quality living.

The towns of Grass Valley and Nevada City sit in the foothills of the Sierra Nevada Mountains, at an average elevation of 2,500 feet. The surroundings vary from rolling hills to rugged peaks, with plentiful forests of oak, pine, cedar and fir. Residents enjoy four gentle seasons, with homes perched above the fog line, yet below the heavy snow line.

Grass Valley is the larger town with almost 10,000 residents, and nearby Nevada City adds another 3,000. Conveniently close to Interstate 80, trips to Reno (1-1/2 hours) or Sacramento (1 hour) or San Francisco (3 hours) are a piece of cake for those who crave action from time to time. However many dynamic cultural activities are available right here, including classical music festivals, concerts and theater productions. Several theatre companies entertain with productions almost the year-round. A community college is scheduled to open here in 1995.

For outdoor recreation, the region is filled with lakes, streams, parks, campgrounds and hiking trails. Winter skiing is only an hour away at half a dozen resorts, and the short drive makes returning home after a hard afternoon's skiing less of a chore. Summers see very little rainfall, so you'll have plenty of sunshine to accompany you on fishing trips and picnics. There is one public golf course and three private ones.

Nevada City, by the way, has an exceptionally active senior center, with plenty of activities and volunteer opportunities galore. The "Gold Country Telecare" network keeps folks in touch by phone for problem solving, assistance and counseling. Telecare volunteers are available for seniors who can't afford to hire someone to fix a leaky faucet or to repair porch steps. Legal and tax questions are covered by other volunteers and still others make sure seniors don't miss an appointment with the dentist, shopping or recreational activities. Medical care is excellent, with a non-profit hospital with a 124-bed acute care facility offering state-of-the-art diagnostic, surgical and therapeutic equipment.

Scattered around the countryside are any number of smaller communities, historic places like Rough and Ready, Gold Run or Colfax, away from town but only a few miles from shopping. Before you settle on a gold-mining location, you must see 'em all!

AMADOR/GRASS VALLEY				Rel. Humidity: Jan. 71%, July 28%	
	Jan.	April	July	Oct.	Rain	Snow
Daily Highs	54	62	85	71	40"	5"
Daily Lows	35	38	54	44		

Paradise   About 100 miles to the north of Amador County, the Feather River yielded another rich harvest of shining metal. Scattered above the canyon, on a place called Nimshew Ridge, a collection of little villages and mining camps sprang up, with vivid names like Dogtown, Toadtown, Poverty Ridge and Whiskey Flats. At Dogtown (now Magalia) a prospector uncovered a 59-pound gold nugget back in 1859. Several nuggets weighing up to nine pounds each turned up later, but after the Dogtown nugget, everything else seemed anticlimactic.

Apparently, folks grew tired of explaining why they lived in Whiskey Flats or on Poverty Ridge, so they agreed to form one town and call it something more romantic: "Paradise." Thousands of modern-day retirees believe they've found their paradise here. Forty-nine percent of the residents are over 55 years old.

Paradise and nearby Magalia share a particularly scenic location. Heavily forested, sitting at an altitude of 2,000 feet, the area is below the snow belt, yet above the Sacramento Valley's smog level.

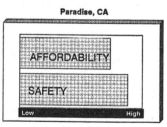

Paradise, CA

(There isn't really that much smog in the valley except when farmers burn the rice fields every fall.) This higher altitude also means ten-degree lower summer temperatures than the valley floor below.

Being below the snow belt doesn't mean that Paradise is snow free. Around these parts, higher elevations (over four thousand feet) are generally covered with snow most of the winter. When winter rains fall on Paradise, it's a good bet that it'll be snowing in Stirling City, some 20 miles away and a thousand feet higher. But, when conditions are right, Paradise's rain turns to snow. At this altitude, snow doesn't come down in small flakes and particles, it forms large puffs the size of golf balls. Very soft and fluffy, it piles up incredibly fast. What might be a four-inch snow in Stirling City becomes 12 inches in Paradise or Magalia. Oldtimers tell of three feet of snow falling overnight. However, this type of snow melts quickly the moment the sun warms things up. Even in the coldest months, afternoons are usually warm enough for a light sweater to feel comfortable, and golf courses are open year-round.

Contractors take care to build homes without disturbing the trees any more than necessary. Building lots are large, usually a quarter to half an acre, sometimes several acres, and houses are scattered so that it's hard to believe there could be 40,000 people living in the area. With low housing density and lots of forest, Paradise is a sanctuary for wild animals, since hunting is prohibited in town. Deer and raccoons saunter about town insolently, as if they were taxpayers.

Adequate shopping facilities, with several tastefully done centers, make for convenience. Cable TV is available and so is that ultimate mark of civilization: home pizza delivery. A drawback is that Paradise lacks both public transportation and intercity bus service; an auto is necessary.

As a normal response to a large retiree population, health care is unusually good. There's a 109-bed hospital, two convalescent hospitals, three medical care centers, plus several residential care and guest homes. This large population of retirees means lots of organized activities and clubs. In addition to the usual AARP organization, there is a Golden Fifties Club, a Retired Teachers Association, a senior singles club and a couple of senior citizens' political action coalitions.

Paradise-Magalia is a peaceful and safe place, ranking seventh highest in our safety research. Many local cops, like retirees, are from Los Angeles. When Paradise organized its own police force, the city recruited in Southern California. One ex-L.A.P.D. officer said, "What a difference! Here I spend my time helping people instead of dealing with criminals. In Los Angeles it was always 'them' against us."

Because almost half the population lives on fixed incomes, housing costs and rents haven't been pushed to the ridiculous highs of some other parts of California. Home prices start at around $60,000 for a modest place to over $200,000 for something with a spectacular view of the Feather River Canyon below Nimshew Ridge. Rentals for two- to four-bedroom homes range from $310 to $650 a month, with mobile homes (on residential lots) renting for $250 to $400. Mobile home parks are plentiful and space rents quite affordable.

PARADISE			Rel. Humidity: Jan. 63%, July 21%			
	Jan.	April	July	Oct.	Rain	Snow
Daily Highs	52	71	92	85	45"	18"
Daily Lows	32	45	61	48		

Chico   In contrast, only a 20-minute drive from the mountain city of Paradise is the flatland city of Chico, another excellent retirement location. Although its population is about the same as Paradise's, the two places are a world apart. Chico is a typical Sacramento Valley town, with live oaks and huge ash trees shading quiet streets on topography as flat as a table.

The thing that lifts Chico above most small, agriculturally centered valley towns is its university and vibrant academic timbre. Precisely because of the town's laid-back atmosphere, away from the distraction of big-city life or surfing beaches, Chico State University is preferred by many California parents when helping their kids select a school. Like all California state universities, Chico State encourages senior citizen participation with free and reduced tuition rates. Cultural events, such as concerts, plays, lectures and foreign films, are plentiful and, more often than not, free.

Many good home buys in Chico are found in older neighborhoods and in some more recent developments on the edge of town. Typical construction is frame with stucco finish, favored because of its resilience in earthquakes. (A brick building tends to crack and suffer damage; a frame house simply twists and rolls with the 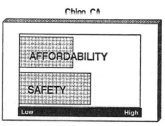 shaking.) Because of the university, housing prices are higher than in ordinary Sacramento Valley cities, and inexpensive rentals are either snatched up by students or are located in student neighborhoods where stereo music is commonly played at a volume that blisters wallpaper.

Retirees living in Chico point out the advantage of being close to the mountains—with good fishing, hunting and camping. A short drive takes you to the natural beauty and the recreational opportunities of the Feather River Canyon wilderness. Skiing is enjoyed at Inskip, about 40 minutes away, and some of the best striped bass in the West are caught in the nearby Sacramento River. Incidentally, fishermen haul monster sturgeon from this river, many fish tipping the scale at over 200 pounds! Since sturgeon is a game fish and not sold commercially, few people have ever tasted a succulent steak from one of these large creatures. It's like no other fish you've ever tasted—as firm as lobster and as juicy as a filet mignon, yet with a flavor closer to frogs' legs than fish.

Chico weather, as in all Central Valley towns, is both a blessing and a drawback, depending on your opinion of how hot summers should be. You can find days on end with temperatures approaching 100 degrees. Balance that against the warm, seldom-frosty winter days, and I believe Chico's weather comes out a winner. After all, when the summer gets going, that's the time for you to get going for the nearby mountains for a picnic beside a cool stream or a day's prospecting and panning for gold in the Feather River.

CHICO			Rel. Humidity: Jan. 59%, July 19%			
---	Jan.	April	July	Oct.	Rain	Snow
Daily Highs	54	73	98	79	22"	1"
Daily Lows	36	44	59	47		

Dunsmuir The Sacramento River, which passes through Chico on its way to San Francisco Bay, has its origins farther north, past Redding and beautiful Lake Shasta, in the mountains not far from the town of Dunsmuir. Dunsmuir sits in a canyon, overlooked by ridges covered with Christmas-tree pines and segmented by streets that climb steeply from river bottom to the interstate highway above town. Year-round, the town enjoys a spectacular view of snow-covered Mt. Shasta in the distance.

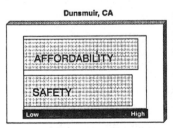

This ancient volcano, is one of the highest peaks on the continent and offers some pretty fair skiing at a place called Snowman's Hill.

Dunsmuir is an old town, with few homes younger than 50 years. A sense of history permeates the old-fashioned downtown section, with its one main street. Here the bus station is still called the "stage stop" by older residents, and the Greyhound bus is called the "stage." Although some mining went on in the area, Dunsmuir originated as a roundhouse and repair service for passing trains, providing fuel and water for the locomotives and food for the dining cars.

With the decline of steam engines, the original purpose of the town faded. Some railroaders moved away when they lost their jobs; others retired and stayed there. Thus began a continuing tradition of Dunsmuir as a retirement location. When the railroaders left, the bottom dropped out of the real estate market, which didn't have far to drop, since property was always quite reasonable. Retirees found this an ideal location—great fishing, economical living, a gorgeous view from the front porch every morning and unforgettable sunsets.

Lurking trout, sometimes large native ones, tempt the fisherman to the shores of the Sacramento River. Wild blackberry bushes on the banks yield delicious makings for cobblers, should the fish not be biting that day. The river has recovered nicely from a horrendous pesticide spill a couple of years past. Once again the odor of rainbow trout frying for breakfast fills the morning air.

Because Interstate 5 bypasses the town by a quarter-mile, the pace along the town's main street is leisurely and unhurried. Dunsmuir's northern location and 2,300-foot elevation ensure at least a couple of good winter snowstorms. Since I spent one winter here, working on the old *Dunsmuir News*, I can attest that snow here is a special sort—soft, fluffy and pretty (as long as you don't have to shovel the blasted stuff). But it does pile up quickly. The canyon turns into a billowy white winter fantasyland for a day or two, until a warm rain clears it all away.

DUNSMUIR			Rel. Humidity: Jan. 62%, July 23%			
	Jan.	April	July	Oct.	Rain	Snow
Daily Highs	50	53	90	68	30"	18"
Daily Lows	30	36	58	39		

Fall River Mills/Burney   One last example of gold country retirement is called the Intermountain Area and nestles between the Sierra Nevada and the Cascade mountain ranges in the northeast corner of California. This is just one of many such picturesque and unspoiled areas of the state with inexpensive living. The highway east from Redding winds past several abandoned mines as it makes its way to the towns of Burney and Fall River Mills. Today, gold mining is no longer an economic force, having been pushed aside by wild-rice farming in Fall River Mills and lumber mills in Burney.

Tall Douglas pines shade Burney's streets and homes. A recent forest fire devastated large tracts of forest, but firefighters heroically stopped it before it could damage the town. Twenty miles away, in a sharply different terrain, are Burney's sister towns of Fall River Mills and McArthur. The panorama in these towns is a wide, grassy valley circled by tree-clad mountains. A remarkably clear stream (the Fall

River) wells up from the depths of a volcanic formation a few miles away and collects the waters of a dozen sparkling trout streams as it meanders through the valley. The views are enhanced by Mt. Lassen (10,466 feet) to the southeast and by majestic, snowcapped Mt. Shasta (14,162 feet) to the northwest.

"Fall River Mills," I hear you saying. "Never heard of it. Why would anyone want to live there?" Well, you've heard of one of Fall River Mills' earlier residents: Bing Crosby. With all of the country to choose from, Bing bought a ranch there as a place to raise his boys. (Another Hollywood personality owns the ranch now; I won't say who, because local people don't like to bring attention to the town that way.)

Bing's favorite sports were golf and fly fishing. The superb trout streams throughout the Intermountain Area satisfied the latter interest, but Bing could not survive without golf. This explains the existence of a beautiful 18-hole championship golf course located just west of Fall River Mills on the main highway. It's reputed to rank among the top 50 courses in the United States. The unique layout of the course poses a challenge to professionals and amateurs alike. There is a restaurant, a clubhouse and a pro shop, with other facilities planned for the future.

Fall River Mills/Burney, CA

AFFORDABILITY

SAFETY

Low   High

Between these two towns you'll find most of the services available in a city, while they cling to an away-from-it-all atmosphere. Burney has a bustling "downtown," complete with shopping district; Fall River Mills is scattered over several miles of highway and ends at an even smaller town: McArthur. Even though the nearest city of any size, Redding, is an hour's drive away, the Intermountain Area is self-sufficient with shopping centers, banks, restaurants and a hospital.

Those looking for a low cost of living would be hard pressed to find a better bargain. Three-bedroom houses sell for as little as $65,000 in Burney. Since land is inexpensive, small lots are rare. Fall River Mills property is a bit higher due to a recent real estate shortage. In a small place like this, just a few buyers can create a scarcity.

The Mountain Senior Center, located in Burney, is a complex consisting of single-family homes and one-bedroom apartments situated within easy walking distance of shopping and medical facilities. It also features a park, community center and RV storage, all designed for use by people 55 years or older. Free bus transportation is also available to seniors throughout the Intermountain area for special needs.

The waterways of the Intermountain Area offer many varieties of fishing. Choose from deep, cold lakes or mountain streams for bass and trout; try the warmer waters for catfish and crappie. Lakes Britton, Eastman, Fall River, Baum Crystal and Iron Canyon are a lure to all types of fishermen. With a short drive to the northwest, fishermen will find other hot spots on Bear Creek, Medicine Lake, McCloud River and others. Two wild trout streams—Hat Creek and Fall River—offer trophy trout to the dedicated fly fisherman or those fishing with artificial lures. (Live bait is prohibited.)

FALL RIVER MILLS/BURNEY			Rel. Humidity: Jan. 59%, July 24%			
	Jan.	April	July	Oct.	Rain	Snow
Daily Highs	40	74	91	69	40"	25"
Daily Lows	28	47	68	46		

Northern California Coast

The northern California coast is highlighted by the urbanity and sophistication of the San Francisco Bay area. But "the City by the Bay" shouldn't be your only stop on a tour of this area's retirement possibilities. After you cross the Golden Gate Bridge going north, Highway 1 winds through some of the most peaceful and rural landscapes to be found anywhere. The towns are small, neighborly and uncrowded. The only large town on the California stretch of coast is Eureka, the next "metropolitan" area being the Coos Bay-North Bend area in Oregon. Several picturesque villages sit along the coast, interspersed with forest and grazing land, sleepy and laid-back just as they should be. Small, family-owned wineries and their tasting rooms make for interesting visits. If you are looking for discos, beach parties and tourist traps, you are much too far north.

Along this coast the traditional industry has always been lumbering, which appears to be in a permanent state of depression all over the West. The second industry is fishing, much of which is done by amateurs or people just out for fun. Since neither industry is hiring workers, jobs are scarce and younger people are leaving for the cities. That means housing is affordable. The moral of this story is, if you need to work part-time to make ends meet, forget about the northwest coast. If you can satisfy your need for work through meaningful volunteer jobs, you will do just fine.

If you are members of that class that hates hot summers and cold winters, you've come to the right place. Frost is all but unheard of, with 40 degrees just about as cold as it ever gets in January. Highs in January—in Eureka, for example—average 53 degrees, but the July and August highs rarely top 70 degrees! Compare that with *your* town's average July temperatures. Every night of the year you will sleep under blankets; an air conditioner would be a waste of money. On the other hand, since lows are never subfreezing, many homes don't have central heating systems, depending upon a wall furnace or fireplace for comfort.

California's Napa Valley wine-producing country and its delightful little towns and villages are great for retirement. People choose places like Calistoga, Healdsburg or St. Helena, just to name a few. For quality living at moderate costs, the Napa-Sonoma region merits closer investigation. But there's a lesser-known wine country—just as pretty and less crowded—not far away, on the Mendocino Coast, with the Pacific Ocean on one side and the low coastal mountains on the other.

San Francisco   Even folks who don't care for California fall in love with this fabulous city of cities located on beautiful San Francisco Bay. No other city I've seen—anywhere I've ever visited—compares with it for breathtaking scenic vistas, restaurants, architecture, cultural ambience and excitement. If you haven't guessed it by now, I'll admit that this is my favorite city in the whole world.

It's a great place to visit, and anyone who passes up a chance to spend some time here is missing a wonderful experience. Although I generally recommend against retirement in a large city, in the case of San Francisco, I'll have to make an exception. Not for just anyone, mind you, because it's expensive, it's crowded and has unsafe neighborhoods. But the excitement of San Francisco, its sophisticated ambience and glamorous setting make it all worthwhile, for some folks anyway.

The "City"—as it's called hereabouts—is composed of neighborhoods, each distinct and sometimes radically dissimilar from the others.

Our favorite activity is exploring these neighborhoods (or districts). Cow Hollow is so different from the nearby Marina District that you can tell where you are just by the types of restaurants. Chinatown, Japantown, the Fillmore, the Financial District, the Mission District, Fisherman's Wharf, Potrero Hill, Twin Peaks, the Tenderloin, Castro Street, Pacific Heights, the Western Addition, the Sunset District—all these places are special to San Franciscans. Each has its distinctive flavor and color, sometimes even a different language. You'll encounter Irish enclaves, where in pubs you'll hear a strong brogue spoken over glasses of Guinness stout, other areas where Italian or Spanish is the lingua franca, and of course, Chinatown, with its myriads of restaurants, shops and mysterious alleyways.

Saratoga, CA

Restaurant exploration is one of the favorite pastimes here. In the Mission District you can order *papusas, enchiladas, empanadas, gallo pinto* and even a hamburger or pizza. Chinatown is my favorite: *dim sum* breakfasts with shrimp rolls, steamed dumplings with quail eggs poached over the tops, *char siu, hoc gau, siu mai*, and on and on. (Okay, I also admit that restaurants are a major factor in my evaluation of San Francisco neighborhoods.)

San Francisco's suburbs are exceptionally high-quality places for retirement, but only for those who can afford the high cost of housing. The nicer neighborhoods are costly, but enjoy higher levels of personal safety. Rents are also steep, but not in proportion to the cost of buying property. For example, we have friends who live in a lovely home with a marvelous view of the bay. The value of the property is $550,000, yet it rents for only $1,800 a month. Although this may sound like a formidable rent, it amounts to a 3.2 percent return on an investment of $550,000. Even municipal bonds pay bigger returns than that, which leads me to question the wisdom of real estate investment here.

In short, unless you can afford to pay $1,200 a month or more, San Francisco is best visited rather than chosen as a retirement location. If the idea of high rent doesn't put you off, the City by the Bay is an excellent place for a six-month or longer adventure in dining, theater, museums and walking tours. However, when choosing an apartment, make sure a garage parking space is included. Otherwise you will spend your six months looking for a parking space.

My personal preference for quality retirement in this area is in the southern portion of the San Francisco Bay, places like Los Gatos or Saratoga (which ranked number *one* in our safety research). On the edge of the Santa Cruz mountains, with wooded hills, even some redwood groves, these offer some of the prettiest home settings with a climate at least ten degrees warmer than San Francisco. When the coast is fogged in, you can be sure of sunshine in Los Gatos and the Santa Cruz mountains. To get to the City from here requires about a 50-minute drive, and to the ocean beaches in Santa Cruz about 25 minutes.

SAN FRANCISCO			Rel. Humidity: Jan. 66%, July 59%			
	Jan.	April	July	Oct.	Rain	Snow
Daily Highs	56	63	71	70	20"	—
Daily Lows	42	47	54	51		

Mendocino/Fort Bragg The Mendocino Coast is accessed only by a slow, two-lane coastal highway; most casual tourists and hurried travelers choose to travel inland, along multi-lane, high-speed Highway 101. This leaves the towns along the coast untouched by those who aren't specifically interested in enjoying the special ambiences of this area.

Mendocino Coast, CA

AFFORDABILITY

SAFETY

Low   High

Founded in 1852 as a mill town, Mendocino started with a Cape Cod flavor that has been carefully preserved. This is a community of artisans, which accounts for the many art galleries and boutiques in the town. It's a small place, unincorporated, with approximately 1,100 residents, although there are over 8,000 in the surrounding area. The village sits high on a bluff, surrounded on three sides by the Pacific Ocean. Hollywood filmed several motion pictures here, taking full advantage of Mendocino's picturesque setting.

Popular with tourists and those looking for beautiful seascapes, the basic business here deals with art in one form or another. Mendocino is popular with those looking for quality living in a rural, cool (but not cold) climate. Housing prices are not as inexpensive as you might expect; well-off San Franciscans like their weekend homes here. Single-family homes of two to three bedrooms range from $175,000 to $378,000. Rentals vary from $600 on up. Expect to pay $1,200 rent for a place with a gorgeous view. But when you leave the immediate vicinity of the town center, prices drop considerably.

Ten miles north of Mendocino on Highway 1 is the working community of Fort Bragg, a lumbering and fishing community of over 6,000 residents. A no-nonsense business section makes Fort Bragg the place where people come for necessary services and shopping. It's an exceptionally clean and attractive place, more modern in appearance than Mendocino. Several local performing arts companies produce concerts, stage plays, musicals and reviews. San Francisco Symphony musicians join local musicians for the Mendocino Music Festival in July.

Housing costs are in line with local wages, thus less expensive than Mendocino. Both communities are attracting retirees as well as artisans, many coming from the San Francisco and Los Angeles areas.

MENDOCINO/FT. BRAGG			Rel. Humidity: Jan. 66%, July 59%			
	Jan.	April	July	Oct.	Rain	Snow
Daily Highs	53	54	64	63	39"	1"
Daily Lows	41	44	52	49		

Eureka/Arcata   This is another area that owes its origins to the gold rush. In 1850 its location on Humboldt Bay made it ideal as a port to supply mines east in Trinity County. Eureka flourished overnight as gold seekers poured into the port fresh from San Francisco. Arcata, on the north side of Humboldt Bay, was also founded in 1850. Brett Harte put in a brief stint as editor at a newspaper here until some local toughs took exception to his writing. He hopped a steamboat for San Francisco, where he achieved fame for his tales of life in the mining camps.

After the gold fields played out, prospectors stayed and looked for steadier work as fishermen, farmers and lumberjacks. The stately redwoods became the backbone of the economy in the late 1800s. Victorian homes built of almost indestructible redwood lumber grace the landscape of Eureka and the surrounding communities. These old homes are showcases for now-forgotten arts of carpentry. Since many early settlers were lumber barons, you can imagine the care and attention to detail with which the artisans constructed the homes. For this reason, the town has been declared a State Historical Landmark.

Humboldt Bay fishing highlights Eureka's economy nowadays. More than 300 fishing vessels call this home port and land more rockfish, crab, oysters and shrimp than any other place in California. Strolling along Eureka's quaint Old Town waterfront is a favorite activity, breathing in the fresh sea air, watching boats returning with catches of salmon and tasty Dungeness crab.

Although its population is less than 30,000, Eureka is the center, culturally and commercially, of another 45,000 residents in the immediate urban area. Approximately 86 percent of Humboldt County's 117,000 population lives within a 20-mile radius of Eureka. The famous Redwood Empire forests begin near the edge of town and climb the mountains beyond and into the Trinity Alps, with backdrops as high as 6,000 feet. Although this is primarily a mountainous region encompassing six wild and scenic river systems and stands of majestic redwood groves, Eureka itself is located on a level coastal plain. Eighty percent of the county is forested public lands.

The weather here, typical of beach towns along the coast north to Washington, is a place for retirees who hate the thought of hot, steamy summers or icy, frigid winters. Except for more rain in the winter months, there's little difference in the weather year-round. A sweater feels comfortable almost every evening of the year, and noonday weather is seldom, if ever, hot enough to make you sweat. Air conditioning is something people here read about. Winters are mild enough that many homes heat with fireplaces or wood stoves. Many older houses have fireplaces in every room. Rainfall here is around 38 inches, a lot for

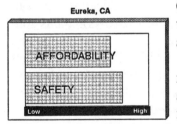

Eureka, CA

California but much less than most Midwestern and Eastern cities. Snow shovels are as unnecessary as air conditioning.

Located on Highway 101, a main north/south artery, the Eureka area also has an airport with regional carriers for short flights to San Francisco and other important local cities. The airport is located a few miles north of Arcata, about 15 miles from Eureka, and is served by a bus shuttle.

Three excellent hospitals serve the area, one each for Eureka and the neighboring communities of Arcata and Fortuna. Arcata's hospital can boast that its staff makes house calls, since they operate a home care service for those who need ongoing treatment outside the hospital. The service is carried out by registered nurses, home health aides and physical therapists under the direction of a physician.

The Eureka Senior Center, housed in an old grammar school building, is one of the most extensive and comprehensive we've seen. From classes such as arts and crafts to an Alzheimer's day care center, the services are superb. The Retired Senior Volunteer Program counts on more than 700 retirees who contribute their skills and interests in service to the community.

Fishing, of course, is a favorite sport here, with salmon, albacore and Dungeness crab catch. With generally benign weather, some kind of fishing, crabbing or clamming is possible all year. For those who get seasick, the country immediately behind the town, continuing 100 miles or so, is full of great trout streams. Deer, river otters, herons and other wildlife are plentiful, for much of the Coast Range and inland Klamath Mountains are jealously preserved as wildlife areas.

Nearby Arcata (pop. 17,000) is the home of Humboldt State University, one of the area's economic mainstays. With a good reputation as a serious school, the university is also the source of many cultural and intellectual events open to the public. In addition, there is the College of the Redwoods, a two-year school, and Eureka Adult School, with many community locations. The academic atmosphere complements the old-fashioned, Victorian atmosphere of the area, a place where mountains, forest and blue Pacific all come together.

Along this northern coast, all the way to Washington state, low wages and living costs are the rule. As a result, housing is quite reasonable—probably as low as you might expect to find anywhere on the West Coast. It's not difficult to find homes selling for $60,000 or less. For $75,000 and up you can buy a new place. We looked at several Victorians—our favorite had high ceilings, a claw-foot bathtub and an antique wood cookstove, three bedrooms, going for $94,000. Mobile homes are located away from the city's residential sections and seem to be in abundant supply, because they sell at very reasonable prices. In the countryside, many place mobile homes on spacious wooded lots. Except for Arcata, where students compete for housing, rentals are readily available.

A place famous for Victorians is Ferndale, a short drive south of Eureka. Started in the late 1800s as a prosperous dairy center, the early settlers built some splendidly ornate homes that became known as Butterfat Palaces. Even though the town is a tourist attraction, it's mostly a "stop-for-lunch, look around and get-going-again" sort of tourism. Retirees find it a place to stay. Ferndale, like the other towns around Eureka, preserves a small-town atmosphere of neighborliness. Bed and breakfast places are popular.

EUREKA/ARCATA			Rel. Humidity: Jan. 56%, July 66%			
	Jan.	April	July	Oct.	Rain	Snow
Daily Highs	53	55	61	60	39"	—
Daily Lows	42	44	52	48		

The Southern California Dream

When most folks think about California, they conjure images of Hollywood, surfboards, swimming pools and Cadillac convertibles. They picture southern California towns like Santa Barbara, Beverly Hills or San Diego with broad, palm-lined boulevards, pastel-colored mansions and ultra-modern apartment buildings. Easterners imagine southern California as a place to fantasize over, not a practical place to live.

However, even though some of these images are indeed true, hundreds of thousands of retired folks will tell you they wouldn't consider living anywhere else. Don't misunderstand: this is not a place to look for bargain living; most southern California locations are not cheap places to live. Overall, Los Angeles home prices are 61 percent over national averages! Yet, there are some excellent southern California communities where housing is comparable to many parts of the country—not next door to movie stars, but certainly in pleasant, safe neighborhoods.

Southern California living costs aren't out of line; after all, groceries, clothing, automobiles and items like that cost about the same, no matter where you live. Competition for consumer business keeps prices competitive in the Southland (as folks here like to refer to their home). You'll find the Los Angeles area always has among the lowest gasoline pump prices in the state. And, because the climate is mild to warm, neither air conditioning nor heating costs make drastic dents in the budget.

Why do people keep coming to southern California? Primarily because of the weather, but also because of the wide variety of things to do and sights to see. Places like Los Angeles and Santa Barbara owe much of their early growth to retirees coming to visit and to stay. Land promoters used to run cross-country passenger trains with free tickets just so retirees could investigate southern California as a retirement haven. When the unsuspecting retirees were hooked on the lovely orange grove dreamland, the slick promoters would sell them building lots for as much as $175 per parcel and then a house for an additional $3,000— places that wouldn't sell for much over $375,000 today. Unscrupulous!

San Diego San Diego, with a population of well over a million, is an excellent example of a city in transition from old to new. The downtown section, once rather ordinary and deteriorating—as most U.S. cities are lately—has been transformed into an exciting, welcoming city center. Trees, landscaping and careful planning are doing the trick.

The attraction here is its superb weather—statistically, it has the best climate in the continental United States. It never freezes or snows, and it rains a scant 11 inches a year—just enough to keep shrubbery and flowers fresh. A constant breeze from the Pacific pushes heat into the desert and nullifies cold snaps. There is no smog or air pollution, and little need for air conditioning. This explains the region's exceptionally low utility costs, 26 percent below national averages.

The San Diego area has an unusually large percentage of retirees. There are more than 100 senior citizens' organizations, with membership totaling over 100,000. Numerous life-care centers and seniors-only apartments and housing complexes are scattered around the region.

The big drawback with San Diego is expensive housing, one of the highest in the nation. The median price of a single family home is almost $190,000. Selling prices of homes are inflated, rents are costly, and mobile home parks are scarce and ridiculously expensive; many have been converted to commercial use, with tenants forced to look for other, non-existent parks. The inflated cost of keeping a roof over your head drags the overall cost of living index up as well.

However, like Los Angeles, it isn't necessary to live in the city itself to enjoy the weather and ambience. At the eastern edge of San Diego the country turns into desert hills, with dramatic boulders and rock formations garnished with cactus and desert brush. Within easy shopping distance from San Diego are the towns of El Cajon, Alpine, Lakeside and several other smaller communities. Land is far less expensive and lots tend to be spacious, sometimes large enough to keep horses. Riding trails take off in all directions to wander through the empty mountain country. Although housing is less expensive, the tradeoff is warmer summers and cooler winters.

From your suburban home you can run into San Diego to enjoy professional sports: the San Diego Chargers, the Padres, the Hawks, or the Andy Williams PGA Open. San Diego State brings collegiate football as well as the usual artistic presentations, and the San Diego Opera, Theater and Symphony are nationally renowned.

As an example, of a nearby retirement location, El Cajon (pop. 86,000) maintains a separate identity, self-contained as far as retirement living is concerned, yet is only 15 miles via interstate to downtown San Diego. Senior citizens account for about 19 percent of El Cajon's population and enjoy numerous services provided by the East County Council on Aging and Grossmont Hospital. Two other hospitals are there, including a Kaiser Foundation facility.

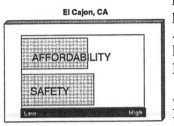

For those who like dry, warm weather, El Cajon is a good prospect for retirement. It isn't all that hot, either. According to the U.S. Weather Bureau, the maximum temperatures for July average 88 degrees (at only 28% humidity), and January high temperatures average 67 degrees. How does that compare to your summer weather?

Northeast of San Diego about 30 miles is the town of Escondido (pop. 80,000). The climate is similar to El Cajon's—dry and pleasant—but it is situated in rolling, grassy country. Low mountains loom in the background and ranches and homes on acreage lots dominate the outlying areas of Escondido. Many homes have horse stables. Houses and condos rent for considerably less than in San Diego, with homes selling for 25 to 50 percent less than similar homes in the city. Escondido offers most amenities retirees demand, such as a hospital, an excellent senior service center, a community college and adult education programs that are free to those over 60.

SAN DIEGO AREA			Rel. Humidity: Jan. 56%, July 66%			
	Jan.	April	July	Oct.	Rain	Snow
Daily Highs	65	68	76	75	9"	—
Daily Lows	48	55	65	60		

Los Angeles This is where the southern California dream started. Retirement became big business back in the 1880s when promoters began capitalizing on its ideal climate. From that time on, retirement remained big as the town grew larger and larger. But Los Angeles didn't simply grow larger, as most cities do; it grew quite unpredictably, spreading out in this direction and that, until the result is a city that looks different and is different from any other major city in the world.

Recently an Argentinian couple came to visit us. We met them at the Los Angeles airport and treated them to a sightseeing tour. They were excited at the opportunity of finally seeing fabulous Los Angeles. But after an hour of driving around, they became puzzled. "But, where is the city?" they asked. "We were expecting tall buildings. Everything here is small!" We drove through Hollywood, Beverly Hills and all the other obligatory areas, and they found few places that matched their image of what Los Angeles should be. To them, a real city should resemble Buenos Aires, Paris or New York. There should be tall, elegant apartment buildings, graceful skyscrapers, fancy restaurants with sidewalk cafes and all the metropolitan delights that combine to make a real city. Instead they found single-family homes and one- and two-story commercial buildings. Occasional tall buildings seemed lonely and out of place.

In most large cities of the world land is at a premium, far too valuable to waste on lawns and landscaping. Buildings start at the sidewalk and rise as high as possible. When room is left over for a lawn, it is placed *behind* the house and jealously guarded for the family's personal use. To be sure, L.A.'s city center does have a group of high-rises, but they are for commerce, not for people to live in. They stand out like lost visions, mistaken attempts to create something impossible: a real city.

There is, of course, a downtown section, but it isn't the same as in other big cities. People don't go "downtown" for Christmas shopping or to seek out those special restaurants as they do in New York, San Francisco or Buenos Aires. People avoid the central downtown and go to the nearest shopping mall instead. Like satellites, a garland of smaller cities surround Los Angeles. Each features its own "downtown" focus, which could be a giant shopping mall, and in turn each is surrounded by even smaller shopping centers and neighborhoods.

This ring of small towns is where retirement is best considered, not in Los Angeles proper. The FBI crime charts show that some of the towns circling Los Angeles are quite safe. Hermosa Beach, Agoura Hills and Redondo Beach for example, rank in the top levels of personal safety. People who live here seldom if ever venture into less safe zones; they have no reason to do so.

There are so many delightful communities here that it's impossible to list them. If the weather here is a strong enough magnet, it's worth spending time driving and looking from Capistrano in the south to the

San Gabriel Mountains to the north or out to the desert-like settings in the east as far as San Bernardino. By the way, the smog problem disappears as you leave the Los Angeles Basin, as does the population density. Nice mobile home parks are increasingly plentiful the farther you travel from Los Angeles.

The area's superb year-round climate makes outdoor recreation practical, with golf, tennis and swimming available in most every neighborhood. Wilderness areas are but one or two hours' drive from city hall. Gold panning in the San Gabriel Mountains, skiing and trout fishing at Lake Arrowhead and Big Bear or rockhounding in the desert—all these and more are available. Fishing off the piers, jogging, walking or loafing on the beaches add another facet of outdoor recreation: the ocean can be enjoyed to the limit. Sailboats and fishing craft can be berthed at numerous places along the coast.

Those who locate away from the city will find that Los Angeles itself offers cultural advantages found only in big cities. World-famous art galleries, museums and symphonies are easily accessible, as are theaters, universities and all types of senior activities. It's a great place for short visits. Most satellite towns have community colleges and none are very far from a state university branch.

The Los Angeles area is not an inexpensive place to retire, yet it doesn't have to be prohibitive. Everybody there isn't rich; it takes some shopping to find a comfortable niche, a place where housing prices aren't off the wall. Nothing here is cheap, but compared with San Diego or Santa Barbara, real estate can be reasonable. But it's important to look beyond housing prices here; the quality of a neighborhood is far more important than affordability. The bottom line around Los Angeles is: if you can't afford to live in a safe neighborhood, forget it.

LOS ANGELES			Rel. Humidity: Jan. 50%, July 53%			
	Jan.	April	July	Oct.	Rain	Snow
Daily Highs	65	67	75	74	12"	—
Daily Lows	47	52	63	59		

Santa Barbara   Santa Barbara started as a retirement center, when wealthy people from Beverly Hills and Hollywood "discovered" it early in the century. Movie stars—whose income was matched only by real estate developers and other money-heavy people—found Santa Barbara the ideal place to get away from it all. Maintaining a weekend house in Santa Barbara, which would later become a retirement home, became the thing to do.

Santa Barbara is indeed a lovely setting, set on a narrow coastal plain and overshadowed by the tall San Rafael Mountains. Miles of prime beaches line the coast. With typical southern California flair, the newly rich built mansions and lavish homes overlooking the beaches, in the town and up the sides of the mountains. Stucco Spanish and Moorish palaces with red-tiled roofs and swimming pools soon made Santa Barbara a re-creation of Beverly Hills dreams. No expense was spared in construction or landscaping. Decorative trees and plants from all over the world graced mansions and even ordinary homes. Today this land-scaping has matured into a virtual arboretum.

The tradition of costly housing has endured over the years. Although Santa Barbara is one of the highest-quality retire-ment areas we've looked at, it is also one of the most expensive. The local newspa-per shows most two- and three-bedroom houses renting for more than many retired couples earn. A few places can be found

Santa Barbara, CA

for around $1,000 a month, but they are described as "cottages" or "charming" (translation: cramped). Most house rentals fall into the $1,300 to $1,700 range. At $1,700 a month, that means $20,400 a year just for rent. In Montecito, a small neighborhood on the southern edge of the city, rents range from a low of $2,400 to $5,900 a month ($5,900 computes to $70,800 a year, not counting gas, electricity and an occa sional meal). Even studio apartments (translation: one room and a hotplate) rent for $500 to $600. We didn't have the heart to ask how much it costs to purchase a home.

If you are one of the lucky persons who can afford this kind of housing cost, you will find that Santa Barbara is a marvelous place for retirement. Its major university is a source of cultural and intellectual stimulation, and it has excellent services for senior citizens. Seven senior centers serve the community.

Santa Barbara is my favorite southern California town to visit, and I've always suspected I'd like living there as well. If it sounds good to you, don't let my assessment of the real estate situation scare you away. If you look hard enough, you can usually find something affordable, if not in the city of Santa Barbara itself, then in the more reasonably priced towns nearby. For example, if you drive north through Santa Barbara, you'll end up in the community of Goleta. This unincorporated area is contiguous with Santa Barbara, but rather less stylish and much more affordable. You'll find both retirees and families here, enjoying the lower cost of living, while taking advantage of all this lovely area has to offer.

Pismo Beach/Five Cities Area   Once the butt of many Jack Benny jokes, Pismo Beach is today having the last laugh. People are discovering that it's a very pleasant place to spend a vacation, plus it's a great place to retire. Located about 200 miles north of Los Angeles, Pismo Beach has a population of around 6,000. It's just one of five adjoining towns spread along the beach and near-inland areas that gives the Five Cities its name. (By the way, the word "pismo" comes from the famous pismo clams that at one time seemed to almost pave the long stretches of sandy shoreline.) Pismo Beach is a typical example of smaller beach-retirement towns on the California coast.

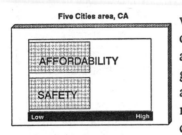

Five Cities area, CA

Until recently, the favorite sport here was digging into sand at low tide in search of the large, succulent clams. Both locals and tourists still do, but today's clam diggers aren't like the crowds of a few years ago. Too many clam forks have thinned the mollusk population considerably. But clams are still there for the persistent, and fishing is still great from the long pier that juts out past the surf (no license required). Bottom fish, such as ling cod, red snapper and sand dabs, are favorite catches. Fishing and clamming are year-round sports. Boat launching facilities are available at nearby Avila Beach, just north of the Five Cities.

Pismo Beach is one of the few places along the California coast where it is permissible to drive a motor vehicle onto the sand, and there are several ramps that give access to the beach. Huge, undulating sand dunes are meccas for four-wheel-drive vehicles and dune buggies. Converted Volkswagens, Jeeps and other souped-up contraptions zip up and down the dunes like motorized roller coasters (away from the more quiet beach crowd, of course). Another favorite beach activity is horseback riding. A couple of stables rent horses for leisurely rides along the surf line. Golf is popular, with several courses in the area.

The loosely connected communities that together comprise the sprawling, lightly populated Five Cities area are Shell Beach, Oceano, Grover City, Arroyo Grande and Pismo Beach itself. Arroyo Grande is away from the beach, but it is the largest (pop. 11,000) of the Five Cities and is considered part of the "metropolitan" area (pop. 30,000). Housing is naturally more expensive along the cliffs or anywhere an ocean view fills your picture window. Still, for a California beach area, Pismo Beach is surprisingly affordable. Brand-new, two-bedroom condos can be had for $68,000 and up. Nice two- or three-bedroom homes range from $75,000 and up. Although these prices may not seem affordable to people moving from some areas of the country, for the West Coast they are cheap. Some very expensive homes sit on the cliffs of Shell Beach, homes with gorgeous views and walled privacy. Yet, just a block or two back from the ocean are many modest homes with low-maintenance yards along neat, comfortable-looking streets. Numerous mobile home parks with low monthly rents dot the area. One reason for the reasonable housing market is the exodus of workers who labored on the nearby Diablo Canyon nuclear power project. When the plant was completed, the housing market dropped considerably.

As you might expect, where there are large numbers of retired folks, you will find active senior citizens organizations. Pismo Beach supports several organizations, ranging from grandmothers clubs to a singles club for people over 60. There is an active R.S.V.P. chapter, Meals on Wheels and a senior citizens' ride program. You will find plenty of opportunities to get involved in volunteer projects.

San Luis Obispo   Just a 15-minute drive north of the Five Cities is the university town of San Luis Obispo, with a population of nearly 40,000. The school sponsors a multitude of cultural events, such as plays, lectures and concerts, many free to senior citizens. One of San Luis Obispo's most popular sites is Mission Plaza, a place for special events such as the Mozart Festival and the Central Coast Wine Festival. (Locals consider the "Central Coast" to be anything between Santa Barbara and San Luis, whether on the coast or a few miles inland.)

The relaxed, intellectual atmosphere generated by the presence of the California State Polytechnic University makes San Luis Obispo a pleasant retirement location for those who don't *have* to be able to walk to the beach (yet the ocean is only a 13-mile drive from the town). The advantage of living away from the shore is more sunshine and more comfortable evenings, which can be shirt-sleeve weather rather than the typically cool, sweater affairs in nearby Pismo Beach.

As in other university towns, San Luis Obispo enjoys a vibrant combination of services and facilities that satisfy tastes and requirements of students and retirees alike. Interesting yet affordable restaurants, bookstores that stock more than just best sellers, and foreign and award-winning movies that other towns would never think to present, are just a few of the items that retirees say they like about living here.

San Luis Obispo, being a much larger community than the Five Cities area, naturally offers more senior citizens' activities. From bowling leagues to golf tournaments, the sports sector is covered. Woodcarving, folk and square dancing, lectures and all sorts of social activities are there for your participation.

CENTRAL COAST AREA			Rel. Humidity: Jan. 55%, July 63%			
	Jan.	April	July	Oct.	Rain	Snow
Daily Highs	64	68	72	74	13"	—
Daily Lows	43	48	53	51		

Chapter 9

Pacific Northwest

The conventional image of Oregon and Washington is a place of continual rain, where long-term residents develop duck feet and where ducks wear galoshes. I admit that I once believed this myself. Years ago, when I accepted a job by telephone on a newspaper in Pasco, Washington, my expectations were of green, verdant mountains towering over lush river valleys with misty waterfalls and leaping trout. There are, of course, scenes in the Northwest exactly like that. But when I arrived in Pasco, I discovered that particular part of Washington is practically treeless! As far as the eye can see, it's rolling hills of wheat, scrub grasses, and an occasional, thirsty-looking sagebrush.

An interesting thing about Washington and Oregon weather is that places 50 miles apart can have climates and topography so different it's hard to believe you're in the same state. The extreme eastern parts are high mountain country, with tall evergreen trees, harsh winters, snow-covered peaks and great skiing. The central portions have scanty rainfall—about half that of Kansas—with a mild four-season climate and light snowfalls. The Pacific coast catches enough rain to keep everything perpetually green—even though it may snow occasionally. The ocean moderates temperatures far inland, since the warm Japan Current flows by the coast, sending temperate breezes inland and keeping freezing weather to a minimum. With a steady, year-round mildness, the climate approaches perfection for those who detest hot, sweltering summers. All but the higher elevations escape the Montana-like winters you might expect at this latitude. There's even a conifer rain forest on the Olympia Peninsula, the only one in the northern hemisphere. Rainfall here is up to 140 inches a year!

Despite Washington and Oregon's reputation for rain, statistics show that Olympia, Washington, has about the same yearly rainfall as Orlando, Florida (51 inches), and Portland, Oregon, averages 37 inches of rain each year, about the same as Buffalo, New York (except that Buffalo also receives 92 inches of snow). Rainfall in places like Ashland or Grants Pass is around 30 inches a year or less—about the same as San

Antonio, Texas; half as much rain as most parts of Florida—enough to keep things green, but not enough to raise the humidity or interfere with fishing.

Some of the best housing bargains in these states, Washington and Oregon, escaped the inflationary real estate madness that swept some sections of the West Coast. Then, when the economy was staggered by the near-collapse of fishing and lumbering, already reasonable prices tumbled. The overwhelming majority of acreage in both states is publicly owned, with national forests and deserts open for hiking, camping and general enjoyment.

Oregon

Oregon's biggest drawback? In a single word: taxes. Oregon property taxes are as high as California's. However, since the value of property is less, you pay less than in California for a comparable home. Recently, angry Oregon voters joined together in a tax revolt; they passed an initiative that mandated a reduction in property tax rates. However, in their enthusiasm for passing the bill, they failed to close all the loopholes. As tax rates dropped, the tax assessors simply increased homes' assessed valuation. It happens that we owned a piece of property on the Rogue River, and our tax bill went up more than $200 the first year of the "tax cut"!

OREGON TAX PROFILE

Sales tax: no
State income tax: graduated from 5% to 9% over $5,000; federal income tax deductible to 7% on $25,000 and over
Property taxes: because of a ballot "reform" measure, property tax rates go down every year while assessments go up; there's no way to predict future rates; current may be about 1.6%
Intangibles tax: no
Social Security taxed: no
Pensions taxed: $5,000 exemption for government pensions for low income; private fully taxable
Gasoline tax: 24¢ per gallon, plus possible local taxes

It's not as bad as it sounds, though. The complete picture is that high property taxes are offset by not having an Oregon sales tax and by exceptionally low automobile licenses. For example: last year we purchased an RV to complete the research for this book. As Oregon residents, we saved almost as much on sales tax and license plates as we paid out in property taxes. In some states you pay both high property taxes *and* sales taxes.

While lacking surplus tax money to spend on senior citizen services, the state of Oregon does a lot with what it has. Using volunteers, they've maintained a surprisingly high level of support for those in need. A state medical plan is considered a model for bringing health care to all who can't afford it. One innovative and cost-cutting program that makes a world of sense and compassion encourages the elderly to remain in their own homes or stay with private families, rather than in expensive, impersonal rest homes.

Wine Country

Although lacking the glamour of California's Napa Valley wine country, Oregon equals the best when it comes to quality and exciting wine-tasting tours. Throughout the inland valleys, grapes are grown on small acreages with little, family-operated wineries producing a wide variety of vintages. Eighty wineries are scattered the length of the state, but the greatest concentration is found south of Portland to Roseburg.

Oregon's wineries aren't large in size or production, but their wine quality is gaining worldwide recognition. When an Oregon Pinot Noir bested dozens of French Burgundies in a tasting in France in 1975, winemakers from California and France took notice. They found that Oregon's soil and weather make it perfect for production of this special grape. Winemakers from California and France are now planting their own vineyards there. The state of Washington, too, has a formidable wine industry underway, gaining national reputation with each harvest.

Ashland celebrates Oregon wine with a Winter Food, Wines and Arts Festival, held the first weekend in February. Because most wineries are small and located away from main highways, roadside signs seldom announce their whereabouts. Information and maps may be obtained from the Oregon Wine Advisory Board, 701 N.E. Hood Ave., Gresham, OR 97030, (503) 228-8336.

Oregon's Inland Valleys

North-south Interstate 5, as it traverses the state, travels through a string of exceptionally desirable retirement locations: from Ashland, near the California border, to Portland, on the Columbia River at Oregon's northern edge. From our point of view, this entire region offers more of what retirees say they want than any other part of the nation. Yet few people outside the West Coast ever hear much about this part of the country. Californians have, much to Oregonians' chagrin, and they come here with open checkbooks, snapping up bargain retirement homes like alligators in a chicken ranch.

The landscape changes quickly as you cross into Oregon from California. Suddenly everything looks green, even in the middle of summer when most of California turns golden tan. Tall pines cloak the hills, and meadows are lush with grass, cows standing knee-deep in clover. It's easy to imagine early pioneers' amazement as their covered wagons rumbled along the Oregon trail to California, and to understand why so many of them stayed right here! Although rainfall in most inland valley locations averages only 25 to 37 inches, enough moisture falls in the summer to keep things fresh. Without enough frost in winter to kill the grass, fields are even greener in December through March, because that's when more rain falls.

The operative climate word here is "mild." Although an occasional light snow may fall, it seldom stays around more than a few hours because of warm afternoon temperatures. January lows are typically around 30 to 40 degrees, with highs of 50 to 60 degrees. Since it rarely freezes, few homeowners bother to insulate their water pipes. A recent cold snap caught them by surprise, giving plumbers scads of overtime work.

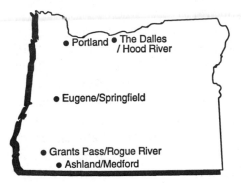

Outdoor recreation is accessible year-round. Golf courses never close; fishing is possible in all seasons; bicycling and walking will lure you outdoors to do healthy things instead of watching TV. Summers are mild, with average highs in the 80s, although July and August do have their share of over 100-degree days. These are tempered by a low, 38 percent relative humidity.

Oregon offers two other favorable conditions: housing prices and medical services. True, other parts of the country offer reasonable real estate prices, some considerably lower, but few places are as suitable for retirement. And, medical care here is wonderful, with excellent hospitals in each of the larger towns.

Ashland/Medford These two cities are about 15 minutes apart along Interstate 5. They share a pleasant countryside of gently rolling hills, with sporadic remnants of the thick forests that once covered the area. Rich farmland and dairy farms spread out beginning at the edges of the towns. Off in the distance, about 30 miles to the east, the forest-covered mountains of the Cascade Range are sometimes covered with snow in the winter, with Mt. McLaughlin rising majestically in white-frosted splendor. On the south, another 30 miles distant, is Mt. Ashland, which

286

dominates the Siskiyou Mountain Range. Skiing is available there from Thanksgiving through April, with up to 22 runs operating (snow permitting). Elk, deer and other wildlife abound in the area. With 13 lakes only a short drive in any direction from Ashland and Medford, recreational activities are abundant.

Medford (pop. 46,000) and Ashland (pop. 17,000) are traditional retirement choices not only for Californians but for folks from all over the country who appreciate a blend of culture, year-round outdoor activities and affordable housing costs. Medford is the commercial center, Ashland its academic counterpart. This area enjoys a very low crime rate, with Ashland ranking in the top 25 percent of towns nationally in personal safety. Here, you'll find small-town living combined with city conveniences.

Ashland is often chosen for retirement because of the enriching cultural atmosphere of Southern Oregon State College. It's also the site of a nationally acclaimed Shakespearian festival. This has expanded from a once-a-year event into a year-round production in three theaters, with contemporary theater and other popular entertainment in addition to classic presentations.

A few miles west of Medford is the historic town of Jacksonville, site of another famous festival. The ongoing Britt Festivals are the oldest outdoor music and performing arts festivals in the Northwest. Five events are presented each summer, featuring world-class artists. Concertgoers combine theater with picnics, sipping wine and sampling cheeses while they relax and listen to classical music, jazz and bluegrass or watch ballet and light opera.

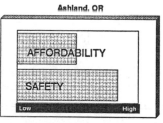

Ashland, OR

Once the site of a major gold strike, Jacksonville lost its chance to become the largest town in southern Oregon back in 1883 when the Oregon & California Railroad pushed its tracks northward. When the railroad requested a $25,000 "bonus" to place a station in Jacksonville, the city fathers unwisely refused to pay. Instead, the station was built at a crossroads called Middle Ford. Middle Ford shortened its name to Medford and grew while Jacksonville languished. In some ways this was fortunate, because "progress" passed the town by, saving its historic old buildings from the wrecking ball.

Jacksonville's shady, tree-lined streets, 130-year-old brick hotels, commercial buildings and restored Victorian homes assured its designation as a National Historic Landmark Town in 1966. Antique stores, boutiques and interesting restaurants line the main street while quiet residential neighborhoods are set back from the commerce. Except for during the festivals, Jacksonville is basically quiet, a place many folks have selected for retirement. The surrounding countryside and north toward the community of Gold Hill are perfect for horses, with pastures and breeding ranches spaced at frequent intervals.

ASHLAND/MEDFORD			Rel. Humidity: Jan. 71%, July 26%			
	Jan.	April	July	Oct.	Rain	Snow
Daily Highs	45	64	91	69	20"	8"
Daily Lows	30	37	54	40		

Grants Pass/Rogue River   Downriver towards Grants Pass, the scenic Rogue River flows through through several small towns and communities where retirement is a pervasive theme. Mobile home parks and cozy-looking houses sit in close proximity to the river, allowing sportsmen to enjoy record steelhead and salmon fishing just a few yards from their back doors.

Eight miles to the south of Grants Pass is the city of Rogue River (pop. 6,000), a delightful little community sitting where Interstate 5 and the Rogue River intersect. Quiet streets, shaded by mature trees, provide inexpensive homes, condos and small apartments for those who prefer to be within walking distance of stores and the library. To the east, a vast countryside of small farms and forested homesites captivate the get-away-from-it-all crowd. We have California friends who recently purchased 38 acres of woods, pastures and abandoned mining claims, with a two-story home for $125,000. Love it!

The river wends its way downstream to Grants Pass, a traditional retirement area for Southern Californians. With about 17,000 people living within the city limits, Grants Pass supports enough commerce to take it out of the realm of a small town. Yet it is surprising how often residents drive 45 minutes to Medford for heavy-duty shopping.

Houses in town are predominantly older, frame buildings, mostly single family, neat, well cared for and affordable. Newer houses tend to be away from downtown, built on an acre or so, with trees and natural shrubbery planted as low-maintenance landscaping devices. Like the area around the city of Rogue River, a great number of retirees choose to retire out in the more rustic places. Oregon is becoming mountainous at this point, with forests and rugged hills covering much of the landscape. A 15-minute drive from Grants Pass downtown takes you to wonderfully secluded and wild-looking properties where you will be plagued by deer eating your flowers and black bears raiding your garbage cans.

The Grants Pass retirement community is exceptionally active, engaging a large number of volunteers in worthwhile programs. This is important, because without sales-tax revenue, Oregon has little money to spare for senior services. If some things are to happen, they must be done with volunteer labor. Since part-time jobs are exceptionally competitive (due to low unemployment levels), those who need meaningful work to feel fulfilled will have plenty of opportunities. Isn't it a good feeling to know that at least *somewhere* people still consider you vital and dynamic?

After the river leaves Grants Pass on its way to the ocean, the going gets rough. Whitewater enthusiasts who have braved rapids all over the world will tell you that rafting Oregon's Rogue River is the ulti- mate whitewater experience because of the river's incredible beauty. Congress desig-

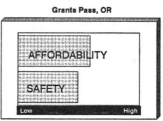

Grants Pass, OR

nated it as the first of the nation's protected rivers under the Wild and Scenic Rivers Act of 1968. Here is where Zane Grey chose to build his home and to write many of his famous western novels. Many scenic descriptions in his books were inspired by the picturesque Rogue River country. Moviemakers have found inspiration as well, with Hollywood crews making the trek to Grants Pass to take advantage of the scenery. My wife and I have rafted the river four times, and will make it five if anyone suggests doing it. The river trip is not really all that bad, provided you go with an experienced boatman. None of the rapids are past class three, which means even cowards like me can have fun.

GRANTS PASS/ROGUE RIVER			Rel. Humidity: Jan. 71%, July 26%			
	Jan.	April	July	Oct.	Rain	Snow
Daily Highs	47	69	96	69	28"	4"
Daily Lows	32	40	56	42		

Eugene/Springfield   Located halfway up the state, this area catches 40 inches of rainfall a year, half again as much as in the southern part of the state. This ensures that the twin cities of Eugene and Springfield stay green all year, but it's still below Midwestern and Southern rain patterns. Spring, summer and fall are gorgeous.

The biggest "industry" here is the University of Oregon, with an enrollment of nearly 16,000 students. Like Ashland, university life and the excitement of learning and culture spill over into the community. Ongoing schedules of lectures, concerts, plays and sports offerings, many of which are free, provide a constant source of interest for the retirement community. The Hult Center for the Performing Arts houses two theaters—a concert hall and a playhouse—which feature plays, concerts and performances by local, regional and national talent.

Eugene's business center features a large pedestrian mall for pleasant shopping convenience. Toward the outskirts, a surprisingly large mall presents about any kind of shop or store imaginable. As a university town, Eugene's residential streets are restrained, with plenty of older homes providing housing for students and retirees alike at reasonable prices. Across the river in Springfield, housing costs are about 10 percent lower, and its downtown makes up for lack of size with extra charm. By the way, Springfield enjoys one of the best senior centers we've encountered in Oregon or anywhere, for that matter. Facilities are excellent, the staff dedicated and retirees unanimously pleased with their center.

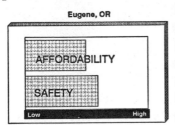

Eugene, OR

The weather here is mild enough for senior citizens to enjoy the outdoors all year. On the average, only 15 summer days a year reach or exceed 90 degrees. Much outdoor activity centers around the Willamette River, which runs through Eugene and Springfield, providing trout fishing, picnicking, miles of bicycle trails and river walks. For ocean fishing, clamming and beachcombing for driftwood or Japanese glass fishing floats, Pacific beaches are just a 90-minute drive west through beautiful low mountain country and the Siuslaw National Forest. A short drive in the opposite direction is the Deschutes National Forest, crowned by the Mt. Washington and Three Sisters wilderness areas. To the north, similar towns suitable for retirement await your investigation, places like Corvallis, Albany and Salem (Oregon's capital city). Some of the state's best trout fishing can be enjoyed toward the east, after a scenic drive to the Diamond Lake area.

EUGENE/SPRINGFIELD			Rel. Humidity: Jan. 75%, July 40%			
	Jan.	April	July	Oct.	Rain	Snow
Daily Highs	46	60	82	65	40"	6"
Daily Lows	33	34	50	41		

Portland Reno, Nevada, bills itself as "The Biggest Little City in the West"; Portland turns this around, claiming the title of "The Biggest Small Town in the West." And it is big, with a million people living in its urban area; the city limits alone include about half a million population. Portland spreads from the foothills of Mount Hood to the plains of the Coast Range, covering a four-county area.

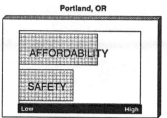

Portland, OR

Portland works hard to maintain its small-town atmosphere and its second motto: "City of Roses." Fortunately, the city's founding fathers incorporated a large number of parks, some quite large, which contributes to a feeling of uncrowded spaciousness. Rolling hills and lots of shade trees extend this feeling into Portland's neighborhoods.

Unlike many American cities, where shopping malls have destroyed downtowns by luring consumers into the suburbs, Portland has managed to keep its central core alive and well, a pleasant place to visit or shop. During the 1970s, the city built a transit system and instituted a system of free public transportation in a 340-block downtown area, known as "Fareless Square." A combination of pedestrian-only streets and free buses makes shopping downtown Portland a pleasure. Well-preserved buildings, upscale shops and restaurants, plus good law enforcement complete the picture of a "small-town big city."

Because Portland's climate, sophisticated setting and hilly picturesqueness are reminiscent of San Francisco, Portland draws many retirees from that area. Coming here from one of the most expensive parts of the country is a pleasant surprise for ex-San Franciscans. Lovely Victorian homes, which would cost a fortune where they came from, can be purchased for California tract-home prices. At least one San Francisco publisher and several authors we know of have made the switch to Portland from "Baghdad by the Bay."

PORTLAND			Rel. Humidity: Jan. 74%, July 45%			
	Jan.	April	July	Oct.	Rain	Snow
Daily Highs	44	60	80	64	37"	6"
Daily Lows	34	41	56	45		

The Dalles/Hood River The drive up the Oregon side of the Columbia River from Portland is another scenic marvel. A half-dozen historic little towns space themselves along the way, with the huge river flowing past, carrying fishing boats, cargo barges and windsurfers. Two places in particular make wonderful retirement locations: Hood River (pop. 17,000) and The Dalles (pop. 11,000).

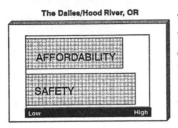

Sitting on gentle slopes overlooking the vast river, both have satisfying downtown sections and reasonably priced property. Numerous homes in The Dalles are listed below $70,000, many in the $50's and $60's. We looked at a three-bedroom home situated on a bluff overlooking the river and the Columbia Gorge for $59,000. From one side of the property, we could see the top of Mt. Hood where residents can enjoy great skiing, in addition to their local river fishing and boating.

THE DALLES/HOOD RIVER			Rel. Humidity: Jan. 75%, July 45%			
	Jan.	April	July	Oct.	Rain	Snow
Daily Highs	42	60	90	63	37"	5"
Daily Lows	31	38	52	41		

Oregon Coast

A wonderful, often overlooked, retirement area is found along Washington and Oregon's Pacific coast. North along Highway 101, an inviting string of small towns dot the shore—starting with Brookings, just across the California state line, to Astoria, on Oregon's northern border and on up to Washington's Grays Harbor.

Ask people who retire along this picturesque stretch of coast, and they'll most likely give "wonderful year-round climate" as a major reason for their decision. Forget about air conditioning and snow shovels. Since it seldom freezes, sweaters or windbreakers are the heaviest winter clothing required. Because mid-day temperatures rarely top 75 degrees, folks here sleep under electric blankets year-round.

It's this stretch of Pacific Coast that earns Oregon and Washington a reputation for being rainy. Gold Beach is perhaps the wettest of all with almost 80 inches per year. Most of it falls in the winter, which would fall as snow somewhere else. The rest of the year is generally sunny and dry. This is a great place for part-time retirees, those seeking to escape Arizona's scorching July and August, or Florida's muggy summers.

Overcrowding? Coast residents have plenty of elbow room. Along Washington-Oregon's 500-mile stretch of Pacific coastline, you'll only find about 20 towns, plus a scattering of villages. Most have between

1,000 and 5,000 friendly residents. The only cities are Coos Bay, Astoria and Aberdeen—and they are just barely large enough to be called cities. Most beaches are deserted, with unrestricted public access guaranteed by state law. Five or ten minutes' drive inland takes you to a low mountain range, the Cascades, with thousands of square miles of wilderness—almost all publicly owned, or in national forest.

Good fishing is another plus—both ocean and river. Steelhead, chinook salmon, and rainbow trout lurk in streams flowing from nearby mountains. Clamming, crabbing and whale watching are popular activities. The open countryside is perfect for camping, picnicking or beachcombing, as well as golf and horseback riding. Whitetail deer are plentiful, plus an occasional black bear or cougar. A large proportion of beachfront is dedicated to public parks and campgrounds, in the midst of the most beautiful seascapes to be found anywhere in the world.

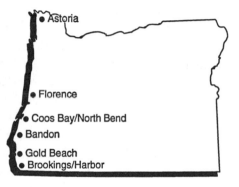

Brookings/Harbor   Just across the California line are the twin towns of Brookings and Harbor. An estimated 30 percent of the population here are retirees. That seems like a low estimate, because retirement is big business along this coast.

Residents love their unusually mild climate, optimistically referring to the area as Oregon's "banana belt." There's some justification, since flowers bloom all year; about 90 percent of the country's Easter lilies are grown here. Rhododendrons and azaleas bloom wildly in the late spring, and an Azalea Festival is held every Memorial Day. Frankly, however, the banana crop doesn't do well at all.

When we asked one man why he chose the Brookings-Harbor area for retirement, he invited us into his small travel trailer for coffee. "This is my home," he said proudly. "It's only 25 feet long, but it's all I need as a bachelor and fisherman. My rent is $100 a month, and this trailer cost me $2,800. Paid more than that for my boat. So here I am, gettin' by on my government money and goin' fishin' anytime I care to, which is almost every day."

Like all Oregon coastal towns, Brookings and Harbor have plenty of things for retired folks to do, both organized and do-it-yourself. The main problem, as far as I am concerned, with these smaller towns is the distance from large shopping centers. People who live here insist there's an adequate supply of hardware stores, grocery markets and the like, but I suppose some of us are spoiled and want huge selections of everything.

Gold Beach/Bandon   The mighty Rogue River empties into the ocean at Gold Beach. A road follows its course for a few miles inland, passing many retirement places favored by fishermen who prize the steelhead and salmon that pass their doors every day. Some folks just can't be satisfied with ocean or river fishing. They have to have both. Behind the town stretches mile after mile of forested wilderness, with trout, steelhead and salmon streams and deer hunting.

Gold Beach has an interesting history. It derived its name from an incident that started a frantic gold rush back in the '49er days. A prospector passing through the area discovered a small quantity of gold mixed in with beach sands. He panned a tiny bit of color and casually mentioned the fact to some other miners. As the word spread, the story expanded until gold mining camps all over California and Oregon fluttered with news of a place where the ocean's waves placered nuggets of gold from the sand, the beach strewn with riches, there for the gathering. Mining camps in California's Mother Lode all but emptied as miners frantically rushed to the "gold" beach.

Actually, gold is rather common on Oregon and California beaches, usually found in black streaks of magnetite sand mixed in with beach terraces. The problem is that it is very fine and difficult to separate from the coarser sand. Back during depression days, when many people had nothing else to do, a lot of gold was gleaned from the beaches, but it was tedious work.

The gold stampede in Gold Beach was short lived, but some miners, tired of jumping from place to place in search of riches, decided to retire from gold panning and settle down. They started the first retirement community on the Oregon coast. The tradition continues today, with retirement becoming a significant industry.

Single-family homes, cottages and mobile homes are the general rule, with people living in multi-generational communities rather than strictly adult developments. Prices are affordable. Typically along this coast, the median home price is $65,500, with 27 percent of the homes valued at less than $50,000. Rentals go from $250 to $500.

Gold Beach and the towns to the north all sit along Highway 101, and are serviced by a Greyhound Bus connection. There is an airport, but no regular passenger planes land here. A small hospital with an emergency room takes care of Gold Beach's medical needs.

As you drive north along the Oregon coast and catch a glimpse of the coast at Port Orford, you will see the ultimate picture-postcard scene. Dramatic rock formations jut from the sea, catching the force of waves, sending spray flying, and then the swells continue on to become gentle breakers on the sandy beach. Beaches here are known for semiprecious stones such as agates, jasper and jade as well as being places to look for redwood burls. Both Port Orford and Bandon (27 miles up the road) are truly retirement communities. A local real estate broker claims that 68 percent of his clients are retired.

Bandon (pop. 1,600) deliberately cultivates a "quaint" atmosphere, with period restaurants, art galleries, ceramic studios and small shops of every description. It's gained a reputation as an artists' colony. The local chamber of commerce coordinates activities for retirees, with monthly dinners, art shows, and an annual cranberry festival.

One of Bandon's more popular attractions is a floating dock that extends out into the water, especially for catching Dungeness crabs. Eager fishermen drop baited crab traps to the bottom and wait for fat crabs to scurry inside. Then, with quick hand-over-hand pulls, up comes the trap, often with half a dozen or so tasty crustaceans, each weighing a pound or two. The market price, last time we went crabbing, was $3.85 a pound!

Because views are so spectacular there, ocean-front property is scarce and expensive, with homes commonly selling for as high as $300,000. However, if a seascape is not essential in your choice of homes, away from the ocean's edge and up nearby rivers you'll find homes for as little as $41,000. And $79,000 will buy one of the more expensive places.

Coos Bay-North Bend   The twin cities of Coos Bay and North Bend are the major population centers of the Oregon coast. Although each has its own municipal government, police department and services, the two towns for all practical purposes merge into one, with a combined population of 25,000. It's difficult to determine where one ends and the other begins. Since the municipality of Coos Bay is the larger, folks usually refer to both towns as Coos Bay. The town seems larger than 25,000, though, probably because it's a trading center for an area extending 50 miles north to Florence and 100 miles south to Brookings.

Coos Bay-North Bend is situated on the blunt end of a peninsula, with Pacific beaches on one side and the waters of Coos Bay on the other. The mountains of the Coast Range, heavily timbered and colored a shadowy blue-green, make a pretty background for the town. The mouth of the bay is crossed by graceful McCullough Bridge, where a third town, Charleston, makes up another integral part of Coos Bay. Fishing and lumber are the major industries, with fine harvests of salmon, tuna, crab, shrimp, oysters and clams. Because the well-protected harbor is navigable by ocean-going vessels, Coos Bay claims to be the world's largest forest products shipping port. But since lumber isn't the hottest item going nowadays, things are rather slow.

The Oregon coast is big on parks. Within a six-mile drive of Coos Bay are four exceptional ones, including Cape Arago, the site where, according to the local chamber of commerce, Sir Francis Drake first set foot on the North American continent. Deep-sea fishing, crabbing and clamming are favorite pastimes. Just north is the lower entrance to famous Oregon Dunes National Recreation Area, with 50 miles of unspoiled beaches, woods and marvelous sand dunes. This is a great place for picnicking, camping and beachcombing. A current sweeps ashore, bringing all sorts of treasures, some from as far away as Japan. Among the prizes are weathered redwood burls, which make marvelous natural sculptures. The smaller ones are made into lamps; larger pieces are cut into slabs, polished and turned into table tops. One retiree I spoke with, a man from Parma, Idaho, turned his woodworking hobby into a rather lucrative business by creating artistic lamps, clocks and furniture from redwood burls. "I sell all I can make," he said. "Problem is, I keep too busy to go out and look for burls—have to buy 'em nowadays."

Florence   Florence isn't that much different from its neighbors, but we like it because it's only 60 miles to Eugene, with its larger-city shopping, university, and excellent cultural and entertainment opportunities. Housing here is a good value; the cost of living is low, and personal safety is high. Excellent Senior services and a helpful chamber of commerce make Florence an easy place to settle into for retirement.

An interesting phenomenon along the coast is the large number of freshwater lakes. Groundwater flowing from the mountains tries to find its way to the ocean, but sand dunes trap the water in low-lying areas to form freshwater lakes sometimes just a few hundred yards from the ocean. Within a few miles of Florence, the Oregon Fish and Wildlife Department stocks two dozen lakes with game fish. Some are loaded with cutthroat trout and restricted to barbless hooks, flies and lures—no bait permitted. Other lakes feature prize-winning bass and still others are reserved for sailboats. Homes built on the shores of these lakes offer dramatic views at bargain prices.

OREGON COAST				Rel. Humidity: Jan. 73%, July 49%		
	Jan.	April	July	Oct.	Rain	Snow
Daily Highs	53	54	62	58	65"	1"
Daily Lows	41	44	51	48		

Astoria   The second-largest town on the coast (pop. 15,000), Astoria sits at the northern edge of the state, where the mighty Columbia River empties into the Pacific. Hilly and verdant, Astoria is fortunate to have many picture-book Victorian homes. An active senior citizen center helps newcomers get settled. Nearby beaches are famous for long-neck clams (have to dig fast to catch 'em) and Dungeness crab for delicious cioppinos. Portland is a two-hour drive for those who need a "big-city fix" once in a while.

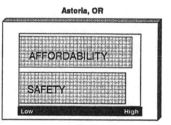

This was the site of John Jacob Astor's fur trading post back in 1811; within a few decades, Astoria developed into a thriving seaport. The affluence of that time shows today in the stately Victorian homes scattered about the town, imparting a formal, but comfortable visage to Astoria. Its small town atmosphere is affirmed by an exceptionally low crime rate, falling in the top 15 percent of the United States' safe places.

ASTORIA				Rel. Humidity: Jan. 77%, July 50%		
	Jan.	April	July	Oct.	Rain	Snow
Daily Highs	47	56	68	61	70"	5"
Daily Lows	35	40	52	44		

Oregon High Country

On the other climatic extreme, let's look at places that not only enjoy four seasons, but experience true-blue winters as well. The town of Bend, for example, averages 46 inches of snow every year. That's less than Albany (New York) with 65 inches or Flagstaff (Arizona) with 97 inches, but it still seems like a lot to me!

However, many retired folks point to their winter season as one of the things they like about living here. "It took a while to get used to driving on snow," said one lady who had lived most of her life in

Monterey, California. "But after a couple of days, I was out there with the best of 'em."

Sunriver/Bend   An example of retirement for active folks is a development like Sunriver. About a 20-minute drive from downtown Bend (pop. 20,000), Sunriver is a self-contained resort community of 3,300 acres. About 1,300 homes have been built there, ranging from nice to ultra-deluxe. More than 650 condominiums are scattered throughout the property, with undeveloped forest serving as green belts. A shopping mall and full complement of services make the community nearly self-sufficient.

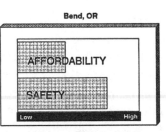

The interesting thing about the layout of the resort is that each house has plenty of land separating it from the next one, so even condos don't seem crowded. Hiking paths and 80 miles of paved bike trails pass by each living unit. Two 18-hole golf courses, 26 tennis courts, two swimming pools, hot tubs, stables and a racquet club provide summer sports for active retirees. Winter sports are skiing at nearby Mt. Bachelor and cross-country skiing over the hiking trails and golf courses.

Of the 1,500 full-time residents, better than half are retired, most from other states. Retired couples are even more strongly represented among the many part-time owners. They spend part of the year there—whichever is their favorite season—and rent their property for other season. A close family friend owns a house there, but spends most of her time in Monterey, California. "One of the advantages of owning," she says, "is that if my kids don't want to use the place in the winter ski season or for summer golf, I just call the management company and they generally find tourists who are happy to pay $90 a day for my place." The winter ski tourists and the summer fishing and golf enthusiasts just about cover our friend's payments. This is done through one of several management companies that advertise the rentals, collect the rent and clean after each tenant leaves.

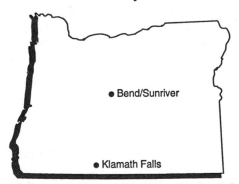

Something that needs to be stressed about places like Sunriver: they aren't full-service retirement communities. Sunriver isn't a place where

298

you can expect doctors to visit or home care workers to look after you. Instead, this is a place for active and alert people—the kind who won't mind an average of two feet of snow during winter or who might like to try cross-country skiing. Why is this any different from places in Idaho and Montana? Because, despite the snow, the Oregon High Country doesn't get the severe low temperatures, and spring comes earlier and fall stays longer.

The city of Bend is also a place for retirement, particularly for those who would rather not put as much money into housing or who need to be closer than a 20-minute drive to major shopping or medical services. However, real estate prices are not truly bargains, due to the pressures newcomers place on the market. Bend manages to blend urban sophistication with a relaxed quality of life. It brims with city parks and activity. Within 30 minutes of town, folks can enjoy a choice of nine golf courses, some of the best alpine and nordic skiing in the Northwest, and whitewater rafting or rainbow trout fishing on the Deschutes River.

SUNRIVER/BEND	Jan.	April	July	Oct.	Rel. Humidity: Jan. 62%, July 64% Rain	Snow
Daily Highs	37	56	84	62	10"	46"
Daily Lows	18	30	54	34		

Klamath Falls   An overlooked retirement area, but not overlooked by bargain-hunting California retirees, is Klamath Falls. About 18 miles from the California border, Klamath Falls offers a high-desert climate similar to Bend, some 137 miles to the north. Fishing and hunting are great, with camping, nature trails and sailing on the huge Klamath Lake providing a full range of outdoor activities. Land-locked salmon and steelhead grow to outstanding sizes. Local fishermen claim that the average trout taken from the water measures 21 inches.

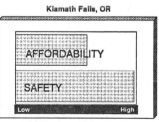
Klamath Falls, OR

The climate is dry, with 280 days of sunshine and crisply cold winters. There's far less snow and cold in Klamath Falls than in Bend, but winters are really winter. Notice the exceptionally low summer humidity (35%).

The big drawing card for most retirees (besides excellent trout fishing) is affordable real estate. Housing seems as low priced as anywhere we've investigated, and considering the quality of the area, it's perhaps one of the best buys in the country. Another economic benefit here is an unusually low cost of utilities, more than 25% below national averages. This helps offset higher heating bills in the winter.

KLAMATH FALLS			Rel. Humidity: Jan. 62%, July 35%			
	Jan.	April	July	Oct.	Rain	Snow
Daily Highs	38	59	85	64	14"	12"
Daily Lows	22	33	54	36		

Washington

Oregon has traditionally attracted more West Coast retirees than Washington; however, this is changing. More and more retirees are traveling just a little farther to investigate Washington. They are pleased to find pleasant living conditions, a mild climate and moderate housing costs. The state's electronics industry has brought workers from all parts of the country, thus creating a varied social composition around the larger cities.

WASHINGTON TAX PROFILE
Sales tax: 6.5% to 8.2%, food, drugs exempt
State income tax: no
Property taxes: average 1.8% of assessed value
Intangibles tax: no
Social Security taxed: no
Pensions taxed: no
Gasoline tax: 23¢ per gallon, plus possible local taxes.

Worthy of special mention is Washington's philosophy on state income taxes: it's one of the few states in the country that does not collect income taxes! Furthermore, it's one of those states with laws prohibiting other states from placing liens to collect taxes owed to that other state. Another good idea here is property tax breaks for the elderly. Under state law, seniors age 61 and over with incomes under $26,000 are entitled to a full exemption from special assessments, and those earning less than $18,000 can be exempt from a portion of regular property taxes.

Seattle Area Seattle is a large city, with all of the advantages and disadvantages of a metropolis, yet it is one of the more beautiful cities in the country. Because of its location on the water, its winters are mercifully mild and its summers pleasantly cool. As you might expect from a big city, crime rates are a little higher than in surrounding communities, but for an urban area the safety factor here is reassuring. Most local neighborhoods in Seattle are as safe as you can find anywhere.

Seattle, WA

It's the high-quality towns near Seattle or on Puget Sound's network of bays, coves, straits and inlets that makes this such a great retirement choice. Places like Bellingham, Burlington or Olympia—to name just a few—share in Seattle's climate and scenic beauty, but also offer the benefits of small-town living. Anacortes, for example, located on a peninsula jutting out into the bay, enjoys the twelfth-lowest crime rating in the country. Edmonds is another attractive area, sitting between Seattle and Everett; its downtown is right on the water, with a beach and ferry terminal at the end of the main shopping street.

The San Juan Islands, in the northern portion of Puget Sound, are one of the scenic wonders of the entire country. Real estate prices are a bit high here compared with some of the other island complexes nearby, but the quality lifestyle possible here makes it worthwhile. Whidbey Island, another favorite retirement area, has the advantage of being accessible by highway bridges rather than ferry boats.

SEATTLE AREA				Rel. Humidity: Jan. 73%, July 49%		
	Jan.	April	July	Oct.	Rain	Snow
Daily Highs	44	57	75	60	39"	7"
Daily Lows	35	41	55	46		

Aberdeen   The largest town on Grays Harbor (on Washington's central coast) is an excellent example of a place where retirees can take advantage of a downturn in the economy. In doing so, they will be contributing to the comeback of a nice area. Grays Harbor inhabitants depended upon fishing and lumber for its prosperity. Both occupations paid well and the area flourished. Then came an invasion of foreign boats, with 30-mile-long drag nets, who began cleaning out the fish. At the same time, Japanese factory ships buy the area's raw logs, processing them with low-paid Filipino workers and selling finished lumber products to our consumers, bypassing local lumber mills and factories.

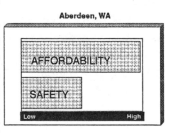

Aberdeen, WA

Thanks to this double blow, Aberdeen's economy fluttered to a standstill. Fishing boats stayed in port, and businesses closed down. As people left the area, houses went on the market, but few buyers were interested.

Not long ago, perfectly liveable homes were offered for as little as $15,000. The economy has picked up some with a WalMart store under construction and dredging of the port to make it competitive as a Pacific Rim exporter. But the buyer still has a tremendous edge. According to

301

an Aberdeen real estate salesperson, "You can buy a pretty nice place for under $50,000." Then he added, "I sold a place the other day for $12,500. Problem is, part of it fell into a neighbor's yard just before closing." Part of Aberdeen's recovery has to do with retirees moving in to take advantage of the great real estate bargains. For some reason, however, nice apartments aren't too plentiful.

Aberdeen has great senior services, equal to the best we've seen. The surprising thing about these community services, not just in Aberdeen, is that so few retirees take full advantage of them. We asked the center's

director what she considered to be her biggest problem. She replied, "Getting the news out that we exist! Folks just have no idea of what we offer. Many of our services are free, some have a nominal cost, others have a sliding fee, according to the ability to pay. Some items are limited to lower-income folks, but most are available to all. Yet, we can't seem to spread the news!" Available services range from free health care to legal services and Alzheimers support groups.

A possible disadvantage for some is an exceptionally high rainfall, almost 70 inches a year, but almost all falls during the winter. One enthusiastic Aberdeen booster said, "I have to admit, I get pretty tired of that steady drizzle all winter. May is also sometimes drizzly, but oh, the gorgeous flowers are fabulous. Even the most tumble-down house looks great with a flowering bush in the yard!" She pointed out another possible drawback here, in that it's sometimes difficult to find a physician still accepting new patients. However there are some in Hoquiam, next to Aberdeen. On the plus side, there's an excellent bus system (25 cents fare), and a bus to Olympia for only $1.

ABERDEEN	Jan.	April	July	Oct.	Rain	Snow
			Rel. Humidity: Jan. 77%, July 50%			
Daily Highs	47	56	68	61	70"	5"
Daily Lows	35	40	52	44		

Pasco Area Earlier in this chapter I poked fun at Pasco because of its dry, desert-like surroundings. Actually, it's a highly productive wheat-producing area and has grown immensely over the years since I worked there. Most neighborhoods are new here, a consequence of fast growth during the past two decades, and an overall prosperity is evident.

Although Pasco may not live up to the damp and green expectations most folks have of Washington, there are certain advantages to living in the eastern part of the state. Besides being a place that actively seeks retirees, the Pasco-Kennewick-Richland area offers great real estate prices and an interesting climate. Even in the coldest part of winter, when the temperature dropped to 20 degrees in the morning, I could be fishing that same afternoon on the Columbia River bank, in my shirt-sleeves. Like rain, snowfall here is slight; it didn't

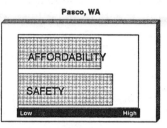

Pasco, WA

snow at all the winter we lived in Pasco. Sunshine was plentiful and being outdoors was a pleasure year-round. A low-humidity summer rounds out the weather picture. Fishing for salmon and sturgeon are favorite outdoor sports.

PASCO AREA			Rel. Humidity: Jan. 71%, July 25%			
	Jan.	April	July	Oct.	Rain	Snow
Daily Highs	37	64	89	65	16"	6"
Daily Lows	20	35	53	35		

Vancouver   Although in the state of Washington, just across the Columbia River, Vancouver is essentially part of Portland's metropolitan area, a bedroom community, so to speak. Yet the city stands alone in several respects. For one thing, its commercial centers are self-sufficient and residents don't think in terms of "downtown" being in Portland; Vancouver has one of its own, thank-you. Residential neighborhoods here tend to have larger lots and smaller home prices. The most significant difference, though, is in taxes. As we have discussed, the state of Washington doesn't collect state income taxes, yet also provides substantial property tax relief to low-income senior citizens. However, the state does have a sales tax. Vancouver residents handle this quite well; they simply cross over the mighty Columbia to sales-tax-free Oregon to make their major purchases, much to the dismay of the state of Washington and Vancouver merchants.

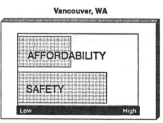

Vancouver, WA

The Vancouver Parks and Recreation department presents an awesome array of services and programs for seniors. Its Marshall Luepke Center offers a series of tours that would put a travel agency to shame.

Upriver on the Washington side of the Columbia are several delightful little towns strung along a winding, scenic road. Camas, Washougal and Skamania are close enough to the city for convenience, but not so close to feel overwhelmed by it. The river's bank rises from the waterline, with streets forming tiers which provide scenic views for the towns' homes. There's an exceptionally peaceful air about this stretch of river, a combination of woods, meadows and steep hills that invites retirement.

Goldendale Oregon has a reputation for disliking outsiders, particularly Californians, but Washington is supposed to despise Californians even more. Although this may be true to a certain extent when it comes to wage-earners coming here to compete for scarce jobs, when it comes to retirees who spend dollars, Oregonians and Washingtonians welcome you with open arms. This is particularly true in the smaller towns, where the citizens are spending tax money to lure newcomers into their communities.

For example, the town of Goldendale has embarked on a campaign to draw retirees (even Californians) into their midst. Located a few miles north of the Columbia River, Goldendale's economy has been on the decline for several years. Replacing regular industry with retirees, the non-polluting industry, seems to be a solution.

Goldendale, WA
AFFORDABILITY
SAFETY
Low   High

With the population dwindling, the civic leaders placed classified ads in major California newspapers, urging retirees to resettle there. The ads boasted of Goldendale's low taxes and utility costs, and good recreation and health facilities. The last we heard, over 30 families moved here because of the campaign. About 20 other small towns in Washington have joined in the advertising program. Be aware that this is out of the Pacific Coast's "green belt" of forest and heavy rainfall. Goldendale participates in typical eastern Washington weather patterns, with half to a third of the rainfall along the coast. Also, it's somewhat isolated in that the nearest airport is 70 miles away in Portland. But there is intercity transportation in the form of Greyhound service.

Chapter 10

Hawaii, Anyone?

Hawaii! The very name creates excitement. Visions of swaying coconut trees, blue Pacific surf and sandy beaches paint tantalizing pictures of idyllic retirement. Yet, most folks push these visions aside as frivolous daydreaming. The common belief is that Hawaii is only for the filthy rich. There's a lot of truth in that, for Hawaii can be extremely expensive, particularly in the area of housing. In some neighborhoods, million-dollar homes are ordinary.

But the interesting thing is that living in Hawaii doesn't have to be super expensive. The vast majority of Island residents are not rich, do not live in million-dollar mansions. The fact is, if you can afford to live on a comfortable scale in your home town, without worrying about watching your expenses, chances are you can do okay on one of the Hawaiian islands. Of all the places we researched for this book, Hawaii surprised us the most. You can't live just anywhere, and you'll have to make tradeoffs in your lifestyle, but you needn't be a millionaire to retire in Hawaii.

Hawaii is pricey; tourists can vouch for that. The first thing you'll hear them say when they return from their three-week vacation is, "My God, but it's expensive over there! Everything costs twice as much!" But as a retiree you won't be living like a tourist. You'll be bargain shopping, just like local residents.

When we asked one couple how they managed to retire in Honolulu—in a $600,000 home on a $25,000-a-year retirement income—the wife replied, "Just do as we did. Buy your home 33 years ago for $18,000 on the G.I. bill, for $500 down." She makes it sound so easy. But for most of us, it's a case of being 33 years too late and $600,000 short. Furthermore, even if you're accustomed to living in a $600,000 home on the mainland and can afford to buy one in Honolulu, you'll be disappointed in its quality because the *average* sales price for Honolulu homes is $650,000. A comparable place in Florida might sell for $90,000.

Inflated real estate is the major culprit in sending Hawaii's cost of living soaring above the palm trees. In the Waialae/Kahala area (where my friend has the $600,000 house) the median price is $1.6 million! The topper is: many homeowners don't own the land their homes are standing on; it's leased ground! Rents in an ordinary Honolulu neighborhood start around $1,200 a month and can easily top $2,000 for a small place.

Are wages so high that local people can afford expensive housing? No. Although employment is probably at the highest rate in the nation, wages are surprisingly normal. In fact, a common complaint on the island of Oahu is that working people need to work two jobs to survive. Then, how can local people afford to buy houses? Most of them can't. If they didn't buy 20 years ago, and have scads of equity, chances are they'll never be able to afford even a median-priced home. The same conditions found in San Francisco, Scottsdale and Washington, D.C., exist in Hawaii, only on a more exaggerated scale.

The interesting part about all this is the lack of For Sale signs around the neighborhoods. Instead of taking their profits, most people are sitting tight. A long-time resident said, "Sure, I could make a big profit on my home, but I would either have to dump the profit back into another house or else I'd have to move away. I'm staying right here!" I know of one working-class family who did sell; they took their profits to Oregon, where they bought a much larger home, invested in a money-making restaurant and banked a half-million dollars. But they miss Hawaii!

Two reasons account for the super-inflation of Hawaiian real estate. The first is obvious: Hawaii's an exceptionally desirable place to live; the more people move here, the higher the demand for homes. Second: real estate is continually pushed higher because of the depressed dollar on the world market. Investors from other countries see our dollars and our properties as incredibly cheap bargains. During our last visit, Honolulu newspapers told of an investor from Japan who rented a limo and cruised about town looking for For Sale signs. Every time he found one, he sent his secretary inside to purchase the house at whatever the asking price. They were so cheap (to him) that he bought 123 homes in a little more than one week, never bothering to get out of the limousine.

With this kind of pressure on the real estate market, prices are going to stay high. Therefore, Honolulu is not a retirement option for folks without a great deal of money to invest in a house or a high enough income to pay up to $2,000 a month rent without shuddering. Today, about the only mainlanders who can afford Hawaiian real estate for retirement are those lucky folks who bought a $20,000 house 30 years ago, and can cash it in today for $300,000. Yes, there are places in the Islands where that amount will buy a nice place.

More About Real Estate

The real estate market on the islands we visited was very dynamic, climbing steadily upward. At the time of our research, many areas of the mainland were undergoing slumps in the real estate business, with prices dropping. The Hawaiian reaction seemed to be a slowdown in sales, but very little if any dropping of prices. We visited many open houses and saw enthusiastic potential buyers at every one.

After retirees buy a piece of island property, they tend to start wheeling and dealing—trading up or down, sometimes even going into the real estate business themselves. All the salespeople we talked with had come over as tourists or retirees in the not-too-distant past and before long found themselves selling Hawaii property to other tourists. In fact, we were so caught up in our research that we came very close to buying a lovely condo on the Big Island! Fortunately, at the last moment we remembered our oft-repeated admonition of *try living here before you buy,* and we demurred.

Tips on Locating

A friend who has lived on Oahu for the last 26 years gave us a few tips on where to locate and what to look for.

> First of all, don't be too anxious to have a house directly on the beach. It's wonderful to hear that wind and surf through the bedroom window, but that same wind blows sand and moisture into the house. Sand damages carpets and damp salt air speeds corrosion and mildew. You'll soon grow tired of scraping green mold off your shoes and painting your house with salt-proof paint.
>
> Another caution is not to get too close to those steep-walled mountains that jut almost straight up from the Hawaiian coastal plains. It isn't that they might fall, it is that the steep mountains deflect the trade winds, leaving homes in the shelter of the mountains without cooling breezes. To make matters worse, the mountains cut off the sunshine and never give the houses in the shadows a chance to dry out completely. Finally, the difference in rainfall can be dramatic, just within a distance of a few hundred yards. It can average 40 inches of rain a year away from the mountain shadows, but up to a hundred next to the mountain.

Speaking of rain, although it may rain normally in most neighborhoods—say 30 inches a year—a couple of miles away, up in the mountains, it could rain *400* inches a year. An exceptionally heavy series of rains can quickly turn certain low-lying neighborhoods into lakes. A tipoff is when many homes are built on tall pilings. You could be buying a home in a drained swamp, which returns to that state periodically. Even though your home may be built high enough to miss water damage, your car and anything left at ground level can be hurt.

Another thing to watch for is single-wall construction, very common in older homes. This construction means only one layer of wood between you and the outside world—no wallboard or insulation. This permits free passage of outside noise and conducts sunshine into heated interiors. The tipoff that a house is single-wall is vertical plank construction with a horizontal board running along the wall, just under window height. Later building codes prohibit this kind of fabrication. Single-wall isn't necessarily bad—with Hawaii's balmy weather, insulation isn't crucial—it is just an indication of inexpensive construction and justifies a lower sales price.

What is bad is any evidence of termites. It isn't the flying types that are dangerous, just those that live in damp ground. A friend who lives on Oahu claims termites can totally destroy a house in a matter of weeks. Apparently, this is one of the reasons houses are commonly built on pillars—to prevent the hungry little rascals from sneaking their tunnels into your floors and walls.

Renting Versus Buying

Yes, rents are high on the islands. If you want a condo for a week or two, expect to pay at least $150 a night for something nice—$75 on the Big Island. For longer term, the same condo might cost from $1,000 to $1,500 a month. However, since so many folks use their condos during the winter and want to rent them out during the summer, rents are considerably lower in the off-season. Because so many non-residents own property, there is rarely a shortage of rentals—long or short term.

If you rent in a non-tourist area—a working-class neighborhood, if you will—the story is again different. We saw apartments renting from $550 to $900, depending upon the island and the location. Although this may sound expensive to people living in many parts of the country, there are towns where $550 would barely rent a one-room efficiency with a view of an alley (try San Francisco or Boston). Of course, $1,200 to $2,000 is considered ordinary rent in some spiffy neighborhoods. Again, this isn't unusual in some places back home. I have friends whose monthly rent on a tiny apartment in Manhattan is over $3,000.

We met a couple on the island of Maui who related an interesting experience of renting rather than buying. They vacationed regularly in the islands, they knew they wanted a condo on Maui, and they knew exactly where they wanted to buy. When they sold their home on the mainland, the equity provided more than enough cash to buy anything they wanted. The husband explained:

> At first we felt uneasy renting. It costs $1,200 a month for our little two-bedroom place. That shocked us, because that was three times what the payments were on our four-bedroom house back in New York. Then, while we were waiting for some CDs to come due so we could pay for our condo, we did some figuring. The $250,000 at 8 percent earns around $1,200 after taxes. That covered our rent, so we were breaking even. We realized that $1,200 was what we would lose in income by owning instead of renting. But that wasn't all. Taxes were $75 a month, leasehold payments $100, and maintenance fees were $360. That meant we would have to come up with an extra $535 a month to own rather than rent!

His wife added, "All together, we're saving $6,420 a year by *not* owning our condo!"

Caution: Fee Simple vs. Leasehold

The history of Hawaiian real estate is very tangled and complex. Because early European settlers grabbed as much acreage as they could and turned it into sugar cane and pineapple plantations, land is scarce and considered very valuable. Landowners, rather than selling the land, prefer to lease it for periods of 60 or more years. Every 30 years or so, the lease comes up for renegotiation. Therefore, you may own your house, but someone else owns the land. This arrangement is called a *leasehold*. If you own the property outright, it's called *fee simple*.

The differences between leasehold and fee simple are very important. We've heard some absolute horror stories concerning leaseholds. One person told of having a $400-a-month leasehold, and upon renegotiation discovered that the lessor wanted $12,000 a month from then on! We understand that the government is trying to control abuses like this, but it's quite important to know what kind of lease you are signing. Another problem is that when a leasehold has less than 30 years remaining, banks are hesitant to finance the property. So, although your purchase could be financed without problem, you may run into trouble when you get around to selling.

Is Hawaiian Retirement Practical?

Because of our personal prejudices, making recommendations on retirement in Hawaii is difficult. We love the climate and we've had very positive experiences dealing with the local people. We've never seen a place where smiles appear so spontaneously and seem so genuine.

The fact that we enjoy the islands doesn't mean others will like them. A friend who moved to Honolulu a few years ago—not for retirement, but in search of a job—painted a different picture of life on the islands. She said, "Yes, if you spend your time with other retirees, and if your dealings with the local people is as a customer or client, you will love the place. But as a worker, I've encountered resentment and even prejudice, simply because I am an outsider. They feel I am taking a job away from a Hawaiian." Her experience is personal, but should be considered if you are thinking of part-time jobs during your retirement.

One problem that comes with living on an isolated island is that you may become *rock-happy*. This is akin to cabin fever or going stir-crazy. It happens when you start feeling confined, when you realize there is no getting away, and that a three- or four-hour drive in any direction will put you right back at your garage door. People claim that the sickness sets in after about three years of bliss.

> **HAWAII TAX PROFILE**
> **Sales tax:** 4%, drugs exempt
> **State income tax:** 2% to 10% over $20,500; can't deduct federal income tax
> **Property taxes:** residents over 60 receive $80,000 exemption, over 65 $100,000; taxes about 0.7% on assessed valuation
> **Intangibles tax:** no
> **Social Security taxed:** no
> **Pensions taxed:** no
> **Gasoline tax:** 16¢ per gallon, plus local taxes from 8.8¢ to 16.5¢

Folks who have lived here for long periods of time claim the only cure for being rock-happy is a trip to the mainland. One of the most popular flights is to Las Vegas. Apparently, the mind is soothed by vast expanses of gambling casino, fields of green-felt tables and cocktail waitresses swaying in the background like coconut trees on the windward coast. Apparently, those who can afford to make periodic trips to the mainland often don't care whether they go or not. It's those who *cannot* afford to leave the "rock" who get the rock-happy sickness the worst.

Another aspect to our view of retirement in Hawaii is that we've lived in a fairly high-cost-of-living part of the country for many years. We're used to high housing costs. What we might view as economical or affordable housing may contrast sharply with someone who is used to far lower costs. Because we can afford it doesn't mean everyone can.

Therefore, our conclusions are favorable. Although Honolulu and the island of Oahu might be out of range for us, other places—particularly the Kona area of the Big Island—would suit us as places where we could retire. However, our philosophy of retirement involves keeping a home base and spending time elsewhere, depending upon the season. We will surely be spending at least some of our time on the islands—perhaps renting a condo or townhouse during the off-season.

Grocery Prices

You may well expect prices to be higher in Hawaii, since most goods have to be brought in by ship or airplane. When vacationing tourists visit Honolulu, they often rent condos for a week or two and do some of their own cooking to cut expenses. When they return they'll say, "We couldn't believe the price of groceries! They're double the cost at home!"

And it's true; if you shop in the tourist areas, food items can easily cost twice as much or more. At a corner deli in Waikiki, a head of cabbage was priced at $3.75 and a dozen eggs at $4.00. Other sundries were proportionally tagged. If you check only prices around the tourist hotels, you'll wonder how in the world islanders can afford to feed themselves.

Obviously, folks who live in Hawaii year-round won't be shopping in tourist-oriented enterprises. Just as you shop for the best prices where you live, islanders patronize ordinary supermarkets, far from the hotel strip. The surprising thing is how close to mainland prices groceries are—at least on the three islands where we did our research. We visited four large supermarkets to compare prices: a well-known chain store on the windward side of Oahu; the same chain supermarket in Kaanapali, Maui; the largest market in Waimea, Hawaii, and a supermarket a few blocks from the tourist area of Kona, Hawaii. We found price variations among these stores on identical items, but no more than you might find between stores on the mainland. The closer to tourists' condos, the wider the price variations.

Although some items were considerably more expensive in Hawaii, the surprising thing was that so many items were not much higher or about the *same* as on the mainland! What happened to the extra costs of shipping? Products such as mayonnaise, coffee and ice cream were priced about the same as back home, as were things like paper goods, soap and pasta. Meats—which we expected to be sky-high—turned out to be *less* than at our neighborhood supermarket!

Some items, however, are much more costly in Hawaii, particularly eggs, milk and fresh vegetables. That milk is expensive is understandable. Land that isn't already planted in pineapple and sugar cane is so expensive that devoting it to dairy cattle would be inappropriate. But the curious thing is the high cost of fresh vegetables. They cost far more than at home, often twice as much or even more. This was particularly true on Oahu and less so on Maui and the Big Island (Hawaii). One would imagine that Hawaii's lush fields and fertile backyards should yield such a high volume of quality produce that people would be almost giving food away. But that isn't the case.

Part of the problem is that some fruits and vegetables don't do well in warm, tropical climates; others suffer from a Mediterranean fruit fly infestation that Hawaii has never been able to overcome. That I understand, but what about vegetables such as lettuce, cabbage or broccoli? Whatever the reason, high prices prevail at the supermarket. Pineapples are the one item that seems to be cheap (and high quality).

When we returned to the mainland, we visited our local supermarket in California to compare prices. Our conclusions are that the Hawaiian grocery bill needn't be a barrier to living in the islands. By shopping shrewdly and planning meals around weekly specials, we feel that we could keep our grocery bills to within 10 to 15 percent of our California budget.

Other Prices

Clothing prices seemed to be pretty much the same as on the mainland. How could this be? Because, like so many products that we used to make in America, most wearing apparel is now manufactured in the Orient. Shipping costs to Hawaii are lower, since it's closer to the factory.

The same is true of automobiles. It costs less to ship a Honda to Honolulu than it does to ship a Mitsibushi to Minneapolis. Furthermore, since the islands have very few miles of highway, cars tend to last a long time. If it weren't for rust and corrosion related to saltwater breezes, autos would probably never wear out. As it is, many old clunkers are still running around happily carrying their owners on short runs to the beach.

Gasoline is one item that costs much more than on the mainland. During a time when regular no-lead was $1.25 a gallon on the mainland, on the islands it varied between $1.50 to $1.75, depending upon the nearness of competing gas stations. However, since you cannot drive very far without returning to the same spot, gasoline shouldn't be a crucial portion of your budget.

The Bottom Line

If you are the type who likes to put down roots, and if you need to own property, and if you want to live in an idyllic climate and, finally, if you can afford a large investment in real estate—then you must investigate the Hawaiian Islands. If you like warm winters and the sight of palm trees swaying in the breeze, yet you can't afford $150,000 for a condo, perhaps Florida is a better choice for you. It isn't Hawaii, but no other place in the world is.

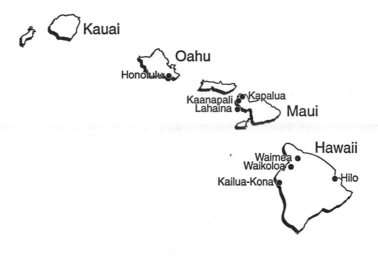

Oahu

The best-known islands of the Hawaiian archipelago are Oahu, Kauai, Maui and the Big Island of Hawaii. But in reality, these make up only a small portion of the Hawaiian Islands: 132 islands, shoals, atolls and reefs stretch from tiny Kure, more than 1,500 miles away, to Loihi, an undersea mountain next to the Big Island that is still building. One day Loihi will be Hawaii's newest island. For all I know, there may be a promoter selling lots on Loihi, so please be cautious.

The secret to living on Oahu is simple: you don't *have* to live in Honolulu. In fact, that's a place I'm not sure I'd choose for a residence even if property were cheap! Too many cars crowd the streets, too many tourists fill the beaches and too many high-rise hotels line the avenues.

Just 35 to 45 minutes from the hustle and bustle of Waikiki Beach, are some lovely communities that have all the attributes of small town U.S.A. The Kailua and Kaneohe areas are good examples, with almost no buildings over two stories high and single-family homes the norm. Each has a population of over 30,000. You'll find exceptionally low crime rates, light traffic and friendly neighbors. Beaches are seldom crowded—often empty—in sharp contrast to the elbow-to-elbow tourists on Waikiki beaches. The bonus is a year-round climate that is as nearly perfect as can be found anywhere in the world.

Homes here sell for less than one-half Honolulu prices. Condo prices are around $200,000—not cheap, but not that much higher than many quality mainland neighborhoods. A comforting note is if you do invest in Hawaiian real estate, the odds are overwhelming that you can get your money back (plus profit) later, should you return to the mainland.

313

Drive another 20 minutes and prices drop even lower. On Oahu's north shore the median price for homes is around $300,000 and condos, $140,000. Now, we are approaching the ballpark for many mainlanders. For folks living in many parts of California, these prices sound normal. Don't misunderstand; I'm not suggesting that these homes are inexpensive or are superb buys. A house for under $300,000 is often located in a neighborhood where I'd feel uncomfortable living. Too many homes are flimsy, single-wall construction and sit on leased land.

How is it possible then, to retire in Hawaii without being wealthy? Remember, I said you could live *modestly*. By modestly, I don't mean wearing high-neck bathing suits with long drawers—but modestly as in wearing bathing suits with patches on the seat.

To test living on Oahu on our normal budget, my wife and I felt that $750 a month was about as much rent as we would like to pay; that's what a small apartment rents for in our California home town. We quickly found a place called Punaluu on the North Shore. It was a one-bedroom condo right on the beach with a swimming pool, off-street parking and a secured building. The monthly rate was $750. Had we wanted to buy the condo, it was listed at $125,000. The neighborhood was quiet, with a couple of grocery stores located within walking distance (plus a convenience store on the premises) and near long stretches of semi-private beachfront. (All Hawaiian beaches are open to the public.) About 40 percent of the condo owners live here year-round; the rest spend the winter months here and rent out their units for the rest of the year. Rents vary between $600 and $950, depending upon the amenities and views. Although we had a rental car, bus service is excellent. Those who live here part of the year have automobiles and store them in reserved parking spaces with waterproof covers when they are staying on the mainland.

Living in the condo as if we owned it and shopping in local markets gave us an insight as to what it would be like to actually live on Oahu as a retiree. We got by just fine on about what we would have spent living at home under similar circumstances. Well, we probably would have rented a larger place on the mainland and dined at more upscale restaurants. But the gorgeous weather and lovely beaches nearby balanced out our lifestyle, probably on the plus side.

HONOLULU			Rel. Humidity: Jan. 62%, July 51%			
	Jan.	April	July	Oct.	Rain	Snow
Daily Highs	80	83	87	87	23"	—
Daily Lows	65	69	73	72		

Maui

Maui is the second largest of the islands and is famous for its marvelous beaches and fantastic views. A few years ago, Maui was a haven for those seeking tropical splendor at cut-rate prices. Property was cheap and the living was easy. Hippies and counterculture refugees from bourgeois boredom passed the word: *Like, Maui is where it's at, man!*

Things have changed. Somehow, the word must have gotten out to the bourgeoisie, because they've invaded Maui with a vengeance—fully equipped with plaid polyester shorts and matching golf clubs. With their middle-class values they also brought higher prices, which forced many counterculture folks to go tripping off to discover new island paradises.

Kapalua-Kaanapali   Most retirees—and mainlanders in general—prefer the western coast of Maui. The luxury areas of Kaanapali Beach and Kapalua are particularly popular, with elegant condos, hotels and expansive golf courses at every crook in the road. Ritzy shopping centers, art galleries and restaurants instill feelings of awe in the most blasé shoppers. The beaches are tops, and the islands of Molokai and Lanai make a wonderful backdrop for sunsets.

We felt fortunate that we had studied Honolulu real estate prices before coming to Maui, because that made property seem reasonable. We stayed at a condo in Kaanapali Beach, a two-bedroom affair with a great view of the ocean. Humpback whales were arriving after their annual voyage from Alaska, and they were leaping from the water in spectacular expressions of joy that the trip was finally over. A couple in a nearby condo had also just arrived from Fairbanks, Alaska, for their winter migration, and although they weren't leaping for joy, they obviously felt like it!

Based on Oahu prices, we estimated the cost of the condo to be at least $500,000. We figured that any offer less than that might be grounds for calling the police. To our amazement, the owner informed us that a unit like that could be purchased for less than $350,000—furnished. A few weeks earlier, this would have sounded like a lot of money, but now it seemed like a steal. You would have to see the luxurious layout to realize what a bargain one of those condos was.

In our forays to the supermarket to supply our condo's kitchen, we found groceries a bit cheaper than on Oahu, but not remarkably so. Vegetables, eggs and milk were expensive, just as we had expected.

Lahaina A couple of kilometers to the south is the historic whaling village of Lahaina, a place praised by Melville, Mark Twain and other famous people over the years. The picturesque old buildings are a natural attraction for artists and photographers. Art galleries and numerous artists at work with easels are common sights. Condos and homes are less expensive here, some selling in the neighborhood of $150,000, although we did look at one place for $475,000—nice but way out of range for most mainlanders.

Lahaina has a very comfortable feeling, but the downtown center suffers from steady streams of tourists wandering around buying souvenirs. The town of Maalea, a bit farther south, is another comparatively inexpensive place. There we found a beautiful two-bedroom condo, right on the beach, selling for $225,000 and a one-bedroom unit for $175,000. These units are usually placed in the hands of rental agents for the times when owners are traveling elsewhere. A rental agent swore that she could keep them rented at an 85 percent occupancy rate for $125 a night.

On the "south coast" (still on the western side of the island) are Wailea and Makena, with a good share of expensive places. With the islands of Lanai and Kahoolawe across the water, it is a magnificent place for Hawaii's legendary sunsets. Long stretches of beach and spectacular surf make this a favorite with mainlanders.

The Big Island

It was here, on the Big Island of Hawaii, that the Polynesians first came ashore, probably landing on Punaluu Beach on the southern end of the island. All around the island you can discover traces of the ancient Hawaiian civilization. Petroglyphs, temple mounds and burial grounds recall the days of the Hawaiian monarchy, from the time before the Europeans entered the picture.

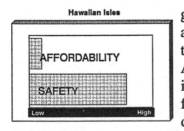

Hawaii is called the Big Island for good reason, with 4,038 square miles, about twice as large as all the others put together, it's about the size of Connecticut. And the Big Island hasn't stopped growing! In an awesome display of nature, lava from the Kilauea volcano has added hundreds of acres of land surface since its eruption a few years ago. The growth continues daily. As the lava flow pushes into the ocean to build more land, it also destroys homes and buildings that lie in its path.

Hawaii is famous for these "drive-in" volcanoes. You can usually drive to where the molten lava moves down the volcano's side and crosses the highway. You can park, walk over to the lava flow and take pictures of the glowing, taffy-like material as it moves toward the sea at 2,000 degrees Fahrenheit.

This process of land building started eons ago when a crack in the ocean floor, some 18,000 feet below the water's surface, opened and began oozing molten lava onto the ocean bottom. It grew ever higher, pouring magma down its sides until the crater's mouth finally broke through the surface of the water and began preparing for an onslaught of tourists. The process of discharging melted basalt continued until the volcano reached its present height of almost 14,000 feet *above* the ocean's surface. Some claim that if you measure from the ocean floor to the snow-covered top of Mauna Kea, it becomes the highest mountain in the world.

Our Favorite Hawaiian Island

Of the islands we visited, the Big Island is, without a doubt, our favorite. You'll find almost every climate and topography imaginable, from tropical rain forests—with lush, jungle-like vegetation—to deserts and snow-covered peaks. On the Kona coast, where most retirees settle, rainfall is about 40 inches a year—about the same as a typical midwestern U.S. location. Yet at the Kona airport, just a few miles north, only 10 inches of rain falls each year. This lower rainfall doesn't mean water shortages as it might on the mainland, because about 400 inches a year fall in the mountains, just a few miles to the east. This water flows in underground streams and is tapped by wells. At the other extreme, Hilo (on the eastern coast) gets over 140 inches, and residents claim that some years the rainfall measures over 200 inches!

During the winter months you can ski the slopes of Mauna Kea in the morning, travel through sugar cane plantations, desert and cactus land during midday, go scuba diving in the afternoon and watch glowing rivers of red lava flow in the evening. Because traffic is light and the roads are good, all these activities are possible with a minimum of hassle.

Notice that I said the Big Island has *almost* every climate and topography imaginable. It seriously lacks something other islands are famous for: beaches. In fact, it has almost *no* beaches! This singular lack clearly makes the Big Island unattractive to many Hawaii fans, especially those whose idea of an ideal holiday is lying on warm sand and soaking up sunshine. On the island of Hawaii, most of the coast is black, jagged lava rock. You can spread your towel on the lava, but you won't be comfortable lying back and enjoying the sun.

Beaches are scarce here because the Big Island is the newest of the islands. Just a few millions of years old, Hawaii is still in the process of becoming an island. The coastlines are twisted rivers of lava rock that have flowed into the ocean; waves and water action haven't had time to break the rock into fine grains of sand. In a few places the lava has disintegrated into black sand—sometimes green or red, depending upon the chemical composition of the lava—but regular old Malibu-type sand is rare. Instead of waves lapping against sand, the ocean's edge is usually boulder-sized black rocks or sharp, formidable cliffs.

At first, it might seem that a lack of beaches should be a drawback. But, there are two major benefits. The first is that the surf and views are truly spectacular, with blue-green waves crashing incessantly upon the black cliffs and jagged boulders. The sounds and sights are infinitely more exciting than the quiet ripples of Waikiki Beach or the leeward side of Maui.

The second benefit is that this scarcity of beaches also means a scarcity of surfers, beach bums and disco maniacs. Tourists and retirees come to the Big Island for gentler, kinder forms of entertainment. The end results are highways without heavy traffic and lots of empty country. As a matter of fact, this enormous piece of land has a population of only 117,000. Honolulu has more than that along one street. The island's largest and only city is Hilo, with a mere 47,000 residents. The rest are in towns and villages.

Another result is the age composition of the tourists and residents. Without surfing, discos and other things that attract youngsters, the Big Island has a quieter, more reserved feeling. Your next-door neighbor is more likely to be your age; your dinner companions will not be youngsters. Hotels are quieter, and more folks live here year-round instead of coming for a hectic fun-packed vacation.

Hilo The quiet, laid-back atmosphere of the Big Island and the light-weight population of tourists are some of the charms of Hilo. Another big plus is the affordability of housing. When you hear people say that Hawaiian real estate is out of sight, you can be sure they aren't talking about the eastern side of Hawaii.

The city of Hilo, for example, boasts of housing prices that compare favorably with all but the most inexpensive places in the United States. You can buy a four-bedroom home on an acre of ground for $100,000. A three-bedroom place can be found for $80,000, or a country cabin on three acres for $45,000. A one-bedroom apartment with a view of the ocean rents for $350 a month, or a studio apartment for $285. Any number of homes are listed for rent in the local newspaper at rates from $250 to $750 a month.

I'm not saying I would prefer living in Hilo to the other side of the island. It is a neat, clean city, with many interesting, historic buildings (reminiscent of Lahaina on Maui), and some absolutely gorgeous homes and townhouses adorn the coast. But it rains too much for me. As a Californian, I am used to zero rainfall during the summer months, so I don't think I could adjust to an average of 11 inches a month. Obviously, the folks who live in and around Hilo would disagree with me, since about half the entire island's population chose to live here. Except for Kailua-Kona and Waimea—both under 10,000 population—most other towns on the Big Island barely qualify as villages.

HILO			Rel. Humidity: Jan. 66%, July 58%			
	Jan.	April	July	Oct.	Rain	Snow
Daily Highs	80	80	83	83	128"	—
Daily Lows	63	65	68	68		

Kailua-Kona   This is our favorite part of the Big Island as well as the attraction for most other retirees. Yes, you'll find tourists—droves of them—but the scene isn't nearly as hectic as on Oahu or Maui. The panorama is typically Hawaiian and tropical, with palms, broad-leaf plants and flowers everywhere. Lovely homes, condos and townhouses command views of the coast and few have either air conditioning or heaters; neither are really needed.

In short, Kailua-Kona has everything you need for Hawaiian retirement (except beaches) with an added bonus: reasonable housing costs. For $150,000 or less, you can find a very livable condo or townhouse with swimming pools, tennis courts and a view of the ocean—a place that would cost $450,000 in Honolulu. It's true that you can find something less expensive in or near Honolulu, but would you be happy living in a poor man's home near a rich man's neighborhood? I wouldn't.

We looked at many places, mostly condos or townhouses, and we tried to stay below the $150,000 range. There were two reasons for this. First, that seems to be the average price range, and second, these are the easiest to rent, should you decide to live here part-time. These places rent for $65 to $75 a night; several reliable companies specialize in handling short-term rentals. Often the condominium's office is set up like a hotel desk, with the manager renting condos for the owners. (The fee varies from 10 to 20 percent of the rental.) With the nearby Kona Hilton renting rooms at $140 a night, the $65 rate looks great to tourists who want more than just a hotel room.

In early 1991, when we visited Kona, there were over 130 condos or townhouses on the market, ranging from $65,000 for a studio without an ocean view to $399,000 for a deluxe three-bedroom place right on the ocean. There were nine one-bedroom places with ocean views selling for $79,000 to $99,000 and several two-bedroom condos under $150,000. The median price of a one-bedroom condo was around $140,000. Compare that with $230,000 median price for Honolulu, and you'll see why we like Kona.

Waikoloa/Waimea　Farther up the coast, a series of super-expensive golf/country club projects are sprouting. My impression is that they are being built by Japanese investors and may be designed for tourists from Japan. Although they are beautifully designed, they are not only expensive but also are isolated from the rest of the island. However, that may not mean much to a golf nut, whose main interest is finding the best courses to play. These new courses are said to be superb.

But inland a bit, at an elevation of 1,000 feet, is Waikoloa. This also has dry weather, which, combined with the altitude, boasts one of the finest climates on any of the islands. This is a fairly new condo and townhouse project, and it is well laid out. We looked at several places right on the golf course that were selling for under $150,000 for two-bedroom units. There's a shopping center and all the amenities nearby.

Normally, I would say Waikoloa would also be too isolated, except that the town of Waimea is only 16 miles away. Even though Waimea is so close, its rainfall patterns are remarkably different. I believe it is close to 30 inches a year, which is enough to make wonderfully lush farming and ranch country. In some ways, Waimea looks like a prosperous farm town in the Midwest. It has less than 5,000 inhabitants, and it isn't tourist oriented at all. Single-family homes are the norm, with tidy yards and comfortable-looking neighborhoods. It's at a higher altitude and enjoys an almost temperate climate, with springtime every day of the year.

Most homes are in the $200,000 to $250,000 range, with some as low as $175,000 for a three-bedroom place. When we were there, an older five-bedroom, two-bath place on acreage was offered at $149,000, and a two-bedroom, two-bath place at $140,000.

Chapter 11

Education in Retirement

Toby didn't graduate from high school. He joined the Marines in his senior year and went off to Korea to fight for his country. When his enlistment was up, he thought about trying to get into college, but without a high school diploma, it seemed complicated. Besides, he needed money and an automobile, so he took a job as an apprentice electrician. When he was 23, he and Suzanne fell in love. She was completing her last year at the university as a history major. They married, bought a home and Toby started a business. Suzanne didn't have time to continue her education; she had too much work at home with children plus keeping books for their business to think about graduate school. She resolved that someday she would go back to school. But the opportunity never came, not until after retirement.

We met Toby and Suzanne in England, in an Oxford pub, one quite popular with university students. Known for its steak-and-kidney pie and selections of British ale, this establishment was said to be one that Bill Clinton patronized when he was a Rhodes Scholar at Oxford.

Toby certainly looked academic, wearing a tweed jacket with suede leather elbows. He sipped a glass of sherry as he paged through a book on Neolithic and early Bronze Age Archaeology in Britain. Suzanne's briefcase brimmed with books, journals and notes for a paper she was preparing, titled *Linguistic Anomalies in the Dead Sea Scrolls*. Were it not for their American accents, we would have assumed them to be Oxford graduate students or professors. Because they were of retirement age, we became curious.

We introduced ourselves and asked if they were going to school here. Toby grinned broadly and said, "Yep. I can't believe it. *Me,* going to Oxford! Suzanne's studying 'Origins of Western Religion,' and I'm taking Adult Ed classes in art and archaeology. We're having the time of our lives."

Suzanne described her research project, adding, "I always loved college, and I felt bad about not continuing. So, when Toby retired, we decided to try school, see if it was comfortable. I'm a little over my head here, but I don't care. It's so exciting!"

"First, we went to Harvard," Toby explained proudly. "We rented an apartment in Cambridge, Massachusetts for seven months while Suzanne took a couple of classes at Harvard. The thought of going to a university scared me, so I tried an Adult Ed class called 'Art Appreciation.' That was easy, so I signed up for an artist's workshop, and discovered I have a talent for sculpture.

"The interesting thing about adult education classes in a university town is: most instructors are full-fledged university professors who are moonlighting—either for extra money, or because they love to work with small groups of students. Also, most people in the class are close to my age, some even older. Half the fun is interacting with such an interesting group. Almost always, some students in the class are professors themselves, specialists in other fields."

Suzanne laughed and added, "Most Oxford students only see the professor from the back of a lecture hall. Harvard students too, for that matter. They're so isolated from one another that a professor wouldn't recognize a student outside the lecture hall if he stepped on her toes. Yet Toby here, he drinks tea and chats like an old army buddy with his Adult Ed teacher, who just happens to have a doctorate in Physical Anthropology, a world-famous expert in his field."

"What I like is, it's stress-free," Toby said, "because I don't have to worry about grades. They don't give any. And to qualify for a class, all I have to do is pay £28 tuition (about $34). Nobody asks if I've taken any prerequisite classes or even if I graduated from high school. The best part is how I feel about myself. I used to feel insecure around folks with lots of education, but not any more. What the hell, I've been to Oxford!"

He also pointed out that in a large university setting—places like Oxford and Harvard—the professors generally don't mind if non-students walk into the lecture hall and sit in on lectures, provided there's room. "When I don't have anything better to do, I'll drop into a lecture hall and see what's happening. I admit, sometimes I haven't a clue to what the professor is saying, but most of the time it's very stimulating."

Suzanne described the apartment they rented for a year, from a professor on sabbatical, for $1,000 a month. "It's a lovely, two-bedroom place with everything, including a washer and dryer. He even let us use his Macintosh computer for our studies. We could have rented a studio for about $400, but the extra bedroom makes a wonderful study space." She added that when their lease is up in June, they plan to go to Paris and study French at the Sorbonne. "The summer sessions there are open to anyone, and they offer courses for absolute beginners. Then, in the fall, it's back home to the U.S.A. We've decided to look for a college town for our permanent retirement home, maybe Boulder, Colorado."

Educational Opportunities

Scientific research shows that as we age, we don't necessarily lose our capacity to learn. The common belief that memory and retention inevitably fade is simply not true. Those who choose to regularly exercise their mental processes hold up quite well, thank-you.

A recent study at Pennsylvania State University dramatically proved this. They took people whose mental functioning had markedly declined and placed them in an intensive learning program. The decline reversed itself and their mental faculties improved remarkably.

Throughout the country, dynamic seniors with active lifestyles are going back to school. This time around, they sign up for subjects they *want* to study, rather than what's *required* to get a degree. By exercising their minds and enjoying stimulating companionship in an academic setting, senior students will extend their intellectual lives and greatly improve their quality of life. In doing so, they'll make new friends, those of a like mind, those with lifestyles to match theirs.

Adult education facilities are expanding to keep up with this demand, and more than two-thirds of U.S. colleges and universities offer reduced rates or even free tuition to older citizens. Some communities develop special centers, schools and programs tailored to older adults' needs. You won't feel like the proverbial sore thumb in a setting where you have company your own age.

Besides intellectual stimulation, other advantages accrue to retirement in a college or university town. Most schools provide the community at large with a wide selection of social and cultural activities, benefits which wouldn't exist without the school's presence. You don't have to be a registered student to attend lectures and speeches (often free) given by famous scientists, politicians, visiting artists and other well-known personalities. Concerts, ranging from Beethoven to boogie-woogie, are presented by guest artists as well as the university's music department. Stage plays from Broadway musicals to Shakespeare are produced by the drama department, with season tickets often less than a single performance at a New York theater. Some schools make special provisions to allow seniors to use their recreational facilities. Art exhibits, panel discussions and a well-stocked library are often available to the public. (You can't check out library books or magazines, but you're usually free to browse the stacks.)

Next to volunteer work, the best way to make friends in a new community is by taking classes. College or adult education, it doesn't matter. You'll find yourself amidst a group of lively, interesting people—the kind you would like for friends. If you have a specialty of some sort, an even faster way of getting known is to offer to teach a class; community colleges and adult education programs are often strapped for cash to hire full-time teachers and therefore welcome the opportunity to add classes with part-time or volunteer teachers.

Once, when my wife and I moved to a small Oregon city, I taught a couple of community college classes in freelance writing. Not for the money—which was almost nothing—but for the opportunity of meeting townspeople with a common interest in writing. The class was a resounding success, for we made half a dozen friends and received an invitation to join a local writer's group. Our entrance into the town's social life was immediate and satisfying.

Nervous about going back to school? Never been in a college classroom? Don't worry, for a mature adult it's a snap. You'll find that teachers are usually closer to your age than to most students. Although professors may talk down to younger students, they'll usually treat you like an equal. I remember occasions when I would disagree with something the professor said, and would receive the reply, "Why don't we have a cup of coffee after class, John? I'll try to convince you that I'm right." But if a 19-year-old would timidly say, "I'm sorry sir, I don't quite understand," the professor would fix the student with an indignant stare and ask, "Why don't you try reading the damned textbook?" That's an advantage of being an older student. Also, the professor often paid for my coffee.

If you're tense about a university setting, start off with adult education courses and work up. My experience has been that all Adult Ed classes have plenty of mature students, often a majority. Community college university-level classes also have a good percentage of older students.

Most schools allow you to audit a course, that is, take the class but not have to worry about quizzes, tests, finals or term papers. You get the benefit and fun out of a course without the tension of having to make good or having to participate in class discussions. How to choose a class? My method is to browse the college bookstore for textbooks that look interesting, and then ask questions about the instructor for that course. If several ex-students recommend the professor, I consider registering.

Classes like ceramics, jewelry-making or music appreciation are wonderful ways to break into the academic milieu, but after a while, despite their enjoyment and satisfaction, you could find them superficial. Delving into deeper, more challenging subjects will really exercise your intellect. Don't hesitate to sign up for classes like "Theoretical Existential Phenomenology." Okay, you don't quite understand what the professor is saying, but then maybe the professor doesn't understand, either. (That's what I've always suspected.) Just making a commitment toward trying to understand, does worlds for your self-esteem and puts you in touch with interesting fellow students, who probably don't understand Existential Phenomenology either.

All educational settings are not the same. Sometimes school districts are short on funding and have cut way back. In this case you may find that community college courses are oriented toward job preparation for young adults. Unless you want to learn welding, consider the local university instead. Visit the school's administration offices and ask for a catalog of classes.

A painless way to break into an academic setting with students exclusively your age is through programs like Elderhostel.* The variety of programs and subjects is absolutely bewildering. These courses typically involve traveling to a university campus, lodging in student dorms and using the school's facilities for study. The noncredit courses generally last a week or two and are restricted to adults age 60 and older. Tuition isn't exactly cheap. It can run about $300 a week, but that includes meals, lodging and field trips This is an excellent way to check out a town, as well as the school, and judge whether you'd like to retire here, for what you would spend for a regular vacation.

University Towns: A Sampler

Let's take a look at a few places where folks retire primarily because of a college or university setting. Of course, the majority of the towns listed in this book have community colleges; most are near a university, or close to a city with one. You can take advantage of continuing education just about anywhere you choose to retire. It's just that in some towns, the university is the centerpiece of local attention, the focus of social and cultural activities. This creates a situation where everyone can participate in the excitement and movement generated by the university.

* Information: *Elderhostel*, 75 Federal St., Third Floor, Boston, MA 02110, (617)426-7788.

Oxford, Mississippi   A century and a half ago the founders of Oxford chose that particular name for their future city, because they fully intended for this to be the site of a great university. They figured that by naming the townsite "Oxford," they couldn't go wrong. Whether or not the name influenced the state of Mississippi when it came time to issue a university charter, the founders' wishes came true in 1848 when 80 students enrolled in the University of Mississippi's first class. Today the campus of "Ole Miss" spreads over 1,800 acres, and its 185 buildings host 11,000 students.

In a true university town, all aspects of everyday life are affected one way or another by the school. Those who don't participate directly in the school usually have connections in their business or social lives that have to do with the university. The entire community is invited to join in ongoing events, such as The Living South Festival, the William Faulkner Conference or the Ole Miss Jazz Reunion. Something is happening every week, and practically every day or night of the week. The Oxford Conference for the Book draws writers, authors and literary fans from all over the world. As part of the agenda, best-selling author Barry Hannah held a fiction-writer's workshop, sharing his expertise and techniques with beginning and advanced authors.

A well-received weekly event, sponsored by the Center for Southern Culture, is the "Brown-Bag Lunch Program," with interesting lectures on a wide range of topics. The public is encouraged to bring edibles and refreshments as they enjoy an educational lunch hour. One retiree who is addicted to brown-bagging says, "You get a mini-education from attending these lectures. I look forward to every meeting." The university also presents lectures on every conceivable subject, mostly open to the public and free. Retirees find Oxford a wonderful place for education; by state law, anyone over the age of 55 can take three hours of classes for credit tuition-free, and can audit as many classes as they care to.

(Oxford is described in more detail in Chapter 5.)

Chapel Hill, North Carolina   "There are so many things to do here, we wore ourselves out when we first retired in Chapel Hill," said a retired couple from New York. "Eventually, we slowed down and began to be more selective about which lectures we would attend or which sports event to watch. However, through all of these activities, we've made some pretty solid friends. And, they're all dynamic, interesting people, every one of them."

Because of Chapel Hill's university atmosphere, more Ph.D.'s retired here than in any other city in the United States. Some come to teach, then stay on to retire. Research Triangle Park—the largest research park of its kind in the United States—draws scientists from all over the world, who also buy into retirement here. Others come to visit academic friends and fall in love with the special dynamics of the "University Triangle," so-called because three major universities, five four-year colleges and eight two-year colleges are grouped within a few miles of each other.

Senior citizens can audit university classes on a space-available basis (as is the case anywhere in the state). Fees are minimal. For example: Duke University, in nearby Durham, charges $90 for its continuing education program, which includes as many classes as you feel up to taking. Because of the unusual number of retired college graduates here, the interest in continuing education is very high. One group developed their own "free university" programs in which retirees teach their own specialties to others. It's an exceptionally successful program, and according to participants, it's in danger of swamping because of its phenomenal growth.

The university's extensive campus is as beautiful as the school is prestigious. However, one thing that impressed us greatly was an over-whelming feeling of welcome and friendliness. No less than three times in half an hour—as we strolled about the campus paths, gazing at ivy-covered halls and landscaped grounds—passing students misunder-stood our starry gaze for bewilderment. They paused to ask us if they could help give us directions.

(See Chapter 3 for more information on Chapel Hill and the University Triangle.)

Columbia, Missouri   When their youngest daughter graduated from high school, ready for college, Charles and Bernice decided it was time for Charles to take his Air Force retirement and look for a suitable college. But Charles had an educational plan of his own. He wanted to study law. In checking out retirement locations, they concentrated on several conditions. First they looked for a Midwestern university, one which offered a good liberal arts education for their daughter as well as a prominent law school for Charles. They also wanted to locate away from a big city, yet near enough to take advantage of the professional sports and cultural events offered by a city. Of course, quality housing needed to be affordable, and their new home had to be within easy driving distance of a place for camping and fishing, preferably in the Ozarks. It didn't take long to decide that Columbia, Missouri, covered all the bases.

Three well-known institutions of higher learning make education a major industry here. A pleasant aura of intellectualism pervades Columbia. As in all university towns, residents find their lives enriched by the wide variety of cultural, social and sports activities open to them, events which simply would not happen were it not for the schools' presence. If you enjoy concerts, festivals, lectures, visiting celebrities and other fascinating happenings, you'll have no problem filling your social calendar. Stevens College conducts a program called "University Without Walls," that reaches out to the community—retirees in particular—with a wide range of interesting classes.

For those who so choose, continuing education can be a way of combining community service with life-long learning. They'll take advantage of programs offering free tuition in return for volunteer work after graduation. "I'm working with a second-grade class," said one retiree who just finished a course in Master Gardening. "I'm showing them how to plant and care for gardens. And, in another group, we're conducting a children's tree-planting project."

(For more information about Columbia, see Chapter 4.)

Boulder, Colorado Twenty-seven miles northwest of Denver, Colorado's premier university town sits at the base of the Flatiron Mountains. Boulder has a scenic beauty which is complemented by a rich and diverse cultural atmosphere. Home of the University of Colorado, this cosmopolitan city of 82,000 inhabitants is deeply influenced by the school's cultural events and intellectual excitement.

This influence spills over into the heart of the city, along Pearl Street, the center of the renovated downtown pedestrian mall. Mimes, jugglers and musicians mingle with the crowds, adding a touch of magic to the scene, something you'd expect to find in San Francisco or Paris, rather than Colorado. You'll find a selection of good restaurants, galleries and shops, along with flowers and bookstores. This is the site of art festivals and celebrations, a place for people-watching and relaxing.

Among the outstanding cultural events generated by the university is its Shakespeare festival, one of the top three in the country. There's also a nationally praised Bach Festival and the Colorado Dance Festival. Every summer the Chautauqua Auditorium sponsors a film series and dance, music and dramatic presentations.

For those who don't feel up to total immersion in the university's curriculum, an extraordinary senior center operated by Boulder Housing and Human Services gives classes in everything from papermaking to computers, as well as sailboat instruction on Boulder Reservoir and day trips to archaeological sites and theaters in Denver. Coupled with an active volunteer program, this is one of the better programs we've seen.

Boulder's winter looks bad statistically, that is, if you consider snow bad, because Boulder catches even more snow than Denver! December and February receive the heaviest blankets of the white stuff, but like Denver, daily temperatures climb high enough to get rid of it quickly. Most days of the year can be spent walking, biking or with other outdoors activities. Summer makes amends by providing gloriously sunny and comfortable days.

(For more details on Colorado, see Chapter 7.)

Ashland, Oregon   Set in Southern Oregon's gently rolling hills, Ashland is an excellent retirement choice for couples with mixed interests, for those who want more than intellectual stimulation. Outdoorsy, sports-oriented people love this part of the country. Great hunting, fishing and skiing is available in the nearby Cascade Range, with crystal-clear waters teeming with world-class salmon and steelhead trout. Whitewater rafting on the wild and scenic Rogue River draws adventurers from all over the country. One of the best climates in the country makes outdoor sports enjoyable year-round; Ashland's 20 inches of yearly rain is a third to half that of most popular Midwest, Southern and Florida cities. It's wonderfully sunny here most of the year.

Ashland also satisfies the cravings for intellectual stimulation through the presence of Southern Oregon State College. Small for a college town, with about 20,000 residents, Ashland is able to gather all interested residents into an intimate relationship with the school. "It's rare that I go downtown without seeing someone I know," said one retiree. And, Ashland's charming downtown features a wide selection of restaurants and shops, far more than you might expect in a town of this size. Folks from Oregon towns near and far journey here to dine in restaurants serving French country cooking, wood-fired pizza or Thailand cuisine, or perhaps to browse in used bookstores or look at fashion clothing imported from Scotland.

Starting out as an annual summer Shakespeare presentation in an open-air, Elizabethan-era styled theater, the Shakespeare Festival expanded to a year-round event, drawing 300,000 visitors yearly to its three theaters. Performances aren't limited to Shakespeare; modern, classic and experimental drama entertains the public. Everybody in town seems to get into the action, volunteering to help with costuming, ushering, or whatever is needed. Tourists are often surprised to encounter costumed actors on their lunch break, munching hamburgers in a downtown restaurant while discussing their roles in the current stage production.

(See Chapter 9 for more details on Ashland.)

Auburn-Opelika, Alabama   Located in eastern Alabama in a setting of rolling hills and forests, the Auburn-Opelika area (pop. 57,000) is a good choice for retirement centered around continuing education. The charm and small-town warmth is enriched by residents from all over the country, drawn here by Auburn University. In fact a third of the population here come from other states, a large percentage of them retirees.

A drive through the shaded streets of Opelika treats you to the sight of old homes being meticulously restored, a sure indication of the respect local residents have for history. Opelika is the quieter, residential side of the two adjoining towns, with a chamber of commerce that recently won a Governor's award as the most active community in the state for recruiting retirees.

Next door in Auburn is highly-respected Auburn University, with 38 undergraduate degrees, master's degrees in 60 fields, as well doctorate degrees in 38 areas. A National Science Foundation report ranks Auburn among the leading research universities in the nation, and *Changing Times* magazine recognizes the school as among the top universities, combining high academic standards with reasonable tuition costs.

In addition to the university, there's a two-year school, Southern Union Jr. College, with about 1,400 students and Opelika State Technical School, which features extended day programs. Because of its top medical school and East Alabama Medical Center, health care here is superior. Nearby Fort Benning, Georgia, has a medical facility for military retirees, as well as a commissary and post exchange.

As you might imagine, football and basketball fever grasp the attention of locals, with the university stadium seating 80,000 fans and the basketball arena accommodating 12,000 in the winter. Of course there's plenty of opportunity for outdoor sports. One of the famous Robert Trent Jones Golf Trail courses is located here, for top country-club quality at public golf fees. There is one other public golf course, plus a private one. Great fishing is enjoyed at any number of sparkling lakes around the countryside, including 130-acre Lee County Public Lake and 15 miles away on the Chattahoochee River. The climate here is mild, perfect for enjoying outdoor recreation, with short winters, early spring and late fall.

(For more details on Alabama, read Chapter 5.)

Getting a Break on Tuition

Many states have legislation granting free or reduced tuition to senior citizens. Here's a list of the states and their policies. Some states are considering liberalizing these regulations, so check locally for up-to-date facts. The information comes from a report by the U.S. Senate Special Committee on Aging.

Alabama: Most of Alabama's colleges and universities offer free or reduced tuition to residents 60 or over. Some private schools offer tuition discounts, special classes, and access to recreation and cultural programs for retirees.

Arkansas: State schools waive general student fees for credit courses to persons age 60 and older on a space-available basis. State vocational and technical schools also waive fees.

California: Depending upon space, many state colleges waive application and regular-session registration fees for regular credit courses to persons age 60 or older.

District of Columbia: The University of the District of Columbia waives tuition for students age 60 or older in courses for credit or audit.

Florida: Application, course registration and other related fees are waived at state universities on a space-available basis to residents age 60 or older.

Georgia: Waives fees for courses scheduled for resident credit to persons age 62 and older on a space-available basis.

Hawaii: Waives tuition or fees for credit classes at the University of Hawaii to persons age 60 or older, on a space-available basis.

Kentucky: Waives all tuition and fees at state-supported institutions of higher learning to any resident age 65 and older, on a space-available basis.

Louisiana: Waives tuition and registration fees at public colleges and universities to any person age 60 or older. Also reduces textbook costs by 50 percent.

Maryland: Waives tuition to University of Maryland system for up to three courses per term to any retired person age 60 or older, on a space-available basis. Also waives tuition to community colleges to residents age 60 or older.

Mississippi: Waives tuition to residents 55 and older for one credit class per semester, as well as offering unlimited auditing, on a space-available basis.

Nevada: Waives registration fee for credit or audit in any course to persons age 62 and older.

New Mexico: Institutions may reduce tuition fees to $5 per credit hour for up to six hours per semester to residents age 65 or older, on a space-available basis.

North Carolina: Waives tuition at colleges and universities to residents age 65 or older who attend classes for credit or non-credit, on a space-available basis.

South Carolina: Waives tuition at any public college or university for credit or non-credit classes to residents age 60 or older, on a space-available basis.

Tennessee: Waives tuition registration fees at public colleges and universities for credit or audit to residents age 65 and older, on a space-available basis.

Texas: State-supported schools may waive tuition for persons age 65 or older to audit any course, on a space-available basis.

Utah: Waives tuition at institutions of higher learning to residents age 62 or older, on a space-available basis.

Virginia: Waives tuition for auditing courses at any state institution of higher education to residents age 60 or older, on a space-available basis. (Note: there is an income limit of $10,000 for this service.)

Washington: State universities and community colleges may waive tuition to residents age 60 or older enrolled for credit, on a space-available basis.

Chapter 12

RVs and Retirement

Most retirees center their plans around the particular town they choose for retirement. Their plans may include an occasional trip to Florida or fishing trips to the north woods, but the focus is on "our retirement home." Other folks, those with a more keenly developed sense of adventure, eager to travel, fill their retirement days with challenges and excitement. After all, for the first time in their lives they are free to do anything they care to. *Anything*. They don't have to be any place at any particular time, and they can travel anywhere they choose. It's a wonderful feeling not to have to explain or apologize to anyone.

For these more adventurous folks, a recreational vehicle ("RV" to you) can be the ticket to a new lifestyle and a new world of experience. This exciting way of travel doesn't necessarily involve a lot of money, depending on how you go about it. With a motorhome, trailer or camper as your floating homestead, you can tour the country by the seasons, visiting places you've only read about, making new friends at each twist of the road. Part-time RV retirees enjoy two sets of neighbors: those in their home town and seasonal neighbors who share spaces in the winter RV neighborhood.

By and large, people who travel by RV are gregarious and friendly. They *have* to be to enjoy parking shoulder-to-shoulder with their neighbors. Although you may not know your next-door neighbors back home, you'll find few strangers in RV parks. At the beginning of each winter season, when the sunshine parks begin filling up, old friends meet and celebrate a renewal of last year's companionship. "We've been coming here for the last six years," one lady told us, "and we've made more friends in this park than we ever made back home!"

RVs Are Not for Everyone

Buying an RV and setting out to conquer the world may sound like a neat idea, but unless you can adapt to this lifestyle, you could be very disappointed. My advice, if you haven't already tried it, is to rent one for a couple of weeks. It's expensive, but it may save you money down the road. Few things can make you so angry with yourself than a big, sheet metal box sitting in your driveway, unused, neglected and nagging at your conscience.

Full-time RV Retirement

Almost every RV owner fantasizes how it might be to live in the rig for longer periods of time than mere extended vacations. Just take off and never land! Follow the seasons, follow your whims, as carefree as a seagull on the wing! It's an exciting and slightly awesome idea: cutting ties with your neighborhood, putting things in storage and setting sail with no particular port in mind!

Most folks ease their way into it, and this is the advised way to go. They move toward full-timing in stages. Dick March (president of Loners on Wheels, a club for single RV travelers) suggests the following stages or levels of RV commitment.

1. *Weekenders*—have favorite places to visit nearby and who rarely stay more than a couple of days before returning home.

2. *Theme-inspired Travelers*—follow a hobby, i.e., Blue Grass (or other) music festivals, fishing, hunting, genealogy, history, square dancing, and the just-can't-stand-that-ice-and-snow type.

3. *Flea Marketeers*—collect junk and treasures, scrounging garage sales and second-hand stores for merchandise to sell or trade at flea markets. They lose money on every sale, but make it up in volume.

4. *Two-basers*—have one summer base and one winter base, traveling back and forth exclusively between the two bases. Often the home base is their house.

5. *High-profilers*—ego-driven owners of half-a-million-dollar motorhomes with endless electronics, communications, hot tub, wine cellar, and so forth. After spending a fortune on equipment, they delight in boondocking, feeling good about saving money.

6. *Chuck-It-All Full-timers*—totally succumb to the gypsy call of the road. They usually belong to several RV clubs, such as Good Sam, Escapees and other organizations that cater to full-timers. They keep in touch through club newsletters and correspondence via mail-forwarding services. The longer they are full-time, the wider their network of friends. These are the elite of the RV set.

Some folks jump right into RV full-timing and enjoy that lifestyle for the rest of their lives. But statistics show that most return to conventional living within a few years, or they at least establish a home base somewhere. Keep this in mind when preparing for the open road. When you start cutting ties, remember where the ends are, just in case you need to reconnect them someday.

Home Base

Full-timers face a total break with former routines and lifestyles. Unfortunately, even though you can be as free as the proverbial bird on the wing, you will find that you need a permanent nest of some sort. The mail carrier cannot and will not chase your rig down the highway to deliver Social Security checks, income tax forms or state license tags. You need an address for the grandkids to send birthday cards and graduation announcements. If you plan on using credit cards, you'll need a place to receive the bills. You'll also want a phone number where friends and relatives can leave messages for you. Finally, no matter how successful your yard sale, there will always be some things you cannot part with.

The solution is to establish a home base. Most travelers start out bravely, with a firm resolve to remain unattached, but generally end up choosing a home base somewhere. It could be a temporary pause in an RV park to catch up on correspondence and income tax records, or it may be a place they might really want to live someday. Your home base could be an inexpensive house, a mobile home or a reserved space in an RV park—any place with storage, even a large storage shed and a P.O. box. After you have a home base, you can make arrangements to have mail and messages forwarded while you are on the road.

Of course, many don't sell their houses when they hit the road; they keep them as anchors, simply locking them up when they go away. (This is the recommended course of action, at least until you are *positive* you want to be a full-timer.) Others rent their homes, reserving the garage or perhaps a couple of rooms or the basement for storing their things. An arrangement is then made with the renters to forward mail and telephone messages. This makes sense, because you keep ties with your home town and your friends intact. Someday you may tire of the full-time carefree life of travel. Most do, eventually.

RV Parks

Most quality parks have certain features in common: swimming pools, Jacuzzis, shuffleboard courts, sometimes even golf courses. No matter how humble, an all-important part of a good RV park is the clubhouse. It's more than just a place to go for a cup of coffee and to meet other RV enthusiasts. Dancing, bingo, arts and crafts, aerobics, card parties, pot-lucks and group tours are just a few of the organized activities available in the typical clubhouse. There's no excuse for ever being bored.

The number and variety of RV parks almost defy description. Their facilities run from none to luxurious. Many feature golf courses and tennis courts, producing a complete country-club atmosphere. A new trend is members-only parks with locked gates and 24-hour security. Some RV parks sit right on the beach, perfect for surf-casting and splashing around in your bathing suits. There are even parks for nudists, where you can splash around in your birthday suits! At least a hundred of these naturist parks are scattered throughout the United States and Canada.

Space rentals vary from as low as $50 a month to $300, and sometimes higher. Better RV parks commonly charge from $160 to $225 a month. One lady visiting in Florida with her motor home pointed out, "Our park rent is less than our winter utilities when we stay home all winter. So, now we just weatherproof our house and forget it until the snow melts!"

Recently I read an ad in *Trailer Life* for an RV park in Mesa, Arizona. It advertised rates of $49 a week and boasted a host of attractions. I'll list them here so you can see what you get for your $49: clubhouse, ballroom, lounge, library, pool/billiards, card parlor, Olympic pool/Jacuzzi, kitchen/snack bar, four tennis courts, putting green, golf driving cage, shuffleboard and horseshoes, exercise gym, lapidary shop, silversmith studio, woodworking shop, ceramics studio, arts and crafts, ping pong, laundry/ironing rooms and sewing room. If your favorite hobby isn't listed here, you should be arrested and kept off the streets!

Trailer Life, by the way, is *the* publication for RV travelers, whether full-timers or weekenders. It is full of important news for RV owners, features on how to repair your rig, interesting places to visit and general trends in the RV industry.*

RV Clubs

How do you find information, hints and assistance about becoming a full-timer? Join an RV club that specializes in full-time RVers. Supportive members, an informative newsletter, club campgrounds and campouts all over the country make the transition far more fun. Most folks

---

* For subscriptions or other information, write Trailer Life at 3601 Calle Tecate, Camarillo, CA 93012, or call them at (800) 234-3450.

join more than one club. You'll find clubs for every kind of special interest you can imagine. Rockhounds and prospectors, jewelry-makers and quilters, as well as handicapped travelers and computer buffs are all organized, along with just about any other kind of hobby you can imagine. Clubs for single people can change the entire RV picture. *Trailer Life* magazine carries advertisements from most clubs.

The largest RV club of all, Good Sam, started 25 years ago when a Utah trailerist sent a letter to *Trail-R-News* Magazine (now called *Trailer Life*.) The letter suggested that the magazine offer subscribers a decal for their rigs, something that would indicate their willingness to stop and help fellow RVers in distress. The idea caught on and mushroomed into the Good Sam Club.

Since few insurance companies were interested in covering RVs, it seemed only natural that the club should provide policies tailored to members' needs. Before long, Good Sam became the major insurer of travel trailers and motorhomes.

Today Good Sam has more than 750,000 members with 2,200 chapters around the country. In addition to insurance, members receive discounts at hundreds of participating campgrounds, mail-forwarding, trip routing and even RV financing. The club's emergency road service is said to be the only one offered by major insurers to RVs. A subscription to *Trailer Life* magazine is discounted.

Sue Bray, executive director of Good Sam Club, speaking of why folks seem to be fascinated with clubs and RVing in general, said, "People seem to have a longing for a way of life where they could chat with neighbors on the front porch or just sit and watch the grass grow. Modern life doesn't allow that. But going to an RV rally, meeting fellow club members, going to a potluck dinner or an ice-cream social—this replaces something that has been lost in recent years."

Full-time RVers have their own organizations; the best-known and largest is the Escapees, with national headquarters at 100 Rainbow Drive, Livingston, TX 77351. The club publishes a news magazine which presents important news about rallies and get-togethers, new places to park, tips on equipment maintenance and hints for making life easier for people who make their homes on the road. Members report where they are and what they've been doing. SKP members often remark, "We feel like we're part of a large, close-knit family."

RV Clubs for Singles

The conventional picture of retirement bliss is a handsome couple, tenderly holding hands as they gaze lovingly upon their retirement mansion. The husband usually wears a cashmere cardigan and has distinguished-looking gray hair that sweeps back from an aristocratic forehead. (He's never bald as a cue ball, is he?) The wife's hairdo displays a few discretely tell-tale streaks of silver; if the advertisement didn't say she was retired we'd assume she was about 37 years old. This couple is successful, affluent and looking forward to a future of stimulating visitors, gourmet dinners and bridge parties as they entertain brilliantly in their fabulous new home.

We all know that this picture is far from accurate. Besides the fact that most of us men lack aristocratic-looking foreheads and look our age, a large percentage of retirement-aged people lack that loving other person to hold hands with. They face retirement alone, as singles. What happens when your spouse dies unexpectedly, just years before your planned retirement date? All your plans are knocked into the famous cocked hat. This is particularly true of working women; over 60 percent drop out of the work force as singles.The picture is often far from the idyllic scene just described.

"Man or woman, life is a difficult experience to handle being alone," remarked one single man who had just retired. The answer for many single retirees is found in one of several RV clubs that cater exclusively to single travelers. Don't misunderstand; these aren't lonely hearts clubs or swinging singles groups. Far from it. These organizations fulfill a legitimate need in bringing people together for mutual support, assistance and companionship while traveling in RVs. If you join one of these groups looking for romance, you might find it, but most clubs will throw you out if you begin traveling with another person. When they say "single" they mean just that!

Loners on Wheels   The singles club with which I am most familiar is called Loners on Wheels (LoW). Several thousand members strong, the LoWs are adding members steadily as the word gets out. Its newsletter is devoted to keeping its members in touch with each other and to promoting social and travel events. Every issue lists chapter news, tips on RV maintenance and news from individuals as they recount their adventures on the road. The LoW's address is P.O. Box 1355, Poplar Bluff, MO 63901.

Singles-only is a strict rule with this club, and the minute members start traveling as a couple, their membership is terminated. I understand that about 60-65 percent of the members are retired women, often widowed, who universally feel that the club has miraculously rescued them from a life of boredom. One man, whose wife had recently died, said, "It's not surprising that the members are mostly women. At this age, most of the men are gone. It's been a godsend running into a group like this."

My wife and I attended several LoW campfire meetings (by special invitation because we're writers). We were impressed by the loving support and undemanding friendship given by LoW members. Singles have a standing invitation to visit any LoW campout, with no obligation other than a friendly smile once in a while.

Every winter LoWs from all over the country converge upon Slab City (near California's Salton Sea) where they set up camp in the desert. Dance lessons, art classes, campfire get-togethers, breakfasts and other organized and ad-hoc activities make for a pleasant winter. One warm January evening we interviewed some single ladies about their experiences. "How do you feel about safety out here in the desert?" I asked. "How has the club affected your lives?"

One woman, recently retired as a bank teller from an eastern city, said, "During the two years before I retired, I was held up at gunpoint five times! Ask me again how safe I feel here!"

Another lady, a widow from Seattle, said, "If it weren't for this club and all of the wonderfully supportive friends in it, tonight I would be sitting alone watching television in a downtown, two-room apartment." She smiled at her friends and said, "I've never felt safer in my life."

One of the men, a retired accountant from Texas, said, "I belong to another RV club besides Loners on Wheels, but somehow I feel like a third wheel as a single man among all of those couples. Here, I feel like I belong."

Working and RVers

Early in the book I threw cold water on the idea of working part-time in retirement. Unless a person has a unique skill that is in high demand, he or she may be forced to compete with younger people for jobs that are low paying and terribly boring.

However, RV retirement changes this picture somewhat. The number of full-time RVers who earn a good share of their expenses by working is truly surprising. And the heart-warming thing is, many jobs are uniquely tailored for RVers. Although the pay may be no better than ordinary part-time jobs, the work can be interesting and rewarding. Often the work setting is beside a gorgeous lake or in a beautiful resort where ordinary folks pay big money to visit for a two-week vacation. You stay the season for free.

Chapter 13 describes volunteering in state and national parks as a mode of seasonal retirement. These volunteer positions are necessarily limited in number because housing can be provided for only so many people. But when you bring your own home with you, it's a different story. Since many volunteer and paid jobs are seasonal and in rustic locations, employers are delighted to find temporary employees who need nothing more than water and electricity hookups for living accommodations. Then, when the season is over, the workers pack up and move on to better weather, leaving behind nothing but good memories.

State and national parks and resorts need all types of workers: campground managers, bookkeepers, off-season caretakers, maintenance and gatekeepers. Many parks offer free parking and hookups (but no pay) for campground hosts whose duties consist of answering questions from new campers.

Seasonal jobs aren't limited to national or state parks and campgrounds—not by any means. When a migration of snowbirds settles into a popular RV area, almost every business in town needs extra help to handle the increased business. From gift shops to garages, from restaurants to recycling centers, temporary help is needed. RV mechanics and repairmen can write their own agendas when thousands of RVs are in town.

Temporary jobs in RV parks and campgrounds can be assistant managers, clerical staff and grounds keepers. When the RVs pull out, the RV park's staff often drops back to just the manager. Ski instructors are needed in mountain resorts for the winter and fishing guides are essential for the summer. Christmas tree lots love to have commissioned salespeople who can park their rigs in the middle of the trees and watch over them at night. Salespeople follow trade shows or shopping mall promotions, staffing booths and selling items to the public. These traveling jobs would be impractical if you had to stay in hotels and eat in expensive restaurants.

Workamper News

So many employers need temporary workers who supply their own housing, and so many RVers are eager to supplement their budgets with free hookups and extra money, that a specialized newsletter has evolved to bring the two sides together. *Workamper News* appears every other month with 40 pages of classified ads, both employees wanted and situations wanted. The ads are free of charge. (See appendix for address.)

The publication has been used by a wide variety of public and private enterprises with great success. Since the publishers try to weed out phony get-rich-quick schemes, most help-wanted ads are legitimate. Each listing includes location, duties, benefits, how to apply and whom to contact. According to the publisher, often there are more jobs than people to fill them.

Each issue contains several non-paid volunteer job offerings even though publishers Greg and Debbie Robus prefer that there be some compensation involved. Greg says, "We encourage beginners to try one of these volunteer positions first. They're generally of shorter duration and with less responsibility. That way, should you find that you hate working during retirement, you can walk away from the job without letting anyone down."

Greg also suggested that folks who have no experience with RV living might rent an RV and try out working on the road before they go quitting their jobs and jumping into something they may not like.

Southwest Boondocking

The Southwestern desert has become a magnet mecca for RVs, full-timers and snowbirds alike. Yuma, Arizona, for example, doubles its 50,000 population every winter. Most of these are RV travelers. Phoenix draws 200,000 winter residents who add untold millions to the economy. Because of competition, many Southwestern RV parks offer non-stop recreational activities like dancing, bingo, arts and crafts, aerobics, card parties, potlucks—just about any activity that's entertaining, educational and not illegal.

But many RVers in the Southwest shun organized parks in favor of boondocking. Boondocking—in case you aren't familiar with the term— is the practice of finding places to camp without paying overnight fees. "Freebies" is another term. Most RV travelers occasionally boondock, perhaps overnight in a supermarket parking lot when it's too late to find an RV park, or in a relative's driveway when visiting for the weekend. But these Southwestern desert boondockers go much further. They've elevated the game into an art form, the more successful players spending the entire winter without ever paying a parking fee! It can be done easily, and it's fun.

Because so much land in Arizona and California is government property and ostensibly open to everyone, RVers have, from the beginning, pulled off the road wherever they pleased, setting up camp in the cactus and sagebrush. So many were doing this that the Bureau of Land Management (BLM) began charging a small fee for the entire season and encouraging the boondockers to congregate in certain locations. The fee is a mere $25 permit for the year. Although few folks camp in the desert for an entire year on this $25, many thousands spend the entire season from October through April.

Don't misunderstand; these campers aren't a bunch of indigent losers; some rigs you'll see boondocked in the desert cost more than an average house—rolling mansions worth over $200,000. Their owners can afford to be anywhere they care to, yet there they are, happily boondocking among the cactus, proud of saving money and having fun to boot. To be sure, some folks really can't afford a winter vacation any other way, but most happy campers come here for the fun of it. You'll find shabby old homemade trailers and rustic campers perched on ancient pickup beds, parked next to shiny new motorhomes and spiffy fifth-wheel mobile homes. A peppery mixture of palatial and mundane, this is a heart-warming example of well-off and just-getting-by folks being neighbors. RV camping is truly a social-leveler. This is democracy at its most grassroots level.

Slab City The nation's most famous boondocking location is in the desert near California's Salton Sea—a place called Slab City. During World War II, General Patton trained his armored division here, preparing tank crews for the North African campaign against the Nazis. The buildings here were razed after the war, but the cement slab foundations remain—hence the name Slab City. RVs of all descriptions and prices pull off the paved road, head into the desert and park haphazardly, sometimes parking next to friends, other times seeking solitude. As many as 10,000 rigs are estimated to congregate here each winter. By June, all but a handful are gone, for this is a true summer hot spot.

My wife and I visited Slab City on several occasions, the last time in our fifth-wheel trailer in January 1994. We've always been amazed at the wonderful, pioneering spirit of the campers. This must be how it was back in the covered wagon days, for among all this chaos is an admirable framework of community and order. Slab City has no formal law enforcement, yet few lawbreakers. Theft doesn't seem to be a problem. People commonly leave their possessions in camp to "hold their spot" while they go shopping in town or perhaps visit nearby Mexico for a few days, confident that everything will be intact when they return.

Ninety-five percent of the campers are retired folks; some quite elderly. A calm sense of security pervades the camp. Everyone watches out for neighbors. There seems to be an unwritten rule that if any camper isn't seen up and about by 10:00 a.m. neighbors knock on the door to see if everything is okay. Several RV units have CB radios always monitoring channel 23, ready to call into Nyland (the town about two miles away) for medical emergencies or on the rare occasion when someone might want a sheriff's deputy.

The charge for staying for the winter is—nothing. Not even the BLM's yearly permit is required. Some boondockers say their only expenditures for the winter—besides groceries from the market in Nyland—are propane for cooking and the gasoline it takes to make a weekly shopping trip and to dump their holding tanks. Some have solar power panels on their rigs that collect enough power to operate battery-powered TVs and radios. One couple said, "We not only get by on our Social Security check, we *save* some of it each month!" Things may change someday, if the state ever finds a buyer for the property. Recently a private party offered to purchase the land and charge a modest $35 per month for parking. In return, he promised to provide RV dumping stations, garbage pickup and fresh water supplies. My latest information is that the deal fell through.

I have to admit that although I love to visit Slab City and enjoy the very interesting mixture of campers, a long-term visit could grow boring. Neither my wife nor I happen to be the kind who can be happy just sitting in the shade reading books or playing cards with neighbors. For a while I enjoy not worrying about deadlines, fax machines or telephones, but after a while, I miss them. The curse of workaholism!

Quartzite, the Big Roundup Although Slab City is interesting, it is small potatoes compared to the queen city of RV roundups: Quartzite, Arizona. It's often claimed that RVs bring a million people to converge here every winter. That's believable, because RVs are scattered across the desert as far as the eye can see. Other estimates, probably more accurate, peg the yearly migration at 200,000. It's hard to count them because rigs are continually arriving and departing or moving from one boondocking site to another.

For half the year, Quartzite is a sleepy desert town with nothing happening, but when winter approaches, things begin to change. A regular city springs up, complete with entrepreneurs selling wares and services to the flood of RV owners that suddenly appear as if from nowhere. Many "full-timers" earn money by engaging in their own specialties. RVers set up stands in front of their rigs and sell all imaginable kinds of articles, arts and crafts, useless trinkets and essential merchandise. Computer repairmen and knife-sharpeners compete with booksellers and clock repairmen. Clothing is sold, and tailors will even fit new duds for you. An outdoor ballroom called the "Stardusty" (what else?) hosts more than 200 ballroom dancers at twice-a-week dances. A carnival atmosphere and excitement grips the crossroads and doesn't let go until the first hot days of spring. Because of so many supportive neighbors, folks who normally wouldn't dream of boondocking feel secure.

Another large encampment area is located north of Yuma, Arizona, around Imperial Lake and Dam. Government-constructed restrooms, holding-tank dumps and fresh water makes camping comfortable. Campgrounds bear names such as "Hurricane Ridge" and "Beehive."

RV Travel in Mexico

When you read the section on foreign retirement, you will see that I love Mexico and the people who live here. I have been visiting and living in Mexico off and on since I was 18 years old. A few years ago, when my friend Don Merwin and I co-authored a book on retirement in Mexico, we received a flood of letters asking about *RV retirement* there. Frankly, this hadn't occurred to us when we were researching our first book, *Choose Mexico*. We were thinking in terms of permanent living in apartments, condos or houses—not RVs. Readers asked questions like: "Is it practical to take my motorhome into Mexico? Is it safe? Can I find a winter location for my fifth-wheel somewhere around Puerto Vallarta? What about mobile home living?"

These questions and many more deserved answers. As it happened, I know more than a little about RV travel in Mexico. My first trip by RV was towing a 16-foot Aristocrat behind our family's new 1958 Edsel. Since that time, my wife and I have driven a motorhome, a VW Westfalia, a pickup-camper, and finally our present 5th-wheel over at least 25,000 miles of Mexican roads during the past 12 years. The result is another book, *RV Travel in Mexico*, which I suggest you check out at your library or buy from your local bookstore for complete details and tips on Mexico travel. (If your librarian doesn't have it, scold her harshly and insist that she order it forthwith!) The answers to these questions are there in detail and may surprise you. It also lists over 400 RV parks in Mexico as well as prices and starred ratings.

Wintering in Mexico

Since the Southwestern desert wintering places are so close to the Mexican border, it would be surprising if RV owners didn't venture farther south for sun and tourism. And, of course, they have; you will see

RVs and RV caravans in all parts of the republic. Mexico has hundreds of RV parks, in just about any part of the country you'd care to visit.

My favorite, easy RV jaunt into Mexico is Baja California—that part of Mexico south of California that juts into the ocean. It's so popular with RV travelers that sometimes 50 percent of the vehicles on the road are RVs with license plates from the western states and Canada. Especially from Canada in the winter.

In January and February of 1990, we took our motorhome on a leisurely trip down the peninsula, stopping at various beaches and RV parks. Baja roads are like most Mexican highways, adequately paved, but not designed for high-speed driving. Mexican drivers tend to drive slowly, which is okay for RVs, because we shouldn't be tearing up the highways anyway. The worst thing about Mexican highways is that they don't have wide shoulders, often no shoulders at all. This is fine for driving during the daytime, but *not* at night.

We stopped in as many RV parks as we could to interview retirees. (Ninety percent of RV travelers in Mexico are retired.) Over a hundred RV parks are scattered throughout Baja—often in places without motels or other accommodations. Facilities range from super-luxurious, five-star resorts to rustic fishing camps with no amenities other than cold beer and friendly faces. By the way, 99 percent of your RV neighbors will be from the United States or Canada, because Mexicans almost never own RVs. Those who can afford them prefer to stay in first-class hotels when traveling. They don't understand why we think traveling in a small tin box is fun. (I don't either, but it *is* fun.)

Boondocking in Mexico

Beaches on the Sea of Cortez-side of the peninsula are the Mexican equivalent of Slab City. These boondocking beaches provide regular winter homes for hundreds of retired couples. The beach where we spent the most time is called Santispac, just south of Mulegé, about halfway down the peninsula.

Several hundred RVs arrive every November and stay until the weather begins heating up in April. With their rigs lined up along the beach, campfire pits in front, and sometimes a palm thatch *palapa* built for shade, these Americans and Canadians enjoy a bountiful season of companionship, fishing, swimming, hiking, and just plain loafing. Regulars expect to see their friends every November through March. Should someone not appear for the season, the others worry about them and might make phone calls to see what is wrong.

Some beaches are totally free; others are maintained by the local "ejido" (community farmers who own the beach) who charge a dollar or so a night for their services: hauling trash and keeping the beach tidy. The ejido residents also keep their eyes on trailers and palapas left throughout the summer, when the heat makes Death Valley look cool. From the reports we get, theft is no problem. "We leave our trailer, trail bikes and boat here all summer," said one couple. "We put small things inside and chain the bikes to the boat for safety. But we've never had anything stolen, not even when we've forgotten to secure things."

Not all beach camps are free. Some charge a nominal fee, $5 or $10 for an ordinary space with nothing but a patio and connections, to full-facility, luxury places that charge $15 to $30 a day. One of our favorite commercial parks is at Bahía de Los Angeles where a cement patio and an electric hookup costs about $6 a day. The sea provides a bountiful harvest of clams and scallops, not to mention fish for those willing to toss a line in the water. A nearby restaurant serves excellent meals of fish, lobster and tough but tasty Mexican steaks. We've made several friends while camping here, with whom we correspond regularly, asking each other when we plan our next Mexico trip.

Chapter 13

Creative Retirement Options

When interviewing folks for the book *RV Travel in Mexico*, we met a delightful couple who manage to pack two great retirement adventures into each year. They spend the winters beachcombing and fishing in Mexico and the summers at a national park doing volunteer work. Spring and fall are reserved for visiting children or catching up on chores around their house. The unusual part of this arrangement is that it costs next to nothing to enjoy this exciting lifestyle. Actually, they make a little money on the arrangement!

How is it done? It's not at all complicated. When Barbara and Carl retired a few years ago, they had sufficient income to handle a comfortable retirement, but with little room for extravagances. Sound familiar? They own a home with a low mortgage, and they love to travel. The first year of their retirement they hit upon a great scheme, and it's worked ever since.

It goes like this: in the spring they place a classified advertisement offering their home for rent during the summer months. Since it is nicely furnished and conveniently located, they have many applicants from the local university—graduate students and temporary faculty who teach summer classes. They can be quite picky about choosing renters. Then they head for their favorite national park, a gorgeous setting in the northern California mountains. As volunteers, they are welcomed with open arms by the park administration. They are given a small furnished house—the same one each year and absolutely rent free—in exchange for working four hours a day. Barbara works in the souvenir shop and Carl helps the park rangers.

"Four hours makes a very short day," says Carl, "so we have plenty of time to enjoy the forest scenery, do some fly-fishing or hike the nature trails. We have two days off each week and sometimes take a camping trip to one of the state parks over on the ocean." Barbara adds, "It's like a three-month vacation in our own summer cottage. And, the rent from our house covers all our expenses with some left over for savings."

They return home after Labor Day and begin interviewing graduate students to rent their home for the university's winter quarter. Then, on the first of December, they pull their vacation trailer to one of Baja California's many beaches. (The mainland also has lovely beaches, but Baja is more convenient for Californians.) They park next to other winter campers—all Gringo snowbirds just like themselves—and set up camp until the first of March. The number of RVs on the beach varies from 20 to several hundred, depending upon the popularity of the beach and its location. Some beaches are absolutely free, and the most expensive is around $25 a day. (But that is luxurious!)

Their favorite beach—Santispac, south of Mulegé on the Sea of Cortez—is one of the most popular in all of Mexico with RVers. A small daily fee is shared by the families who clean up the beach and watch over RVs while their owners are in town shopping or using the laundromat. One family runs a small restaurant that caters to the campers. Every day a grocery truck tours the beach, selling vegetables, canned goods and other essentials. Clams, scallops and fish are in bountiful supply.

"The same folks tend to come to our special beach every season," explains Barbara. "It's like a big homecoming every time another rig pulls in. With campfires every evening, it's like a three-month beach party." Carl explains, "Since our rent here is next to nothing, we figure it costs us a little more than $300 a month to spend the winter in Mexico. It could be less, but we like to eat breakfast at the beach restaurant and we have dinner in town fairly often."

While Carl and Barbara are actually making money on this arrangement, they point out that finding reliable tenants for your house can be tricky. It can also be expensive should you make the wrong choice and return to find wine stains on the carpet and broken dishes.

National Park Volunteers

How can you do as Carl and Barbara do? Of course, the book *RV Travel in Mexico* will show you how to do the Mexico part. But, to become a national park volunteer, you simply request an application from the National Park Service (NPS) regional office.

The NPS invites you to join their VIP (Volunteers In Parks) program. It tries to make you feel like a VIP because you actually are a very important person when you volunteer. You can be assured of a warm welcome and appreciation for your help in preserving our majestic outdoor wonderlands and helping others to enjoy it.

The program is for everyone—for professionals, housewives, students—but senior citizens are especially welcomed. There is no pay, but the NPS usually provides for incidental expenses such as transportation, uniforms, lodging and subsistence.

Typical jobs involve helping visitors understand both the natural and human history of an area, doing environmental studies or working with wildlife management experts. If you have a penchant for the dramatic, you can have fun in one of the "living history" parks, where you dress in period costume and interpret—by example and dialogue—how people lived in different periods of history. If you are into arts and crafts, you may be asked to demonstrate a skill, such as weaving, candlemaking or glassblowing. Or, you could work with children on a simple arts-and-crafts program. There's a job for everyone.

Not only does the National Park Service need volunteers, but state and county parks often offer volunteer opportunities as well. Some state parks like to have "campground hosts." These are usually retired folks who set up their RV for the summer and give information and assistance to incoming campers. The hosts are usually in two-way radio contact with headquarters, and a quick call will bring instant response from a ranger patrol car. You will be stocked with trail maps, park literature, fishing regulations, and safety suggestions. These jobs don't pay salaries either, but the camp space is free and it is fun meeting new people. Check with your state or local park service for the particulars for your area.

The American Hiking Society publishes an excellent 100 page book listing volunteer jobs, with descriptions of the jobs and the telephone numbers to call for contacts. (It's called *Helping Out in the Outdoors*; for a copy, send $5.00 to A.H.S., 1015-31st St. N.W., Washington D.C. 20007.) It covers numerous city, county and non-profit organizations as well as state and federal. One volunteer reported that he spent only three months at home and traveled all over the country for free the rest of the time. Another said that letters of application brought in several offers within a week.

National Park Service Regional Offices   You may write to these regional Park Service offices for more information. Ask for a volunteer program application.

North Atlantic Office: 15 State St., Boston, MA 02109
Mid-Atlantic Office: 143 S. 3rd St., Philadelphia, PA 19106
Southeast Office: 1895 Phoenix Blvd., Atlanta, GA 30349
Midwest Office: 1709 Jackson St., Omaha NE 68102
Rocky Mountain Office: P.O. Box 25287, Denver, CO 80225

Southwest Office: P.O. Box 728 Santa Fe, NM 87501
Western Office: Box 36063, San Francisco, CA 94102
Pacific Northwest Office: 1424 4th Ave., Seattle, WA 98101
National Capital Office: 1100 Ohio Drive, SW, Washington, D.C. 20242

Foreign Retirement

A common dream of retirement is slipping away to some tropical paradise, or to an old-world setting in Europe. A foreign country where you can enjoy exotic foods, learn a new language, have new adventures—these are not impossible dreams at all. Hundreds of thousands of people are fulfilling their retirement dreams with foreign retirement. The marvelous thing is that living abroad can be inexpensive, depending upon where you choose to go.

A few years ago, almost any foreign country in the world was inexpensive for those of us with dollars in our pockets. It used to be that Social Security could provide an almost luxurious lifestyle overseas, complete with servants, in all but a few countries. But the decade of the 1980s, with its unlimited deficit spending, negative balance of payments and military boondoggles, sent the dollar into a tailspin.

Don't despair; it's still possible to retire in a foreign country on Social Security. But you can't do it just anywhere. There are still countries where retirement living is no more expensive than in the United States or Canada. Furthermore, there are countries where you can retire in semi-luxury for what would amount to a semi-starvation budget in the United States.

Understand, I make these foreign retirement recommendations not on a basis of cheap living, but as places where you can enjoy the company of other North American retirees and where you can experience the unique adventures of foreign living and participating in a foreign culture.

Mexico A few years ago my friend Don Merwin and I decided to expose the world to the joys of living in our favorite foreign country: Mexico. We wrote a book called *Choose Mexico: Retire on $400 a Month*. This book became an instant success. Before long, several other books joined the bandwagon in extolling the benefits of retirement in Mexico. However, nothing ever remains the same; living costs in Mexico have risen considerably. Today, it would require at *least* $800 a month (hence the title of the current, fourth edition, *Choose Mexico: Live Well on $800 a month*) to meet all basic expenses in Mexico. However on that amount, you will live a much higher quality retirement than you could hope for in the United States.

The best part about Mexico retirement is that the government makes it easy to retire there on a part-time basis. A six-month visa, or tourist card, is yours for the asking, and there are any number of North American "colonies" where you can rent a house and savor the enjoyment of foreign living without becoming involved in legalities. I first lived in Mexico on a tourist card over 40 years ago and have returned dozens of times since.

You have your choice of many lovely places to retire in Mexico. You'll find modern cities and delightfully ancient towns with cobblestone streets and buildings dating from the 1500s—settings matched only by Europe's medieval cities. Some of the prettiest beaches in the world make for idyllic retirement lifestyles. Fabulous Acapulco, Puerto Vallarta and Cancun are not only beautiful, but entirely practical for full or part-time retirement.

Mexico isn't all tropical paradise. High mountain villages, desert towns and pleasant suburbs attract travelers and retirees. Picturesque colonial towns have become artist colonies where writers and painters (and those who would like to be artists and writers) congregate to exchange views. Modern cities that perch high on the Central Plateau offer year-round, spring-like temperatures—places like Guadalajara and Morelia. More than 30,000 U.S. citizens live in the Guadalajara area alone.

Costa Rica   This is my favorite foreign country and one of the most beautiful places in the entire universe. Obviously, many other North Americans agree, because there are 35,000 United States citizens living in Costa Rica at this time, most retirees. The country's total population is less than 3 million, which means that per capita, more North Americans call Costa Rica home than any other foreign country in the world.

This little jewel of a country used to be like a closely guarded secret; few tourists ever heard of the place, and when they did, they usually confused it with Puerto Rico. "Oh yes, that's an island, isn't it?" But the secret seems to be out, because more and more folks are headed that way. The pleasant thing is that the Costa Rican government goes way out of its way to make us welcome as retirees. "Pensionados" (retirees) receive all sorts of tax breaks and exemptions in recognition of their contributions to the country's culture and economy.

What makes Costa Rica so special? If I were to name the most important factor, it would have to be the people. They are surprisingly like us in so many ways. Open, friendly and fiercely democratic, the Costa Ricans share a sense of equality that even exceeds our ideals. This is quite different from many Latin American countries, where people are class conscious, shy and reluctant to make close friends with people outside their families. Frequently, while traveling on a bus or train, the person sitting next to me would strike up a conversation—and by the end of the trip I would have a dinner invitation to the family's home. This would never happen in any other Central American country.

Called the "Switzerland of the Americas," the bulk of its population lives high on a mountainous plateau that is swathed year-round with lush vegetation and fluorescent blossoms. The capital, San José, sits at a 4,000-foot elevation and enjoys perpetual spring. This is not an exaggeration: every day is like the first warm day in April, with crystal-clear air and fluffy clouds drifting overhead. Although there's a rainy season, scarcely a day goes by without some sunshine and blue skies. This is one of the few places in the world where you can choose between swimming in the Atlantic or the Pacific, with less than a two-hour drive in either direction.

Three conditions make Costa Rica very different from the other countries of Central America: first, its high standard of living, stability and prosperity; second, its devotion to democracy (which couldn't come about without prosperity); and, finally, the industry and entrepreneurship of its citizens (without which none of the above would be possible). It's an endless circle.

This is a country of small businesses, family-operated farms and almost none of the crushing poverty that characterizes the other Central American nations. The culture and racial stock is very European, with most people descended from Italian, German or Spanish immigrants who settled there in the late 1800s. Those of Italian heritage appear to be in the majority. To prevent military takeovers and dictatorships, the people abolished the army almost half a century ago. Instead of squandering resources on the military, they've built schools, roads, hospitals and other life-enhancing projects. Health standards and literacy rates are among the world's highest (higher than ours), while those in next-door Nicaragua and Panama are disgracefully inadequate.

This is a country where Americans and Canadians feel very comfortable in retirement. It is a country of laws, where property ownership is affordable and strictly protected. The cost of living is favorable, with most prices at two-thirds of what we might expect to pay at home.

As you might expect, I've written a book about Costa Rica retirement, now in its second edition, titled: *Choose Costa Rica: A Guide to Retirement and Investment*. Like *Choose Mexico,* this book is available in bookstores' travel sections and through Gateway Books, and also covers subjects not found in ordinary travel books. This is a how-to-do-it guide to living, retiring and investing. You'll learn how to rent a home or buy property, to hire a gardner or a maid and how to put your money to work or start a business in Costa Rica.

Spain and Portugal   While on the subject of foreign retirement, I would be remiss in omitting another of our favorite places: the Iberian Peninsula (Spain and Portugal). While not inexpensive places to live, these countries are among the true bargains of Europe—at this moment, at any rate. I add that qualification because not long ago, the exchange rate almost trashed the dollar value in Spain (and Portugal to an extent), boosting prices to the already high levels of France, Germany and most other European countries. I suspect that the exchange rate was artificial, because in 1993 a severe adjustment in the financial markets raised the rate from about 94 pesetas to the dollar to 135. This means a 30 percent increase in your dollar's purchasing power. At the moment of writing, most expenses are below those in the United States, and far below those of neighboring countries.

For the average North American, neither Spain nor Portugal are suitable full-time retirement destinations, because of the red tape involved in acquiring residency, and (in my opinion) an inevitable increase in the cost of living until it reaches the normal prohibitive level of the rest of Europe. But in the meantime, both countries are dreamy places for part-time retirement.

Since Spanish or Portuguese visas are good for 90 days, the trick is as follows. Spring is best spent on the Costa del Sol or Costa Brava, in an apartment with a view of the Mediterranean. After the 90 days are up, it's June, July and August in Sintra or Cascais, Portugal. (Incredibly beautiful!) Then, back to Spain for an apartment in Seville, Segovia or Avila. When winter closes in, it's time to head for the Canary Islands (Spanish) or the Azores (Portuguese) for a tropical or semi-tropical sojourn.

Yes, you've guessed correctly; I also have a book in print on retirement and long-term travel in Spain and Portugal. *Choose Spain*—co-authored by Bettie Magee, a knowledgeable, well-traveled retiree of the Iberian Peninsula—covers the same topics as the other retirement-abroad books and is also available at your local bookstore and from Gateway Books.

For an even broader scope of retirement in Europe and other countries, you need to consult the book *Adventures Abroad* by Allene Symons & Jane Parker (Gateway Books).

Peace Corps

Here's another option for foreign travel, one that not only won't cost you any money, but will give you meaningful, fulfilling work to do. Consider the Peace Corps. It isn't as off-the-wall as it might seem at first glance. Many older Americans are having the times of their lives and at the same time participating in programs that affect literacy, health and hunger and help promote world peace, friendship and sharing. Retired singles and couples have put their expertise to work in Africa, Asia, South America, Central America and the Pacific islands.

Perhaps you've always been under the impression that Peace Corps volunteers are a bunch of youngsters who are having an adventure between college and going to work. Not so. The Peace Corps is very interested in older Americans. No other group in this country embodies the years of leadership, skills, experience and proven ability of our senior citizens. Each of us by retirement age has an enormous reservoir of work experience and wisdom that will be lost if we don't share it. What better place to share than with grateful people in developing countries? And, unlike the United States, where the emphasis is on youth, most foreign cultures respect and appreciate age.

Besides the wealth of expertise and experience that older Americans have to offer, they are usually in a better position to *afford* being a Peace Corps volunteer. A youngster right out of college has to think about money, usually big money to repay the costs of education or to get started in the job market. But a retired senior citizen, with Social Security and maybe a company pension coming in, isn't stymied by the low compensation paid by the Peace Corps.

Peace Corps volunteers receive living expenses and a monthly stipend to cover incidental needs, so there is no need to spend savings or other income. In addition, $175 per month is put aside and given to them at the end of the typical two-year assignment. This $4,200 per person comes in handy for making a transition back into life at home. The compensation you receive from the Peace Corps doesn't affect your Social Security earnings any more than does unearned income from savings annuities, dividends or pensions. Since all expenses are paid, many older Peace Corps volunteers bank their entire Social Security, pension and interest income during their two-year tour of duty.

Here is a terrific opportunity to make a contribution to peace, to utilize your life's experience helping others and to have the *time of your life*. If you're married, odds are that your spouse also has some much-needed skill, so there's a chance the two of you might go as a team.

The Peace Corps points out that there are some major benefits of becoming a volunteer. Perhaps for the first time in your life you will be measured by your accumulated life's experience rather than how much you can earn each month. You can live with dignity and purpose in a culture where your age is respected and looked upon as an asset. This respect and knowing that your work is appreciated renews vigor and vitality. And, finally, you have the adventure of creating a new and exciting life. What more could you ask of retirement?

Here are some details about being a Peace Corps volunteer:

SAFETY—Safety is the highest priority. The Peace Corps monitors volunteers' environments constantly. If there's any doubt about safety, volunteers are immediately evacuated.

HEALTH CARE—The focus is on prevention, with every possible safeguard taken to provide quality health care. Volunteers undergo complete physical and dental exams, are given immunizations, preventive medications and health care training. Every country has a medical officer with access to qualified local doctors and medical facilities.

LIVING ALLOWANCE—Covers basic expenses such as food, housing and incidental expenses. Modest but comfortable housing is provided.

TRAINING—Technical and language training is provided during an intensive 10-12 week program. Volunteers' expenses are covered during this training, and their $175-a-month savings plan starts with training, too. Cross-cultural training gives volunteers an in-depth acquaintance with the customs and traditions of the country where they will live and work.

VACATION AND TRAVEL—Volunteers accrue vacation at the rate of two days per month, which can be taken as the work situation permits. Most Peace Corps workers take the opportunity to visit neighboring countries, travel adventures they could never dream of in ordinary retirement. Friends are permitted to visit as long as they don't interfere with the work schedule.

For further information or an application, write to Peace Corps, Room P-301, Washington, D.C. 20526; or call, toll-free, 800-424-8580.

Low-Cost Housing

According to current statistics, more than three million Americans now live in some type of retirement facility. This is an increase of 300 percent over the past 15 years. Additionally, nearly 250,000 live in continuing-care communities. A boom in new retirement housing is evident throughout the country, but construction is not keeping pace with demand. With recent studies showing that the number of Americans over 85 years of age will top 24 million in the next half-century, the problem should be apparent.

However, this retirement facility boom is largely for the upper-middle to upper income groups. These folks can well afford this retirement lifestyle, with payments often topping $3,000 a month for a couple. The fact is, more than 25 percent who reach retirement age are at or near the poverty level. A majority of these are elderly single women. Because their wages were always lower, their Social Security payments are also low—disgracefully low.

The government attempts to do something about low-cost housing through Housing and Urban Development (HUD) programs subsidizing both the construction and monthly rentals of qualifying retirees. However, the outlook here is bleak indeed, with deep cuts in the funding. According to the last figures at my disposal, there were 250,000 low-income retirees on waiting lists for low-cost retirement facilities. The odds were about 15 percent for being accepted.

The largest non-profit provider of subsidized retirement facilities—The Retirement Housing Foundation—can send you a list of its facilities and information on how to apply. It operates over 110 retirement communities in 24 states (and Puerto Rico). The units are HUD approved, and the tenants' rents are subsidized by HUD. Some facilities are not subsidized, which means residents pay a deposit and competitive rents, although somewhat lower than a conventional commercial facility because of the HUD 231c low-interest mortgages.

Retirement Housing Foundation manages a total of 6,926 subsidized units and 3,752 non-subsidized units. These include independent-living arrangements, assisted-living and skilled-nursing units. Information about Retirement Housing Foundation's facilities can be obtained by writing 401 E. Ocean Blvd., #300, Long Beach, CA 90802.

Bibliography

Books

Frommer, A. *New World of Travel.* Prentice Hall, New York, 1991.
A must-read book for travelers. Covers alternative ways to travel, interesting vacations and long-term travel, house-swapping at home and abroad, volunteer opportunities and much more. Out of print, but try your library.

Howells, J. *Choose Costa Rica: A Guide to Retirement and Investment (2nd edition).* Gateway Books, Oakland, CA, 1994.
Long-term travel, retirement, and investment in Costa Rica and Guatemala.

Howells, J. *RV Travel in Mexico.* Gateway Books, Oakland, CA, 1989.
The how-to-do-it book on RV traveling in Mexico. Tips on travel, where to go, how to deal with local people, plus complete listings of over 400 parks in Mexico.

Howells, J. and Magee, B. *Choose Spain.* Gateway Books, Oakland, CA, 1990.
Long term travel and retirement in Spain. Written with a long-time retiree in Málaga, Spain. How to travel, finding apartments, understanding the country.

Howells, J. and Merwin, D. *Choose Mexico: Live Well on $800 a Month (4th edition).* Gateway Books, Oakland, CA, 1994.
How to retire in Mexico and have a gracious, interesting life for very little money. Descriptions of the country and tips on where to retire.

McMillon, B. *Volunteer Vacations.* Chicago Review Press, Chicago, 1989.

Peterson, K. *Home Is Where You Park It.* RoVers Pubs., Livingston, TX, 1994.
The third edition of *the* how-to-do-it manual on full-time RVing, with tips on how to get started and adjust to a new lifetyle.

Peterson, J. and Peterson, K. *Encyclopedia for RVers*, 1992, and *Survival of the Snowbirds*, 1995. RoVers Pubs., Livingston, TX.
Both full of information on all aspects of RV travel. The Encyclopedia features a complete list of services, organizations, publications and essential addresses for RVers. Snowbirds discusses ways live to live rent-free while RVing.

Symons, A. and Parker, J. *Adventures Abroad.* Gateway Books, Oakland, CA, 1991.
First-hand accounts of retirement life in 15 countries, including France, Greece, Thailand, Italy, Mexico, Portugal, Spain, Costa Rica.

Volunteer! Council on International Educational Exchange, 205 E. 42nd St., New York, NY 10017, 1992.
A comprehensive guide to voluntary service in the U.S. and abroad, lists short-term to long-term projects.

Periodicals

Escapees Magazine—100 Rainbow Dr., Livingston, TX 77351; (800) 976-8377.
Bimonthly publication of the Escapee, Inc. (SKP), an organization that specializes in full-time RV travelers. Full of information for any RV owner.

Tico Times—Dept. 717, P.O. Box #025216, Miami, FL 33102.
Costa Rican daily newspaper in English. A must for anyone planning on visiting this country. Year subscription is $46.

Workamper News—201 Hiram Road, Heber Springs, AR 72543; (800) 446-5627.
Excellent publication listing temporary and long-term jobs for RV travelers. Free employment and situation-wanted ads. A 40-page publication every other month. By subscription only, $23 a year.

Chambers of Commerce & Senior Agencies

|Alabama|

Advantage for Retirees—P.O. Box 250347, Montgomery, AL 36125.
Blount County—P.O. Box 87, Oneonta, AL 35121.
Decatur—P.O. Box 2003 Decatur, AL 35602.
Dothan—P.O. Box 638, Dothan, AL 36302.
Enterprise—P.O. Box 577, Enterprise, AL 36331.
Eufaula—P.O. Box 1055, Eufaula, AL 36072.
Florence—104 S. Pine St., Florence, AL 35630.
Gulf Shores—P.O. Box 3388, Gulf Shores, AL 36547.
Ozark—308 Painter Av., Ozark, AL 36360.
Scottsboro—916 S. Broad St. Scottsboro, AL 35768.

|Arizona|

Arizona State Dept. of Economic Security, Aging and Adult Admin.—1789 W. Jefferson, Phoenix, AZ 85007.
Ajo—P.O Box 507, Ajo, AZ 85321.
Bisbee—P.O. Box BA, Bisbee, AZ 85603.
Bullhead City—P.O Box 66, Bullhead City, AZ 86430.
Flagstaff—101 W. Santa Fe Av., Flagstaff, AZ 86001.
Green Valley—P.O Box 566, Green Valley, AZ 85614.
Lake Havasu City—1930 Mesquite Av. #3, Lake Havasu City, AZ 86403.
Payson—P.O. Box 1380, Payson, AZ 85547.
Prescott—P.O. Box 1147, Prescott, AZ 86302.
Sedona—P.O. Box 478, Sedona, AZ 86336.
Tucson—P.O. Box 991, Tucson, AZ 85702.
Wickenburg—P.O. Drawer CC, Wickenburg, AZ 85358.
Yuma—P.O. Box 230, Yuma, AZ 85364.

|Arkansas|

State of Arkansas—P.O. Box 3645, Little Rock, AR 72203.
Bull Shoals—P.O. Box 354, Bull Shoals, AR 72619.
Eureka Springs—P.O. Box 551, Eureka Springs, AR 72632.
Fairfield Bay—P.O. Box 1159, Fairfield Bay, AR 72088.
Greers Ferry—P.O. Box 354, Greers Ferry, AR 72067.
Heber Springs—P.O. Box 630, Heber Springs, AR 73543.
Hot Springs—P.O. Box 6090, Hot Springs, AR 71902.
Little Rock—One Spring St., Little Rock, AR 72201.
Mountain Home—P.O. Box 488, Mountain Home, AR 72653.

|California|

California State Dept. on Aging—1600 K St., Sacramento, CA 95814.
State of California—P.O. Box 1736, Sacramento, CA 95808.
Amador County—P.O. Box 596, Jackson, CA 95642.
Arcata—780 7th St., Arcata, CA 95521.
Chico—P.O. Box 3038, Chico, CA 95927.
Desert Hot Springs—P.O. Box 848, Desert Hot Springs, CA 92240.
Dunsmuir-Mt. Shasta—3000 Pine St., Mt. Shasta, CA 96067.
El Cajon—109 Rea Av., El Cajon, CA 92020.
Escondido—P.O. Box C, Escondido, CA 92244.
Eureka—2112 Broadway, Eureka, CA 95501.

Fall River Mills—P.O. Box 475, Fall River Mills, CA 96028.
Fortuna—P.O. Box 797, Fortuna, CA 95540.
Garberville—P.O. Box 445, Garberville, CA 95440.
Grass Valley—248 Mill St., Grass Valley, CA 95945.
Mendocino/Ft. Bragg—P.O. Box 1141, Ft. Bragg, CA 95437.
Nevada City—132 Main St., Nevada City, CA 95959.
Palm Springs—190 W. Amado Rd., Palm Springs, CA 92262.
Paradise—5587 Scottwood, Paradise, CA 95956.
Pismo Beach—581 Dolliver St., Pismo Beach, CA 93449.
San Diego—110 West C St., Suite 1600, San Diego, CA 92101.
San Francisco—465 California St. #900, San Francisco, CA 94104.
San Luis Obispo—1041 Chorro St., San Luis Obispo, CA 93401.
Santa Barbara—P.O. Box 299, Santa Barbara, CA 93101.
Yucaipa—P.O. Box 45, Yucaipa, CA 92399.

Colorado

State of Colorado—1860 Lincoln St. #550, Denver, CO 80296.
Denver—1600 Sherman St., Denver, CO 80203.
Grand Junction—360 Grand Av., Grand Junction, CO 81501.

Florida

State of Florida—P.O. Box 11309, Tallahassee, FL 32302.
Apalachicola—128 Market St., Apalachicola, FL 32320.
Bonita Springs—P.O. Box 1240, Bonita Springs, FL 33959.
Bradenton—P.O. Box 321, Bradenton, FL 33506.
Cape Coral—2051 Cape Coral Parkway, Cape Coral, FL 33904.
Cocoa Beach—400 Fortenberry Rd., Cocoa Beach, FL 32952.
Daytona Beach—P.O. Box 2775, Daytona Beach, FL 32015.
Ft. Myers—P.O. Box CC, Ft. Meyers, FL 33902.
Ft. Walton Beach — P.O. Box 640, Ft. Walton Beach, FL 32549.
Gainesville—P.O. Box 1187, Gainesville, FL 32602
Key Largo—105950 Overseas Hwy., Key Largo, FL 33037.
Lakeland—P.O. Box 3538, Lakeland, FL 33802.
Marathon—3330 Overseas Hwy., Marathon, FL 33050.
Melbourne—1005 E. Strawbridge Av., Melbourne, FL 32901.
Miami—900 Perrine Av., Miami, FL 33157.
Naples—1700 N. Tamiami Trail, Naples, FL 33940.
Ocala—P.O. Box 1210, Ocala, FL 32670.
Orlando—P.O. Box 1234, Orlando, FL 32802.
Palm Coast—1 Corporate Dr., Palm Coast, FL 32151.
Panama City—P.O. Box 1850, Panama City, FL 32402.
Pensacola—P.O. Box 550, Pensacola, FL 32593.
Port Charlotte—2702 Tamiami Trail, Port Charlotte, FL 33952.
Punta Gorda—326 W. Marion #112, Punta Gorda, FL 33950.
St. Petersburg—100 2nd Av. North, St. Petersburg, FL 33731.
Sarasota—P.O. Box 308, Sarasota, FL 34230.
Winter Haven—P.O. Drawer 1420, Winter Haven, FL 33822.

Georgia

State Office of Aging—878 Peachtree St. N.E., Atlanta, GA 30309.
Brunswick-Golden Isles—P.O. Box 250, Brunswick, GA 31520.
Rabun County—P.O. Box 761, Clayton, GA 30525.
Savannah—222 W. Oglethorpe Av., Savannah, GA 31499.

Valdosta—P.O. Box 1964, Valdosta, GA 31603.

Hawaii

State of Hawaii—735 Bishop St., Honolulu, HI 96813.
Hilo—180 Kinoole St. #118, Hilo, HI 96720.
Kailua-Kona—P.O. Box 1496, Kailua, HI 96734.
Maui Island—P.O. Box 1677, Kahului, HI 96732.

Kentucky

Bowling Green—P.O. Box 51, Bowling Green, KY 42101.
Murray—P.O. Box 190, Murray, KY 42071.

Louisiana

Alexandria—802 Third St., Alexandria, LA 71309.
Baton Rouge—P.O. Box 3217, Baton Rouge, LA 70821.
Houma—P.O. Box 328, Houma, LA 71040.
Lafayette—P.O. Box 51307, Lafayette, LA 70505.
Leesville—P.O. Box 1228, Leesville, LA 71496.
New Orleans—P.O. Box 30240, New Orleans, LA 70190.
Opelousas—P.O. Box 109, Opelousas, LA 70570.

Mississipi

Council on Aging—421 W. Pascagoula St., Jackson, MS 39203.
Bay St. Louis—P.O. Box 103, Bay St. Louis, MS 39520.
Biloxi—P.O. Box 1928, Biloxi, MS 39533.
Gulfport/Long Beach/Pass Christian—P.O. Drawer FF, Gulfport, MS 39502.
Natchez—P.O. Box 1403, Natchez, MS 39120.
Oxford—428 North Lamar Blvd., Oxford, MS 38655.

Missouri

State of Missouri—P.O. Box 149, Jefferson City, MO 65102.
Columbia—P.O. Box 1016, Columbia, MO 65205.
Osage Beach—P.O. Box 193, Osage Beach, MO 65065.

Nevada

State of Nevada—P.O. Box 2806, Reno, NV 89505.
Aging Services, 1665 Hot Springs Rd. #158, Carson City, NV 89710.
Lake Tahoe—P.O. Box 7139, Lake Tahoe, NV 89449.
Las Vegas—2301 E. Sahara Av., Las Vegas, NV 89104.
Pahrump—P.O. Box 42, Pahrump, NV 89041
Reno—P.O. Box 3499, Reno, NV 89505.

New Mexico

Albuquerque—P.O. Box 25100, Albuquerque, NM 87125.
Carlsbad—P.O. Box 910, Carlsbad, NM 88220.
Las Cruces—P.O. Drawer 519, Las Cruces, 88004.
Santa Fe—P.O. Box 1928, Santa Fe, NM 88061.
Taos—P.O. Drawer 1, Taos, NM 87571.
Truth or Consequences—P.O. Box 31, Truth or Consequences, NM 78901.

North Carolina

Division of Aging—693 Palmer Dr., Raleigh, NC 27626.
Asheville—P.O. Box 1010, Ashville, NC 28802.
Blowing Rock—P.O. Box 406, Blowing Rock, NC 28605.
Boone—112 W. Howard St., Boone, NC 28607.
Brevard—P.O. Box 589, Brevard, NC 28712.
Chapel Hill—P.O. Box 2897, Chapel Hill, NC 27515.
Durham—P.O. Box 3829, Durham, NC 27702.
Pinehurst/Southern Pines—P.O. Box 458, Southern Pines, NC 28388.
Raleigh—P.O. Box 2978, Raleigh, NC 27602.

Oklahoma

State of Oklahoma—4020 N. Lincoln Blvd., Olkahoma City, OK 73105.
Bartlesville—P.O. Box 2366, Bartlesville, OK 74005.
Grove—104-B W. Third St., Grove, OK 74344.
Tahlequah—123 E. Delaware St., Tahlequah, OK 74464.

Oregon

Ashland—P.O. Box 1360, Ashland, OR 97520.
Astoria—P.O. Box 176, Astoria, OR 97103.
Bandon-by-the-Sea—P.O. Box 1515, Bandon OR 97411.
Bend—164 N.W. Hawthorne Av., Bend, OR 97701.
Brookings/Harbor—P.O. Box 940, Brookings, OR 97415.
Coos Bay/North Bend—P.O. Box 210, Coos Bay, OR 97420.
Eugene—P.O. Box 1107, Eugene, OR 97440.
Florence—P.O. Box 26000, Florence, OR 97439.
Gold Beach—510 S. Ellensburg, Gold Beach, OR 97444.
Grants Pass—1501 N.E. Sixth St., Grants Pass, OR 97532.
Hood River—Port Marina Park, Hood River, OR 79031.
Jacksonville—P.O. Box 33, Jacksonville, OR 97530.
Klamath Falls 125 N. Fifth St., Klamath Falls, OR 97601.
Medford—101 E. Eigth St., Medford, OR 97501.
Portland—221 N.W. 2nd Av., Portland, OR 97209.
Rogue River—111 E. Main St., Rogue River, OR 97537.
Springfield—P.O. Box 155, Springfield, OR 97477.
The Dalles—404 W. 2nd, The Dalles, OR 97058.

South Carolina

State of South Carolina—P.O. Box 11278, Columbia, SC 29202.
Aiken—P.O. Box 892, Aiken, SC 29802.
Charleston—P.O. Box 975, Charleston, SC 29402.
Columbia—P.O. Box 1360, Columbia, SC 29202.
Hilton Head Island—P.O. Box 5647, Hilton Head, SC 29938.
Myrtle Beach—P.O. Box 2115, Myrtle Beach, SC 29578.

Tennessee

Clarksville—P.O. Box 883, Clarksville, TN 37041.
Crossville—P.O. Box 452, Crossville, TN 38557.
Dover—P.O. Box 147, Dover, TN 37058.

Texas

State of Texas—300 W. 15th St. #875, Austin, TX 78701.
Aransas Pass—452 W. Cleveland, Aransas Pass, TX 78336.
Austin—P.O. Box 1967, Austin, TX 78767.
Brownsville—P.O. Box 752, Brownsville, TX 78522.
Corpus Christi—P.O. Box 640, Corpus Christi, TX 78403.
El Paso—10 Civic Center Plaza, El Paso, TX 79901.
Fredericksburg —P.O. Box 506, Fredericksburg, TX 78624.
Galveston—2106 Seawall Blvd., Galveston, TX 77550.
Harlingen—P.O. Box 189, Harlingen, TX 78551.
Kerrville—1700 Sidney Baker St., Kerrville, TX 78028.
Mission—220 E. Ninth St., Mission, TX 78572.
Nacogdoches—P.O. Box 1918, Nacogdoches, TX 75963.
Port Isabela-Padre Island—P.O. Box 2098, Port Isabela, TX 78597.
San Antonio—P.O. Box 1628, San Antonio, TX 78296.
Wimberley P.O. Box 12, Wimberley, TX 78676.

Utah

Cedar City—P.O. Box 1007, Cedar City, UT 84720.
St. George—97 E. St. George Blvd., St. George, UT 84770.

Virginia

Dept. for the Aging—700 E. Franklin St. 10th Fl., Richmond, VA 23219.
Charlottesville—P.O. Box 1564, Charlottesville, VA 22906.
Hampton—6 Manhattan Sq., Hampton, VA 23666.

Washington

Aberdeen—506 Duffy St., Aberdeen, WA 98520.
Goldendale—228 W. Main St., Room 110, Goldendale, WA 98620.
Pasco—P.O. Box 550, Pasco, WA 99301.
Seattle—600 University St. #1200, Seattle, WA 98101.
Vancouver—404 E. 15th St. #11, Vancouver, WA 98663.

Weather Statistics for Some Major Cities

Town	Average High Temp. Jan.	Average High Temp. July	Average Low Temp. Jan.	Average Low Temp. July	Average Percent Humidity	Total Inches Rain	Total Inches Snow
Albuquerque, NM	47.2	92.8	22.3	64.7	27	8	10
Anchorage, AK	20.0	65.1	6.0	51.1	62	15	68
Asheville, NC	47.5	84.0	26.0	62.4	63	48	17
Atlanta, GA	51.2	87.9	32.6	69.2	60	48	2
Baltimore, MD	41.0	87.1	24.3	66.5	53	42	21
Birmingham, AL	52.7	90.3	33.0	69.8	60	54	1
Bismarck, ND	17.5	84.4	-4.2	56.4	47	15	41
Boise, ID	37.1	90.6	22.6	58.5	22	11	21
Boston, ME	36.4	81.8	22.8	65.1	57	44	41
Bridgeport, CT	36.5	82.1	22.5	65.9	61	42	25
Brownsville, TX	69.7	92.6	50.8	75.6	55	25	—
Buffalo, NY	30.0	80.2	17.0	61.2	55	37	91
Charleston, SC	58.8	89.4	36.9	71.6	62	51	—
Cleveland, OH	32.5	81.7	18.5	61.4	57	35	54
Columbia, MO	36.3	88.6	18.6	66.9	55	36	23
Columbia, SC	56.2	91.9	33.2	70.1	54	49	1
Corpus Christi, TX	66.5	94.2	46.1	75.6	57	30	—
Denver, CO	43.1	88.0	15.9	58.7	34	15	60
Detroit, MI	30.6	83.1	16.1	60.7	53	31	41
Fairbanks, AK	-3.9	71.8	-21.6	51.2	50	10	65
Fort Myers, FL	74.3	91.0	52.5	74.1	60	53	—
Honolulu, HI	79.9	87.1	65.3	73.1	51	23	—
Indianapolis, IN	34.2	85.2	17.8	64.9	60	39	23
Kansas City, MO	34.5	88.5	17.2	68.5	56	35	20
Las Vegas, NV	56.0	104.5	33.0	75.9	15	4	1
Lincoln, NE	30.4	89.5	8.9	65.6	52	26	27
Little Rock, AR	49.8	92.7	29.9	71.4	56	49	5
Louisville, KY	40.8	87.6	24.1	67.5	58	43	16
Miami, FL	75.0	88.7	59.2	76.2	63	57	—
Milwaukee, WI	26.0	79.8	11.3	61.1	61	30	46
Mobile, AL	60.6	91.2	40.9	73.2	60	64	—
Nashville, TN	46.3	89.8	27.8	69.0	57	48	10
Oklahoma City,OK	46.6	93.5	25.2	70.6	49	31	9
Oxford, MS	51.1	92.5	31.2	69.4	55	56	5
Pensacola, FL	60.6	90.1	42.7	74.4	64	61	—
Phoenix, AZ	65.2	105.0	39.4	79.5	20	7	—
Pittsburgh, PA	34.1	82.7	19.2	61.3	53	36	43
Portland, OR	44.3	79.5	33.5	55.8	45	37	6
Raleigh, NC	50.1	88.2	29.1	67.1	58	42	7
Reno, NV	44.8	91.3	19.5	47.7	19	7	24
Richmond, VA	46.7	88.4	26.5	67.2	56	44	14
Salt Lake City, UT	37.4	93.2	19.7	61.8	22	15	58
San Antonio, TX	61.7	94.9	39.0	74.3	52	29	—
San Diego, CA	65.2	75.6	48.4	64.9	66	9	—
Seattle, WA	45.3	74.6	35.9	56.0	49	39	7
Sioux Falls, SD	22.9	86.2	1.9	61.8	53	24	39
Spokane, WA	31.3	84.0	20.0	55.3	27	16	50
St. Louis, MO	37.6	89.0	19.9	68.8	56	33	19
Washington, DC	42.9	87.9	27.5	69.9	53	39	17
Wichita, KS	39.8	92.9	19.4	69.8	48	29	17

Index

Index to Places

For Credit Card ORDERS ONLY - call toll-free
1-800-669-0773
For Information - call 510-530-0299

To order direct, send check or money order to:
Gateway Books, 2023 Clemens Road, Oakland CA 94602

Adventures Abroad $12.95.................................. $_____

Choose Costa Rica $13.95................................. _____

Choose Mexico $11.95..................................... _____

Choose Spain $11.95.. _____

Get Up & Go $10.95... _____

The Grandparent Book $11.95............................ _____

Retirement on a Shoestring $7.95....................... _____

RV Travel in Mexico $9.95................................. _____

To Love Again $7.95... _____

Walking Easy in the Austrian Alps $10.95.............. _____

Walking Easy in the Swiss Alps $10.95.................. _____

Where to Retire $14.95 .... _____

    Postage & Handling

        First book.......................$1.90 _____

        Each additional book..........1.00 _____

        California residents add 8% sales tax _____

                Total $ _____

( ) I enclose my check or money order
( ) Please charge my credit card

      Visa   Master Card   American Express

#_____Exp. Date _____

Name on Card _____

Telephone (   )_____

Please ship to:

Name_____

Address_____

City/State/Zip_____

Our books are shipped bookrate. Please allow 2 - 3 weeks for delivery. If you are not satisfied, the price of the book(s) will be refunded in full. (U. S. funds for all orders, please.)